Tioga
Bradford
Susquehanna
Wayne
Wyoming
Lackawanna
Sullivan
Lycoming
Pike
Luzerne
Monroe
Columbia
Montour
Union
Carbon
Northumberland
Snyder
Northampton
Schuylkill
Lehigh
Dauphin
Harrisburg
Perry
Berks
Lebanon
Bucks
Montgomery
Cumberland
Philadelphia
Lancaster
Chester
York
Delaware
Adams

COUNTY CHRONICLES

There's No Place Like Home!

A Vivid Collection of Pennsylvania Histories

by
Ceane O'Hanlon-Lincoln

Front Cover

"Old RR Station, Dunbar, PA" by Pennsylvania artist Helen Crosby (Warmuth) Alt. Prints of this volume's cover, as well as prints from the covers of other volumes of the *County Chronicles* Pennsylvania history series, may be purchased by contacting the artist at 724-628-9543.

Helen Alt was born in Philadelphia in 1918. She began painting during her high school years, and upon graduation received a scholarship to the Pennsylvania Academy of Fine Arts. Her work has earned her numerous awards. Alt has been a resident of Connellsville, Pennsylvania, since 1946.

Author Ceane O'Hanlon-Lincoln with her cover artist Helen Alt, at awards ceremony, Connellsville, PA
Photo by William S. Warmuth II

Published by

Firefly Publications

Imprint of

MECHLING BOOKBINDERY
Books...made to order

1124 Oneida Valley Road – Route 38
Chicora, PA 16025-3820
www.mechlingbooks.com
1-800-941-3735

Copyright © 2010 by Ceane O'Hanlon-Lincoln

Layout and Design by Kari Anne McConnell

All rights reserved. Published 2010

Printed in the United States of America

No part of this publication may be copied or electronically reproduced by any means, without prior written permission from the publisher.

ISBN-13: 978-0-9841400-0-8
ISBN-10: 0-9841400-0-X
Library of Congress Control Number: 2009937431

Book # _457_ of 1000

This book is dedicated to my father, who loved stories;
To my mother, who loved books;
To my brother, J. Robert Hanlon, Esq., who loves both;
To time-travelers everywhere,
To my husband, Phillip R. Lincoln~
Who bought me my ticket ...
And to all future time-travelers and caretakers of history ...

For those who sleep,
And those who dream,
And those who have awakened ...

"Researching and writing history is such a wondrous process of discovery I can't wait to get started each day."

~ Ceane O'Hanlon-Lincoln

— Acknowledgments —

As always, my greatest debt is to my husband, Phillip R. Lincoln.

To my cherished readers who continually communicate their delightful feedback for my Chronicles, both to me and to my publisher.

To an amazing artist and dear friend, Helen Alt, whose paintings for the covers of my *County Chronicles* charmingly beckon the reader to enter and embark on a magic-carpet ride into Pennsylvania's thrilling past.

To my treasured muses, especially Nancy Stafford, Jean Minnick, Bill Colvin, Arlene Zimmerman, Nancy Sova Hrabak, Patty Wilson, Mabel Shaner, Barbara M. Neill, Sandra Bolish, Cookie Pilla, and Bob Cole.

To Cathy and Gerald Seymour of Paramount Press, Inc., and Pennsylvania artist Robert Griffing for permission to use Mr. Griffing's prints in this volume.

To professional photographers Glenn E. Mucy and John Craig for permission to use their prints in this volume.

To Valley Forge Supervisory Ranger William J. Troppman for his gracious tour of Washington's Headquarters and the park area.

To fellow authors for the permissions to quote from their works.

To all those who supplied precious photographs and memories for this volume.

To the docents of the historical societies and historic sites all across our great commonwealth.

To everyone over the long years who advised, "Write it your own way."

To all the interesting, colorful people I have met and interviewed along the exciting road to history- to each of my dear benefactors, I am profoundly grateful.

To the Native Americans, the pioneers, the immigrants, the heroes herein.

To fellow time-travelers everywhere—

And since we are all travelers in this world and the next—

This book is for you.

— Contents —

Foreword ix

"All aboard for Horseshoe Curve, the Altoona Railroaders
Memorial Museum, and RR Memories!" 1

"The Valley that Changed the World!" 13

"Johnny Appleseed" 29

"Valley Forge, the Legend, Lore and Mystery" 35

"Haunted Pennsylvania: Tillie Pierce,
What a Girl Saw and Heard" 53

"The Story of the 11th Pennsylvania's Sallie" 68

"The Salient Spring of Rachel Carson" 72

"Massy Harbison, Terror on the Frontier" 95

"Louisa May Alcott's Magic Inkstand" 111

"Zane Grey ... Cowboy Secrets" 118

"It Might Have Been, the Story of Billy Conn" 132

"They Came to America, Echoes from Our Past" 146

"Pennsylvania Wilds" 174

"This is Pittsburgh!" 191

"The Right Stuff: Sophie Masloff" 211

"Historic Connellsville ... Hometown Memories" 217

About the Author and "What Readers Have to Say" 238

Selected Bibliography 242

— FOREWORD —

I love history, especially Pennsylvania history. I love researching it. To me, research is like a treasure hunt, because I am forever uncovering gems of yore. Even more, I love writing about our past, for the past speaks to us– *if we listen.*

My books afford time-travel, something about which I often fantasize. Since nothing is ever lost or destroyed, the great Albert Einstein believed that actual time-travel would one day be possible. Of course, visitors to the past would be observers only. History does not offer revision. It proffers lessons.

Immediately after the premier volume of *County Chronicles* debuted in late October 2004, readers began asking me if I had begun the second volume. The fact that my *Chronicles* would be a series had been announced in the Foreword of the first volume, as well as in several newspaper articles round about. Originally, I had intended to stay within the general vicinity of southwestern Pennsylvania; but I decided, after prompting from readers, to loosen those confines.

County Chronicles, the series, discusses historic figures and events that left their dusky imprints across the landscape of our entire commonwealth. I have, on occasion, been referred to as a writer of local history, but I daresay– *all history is local.*

As I did in the first four volumes, I decided to add, at the end of this book, a "Hometown Memories" segment. There are two reasons for this. First and foremost, Connellsville, one of the most historic towns within the Commonwealth, celebrated its bicentennial in 2006. The other reason is that our southwestern corner of the state has, for far too long, been the forgotten segment of Pennsylvania. As a writer of Pennsylvania's vibrant past, I naturally want to share with readers a bit about *my* neck of Penn's Woods, which is replete with history and scenic delight.

In keeping with the first four books, this volume of the series will *not* be a chronological history, but rather a bright and colorful tapestry of assorted people, places and events that affected and shaped our state's exciting story. Thus, the reader may skip around, choosing a Chronicle according to interest and mood.

My style is conversational, not the documentary style found in most conventional history books, where this fascinating subject is chronicled with dates and events of politics, war and social issues. History is so much more! *It is the full scope of human experiences.* Politics, war and social issues to be sure, but history is also art– both the creative and the performing arts– science, industry and innovations, religion, medicine, significant achievements in every field of endeavor, love and its opposite, fear; the list is virtually endless. There should be no fences around history; it is a spacious realm with a diversity of fascinating vistas.

Each Chronicle in every volume unfolds like a story. That is what history is– the *story* of a small town– perhaps one you've never heard of- or a city, a state or nation; and more than anything else, *history is people.* They throng these pages, leaping to life out of the text, to become, I hope, unforgettable.

The great historian Richard Ketchum once wrote in a book dedication- "History is us."

I sometimes feel as though I know the historical figures about whom I write more than I do most people around me today. After all, I don't get to read other people's mail, personal papers, or their diaries, as I often do with many of the luminaries who have long passed over.

Make no mistake, I do my homework. "History is not history unless it is the truth," the astute A. Lincoln once declared; and History should never hide the truth. Truth can be stranger, more captivating- and ever so much more thrilling than fiction. And let me tell you that after four decades of reading and writing about the past, I have reached another indisputable conclusion: *history is full of surprises.*

I do not presume to apply the lofty title "historian" to my name. To echo an esteemed Pennsylvanian, author David McCullough, I consider myself a writer whose *milieu* is the past. Along with the meticulous research, many of the histories found in this series are seasoned and warmed with nostalgic memories gained through personal experiences and interviews. In addition, each volume of my *County Chronicles* is a convenient travel guide to Pennsylvania's historic sites.

Concise enough to read in one sitting, each Chronicle is complete in itself- ideal for today's busy people who like to read.

I am proud to state that both men and women, teen to senior, enjoy my *County Chronicles.* From the outset of this series, my goal has been to reach a wide range of readers and not just die-hard history buffs. On occasion, I have encountered a wary reader who has expressed doubt: "I didn't like history in school."

"Hold on!" I interpose. "Answer me this: Do you like a good story well told? A story well stocked with mystery, romance, spice, adventure, and lots of action? A cliff-hanger at every page-turn?"

"Sure!" comes the inevitable swift reply.

"Well then," I say, "you like history. You just don't know you do!"

For the reader who seeks the enjoyment of a good story, written history is frequently burdensome, pedantic, even tedious. On the other hand, the historical novel, while often dramatic and compelling, rarely, if indeed ever, can be relied upon for historical accuracy. It has long been my belief that this gap could and should be bridged, that these two literary forms could be wedded to create a marriage possessing vivid drama and historical truth.

And so, drawn from a spectrum of counties, each volume continues to be a vivid- readable- collection of Pennsylvania's true stories, as varied as the people, the places, and the events they depict. Yet they share a kinship. All the stories breathe the same spirit, the spirit that grew out of the great American spirit, to what we now call the "American Heritage."

My main goals with my Chronicles have always been to stimulate pride and appreciation in Pennsylvania's rich, layered history and to spark further interest in the subjects therein. *It is my hope too that readers will keep these numbered, very collectible books in their families, to pass down from one generation to another.*

Greater minds than mine have distinguished history as the most important subject in school. An *unawareness* of history is akin to planting cut flowers. History not only gives us roots, it teaches us valuable lessons. History teaches us how to behave. History teaches us what America stands for- what we should be willing to stand up for! *And more than anything else, history is love of home- and country.*

It is pleasing and headily gratifying to announce that my *County Chronicles* have thus far garnered three major awards, the Athena Award from my hometown of Connellsville, a Citation/Special Recognition Award from the Pennsylvania House of Representatives, and a Congratulatory/Special Recognition Award from the Senate of Pennsylvania for: "... the significant contribution to the citizens of the commonwealth of Pennsylvania. ... Whereas a writer of considerable talent, Ms. O'Hanlon-Lincoln penned [*County Chronicles*] in a most professional manner, with meticulously researched stories of ... history and landscape. ... Ms. O'Hanlon-Lincoln is truly deserving of great respect and gratitude for her book which details this commonwealth's rich history ... ."

The Pennsylvania Senate Library stated: "*County Chronicles* is a welcome addition to the Senate Library ... the history you provide will help anyone researching Pennsylvania."

In addition to the Pennsylvania Senate Library, *County Chronicles* have found several other prestigious homes in: the library and archives at Heinz History Center; the cadet libraries at the United States Military Academy at West Point and the United States Naval Academy at Annapolis; the George C. Marshall Library, the Virginia Military Institute, Lexington, Virginia; and the Special Collections Department in the library at Washington and Lee University, Lexington, to name a few.

Since the release of *County Chronicles Volume III*, I did two television programs, *Faces of Fayette* in my home area, and *PA Books* with host Brian Lockman on PCN, Pennsylvania Cable Network.

The feedback from readers, across the state of Pennsylvania and beyond, has been amazing, and I thank each of you who took the time to pen me your impressions. I have been called a "state-of-the-heart" writer. I write from the heart to reach the heart- *I write for you.*

I so enjoy sharing with you, in each of the volumes of *County Chronicles*, the vast wealth of history that is embedded in Pennsylvania's lush, rolling hills and valleys, majestic mountains, and ever mysterious deep woods.

And what wonderful memories I am increasingly reaping with my Chronicles! Like "Dorothy," I have clicked my heels together thrice and repeated that time-honored phrase, "There's no place like home!"

I hope you find the stories of Pennsylvania's past as captivating as I do. It is my ardent desire that by the conclusion of this fifth volume, those of you who live in Pennsylvania will see home with new eyes, to wit with appreciation and admiration; and those readers from afar will have become cognizant of a magical land- just over the rainbow.

Now, I invite you to open that charming window to the past that beckons on the cover of this book ... enter through the tunnel of time, and embark with me across the turning pages along the yellow brick road to history, as we explore this unique corner of our nation once called "Penn's Woods."

Ceane O'Hanlon-Lincoln
Connellsville, Fayette County, Pennsylvania
April 12, 2009

"In days to come, when your children
ask you what these stones mean,
you shall tell them."
— Joshua 4:7

Central City Vista in autumn splendor, Somerset County, PA
Though this photo was captured in Somerset County, the juvenile red-tailed hawk is soaring over Bedford County.
Photo by professional nature photographer Glenn E. Mucy
This and other images available by calling: 724-379-8370

"ALL ABOARD FOR HORSESHOE CURVE, THE ALTOONA RAILROADERS MEMORIAL MUSEUM, AND RR MEMORIES!"

"Horseshoe Curve just has to be the best train watching in North America!"
– Ceane O'Hanlon-Lincoln

If ever you have a chance to travel to Altoona, Blair County, Pennsylvania, be certain to visit the famous Horseshoe Curve. This railroad engineering marvel in Pennsylvania's gorgeous Allegheny Mountains is a national historic landmark.

The scenic railroad curve *is* shaped like a horseshoe, hence the name. Folks in my neck of Penn's Woods, in the Pittsburgh area, will recognize the name of one of its designers, J. Edgar Thomson. Thomson shares the honor for this engineering feat with Herman Haupt.

The famous Horseshoe Curve

Born in 1808, J. Edgar Thomson is considered an American civil engineer, railroad executive and industrialist. He was president of the Pennsylvania Railroad from 1852 to 1874, when he oversaw the railroad's conversion from wood to coal as a fuel for its steam locomotives. During that smoky age– coal carried coal.

The "Steel King," Andrew Carnegie, another of the period's powerful titans, and his partners opened the Edgar Thomson Steel Works in 1873 in Braddock, Allegheny County, naming it for Thomson, the president of the Pennsylvania Railroad. Bear in mind, readers, that though this no-income-tax era was a dog-eat-dog epoch, the moguls of the time sat on each other's boards and, to some extent, "scratched each other's backs," to control as much industry and finance as they could.

Resultant of the Bessemer steel-making process, the first inexpensive industrial method for the mass production of steel, the Edgar Thomson Works was established on the historic site where, on July 5, 1755, British Major General Edward Braddock met his ignominious defeat during the French and Indian War in the Battle of the Monongahela. Then, French and Indian forces ambushed and nearly wiped out Braddock's flying column, mortally wounding the general himself. If it had not been for the valiant George Washington, who, in a rear-guard action, orchestrated a retreat, none of Braddock's panic-stricken men would have escaped torture and death that fateful day.

One hundred and twenty years later, on August 22, 1875, on that spot that had felt the heat of battle, the site began to experience another kind of heat. Here, the Edgar Thomson Works' Bessemer converter produced its first liquid steel, destined to become 2,000 steel rails for the Pennsylvania Railroad. The PRR was the largest railroad by traffic and revenue in the United States throughout the twentieth century, at one time the largest publicly traded corporation in the world. At its peak, the PRR controlled over 10,000 miles of rail line, employing over 250,000 people.

The Bessemer brought significant changes to the steel and railroad industries. You can picture how the PRR's rails were made if ever you get an opportunity to visit Pittsburgh's Station Square, where you will see at Bessemer Court an authentic "Big Bess" converter, a compelling relic from Pittsburgh's dramatic industrial past. You can read more about the hulking "Big Bess" in "This is Pittsburgh," this volume.

In its heyday, the great Edgar Thomson Works was capable of producing over 225 tons of steel rails per day for the Pennsylvania and other railroads. Today, these works are part of U. S. Steel (born out of the vast Carnegie Steel Company, including the Edgar Thomson Works), and at this 2009 writing, two of its blast furnaces continue in operation.

Now to return to Horseshoe Curve: This railroad engineering marvel has been open since February 15, 1854, built by the prestigious Pennsylvania Railroad and later used by the Penn Central line, then Conrail. Currently, it is owned by Norfolk Southern Railway and used by Amtrak's Pennsylvanian service.

Located in Kittanning Gap at the summit of the Allegheny Front, approximately five miles (8 km) west of Altoona, the Horseshoe bend is a tight arc of approximately 220 degrees. The horseshoe design is, of course, comprised of two separate curves. On the north side, the radius measures 637 feet, tightening to 609 on the south side. Edgar Thomson and Herman Haupt responded with this design because of the great difficulty in constructing a railroad through the summit of the Allegheny Mountains.

From the outset, Horseshoe Curve has been an important location to railroad traffic in the United States. During the Civil War, it was guarded by Union soldiers; and during World War II, Adolf Hitler made it an objective. The Nazis attempted to sabotage Horseshoe Curve via Operation Pastorius.

Staged in June 1942 and targeted at strategic US economic sites, Operation Pastorius was a failed plan for sabotage in a series of attacks by Nazi agents inside the United States. Named for Francis Daniel Pastorius, the leader of the first organized German settlement in America, the operation recruited eight operatives who resided in the States. Two of them, Ernest Burger and Herbert Haupt, were American citizens. The others had worked at various jobs throughout America. I find it ironic that the surnames of the leading designer of the Horseshoe Curve RR site and one of its leading would-be destroyers are the same, though there were no blood ties between the two men.

Their mission was to sabotage the hydroelectric plants at Niagara Falls and the strategic railroad site at Horseshoe Curve, in addition to a list of other targets.

After a crash course in sabotage techniques, the operatives were given nearly $175,000 in American money and put aboard two submarines to land on the east coast of the United States. By June 16, 1942, via two separate U-boats, the operatives were all ashore. Nevertheless, before long, two of the saboteurs decided to back out. When George John Dasch turned himself in to authorities in Washington, DC, he was, incredibly, dismissed as a lunatic, until, in exasperation, he flung the huge wad of cash he had been given to use toward the mission's objectives across the top of the surprised agent's desk. It was then that a horde of G-men descended on Dasch, intensely interrogating him for hours on end.

Over the next two weeks, the other saboteurs were all apprehended and put on military trial with specific instructions from President Franklin D. Roosevelt. All were found guilty and sentenced to death. The President commuted Burger's and Dasch's sentences to life and thirty years, respectively, since they had turned themselves in and provided information leading to the arrests of the others. The electric-chair executions were held in Washington, DC, soon afterward.

In 1966, Horseshoe Curve was designated as a National Historic Landmark and is today part of the National Register of Historic Places.

Here are some other interesting statistics on the Curve. It is 1,800 feet across, and its length is 2,375 feet. In nearly continuous

The Horseshoe Curve funiculars

COUNTY CHRONICLES

operation since it opened in 1854, Horseshoe Curve originally comprised two tracks. It was widened to four tracks between 1898 and 1900. Conrail removed one of the tracks in 1981, and at this writing (2009), the Curve remains in this three-track configuration.

I hope one day soon you will take a beautiful drive through the Allegheny Mountains to Horseshoe Curve. Autumn is the best time, I think, to visit when Pennsylvania's woods are aflame with a gamut of jewel-tone colors.

Looking about, you will appreciate the great challenge the Pennsylvania Railroad had here, the trials and tribulations the workers overcame by completing railroad tracks through this rough, mountainous terrain. With nothing more than sheer muscle and "guts"- that is, the resolve to etch a permanent place for themselves within the framework of their adopted country- several hundred Irish laborers, aided by gunpowder and pack animals, hacked out the track's bed on the slopes of the majestic Allegheny Mountains. There is an old joke that in the mid and late-nineteenth century, there was steam power and Irish power. The result those Irish workers achieved is historic. The once-impenetrable Alleghenies were now conquered- and America had its gateway to the West.

A stairway to heaven for train enthusiasts

Once at Horseshoe Curve, you can either ride the incline, the "funicular," or you can get your exercise by climbing the 194 beautifully landscaped steps to the tracks atop where the surrounding vistas are breathtakingly beautiful. For you railroad enthusiasts, I doubt you will ever have a better front-row seat for train watching anywhere.

It is never a long wait for the next train.

Horseshoe Curve is a train person's wonder. Few railroads, if any, permit visitors to get this up-close and personal to an operating mainline. It is exciting. You will thrill to the panoramic beauty from the trackside observation deck, and, I am certain, ponder the rich, layered history of the site.

Bring refreshments. There are comfortable benches and picnic tables under the lofty shade trees in the small park (constructed by the Pennsylvania Railroad in 1879), the perfect spot to enjoy the view as you wait for the next train to round the great Curve. Listen ... suddenly a distant sound echoes across the valley. And then, within moments, we spot it, a train! A train is coming!

The last time I visited Horseshoe Curve, with my husband and some friends, it was a day in July 2008. Since the afternoon was hot and exceptionally humid, we took the funicular rather than the steps. No sooner did we arrive at the top when a train made its grand appearance.

Below, be certain to take time at the visitors' center, where descriptive displays and stories will help you to better appreciate the work it took to complete such a marvel. The center also houses a gift shop with souvenirs to tempt railroad buffs of any age, including a nice selection of books.

Before we move on to the Altoona Railroaders Memorial Museum, let me relate to you a few details about a couple of the area's most famous train wrecks. The first in our discussion is the one that to this day bears the grisly yet legendary description the "great circus train wreck."

A famous traveling circus of the late nineteenth century, the Walter L. Main Circus, was just beginning a tour through central Pennsylvania in May of 1893, when a horrible accident occurred. During the early morning hours- approximately 5:30- of Decoration (now Memorial) Day, the circus train was making its way down a steep grade of track from Houtzdale (Clearfield County) to Lewistown

What a thrill to see a long train round the great Horseshoe Curve!

Horseshoe Curve's visitors' center houses a wealth of information.

(Blair County) via the Tyrone & Clearfield Railroad, a branch of the Pennsylvania Railroad. The steep grade mentioned above is the same grade the Horseshoe Curve is on- i.e. the eastern slope of the Allegheny Front.

Before its downward spiral, the train, comprised of three passenger sleeper-cars and fourteen other circus cars, rolled along without incident toward Lewistown, where the circus was scheduled to put on a show the subsequent day. The distance between Houtzdale and Lewistown, by train, is only about sixty-five miles, but betwixt those two towns- the geography changes drastically.

From the first moment they started down the mountain, the engineer fought gravity for control of the heavy circus train. Stretching along the tracks for about a quarter of a mile in length, it must have been a spectacle to see, the words, in black, red and gold, across the sides proclaiming- "Walter L. Main's All New Monster Shows."

When the train began the precarious descent above Vail Station, the harried engineer became powerless to abate its rapidly increasing speed, finally losing control five miles north of Tyrone.

This train had a combination of hand and air brakes; and to quote Paula Zitzler, historian and author of *Unscheduled Stop: the Town of Tyrone and the Wreck of the Walter L. Main Circus Train* (2008), it was quite simply "Too much train for the engine."

The train raced wildly down the tracks at a death-defying speed, rocking and reeling on its mad course, sweeping round the railed curves made slippery by the early morning dew. Out-of-control, it sped round a dozen or more curves, including the one at Big Fill, almost continually picking up speed until it was going so fast, one witness said, "It would have been impossible to count the telegraph poles." This from an article by Louis E. Cooke penned in 1922 and printed in the circus magazine *Bandwagon*, Vol. 11, No. 3 (May-June), 1967, (taken from Cooke's circus history) about Walter E. Main and the great circus train wreck.

Cooke was a well-known agent for several famous shows at the turn of the last century, including the *Buffalo Bill Wild West Show, Barnum & Bailey, Miller Bros.*, and the *101 Ranch Show* (of which I wrote in "Tom Mix, King of the Cowboys," found in *County Chronicles IV*). Cooke's biography of Walter L. Main was penned with extensive cooperation from Main himself, as well as from many employees and former employees of the Main show.

In a lengthy August 2008 telephone interview, author Zitzler- who has probably done more research on this subject than anyone- told me, "That train dropped about a thousand feet in ten miles." By this point in time, the ultra-heavy train was literally flying down the mountain!

Past Big Fill Curve, near Gardner's, is a hairpin loop, beyond which there is a straight-track shot into Vail Station. But, to echo Paula Zitzler, this train was destined for a most-dreadful *unscheduled stop*. It never made it into Vail.

When the runaway train hit that abrupt curve, the heavily laden cars flew- factually flew- off the tracks onto their sides, grinding human and animal lives into a macabre mass of misery whilst sending some of the cars with their flesh-and-blood cargo plummeting violently down the steep embankment.

The problem, as touched on above, was that the circus train was much longer and heavier than the average train, and as it headed for the bottom of the hill at McCann's Crossing, thirteen of the weighty fourteen cars (with circus animals and a variety of crew) jumped the tracks, smashing to splinters. Centrifugal force violently swung the circus combination-car (half sleeper, half dining car) sideways on the track, where it cushioned the trio of sleepers behind it, or there would have been a greater loss of human lives. The locomotive and the trio of sleeper-cars were all that remained on the rails.

From my research, I do not think the engineer was initially speeding or in any way reckless. There could have been malfunctioning brakes that factored into the problem. Of that I cannot be certain. But as per author/historian Paula Zitzler, "It was simply too much train for one engine to handle."

Immediately after the crash, Engineer M. S. "Red" Creswell took off down the tracks on foot, running as fast as his shaky legs could carry him to Vail Station, which he could see in the distance. It was initially reported that he ran away, from the scene of the accident. In actuality, he ran to Vail Station to wire for help.

According to circus-train expert Susie O'Brien, circus owner Walter Main had had concerns about the train's steep mountain route and asked Conductor William Snyder to wire ahead to request an additional engine. When Superintendent S.S. Blair asked him how many cars he had, Blair replied that he had sufficient braking power for that train. In the Superintendent's defense, he was new to his job and was going by the book; however, strictly-by-the-book was not the right decision in regard to that particular situation; hence there was not enough braking power to properly slow the circus train during its steep descent. The decision would cost Blair his job and any future railroad employment.

Why Snyder did not explain to his super that those circus cars were longer and heavier than normal railroad cars bothered me; yet, I could find no data, no documentation, to answer that question.

Piecing together remnants of history is like the old game of connecting the dots, the dots being facts. Likely Snyder wired ahead to appease circus owner Walter Main. When Blair told him he had sufficient braking power for the number of cars in his train, Snyder dropped the matter. As a conductor, his concern was keeping the train on time to meet schedule. "He had nothing to do with the mechanics of the train," Susie O'Brien reminded me. I am not stating that this is the whole truth, only how Mrs. O'Brien and I "connected the dots."

My readers are likely wondering why Engineer Creswell had not voiced any concerns to Superintendent Blair about the train's lack of braking power. He did. Blair's reply was: "If you can't bring the train down, I'll send someone who can!" Red Creswell's answer "All right, I am coming" ended the discussion and, as I've noted above, S.S. Blair's railroad career.

All of the accident's human deaths befell circus laborers and crew on the flat cars and in the stock cars. The circus performers and management staff, in the sleepers at the end of the train, were spared death and serious injury.

The Walter L. Main Circus was renowned for its menagerie of exotic animals. When the horrific din of roar and thunder that was the accident quieted, the circus' animal cages lay smashed into kindling. A gigantic gorilla named Man-Slayer, lions, tigers, leopards, wild boars, elephants, and a myriad of other creatures bellowed, roared, screamed and either lay helpless with shattered bones, or leaped forth to liberty in the surrounding Pennsylvania woods.

About fifty (accounts/numbers differ) beautiful horses were killed outright, including the circus' valuable performing horses- all elegant beauties representing years of patient training. Many horses not dead had to be put down, including Snow Flake the famous fire-jumping steed. The white as Snow Flake lay entrapped in the debris, breathing heavily, the whites of her large eyes indicative of her panicked state. Now and again, she made a valiant attempt to rise, but her efforts were in vain. At first, Main would not allow his crew to put his favorite down. He stubbornly held on to the hope that Flake would pull through the ordeal. She did not, succumbing to her injuries the next day.

Main loved that mare, training her himself. The circus owner likened Flake to a dog for the way she followed him around. Whatever Walter sought to teach her, always eager to please, she had willingly learned. In fact, Flake had learned to imitate Main. That was how he had taught her to jump through the fire rings. He did it first, and she followed suit. More than anything else, it broke his heart when the cherished pet-performer, so like a family member, expired.

Along the jumble of wrecked cars, pandemonium reigned. The head of an elephant named Jennie was ensnared in the tangle of a wrecked car. As soon as she was released, the great beast struggled to her feet, shaking off the heavy timbers like they were straw, only to plow through the balance of the wreckage, happily trumpeting her freedom. Jennie had, however, injured her leg and forever after walked with a limp. The larger of Main's two elephants, Lizzie, had not sustained injuries and became, in the wake of the tragedy, a great help with the cleanup.

To quote from Paula Zitzler's impressively researched *Unscheduled Stop*: "A large black gorilla exploded from the wreckage, tossing the pieces of his wagon aside with his powerful arms. Agitated, he ran back and forth, finally settling on a tree stump where he continued to howl and beat his chest."

A tiger, with the jaws of death open to reveal his fearsome teeth, stepped out of the remains of his cage, and catching sight of a zebra, immediately bounded for it. The zebra survived the attack due to the loud, frantic shouts of those nearby, which caused the agitated cat to dash off into the countryside. I have also read that the same tiger attacked a wounded, circus ox.

Tyrone-area lore recounts yet today the story of one of the escaped Bengal tigers. The day of the wreck, a local farmer's daughter, Hannah Friday, was en route to the barnyard to milk her cow, when she espied the huge, orange, black-banded cat emerging from the surrounding trees. Miraculously, the young woman was able to execute a hasty escape, running for her life back to the house. The hungry, snarling tiger ignored her, opting for the cow, and leaping upon its back, quickly killed it. Soon after, a posse set out after the tiger.

As a result of telephone discussions with Susie Lehner O'Brien, Hannah's great-great-niece (who has collected information and memorabilia on the great circus wreck for years and who has worked closely with author/historian Paula Zitzler), I was able to garner several other compelling details of the historic accident. First of all, the Fridays would not have been able to defend themselves against the marauding tiger, since Hannah's father Hiram forbade guns on his property. A Civil War veteran of at least two ferocious battles, he had had enough of firearms. Mrs. O'Brien told me that Alfred Thomas– since he was the only person round about who, as a bear hunter, had a large enough caliber weapon– was the posse member who actually shot the tiger. Thomas fired the killing shot in close proximity to the Friday farm, within the murky veil of Hunters' Woods. Today, the tiger's skull, complete with bullet-hole, hangs on the wall at the Tyrone Sportsman's Club.

Susie O'Brien informed me that a black panther was also shot by a local farmer. The incident unfolded like this: Under cover of darkness, the panther broke into a chicken coop. Upon hearing the noise, farmer Gotleib Wesner, thinking a fox had gotten into his hen house, burst upon the shadowy scene with a loaded shotgun. An eerie splash of moonlight revealed the great black cat with a chicken in its mouth. Wesner's immediate reaction was to let go with both barrels.

I don't know if those shootings could have been helped. They occurred in an era long before the introduction of the tranquillizer gun (circa 1950) for capturing animals. And take into account, readers, that these rural folk depended on their farm animals for their very existence. Horses, for instance, were needed for farm work as well as for transportation in 1893. And one can well imagine the fear that permeated the area over the escaped big cats and other dangerous animals. Mothers kept their children indoors, and most of the men took to toting a gun wherever they ventured.

A woman, walking from Vail Station in the direction of the scene of the wreck, encountered a lion on her route. Spinning part-way round to run, she discovered a hyena within a few feet of her on the road. I think what likely saved her was the fact that she did *not* run, rather she "froze up" and began screaming loudly, causing the stressed lion and hyena to run posthaste, in opposite directions, into the deep surrounding woods.

One lion was easily captured by its trainer, who tossed a lasso over the big cat's mane, securing him with the rope to a stout tree. Simba then lay there content to view the goings-on as if they were everyday occurrences. A second male lion, however, was not so content to be thus restrained, something he surely was not used to; and after being tethered to a tree, ended up strangling in his frenzy to free himself. Other large jungle cats, completely unnerved by the calamity, dashed off into the woods, "looking for new fields," as Louis E. Cooke worded it in his 1922 article.

A great many monkeys escaped, chattering wildly, into the adjacent trees. Snakes, parrots and other exotic birds took off for the safety and shelter of the woods. Several animals that could have run off chose not to, including camels, two elephants, a zebra, a yak, and a variety of others from different parts of the globe.

As bad as the accident was, it was not as bad as it would have been had it happened in the dark of night. If you recall, I mentioned earlier that the crash occurred around 5:30 a.m. As soon as the dead could be pulled out of the wreckage, they were taken to Tyrone. From the outset, the people of Tyrone verified their kind Pennsylvania hearts when they came to the aid of those frazzled circus people.

One of the first to exit the wrecked train was circus owner Walter L. Main, who had been aboard, traveling with his circus. Main was in his thirties at the time of the railway disaster. In a heart-wrenching glance, Main took in the dire situation. All of his years of hard work, frugality, patience and perseverance lay in shattered ruin about him. However, he wasn't about to let this turn of events ruin him. Amidst the horrible mess, calmly and with clarity of judgment, he began barking out orders to his crew in his nightshirt and bare feet. When he finally retired, hours later, his feet were reduced to bloody pulps.

Immediately, the good people of Tyrone provided rooms and hospitality to Mr. Main and his people. This succor extended over a period of approximately nine days– the time that it took the Pennsylvania Railroad to rebuild the cars and wagons and the stouthearted Main to assemble a new outfit and continue on with his tour.

Mind, several of his crew were dead. The catastrophe had claimed fifty or more of his trained horses, as well as a variety of other animals, dead, injured or missing. Some of those animals were never recovered, and not one of his decorative circus wagons had survived. Main placed his losses at upwards of $150,000 (1893 value).

Soon after the calamity, countless telegrams began arriving in Tyrone for the circus owner, proffering financial aid and help of all kinds. Other circuses came to the rescue by promptly shipping Main extra animals and equipment. It was a poignant testament to Walter L. Main's high standing and to the great human spirit in general. This author has always advocated that crises will bring out the worst and the best of humankind.

Walter L. Main, who hailed from Geneva, Ohio, was the son of a schoolteacher mother and a veterinary father. When Walter was a youngster, his father habitually traveled with the circus, during the tour season, as its veterinarian. From the age of twelve, Walter had accompanied him, and that led to his great love of the Big Top. From an early age, Walter dreamed of owning his own circus. He had a difficult time, however, convincing his mother of his plan, who wanted a college education for her son. To appease his mother, Walter made her a deal: If his circus failed, he would then go to college. Thus, from the outset, Main was a determined young man with an unwavering goal to succeed in the circus world he so loved.

The circus' women should be mentioned for their kindness, in the wake of the train wreck, in easing pain and comforting those they could until help arrived from the town. Special mention is in order for the animal trainers, who, within the timeframe they were in Tyrone, did manage to round up several of the scattered, frightened creatures. A keeper named William Jenks was endeavoring to subdue an overwrought lion in the woods near the disaster site, when the great cat seized him with its deadly claws and teeth, ripping off the trainer's kneecap. The profusely bleeding Jenks was hurried by horse and wagon to the hospital in Altoona for treatment.

For weeks after the wreck, locals met wild animals at nearly every turn. I can imagine what it must have been like to encounter a panther en route to a neighbor's back porch! Stories persist to this day about those animals that were never recovered. I have heard many an embellished tale as far west of the wreck site as Fayette County, my home area, of black panthers roaming the mountains of Pennsylvania yet today, descendants of those panthers liberated by the great train wreck of 1893. Not to say that panthers, even black ones, have not been sighted in our abundant Pennsylvania woods– see "Ghostwalkers" in *County Chronicles III.*

During our riveting talks, the knowledgeable Susie O'Brien related to me the story of the missing kangaroo that was sighted, the summer following the accident, by a trapper in the woods several miles from the train wreck. John Swope had never in his life seen such a creature. "He seldom left the woods where he hunted and trapped," O'Brien told me. "The only time he'd go into town was to sell his pelts and purchase a few supplies."

With animation, Swope described the strange being to the folks below in the Huntingdon-County town of Alexandria. A listener dashed over to the library and, returning with a book, pointed to an image of a kangaroo, asking, "Is this the creature you saw?" Swope answered to the effect that "It sure as hell was!"

Walter L. Main had ensured that a list of his missing animals be sent around the entire area for a so-many-mile radius. The kangaroo was eventually captured with the aid of a net not long afterward. "He must have followed the forested Warrior Ridge to the Alexandria area," Susie concluded.

"It took railroad workers just two days to clear the tracks," author Paula Zitzler told me. What is amazing was that those laborers managed, within those couple of days, to clear the wreckage not only from the tracks, but the bulk of it from the field as well.

The dead circus animals were deposited into a huge pit that was dug near the scene of the disaster, after which all the wreckage that was not usable was tossed on top of the carcasses and lit, rendering a giant bonfire, whence the smoke, for miles around, could be seen and smelled. The remains were then covered with the dug-out earth and the pit smoothed over.

Two of the circus employees who were killed were buried in a cemetery in Tyrone. Others were transported to their families and their respective hometowns. Over the years, when a circus passed through Tyrone, it always paused so that the company could pay their respects at Grandview Cemetery, where the victims of the 1893 accident are interred. I must point out that this was not just the Walter L. Main Circus but *any* circus troupe passing through the area. They all paid their due respects to their circus brethren. Mrs. O'Brien told me that she believed the last circus passed through the area in 1958.

In 1951, sixty years after it happened, Cecil B. DeMille incorporated the Walter L. Main circus train wreck into the now-classic film, *The Greatest Show on Earth*, albeit DeMille took dramatic license with the story.

According to an article originally published in April 1993, and written by Suzanne Sickler Ohl, an early member of the Tyrone Area Historical Society, on June 23, 1975, a memorial plaque was dedicated (where the wreck occurred) at McCann's Crossing, lest the tragic episode be lost in the fog of time. About one hundred Tyrone-area folks gathered for the occasion. The plaque's inscription briefly describes the great circus train wreck of 1893, in addition to listing the names of the people involved in the memorial project.

In 1993, in honor of the 100th anniversary of the Walter L. Main circus train wreck, the Tyrone Area Historical Society assembled for a special meeting. Chairperson for the gathering was Susie Lehner O'Brien, the great-great-niece of Hannah Friday, the woman who managed to escape unharmed when a hungry Bengal tiger from the circus rubble jumped on the back of her cow, killing it. Mrs. O'Brien, as touched on above, lives near the accident site and maintains an extensive scrapbook of the historic disaster. Her family has a collection of artifacts found about the wreck locale, as well as other Walter L. Main Circus memorabilia.

The great circus train wreck of 1893 was, if not the worst circus catastrophe in the world at that time, one of the worst. However, it is not the only railroad memory left behind in Tyrone. There are many.

The railroad came through the town in 1849, and Tyrone was incorporated not long afterward. With the railroad came economic prosperity that included the erection of the city's beautiful homes, resplendent with Victorian gingerbread, such as stained glass, ornate staircases and decorative moldings. The distinguished mansions still grace the city's charming tree-lined streets. Today, Amtrak stops in Tyrone, and the railroad remains an integral part of the Tyrone scene.

To learn more about the great circus train wreck of 1893, plus the historically rich railroad community of Tyrone, I highly recommend Paula Zitzler's above-mentioned book, a well-researched, factual account of the 1893 circus disaster.

There was another news-making train wreck in the Altoona/Horseshoe Curve area on February 18, 1947. At least twenty people were killed instantly when Pennsy's/Pennsylvania Railroad's "Red Arrow," their "crack passenger train," Detroit to New York, jumped the tracks about ten miles west of Altoona.

The runaway train sent two engines, the mail car, baggage car, sleepers, and the dining car soaring over the steep embankment. In addition to the dead, many people were injured, some later expiring in nearby hospitals.

This wreck occurred at 3:25 a.m., about two miles west of Horseshoe Curve. The injured were rushed to facilities in and around Altoona, where attendants became nearly overwhelmed with the casualties.

Newspaper men at the scene reported the scattered, twisted wreckage a "weird sight." Railroad workers were laboring to remove the trapped and pinned injured by cutting through the debris, whilst a clergyman was attempting to calm frightened passengers in a car that had plunged over the edge. As stated by one Altoona newspaper, a frantic woman passenger atop was "hysterically screaming for her daughter who was in a car that had plummeted down the 100-foot embankment."

Interestingly enough, a railroad engineer who was killed in the disaster was Michael E. McArdle of Scottdale, Pennsylvania. He had cousins who resided on North Pittsburgh

An old-timey locomotive

Street in my hometown of Connellsville and another relative, a Mrs. Charles Reshenberg, whose home place was only a block from my family's house in Brookvale, a section of Dunbar Township.

Located at 1300 Ninth Avenue, Altoona, the Altoona Railroaders Memorial Museum celebrates over a century and a half of railroading heritage in the Altoona area.

In 1854, when the Pennsylvania Railroad opened the Horseshoe Curve, the Allegheny Mountains were no longer a deterrent to Westward rail travel. In the scenic valley below, the town of Altoona emerged the center of PRR operations; and rapidly, this "Railroad City" became the place to conduct business.

The Railroaders Memorial Museum affords visitors the opportunity to relive the early railroad days, witness how the railroaders lived, and discover the magnitude of the great PRR's early railroad operations.

I truly enjoyed this magic-carpet ride through railroad history, and I want to relate that the museum is open Monday through Saturday, 9 a.m. to 5 p.m. Sundays 11 a.m. to 5 p.m. The price of admission is reasonable, with special rates for children and seniors. At this writing, there are special winter hours, so I suggest that would-be visitors call ahead: 1-888-4-ALTOONA. Or visit the museum online at: www.railroadcity.com.

I cannot conclude this Chronicle without relating to you where we ate lunch our unforgettable day in Altoona. The name of the eatery was Tom and Joe's Diner. Located at 1201 13th Avenue, the place has been an Altoona landmark since 1933– and it is an original!

The blurb on the diner door states that the establishment offers "good homemade food served with a side of sass." The meal was good, the portions generous, and yes, it was served in an entertaining atmosphere. Our waitress was certainly sassy, but it was all in good fun, and we thoroughly enjoyed our time at Tom and Joe's. The regulars who dine there are as delightful as the staff. And it always warms my heart to meet such friendly, helpful fellow Pennsylvanians. You can visit this nostalgic diner ahead of time from your computer at: www.tomandjoes.com.

Start planning your visit to Horseshoe Curve and the Altoona area to experience first-hand Pennsylvania's thrilling railroad past and present. Experience the grand era of trains, gone now but preserved so admirably at the Altoona Railroaders Memorial Museum.

I promise you, it will be well worth the trip.

"THE VALLEY THAT CHANGED THE WORLD!"

"On August 27, 1859, Edwin L. Drake struck oil by drilling near Titusville, Pennsylvania. It was one of those moments that changed the world."
- Kyle R. Weaver, Editor, Stackpole Books

The "Valley that Changed the World," Oil Creek Valley, is, for the most part, located in Venango County, Pennsylvania, extending into Crawford County at Titusville. This northwestern part of Pennsylvania was one of the last areas, if not *the* last region, to be settled. It contained vast forest lands, but little coal or iron, and was comparatively inaccessible. It was a tough wilderness, and the folks who finally settled it were even tougher.

The story of oil in northwestern Pennsylvania does not begin with the "Colonel." Edwin L. Drake did not *discover* oil in 1859, he *struck* it. Long before Drake came to the area, Native Americans collected and made use of petroleum from seeps and pits in the Oil Creek Valley- actually, for *centuries* before, and long before William Penn founded his colony.

Native Americans made use of the oil on the grounds where the Drake Well Museum and Park exist today.

Exhibits at the Drake Well Museum near Titusville discuss how the Indians made use of the oil pits on the grounds where the museum and park exist today. Here, the oil was cribbed (contained) with wooden timbers believed to have been fashioned with stone axes some time between 1415 and 1450. Archaeological studies revealed that these early inhabitants were collecting oil in northwestern Pennsylvania, using sophisticated systems of hydraulic engineering before Christopher Columbus set sail. Though excavations were conducted in 1934 and again in 1970, there are still unanswered questions about these early Indians. Why were they gathering so much oil? What were they using it for?

On one of these Native seeps, 400 years hence, Edwin Laurentine Drake drilled his well- and the world changed forever.

Drake proved that a well could be drilled to produce oil. Little did he or the capitalists who hired him- or anyone- realize the significance of what Drake's operation accomplished. His achievement was not immediately apparent. At that point in time, no one *dreamed* that Drake's well would revolutionize world economics and politics.

But lest we get ahead of ourselves, let us first discuss in brief what use later Indians had for the oil. According to the *Drake Well Museum and Park* guide, the Seneca, of the six nations of the powerful Iroquois Confederacy, used crude oil to preserve animal hides, create paint for adorning their faces and bodies, and for the decorating of sundry articles, such as drums and tunics; but most importantly, they used the oil to protect and heal the skin on their own bodies.

To the Seneca of the area, this gift of Earth Mother was also a commodity. The crude oil they used in trade became known as "Senica/Seneca Oil," and they used it to barter for goods with soldiers at Fort Franklin, the present-day site of Franklin, Pennsylvania. To quote from the above booklet: "Ledgers from 1796 record the fort's inventories of three kegs of 'Senica Oil' [sic] valued at $50."

Remember, readers, there were very few doctors on the frontier; consequently, pioneers made their own remedies, passed down through generations and carried from the old world. They used whiskey for a pain killer and an antiseptic; and they learned remedies, prepared with the gifts of Earth Mother, from the Native Americans. During the eighteenth century, settlers who arrived in the area learned to skim the oil from the surface of Oil Creek, to be used as a medicine for everything from headaches to constipation. Oil was heated and applied to the skin as a treatment for rheumatism, but its most common use was for treatment of the skin- for burns and cuts. Pioneers learned from the Indians to rub it on their horses. The smell kept the flies at bay. They even learned to use it to lubricate the wheels of their wagons. The uses of Seneca Indian Oil were widely quoted, and many a frontier settler kept a bottle of the stuff in his remote cabin. A favorite liniment by the early 1800s, this Seneca Oil is what we call "petroleum jelly" today.

Early entrepreneurs bottled petroleum and exalted it as a cure-all elixir. One of these colorful characters was a canal-boat proprietor from Pittsburgh named Samuel Kier, who, around 1847, started hawking this Pennsylvania-crude preparation in half-pint bottles. He labeled it "Kier's Petroleum," claiming it would cure anything that ailed, including diarrhea, ringworm, eye troubles, even deafness! In spite of Kier's dramatics, like the Native American inhabitants of the area, folks in western Pennsylvania discovered crude oil to be the most beneficial in treating the skin and, when heated, for aches and pains of the joints.

With the passage of time and the advent of the twentieth century, crude oil was used generally to lubricate machinery. Accepted on the Pennsylvania frontier for years for its medicinal uses, crude oil was also burned to produce illumination. Though it rendered light when burned, it gave off a strong odor, not to mention the oily black smoke.

In 1846, Abraham Gesner, a Canadian geologist, distilled what he termed "keroselain" from coal. Others did similar procedures, including Samuel Kier. In addition to his cure-all tonic, Kier began, circa 1850, refining the Pennsylvania crude on his father's property into lamp oil. Kerosene for lamps became a huge industry in the mid-nineteenth century, stimulating the demand for large quantities of crude oil.

At this moment in time, the primary lamp oil was whale oil. However, so many of the poor creatures had been hunted and killed that whales were becoming scarce, and whale oil terribly expensive. That aside, folks needed oil for their lamps "to push back the night" and light their homes.

In December 1854, the Pennsylvania Rock Oil Company of New York was formed for the purpose of developing the oil springs around Titusville, Pennsylvania, for lamp oil- and whatever other possibilities for oil use might surface. I should mention that another name for Pennsylvania crude in that era was "rock oil."

Titusville locals were flabbergasted when the company purchased a tract of land known as the "Hibbard Farm" for $5,000. Hoots of derision echoed throughout the Oil Creek Valley. "Who in their right mind would pay that kind of money for a worthless piece of property a man can't even tramp over without making an oily mess of his boots and pant legs!"

Though oil at that time had its modest uses, the worth of that "mess" was virtually unknown until a Yale chemistry professor, Benjamin Silliman, Jr., conducted a laboratory analysis, concluding that petroleum could well possess significant economic value. Silliman reported that he had been experimenting with the Pennsylvania oil as a lubricant "on watches and fine machinery."

As a result of the astute professor's findings, interest was stimulated in the Pennsylvania Rock Oil Company within a group of New Haven capitalists headed by James Townsend. According to the Drake Well Museum, the group proffered the deal that they would purchase stock if the company were restructured under Connecticut's more liberal incorporation laws. Within a short time, the deal was struck and the paperwork completed. By mid-September of 1855, the new company was launched with $300,000 in capital stock.

As with so many other things in life, progress was slowed due to disagreements. In fact, the New Haven and New York partners were hardly ever in accord. Thus, in 1858, the New Haven associates organized the Seneca Oil Company, straightaway leasing the Titusville property from the Pennsylvania Rock Oil Company. To quote the *Drake Well Museum and Park* guide: "The stage was now set for the appearance of Edwin Laurentine Drake."

However, before the Colonel steps onto what was destined to become a world stage, I'll introduce him to you.

Born in March 1819, Edwin L. Drake came of age on family farms around the Castleton Corners area of Vermont, where he attended local schools. With nothing in his biographical sketch to suggest that he would emerge the father of the modern oil industry, he made no outstanding impression as a youth or a young man. After leaving home at nineteen, Drake drifted from job to job before he accepted a position, from the above-mentioned James Townsend, that would eventually bring him to Titusville, Pennsylvania.

Between 1849 and 1857, Drake was employed by the New York & New Haven Railroad as a conductor, though he had also worked for the railroad as a clerk and an express agent. That seems to have been the longest-lasting job he held to this decisive moment in our story. However, in the summer of 1857, he was forced, due to illness, to resign from his conductor position, opting to settle in New Haven to recuperate. Health would be an issue for the remainder of his life.

During the period when Drake worked for the railroad, he had married, in December of 1845, Philena Adams, who died in 1854, leaving Drake to rear their four-year-old son George. Three years after Philena's passing, Edwin wed, in January 1857, a woman sixteen years his junior, Laura Dowd. Drake's union with Laura produced two sons, Alfred and Charles, and a daughter, Mary Laura.

Whilst residing at the Tontine Hotel in New Haven, Drake had a chance encounter with James Townsend, with whom he subsequently struck up an acquaintance. Enthusiastic about his venture, Townsend talked his new friend into purchasing a small amount of company stock. Apparently, Drake had had sufficient time to recuperate, at least partially, from his illness, and now that he was in need of a job, he accepted Townsend's offer to travel to Titusville to inspect the site and prepare a report to the stockholders.

Though Drake had no background in this sort of endeavor- no experience in drilling- he did not come into the project sans recommendations. In years past, he had observed artesian-well drilling in New York and Pennsylvania; he therefore believed it possible to use similar techniques to harvest oil from the Pennsylvania oil seeps. And let us not discount Drake's free railroad pass that enabled him to travel to Titusville at no cost to the Seneca Oil Company. Townsend hired him on the spot.

Drake made the uneventful journey to Titusville that December (1857), preparing his report that "... the oil seeped into pits and there seemed to be plenty of it." He also did some work on the company's ownership documents, transferring them to the stockholders, who, impressed with Drake's findings, sent him back to Titusville- this time for a longer stay and with a more refined image.

When Edwin Drake stepped off the stagecoach in May 1858, attired in a long swallowtail coat, high top hat, and glossy riding boots, he looked like the salaried agent of an esteemed company. Indeed, the Seneca Oil Company was paying him an annual wage of $1,000. He had also been crowned with the lofty title "Colonel," and though it bore no military significance, it looked impressive on the mail he received from Seneca Oil.

The new, polished Drake stood in the Titusville road and glanced around. Things hadn't changed much, but perhaps *he* could bring about a significant transformation. He had a big job ahead of him- to get oil flowing for the investors.

But how to get the oil out of the ground? Seepage was too slow. Drake decided to dig. On the Hibbard farm, Drake passed several futile weeks digging in the main oil spring, before his crew struck water that flooded the operation. Drake decided next to drill. However, he personally lacked the know-how. He hadn't struck oil yet, but his keen mind struck on an idea. He'd travel to the Pittsburgh area, to Tarentum, to observe how salt wells were drilled. (Some sources say that Drake observed salt-well drilling in western Pennsylvania the previous year.) In Tarentum, the Colonel's plan was to hire an experienced driller.

According to the Drake Well Museum, drilling techniques used to harvest salt brine in the 1840s laid the technological foundation for the present-day oil industry.

To furnish the power for the drilling operation, Drake acquired a six-horsepower steam engine and a Long John boiler. The Long John was a stationary, tubular boiler originally used by steamers. Drake was now set to go except for want of an experienced driller.

The Colonel hired one, but the fellow failed to show up. He then hired a second driller, and he too neglected to report for work. By this time, it was too late in the season to make the long trek via horseback into Pittsburgh again to hire someone personally, so the frustrated Drake had no choice but to shut down operations for the winter. What else could he do? The ground was frozen solid.

However, with the advent of spring- finally- came a driller. "Uncle Billy" he was called round about, and Drake was darn lucky to get him. William A. Smith, a salt-well driller from Tarentum, agreed to work for $2.50 a day.

Billy was also a blacksmith, which meant that he could make the drilling tools that Drake would need. To boot, Smith threw in the services of his teenage son Sam. For the record, it was the white-haired, bearded Uncle Billy who constructed the derrick and the engine house that would result in arguably the world's first oil well. (Canada, West Virginia, and Kentucky contest the validity of "first"; however, this author and many others concede this privilege to the great Keystone State. And it is with pride that I affirm here that Drake Well gave birth to the modern oil industry.)

During the course of the next year, the operation was not without its problems. Water and cave-ins bedeviled Uncle Billy until Drake, who was running out of money, got another bright idea and solved the tribulations with his invention of the drive pipe.

Drake drove, by horse and buckboard, to Erie, Pennsylvania, where he purchased pipe sections made of cast iron, each ten feet long. Back at the Titusville operations, he and Uncle Billy fitted the sections of pipe together, driving the thirty-two-foot pipe through the ground into the bedrock below. This allowed them to drill *inside* the pipe, without the earth collapsing from water seepage. The principle behind this idea is still used today by many companies drilling for hydrocarbons.

Readers, hardly anyone had much faith in Edwin Drake. The locals called his well "Drake's Folly," whilst the Seneca Oil Company continuously lost patience with him. From the outset, Seneca sent very little money to fund the project, finally stopping funding all together, forcing Drake to use what little money he had.

By August, Edwin's money had run out. He was so broke, there was virtually nothing left to feed his family; thus, it was a godsend when two local businessmen decided to help. They guaranteed a loan of $500 for him. It meant food on the table- and he could continue his work at Drake Well.

By mid-August, drilling had progressed to about three feet a day. At the end of the day on Saturday, August 27, 1859, Drake and Uncle Billy were drilling through the layers of sandstone and shale when, of a sudden, the drill dropped six inches. This had not happened before, but Drake and his driller figured the drill had simply dropped into a crevice. The incident bothered them not at all; however, weary from their grueling, hot labor, they acquiesced to aching muscles and rumbling bellies and decided to call it a day.

The next day, Sunday, Uncle Billy went to check on the well, taking his son Sam with him. When he looked down into the shaft, Billy saw a dark liquid floating on the surface of the groundwater. He reached for a piece of tin eave spouting, rolled it, fashioning it into a sort of cup; then, plugging one end, he attached a cord to it and lowered it down into the hole to scoop out a sample. *What he drew up was the first Pennsylvania crude from the world's first oil well.*

Now mind, readers, this was no gusher. The men borrowed a hand pump and filled a wash tub and some whiskey barrels with the black gold. The original well's production is quoted in various sources as ten to twenty barrels per day. But know this: the measure of barrel capacity varied based on barrel size. Drake sank a second well that produced about twenty-four barrels per day; but this was meager compared to what was to follow.

Edwin Drake was not a demonstrative man, and he displayed little excitement over his success. Perhaps he had a "gut feeling" that it would take the oil company years to pay him for his trouble and his accomplishments. Perhaps he knew with some inner light and knowledge that he personally would never benefit from what he did in Oil Creek Valley.

The company sold its Pennsylvania rights in the spring of 1864, finally repaying Drake $507 plus $233 interest for the advances he had made to them. Victory, as it ofttimes is in history, was, for Edwin L. Drake, verily bittersweet.

Though he had been urged to do so, Drake had not been able to afford leases in his own name, nor had he applied for a patent for his grand idea of using cast-iron drive pipe to keep wells from caving in. He likely would have become wealthy if he had patented his invention.

Drake served as justice of the peace for a time and was a founder of Titusville's Saint James Episcopal Church, but harder times were just around the corner. He remained in Titusville until 1863, living a step up from poverty, while others got rich following in his oily footsteps.

When Edwin Drake left the Oil Creek Valley, he was in debt to several people. It was his

Top-hatted Edwin Drake at his well with Peter Wilson, a Titusville druggist and friend (1864). A board-for-board replica of Drake Well stands on the exact site today.
Courtesy the Drake Well Museum and Park

friend and benefactor, Jonathan Watson– the world's first oil millionaire– who bought back from Drake a tract of land at an increased price that allowed the Colonel and his family to leave Titusville in 1863.

Drake then worked as a stockbroker in New York, trying desperately to make money enough to keep his family, pay off his debts, and not fall into complete financial ruin. His stockbroker endeavors failed miserably, and again Drake lost what little money he had.

Life after Titusville was not kind to the former oil man. Poverty plagued him to the point that his unstable health spiraled downward. All that Drake had in savings he had poured into his speculations. The situation grew so bad that his wife Laura (in that long-past era when wives did not earn money) began taking in laundry and sewing as well as boarders to provide support for the family.

It must have been both frightening and frustrating to be in Drake's dire straits, not knowing how he was going to support his wife and children, not knowing if he would ever be well again. What his actual ailments were is not clear in any of the accounts I have read. However, we do know it stemmed from severe arthritis- what more than one source called "muscular neuralgia."

As a result of Laura's letters to old friends in Titusville, those good folks met to raise money for her husband's care. That same year, 1873, they succeeded in persuading the Pennsylvania Legislature to pass a bill providing the "Father of the Modern Oil Industry" with an annual pension of $1,500 for the remainder of his life. To collect his pension, Drake was required to relocate to the Commonwealth. Hence, he moved his family to Bethlehem, Pennsylvania.

In 1870, Edwin Drake penned his account of his achievement. Today, his writings are a fascinating part of the Drake Well Museum's collection. This exceptional man had seen the amazing growth of the oil industry, and he rightfully claimed credit as its founder.

After 1873, Drake was unable to walk. Sadly, he had also lost control of his hands. Sustained missives from his wife to Titusville friends describe his pitiful state and his excruciating pain. After his passing, the pension continued to his widow for the extent of her life. Edwin Drake's days came to an agonizing end in 1880. It would be two decades before his great contribution would be honored.

When Drake died, he and his family were still living in Bethlehem, and that was the location of his original burial site. I can imagine that the broken man passed on, thinking he would be quickly consigned to oblivion. However, those of us who revere the past know that Time is our greatest historian.

About twenty years after Drake's passing, at the turn of the last century, Henry H. Rogers, an executive of the Standard Oil Company, felt strongly that the time was long overdue for public recognition of Drake's significant chapter of history. Underwriting the $100,000 memorial, Rogers orchestrated its construction. Highlighted by a massive bronze statue representing man's effort to harvest the earth's natural resources, the Drake monument was unveiled in all its glory in October 1901.

Edwin's body was disinterred and reburied at Titusville's Woodlawn Cemetery. There, Edwin and his wife Laura rest, side by side, at the foot of this magnificent tribute.

During the 1860s, the oil industry grew with rapidity as word of Drake's oil strikes spread. People from all across the country rushed headlong to the Oil Creek Valley of Pennsylvania, as they had years before (1848-1855) to California for the Gold Rush. Now the stampede was on for the "black gold" rush!

They dashed head-over-heels to lease land and drill wells along Oil Creek. These strikes yielded 1,500 to 4,000 barrels a day. I have seen them referred to as "gushers," but that term is not technically correct. As per Drake Well Museum, Pennsylvania has "flowing" wells rather than "gushers." These are primarily deep wells that are pressurized by natural gas, and, though deep, they have to be pumped after gas pressure is exhausted.

The problem was that most of the early oil men were unprepared for the overwhelming quantities. Consequently, some owners dug holes in the ground; and shades of the region's earliest inhabitants, they cribbed the seeps with timber to store the crude oil. Over time, these seeps extended across several acres. Today, this would be viewed as outrageous. Modern environmentalists would be appalled at the pollution in the Oil Creek Valley during the boom era. But keep in mind that in those early days of the oil industry, every step was an improvised stride. There was no blueprint of any kind, no pattern to follow. Everything had to be invented, tried out, and worked out via trial and error. And much of it was error.

Though, from 1861 to 1865, the country was engaged in the Civil War, the Pennsylvania oil region seemed removed from the bloody conflict. The war did not stop people from coming to the Oil Creek Valley to pursue their quest for getting rich quick. The infamous John Wilkes Booth was one of those people.

Late in 1863, Booth became fearful that he was losing his voice. This was the result of the actor's failure to project his voice properly from his diaphragm. He had heard talk of making a lot of money from oil; and so, in the late spring of 1864, he arrived in the Franklin area with the intention of investing in wells. After dumping his money into one empty hole after another, he took his leave of Pennsylvania. Less than a year later, his madness would lead him to shoot President

Abraham Lincoln. Booth, "full of sound and fury, signifying nothing," was subsequently gunned down by a military search party. To borrow again from the Bard- the evil that Booth did lived long after him.

Perhaps the region's best paying well was the Noble and Delamater. Drilled in 1863, the year Edwin Drake left Titusville, Delamater Well's lifetime production would be over one and a half million barrels of oil.

At Noble and Delamater's beginning, oil sold for four dollars a barrel. However, prices were rising, and the owners netted more than $5 million before increased production drove oil prices down to ten cents a barrel.

Oil prices fell and rose with the boom and bust cycles common to Pennsylvania's oil fields, and I would not be overstating it when I tell you that the area was exploited for its oil.

In the autumn of 1864, Colonel E.A.L. Roberts filed to patent a torpedo as a way of increasing the production of oil wells. The first public test of his torpedo was at one of the Titusville wells that same year. Since so many others claimed they thought of the torpedo idea before Roberts, it took years before the former Civil War veteran and explosives expert was granted a patent. For your information, readers, the Roberts Company patent for shooting oil wells became the industry's first monopoly.

On display at Drake Well Museum, Roberts' torpedo made me even more cognizant of the ever-present danger in those early oil fields. Roberts' torpedo consisted of a tube, about four feet in length and filled with either black powder or nitroglycerin, that was made to fit the bore of the oil well. The torpedo was carefully lowered into the well and secured at the desired level. An iron weight called a "follower," attached to the tube's wire, was then dropped atop the torpedo, and when the weight hit the cap, an explosion occurred. I might add that as soon as the "follower" was dropped, the men in the area would "run like hell!"

One of the most colorful locales of the entire region was Pithole Creek. Here, in January 1865, a trio of wells struck oil; and by autumn of that year, Pithole was producing 6,000 barrels of oil a day- two-thirds of all the crude yielded in the Pennsylvania oil region.

Tests and trials proved that oil could be moved through iron pipelines, and successful operations over long distances came about in 1865. The pipelines were a godsend. Deplorable roads, costly teamster hauling fees, and overwhelming oil production prompted Samuel Van Syckel to lay a two-inch pipe from Pithole to Miller Farm along Oil Creek Railroad, five miles distant. Approximately eighty barrels an hour flowed through the pipeline at a third of the cost of transportation via teamster wagons.

This, as you can imagine, did not set well with the teamsters, who, attempting to protect their jobs, sabotaged the lines- over and yet again. Each time the oil companies repaired the pipeline, the determined teamsters executed their dirty work, forcing the oil companies to hire Pinkerton detectives. The shootouts between the two factions rivaled those of the Wild West. Nonetheless, the Pinkertons, whose logo was an open-eye with the words "We never sleep," thwarted the saboteurs, and the pipeline prevailed.

Pithole's unromantic name emerged from a deep pit or chasm on the hills near the mouth of Pithole Creek. For over a thousand days, beginning in the spring of 1865, this was one of the most principal cities in the entire state. But it was a rough and tumble place whose name could just as well have been "Hell Hole"!

It had all begun with the Frazier Well that in January 1865 started producing 250 barrels a day on a farm near Pithole Creek. By spring, word of the bonanza got out, and the area became a magnet for oil adventurers everywhere.

I'll remind my readers that the Civil War had come to a bloody end in April of that year, and discharged soldiers- Union as well as former Confederates whose lives had been turned upside down by military duty and the ravages of war- came to the Pennsylvania oil fields to strike it rich.

By September of 1865, Pithole boasted a population of 15,000. The wild untamed place had at least two banks, no less than fifty hotels, a daily newspaper, and as indicated by the Drake Well Museum, the third-largest post office by volume in Pennsylvania.

Oil was the lifeblood of the town, and the place literally reeked with it. Oil was everywhere- in the cellars of buildings, in the water supply; it was in the streets, and seemed to hang in the very air, rendering Pithole folks fearful of even striking a match. Smoking in certain areas became a hanging offense. Despite that strong deterrent, explosions and fires were common, and in 1866, a series of fires burned disastrously.

In the town's numerous saloons, whiskey sold cheaply, but clean water was but a dream. Teetotalers had to travel a right-far distance to get a glass of good water or a cup of good-tasting tea, though a glass of what was supposed to be clear, fresh water sold dearly. Drunks and rowdies could be seen everywhere, spewing vile oaths and profanities as they stumbled about the mucky streets. The town had no sewage system; and refined newcomers, their hands rushing to cover their noses with elegant, lace-edged handkerchiefs, exclaimed that Pithole looked and smelled like a cesspool.

In spite of the filth, the place became a mecca for anyone seeking excitement, fast money and/or a new lease on life. Surprisingly, ugly, dirty, reeking Pithole did not lack the finer things of life. Hotels oozed luxury as the surroundings oozed oil, their windows decorated with elaborate hangings, their carpets glinting in the soft glow of gaslight with a sheen that whispered of silk. Theaters, hung with rich velvets and sparkling Tiffany chandeliers, staged Shakespearean plays; and, rough and tough though their audiences were, the actors played nightly in each to a full house.

One memorable production of *Macbeth* starred a buxom young actress named Eloise Bridges whose stage name was "Miss Eloise." Her interpretation of the Bard's arch murderess was, to this author's knowledge, the only one of its kind. Miss Eloise portrayed "Lady M" as an extremely pleasant woman with a harmonious disposition. But most unforgettable, it is said, was her hourglass figure, draped in a filmy, floating nightgown, that stopped the show during the "Scottish play's" famous sleepwalking scene. No small wonder the actress, emitting squeals of delight, was overwhelmed with amorous notes, marriage proposals, and large sums of money during her numerous, whistle-enhanced curtain calls!

Virtually overnight, Pithole had become a boomtown, catering to the needs and desires of the oil men. Eating establishments, saloons, hotels, housing, and brothels shot up all over the fast-growing town. You can well imagine what these hastily constructed buildings were like in the blast of a Pennsylvania winter. Wind and snow whipped through the cracks between the clapboards, whilst those inside shivered to the tune of their chattering teeth.

As with all boomtowns, crime and vice flourished in those of the Pennsylvania oil region. The most infamous of the houses of ill repute was operated by French Kate whose partner in crime was Ben Hogan. Suffice it to say that he called himself, the "wickedest man in the world." That being said, I might add the notorious duo had a fair amount of competition in Pennsylvania's oil region.

Hogan was already a thief when he left New York City, at the age of fourteen, with his parents. The family settled in Syracuse, New York, where Ben fine-tuned his burglary skills. At age seventeen, the street-wise youth went to sea as a cabin boy. His life of adventure was just beginning; and before it would end, he would have a criminal record as long as the proverbial man's arm, including piracy on the high seas. During the American Civil War, he dared to slip slyly in and out of the port of Charleston, South Carolina, as a blockade runner. And I have read in several sources that he also acted as a spy– for both sides.

Hogan arrived in the Pennsylvania oil fields in 1865. It seems he first went to work as a bouncer. Concurrently, he polished his strongman act (something he had in his repertoire for some time) and gave boxing lessons. Not a man to hold down any particular job for long, he drifted from one bar or brothel to another, working as either a bouncer or a card dealer.

Though, by this juncture of his life, Hogan had done plenty of bare knuckle fighting in the oil region, he had not competed in an organized prize fight until the spring of 1866 when he fought Jack Holliday and won. Several Hogan bouts and exhibitions followed in the Pennsylvania oil region and elsewhere.

Ben Hogan was a strikingly handsome man, the "Rhett Butler" type, with ink-black hair and a thick handlebar moustache. Though he was not tall, he was of average height for his era with the broad chest, shoulders, and steel-like muscles of a well-trained boxer. It is amazing to me how he maintained his muscular physique when it is said that he drank heavily and chain-smoked cigars; though his leading biographer, George Trainer, said in 1878 that Hogan was "nearly abstemious." Trainer also wrote that Hogan's exceptional body was due to the raw meat he regularly ate. In any case, "Wicked" Ben was likely an excellent boxer, rarely, if ever, having met with defeat.

The one thing History knows for certain about Ben Hogan is that he loved excitement. He had a reputation for trying anything once, as long as it paid well. And then there were the women. Ben was known for being quite the ladies' man.

He was possessed of great energy and grit; and I suppose, in a misguided way, we could say he possessed executive skills, the gift of entrepreneurship in any event. Several of his fair companions were also his business partners and associates. Of these, French Kate was the most famous- or infamous. In a short time, the pair became the most notorious couple in the oil region.

Flame-haired Kate was said to be stunning, though she was described by many as "tough as nails." Tough or not, she supposedly captured Ben's attention at first sight. At the time they met, Hogan was managing Madam Fenton's Dance House in Pithole. Kate was a young prostitute there. In jig time, the emerald-eyed baggage became his mistress and business partner; and the pair soon owned, among smaller houses, a big bold brothel on Babylon Hill near Tidioute.

To recruit girls for their "rooms of entertainment," the couple placed ads in the newspapers of various cities, offering a "position with a private family to some young lady of good character." A rather prominent incident resulted from one of these ads.

A young woman of seventeen named Rebecca from central New York answered the ad via post, innocently believing it to be authentic. Her letter of response instructed her to report to work at Pithole, Pennsylvania. The address, of course, was included in the communiqué Rebecca received. Upon her arrival in the smelly boomtown, she located the address and introduced herself to her new employers- Ben and Kate. Needless to say, within moments, the young girl realized this was not the respectable family she had expected to meet, and governess most certainly not the job in this house where honky-tonk music blared from the next room, and half-dressed, painted "ladies" paraded in plain view.

Before she could make her getaway, the poor girl was grabbed and held captive in an upstairs room, where she continually refused to cooperate with her captors. She was denied food and told she would starve to death unless she joined their staff of "hostesses." If you think this is far-fetched, wait till you learn of her legendary escape!

Rebecca somehow got hold of a sheet of paper and an envelope, dashed off her plight to her mother in New York, addressed the envelope and tossed the missive out of a window from her upstairs prison. A passerby discovered the letter on the filthy street near Kate's restaurant, and the kind-hearted soul paid the postage to send it on its journey to Rebecca's mother. This was a miracle in itself, since Pithole was sated with sinners galore!

As soon as she received the desperate plea for help from her captive daughter, Rebecca's mother rushed to Pithole. At the entrance of the house of ill-repute, the distressed woman met Ben Hogan, who informed her that no such girl was there, and pushing her into the muddy street, slammed the door in her tear-streaked face. The woman continued to plead, pounding on the locked door to no avail.

Next, the near-crazed mother went to the surrounding authorities, only to find that *no one* was willing to tangle with the notorious Ben Hogan. At wits end, she was directed to the honorable Reverend Darius Steadman (see below), who was not afraid of anything or anyone. He had had no previous dealings with either Kate or Ben, since they did not attend his church (or any church for that matter), and their paths had most assuredly never crossed socially with the good preacher's. However, the reverend did know *of* the pair. And that was all it took for him to galvanize into action.

Brother Steadman rounded up a trio of tough Civil War veterans. Each of the men- the reverend included- armed himself with a brace of loaded pistols, then they directed their purposeful steps to French Kate's bawdy house.

Upon the men's arrival at her door, Kate, seeing the look on their faces, made a hasty exit to the barroom, leaving the situation for Ben to handle. At first, he attempted to pass the entire thing off as feminine foolishness. Failing to convince the armed men of this, Hogan dismissed the subject and ordered them to leave. When that failed, he made the mistake of attempting to forcibly put them out.

As they had in the heat of battle, the hardened Civil War vets stood their ground, and when Hogan reeled about to engage, he found himself staring down the business ends of eight loaded revolvers.

Despite his situation, Hogan stuck to his tale that he had no idea who the girl was. However, with the clicking chorus of hammers cocking, Ben's memory suddenly returned. He grinned, revealing even, white teeth, stroked his glossy moustache, and shrugging his bull shoulders, led the men upstairs, where he instantly released his tearful prisoner.

The wheels in Hogan's wily mind were forever turning. For one of his most prosperous business ventures, he converted a river barge that had seen better days to a floating pleasure palace. The barge was approximately 140 feet long and about 25 feet wide, not really large enough to warrant the fanciful name "Ben Hogan's Floating Palace of Pleasure," though the enterprising man fitted it out in the most grand and elaborate manner, including a large ballroom for dancing. He brought aboard a bevy of his soiled doves, a full and lively orchestra, sumptuous larder, and an enormous stock of liquor.

The Palace was anchored in the middle of the Allegheny River between Clarion and Armstrong counties. In this way, Hogan could avoid legal difficulties. Two boats were kept constantly running back and forth from Palace to shore with paying clientele, these the oil men, merchants, bankers, investors, and anyone seeking "wine, women, and song," the theme of each of Hogan's establishments. After a rip-snorting year or so, the Palace ran against a river snag and sank.

Not all was bliss between Ben and Kate; their fights too are legendary. Kate had learned many things from her partner in crime, and as she warned him, it was more than enough to teach him something. Together, they had raked in about $30,000 in gold (1860s dollars), though Hogan, it is said, gambled it away in New York, causing the feline Kate to shoot at him, shaving off a bit of one ear.

Like Pithole itself, the ill-famed couple went their way- their separate ways- but Ben was never without female companionship, and subsequent mistresses included Kitty Bowers and English Jennie.

After a shocking career in sin, Ben saw the light, sometime around 1878, and got religion. Legend has it that he wandered into a revival meeting at the Park Theatre on Broadway. Listening to a reformed sot recounting the evils of a wayward life, Hogan was instantly "saved." He married a mission worker, after confessing to her his life of crime (though I would wager not all of it), and began assisting in revivals within the Bowery.

According to biographer Trainer, Ben even returned to the oil region of Pennsylvania, Bible in hand (and that renowned Hogan determination in his heart), with the aim of reforming others in that sin-infested area of America. However, no one wanted to sample what Ben Hogan was selling this time round; thus, the self-ordained preacher and his wife headed for the slums of Chicago, where, for a time, they ran a mission together. Eventually Hogan established himself in mission circles.

The question begging is: Did this former pimp and flimflammer really see the light, or was his mission career the ultimate con game? Only Ben could tell us that.

As for French Kate, she seems to have dropped out of sight after Pithole's brief thousand-day boom fizzled out. It is believed she ran off with another man and simply vanished into a black hole of history.

I have read that Kate, who had more than a nodding acquaintance with John Wilkes Booth, was involved in the plot to assassinate President Lincoln, but I could not validate this claim. I have read and do believe, however, that during the Civil War, she acted as a spy; whether for both sides, as her former lover, I know not.

Now let's back up a tad to learn a bit more about Pithole. As the boomtown grew, families of the oil men arrived, tending to smooth some of the town's rough edges. Though there was a school held in the cellar of the Methodist Church, before schools and churches could really take root, Pithole's densely packed wells and derricks- drawing from the same pool- resulted in dwindling oil production. Then the wells went dry. The oil men left, and following them, went the dancehall girls; even many of the buildings, disassembled, were carted off to other spots richer in oil. Hence, the once-bustling Pithole went the way of yore, a colorful chapter in Pennsylvania's thrilling past.

There was one church that had taken root, and it remained for a while. This was the Methodist Church whose minister was the above-mentioned Reverend Darius Steadman. The staunch vicar had preached- with fervent fire and brimstone- from his pulpit that his church would endure long after the sin and sleaze that was Pithole was gone.

Too isolated to convert to a museum, the church was razed in the late 1930s. Be that as it may, during the Centennial Celebration of Oil in 1959, the Methodist Conference dedicated a memorial plaque to the church, placing it on a raised structure constructed from its foundation stones. The plaque reads: "It remained after all else had vanished."

Today, nothing much remains of Pithole. In fact, it is western Pennsylvania's largest, shortest-lived and, by far, most *notorious* ghost town. By the end of 1867, Pithole was, for all practical purposes, dead.

Within a few years all that lingered were cellar holes and odds and ends of lumber and debris to mark the site where one of the great oil boomtowns had once flourished. In 1877, at the end of the oil boom, Pithole was sold to Venango County commissioners for "$4 and change."

Drake Well historians offer, in early October, a ghostly lantern tour through the now-grassed-over streets of the former oil boomtown. There is entertainment by the golden glow of moon and lamplight, as well as the opportunity to visit the Pithole Visitors' Center to view the exhibits. Refreshments are available for purchase. The entrance fees are reasonable; group rates are available; and reservations are suggested, especially for large groups. Contact the Drake Well Museum and Park at 814-827-2797 or go online at www.drakewell.org.

An interesting tidbit I uncovered is that actress/comedienne Lucille Ball's great-grandfather, Clinton Ball, was born near Pithole. In 1865, Clinton was visited by Lady Luck when oil was struck near his Pithole property known as Balltown. Ball sold his farm for three quarters of a million dollars, abandoning the filthy, unpredictable business of rigs and derricks to the gamblers and roustabouts who were rushing to the area. With his windfall, Clinton Ball purchased four hundred acres of rich soil in the "grape belt" along Lake Erie, where Dr. Thomas B. Welch founded America's concord grape juice industry. Becoming a wealthy grower, Ball built a handsome gas-lit house in nearby Fredonia, New York, a beautiful Victorian village that had been gas-lit since the 1820s when natural gas was discovered there. Perhaps there's something to the old adage that money attracts money.

The bustling Oil Creek Valley, once chaotic, profane, filthy and smelly, made millions for many and ultimately changed the world forever.

Let's talk a bit now about petroleum and its products. Among those who rushed to the Pennsylvania oil fields was Robert Augustus Chesebrough, a twenty-two-year-old chemist from Brooklyn. With interest, he observed an oil worker removing a waxy residue from an oil-pumping jack. The aptly named "rod wax" was "worthless except for one thing," exclaimed the innovative New York dandy. "The boys say it heals cuts and burns."

That statement incited the grey matter in the chemist's fertile mind. He took samples back to his lab and got down to work. After months of testing, he was able to extract a usable white petroleum jelly, which he christened "Vaseline." Tests on himself and Brooklyn construction workers revealed that the stuff did indeed aid healing. Now he sought to market this natural wonder.

He rented a small space and went into production. At first, he gave away samples, from a rented horse and wagon. It was a good business move, and orders started trickling in. Next he organized a team of salesmen with horses and buggies, who set out for New England to work their magic. More orders came in, and Vaseline started making a name for itself outside the Pennsylvania oil fields.

By 1870, Vaseline Petroleum Jelly was a household name and a product found in medicine cabinets from coast to coast. On the word of the Drake Well Museum and Park, "America bought it at the rate of a jar a minute."

In 1955, the Chesebrough Manufacturing Company merged with the Pond's Extract Company to form Chesebrough-Ponds, Inc. Yet today this innovative concern makes and markets Vaseline.

We are all quite cognizant of the fact that oil has for decades played a major role in modern daily life. Fuel for automobiles and ships, as well as railroad diesels, in addition to oil-powered generators to produce electricity are the uses that leap to mind. Most of us do not realize the myriad of other everyday uses for petroleum. Here are a few: synthetic rubber tires, plastics for a great variety of everyday items, dishwashing detergent, paraffin wax, refrigerator coolants, adhesives, salves and ointments, aspirin, rubbing alcohol, cosmetics, nylon products, paints, varnishes and lacquers.

The oil boom lasted but twenty years in the Titusville, Pennsylvania area, but the oil industry rapidly went international as Drake's techniques were utilized in other oil-rich areas of America and abroad.

The rich oil heritage of northwest Pennsylvania extends beyond Venango County, reaching into Crawford and McKean counties as well. In fact, McKean County is home to the oldest operating oil refinery in the world, American Refining Group in Bradford, which began production in 1881 at the height of the oil boom. Then, the Bradford Field produced 83% of the country's and 77% of the world's oil. As I constantly remind my readers, they don't call us the "Keystone State" for nothing!

As touched on above, there had been, over the years, several attempts to honor Edwin L. Drake, the "Father of the Modern Oil Industry." Images captured by photographer John A. Mather in the 1890s showed Drake Well's original drive pipe, and these historic photos prompted a movement to preserve the actual site of the birth of the modern oil industry lest it be lost to history.

In 1913, Susan Emery, wife of David Emery, an early oil producer, donated an acre of land, including the original well, to the Canadohta Chapter of the Daughters of the American Revolution in memory of her husband. The subsequent year the DAR erected a limestone boulder affixed with a bronze plaque to mark the site of Drake's well.

In 1931, the American Petroleum Institute raised $60,000 toward constructing a museum on the Drake Well site. The dream hinged on the commonwealth of Pennsylvania accepting the property and funds for development and maintenance. Additional land was acquired, improvements made, resulting in the Commonwealth formally accepting the site in time for the Diamond Jubilee of Oil Celebration in 1934.

The following year, in August 1935, the US Department of the Interior designated Drake Well a National Historic Landmark.

The first museum and library was a single-storey brick building. Today, Drake Well Museum and Park encompasses an admission building and museum shop, a visitors' center, the DAR monument, the famous Drake Well replica, drilling rigs, an oil company office, an oil transportation exhibit, pump station, drilling and pumping machinery, oil pits, picnic pavilions, Oil Creek and Titusville Railroad boarding platform, caretaker's house, and more.

The park's layout with its wealth of exhibits, films, displays and demonstrations is absolutely incredible, and I suggest *at least* three hours to take in everything. Be certain to watch the films offered at the visitors' cen-

The Daughters of the American Revolution Monument at Drake Well

PENNSYLVANIA HISTORIES

Shooting nitroglycerin into wells to increase flow was a common practice in the PA oil fields.

ter; they are informative as well as enjoyable. By taking time for the films, you will better appreciate your Drake Well experience. Maps, dioramas, vintage photographs, artifacts, models, machinery– from the Native Americans' use of oil to the Pennsylvania boom era– will delight those interested in the history of the oil industry, as well as history lovers– or anyone who likes a good story well-told.

Lifelike, life-size figures depict Uncle Billy at work in his blacksmith shop, and visitors will "call on" Edwin and Laura Drake in the Victorian parlor of their humble Titusville home.

At the heart of the park is a replica, built in 1945, of Drake's engine house and derrick. Actually, this is an exact copy, board for board, of the *second* Drake structure.

The first building erected by Drake and his driller Uncle Billy Smith exploded and burned before they began to drill the well, in October 1859, less than two months after they struck oil. Smith, who had not been cognizant of the volatile fumes rising from the oil storage tanks, had been using a kerosene lantern to check the tanks' oil levels. He was lucky he wasn't blown to kingdom come! A replacement building was promptly put up, and Drake Well resumed production in November of that same year.

As stated above, the replica was created in 1945 from photographer Mather's vintage photographs of the second building. Working reproductions of the steam engine and boiler that Drake purchased in Erie, Pennsylvania, were added in 1986 so visitors can witness how

This Colonel Drake Steam Pumper (1868) with its fancy red wheels was used by the Titusville Fire Dept. to combat oil-field fires. Fires were a constant danger, for crude oil contains gasoline and other highly flammable elements.

A 1912 Quaker State delivery truck built by the Hatfield Auto Truck Company of Elmira, NY. The chassis for this model cost $850. Customers were expected to supply whatever body suited their needs. According to the Drake Well Museum, only three trucks built by this company are known to exist.

COUNTY CHRONICLES

THE WORLD'S FIRST OIL WELL

On this site in August 1859, Edwin L. Drake, an agent of the Seneca Oil Company, struck a shallow oil deposit 69 1/2 feet below the surface and began an industry that changed the world.

The Seneca Oil Company sold the property in 1864, and it was eventually purchased by David Emery in 1889. His family deeded the site to the Daughters of the American Revolution in 1911, and they erected a stone monument and maintained the grounds for twenty years. The American Petroleum Institute acquired the site, purchased additional land and turned it over to the state in 1933.

Drake's well house replica was constructed by the commonwealth of Pennsylvania in 1945 and restored from 1984-1986. While both projects were based on historic research and photographs taken in the 1860s, there was little documentation on the actual equipment Drake used. The boiler and engine in the replica are reproductions of equipment used in the 1850s and are similar to what Drake probably used to drill and pump his well. [Displayed at Museum]

Authentic Pennsylvania crude

oil was pumped from the original well. Genuine Pennsylvania crude comes up from the ground (from a well not too distant), and the black gold can be purchased in a small vial at the museum gift shop. The stuff was as black as I had imagined, but the viscosity was not as thick as I thought it would be. Though oily to the touch, it actually resembles black water.

Drake Well Museum and Park is not only extensive but, with no exaggeration, *phenomenal*. My husband and I were completely enthralled with the place and plan to visit again soon. There is just so much to see and learn at Drake Well!

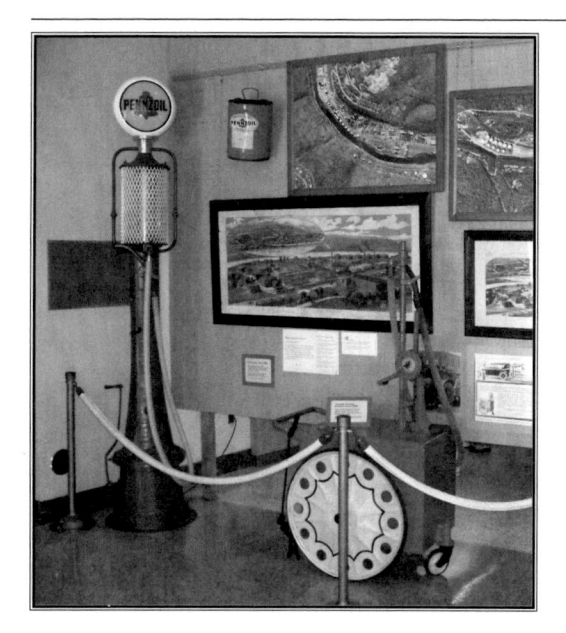

A couple of Drake Well Museum's informative displays

For more information on this fabulous Pennsylvania historic site, please visit www.drakewell.org or telephone 814-827-2797. Most of your questions concerning hours, tours, programs, activities, and fees will be answered.

Among the many oil-related items available for purchase in the museum gift shop, visitors may purchase tickets for the Oil Creek and Titusville Railroad. Travelers can board the train at the park's covered platform during the train's seasonal operation (at this writing) from June through October. Fall is the best time to go when Pennsylvania's lush forests are vibrant with autumn colors. And since most people prefer this vivid season, reservations are a must!

Following a 1912 route, the three-hour trip, in vintage passenger cars, includes guides and an entertaining taped narrative as the train travels through the "Valley that Changed the World." Clean, well-maintained restrooms, snack cars, an open-air gondola car, the nation's only rolling railway post office (postcards available for purchase therein), and beautiful rustic scenery all make this a memorable trip indeed.

We visited Drake Well Museum and Park in the morning; then, after a light lunch in Titusville, we boarded the Oil Creek and Titusville Railroad at the Perry Street Station in town. The fare is reasonable, and the line offers special rates for seniors and children. There are also special family rates.

One very compelling offer is the OC&T RR's Murder Mystery package that includes a delicious buffet dinner, theatre, and train ride with all the mystery and suspense anyone could ask for! The actors join the travelers for dinner, a nice touch to kick off the evening's entertainment. And a word to the wise, don't trust anyone aboard the Murder Mystery train ... anyone can be a partner in crime!

Special overnight packages are also available. Then, visitors enjoy a night in an authentic caboose- renovated to luxurious- at the Caboose Motel situated on the tracks at Titusville's Perry Street Station. Each of the twenty-plus caboose cars (some with cupolas) is self-contained with its own heat and AC units, bath, telephone and television. Decks are equipped with comfortable chairs for evening or early-morning fresh-air relaxation. For more information and/or to book in, call toll-free: 1-800-827-0690. The Perry Street Station is but a five-minute drive to the Drake Well Museum and Park.

For more information about the OC&T RR visit www.octrr.org or telephone 814-676-1733.

After our train ride, we enjoyed a fabulous dinner at The Porter's House restaurant. Formerly called "The Old Mill," Porter's House is located a stone's throw from the Perry Street

Station, at 221 South Monroe Street in Titusville. I think the former name was a bit more telling, because the place was originally a mill where grain was ground for horse feed. But don't let that fool you, this revamped old-mill-dining-place is nothing short of gorgeous, and the food was absolutely scrumptious. Prices were reasonable, the menu varied and quite unique, and the service Pennsylvania friendly. Sadly, as I was proofing this segment of this volume, I learned that this fabulous restaurant had closed. I hope it is only temporary!

Our great commonwealth has had many firsts- among them the birthplace of the modern oil industry in 1859. Come visit- *experience*- the early oil fields of Pennsylvania. Our OC&T train is just about to leave. This is one magic-carpet ride you do not want to miss! Hurry ... the conductor is checking his pocket watch and raising his hand to signal- **"All Aboard!"**

And we're off- to the "Valley that Changed the World."

Drake Well photos by author's husband Phillip R. Lincoln

Courtesy the Drake Well Museum and Park, 202 Museum Lane, Titusville, PA

"Johnny Appleseed"

"Johnny Appleseed was a legendary American who spent nearly half-a-century of his life in the wilderness, planting apple trees. Many people think that Johnny was a fictional character, but he was a real person- in fact, one of the most genuine people who ever lived."
- Ceane O'Hanlon-Lincoln

Johnny Appleseed was born in Leominster, Massachusetts, on September 26, 1774. His real name was John Chapman, but he would come to be known in history as "Johnny Appleseed" because of his ardent quest of planting apple trees throughout the then-frontier- so that no one would go hungry. When all was said and done, this persevering man seeded apple trees in Pennsylvania, Ohio, and Indiana. Though I have also read that he planted trees in Kentucky and Illinois, there is not much evidence to support it.

Chapman/Johnny Appleseed became a legend in his own time, due largely to his kind and generous ways, his great leadership in conservation, and the symbolic importance of apples.

Vital to the settlers on the frontier, apples broke the monotony of game-and-cornmeal repasts. Apples were easy to grow and store for year-round use. They could be eaten off the tree, baked alone or in pies, cakes, strudels or tarts, made into cider (hard or not), applesauce and apple butter, and they could be dried to eat during the winter months when food provisions were low. Did you know that settlers used apple-cider vinegar to preserve their garden vegetables for consumption throughout the winter? Indeed they did- yet another use for the incredible, edible apple!

John's father Nathaniel Chapman was one of the Minutemen who had fought at Concord on April 19, 1775, and in the Continental Army during the Revolutionary War. John's mother Elizabeth Symond Chapman died in 1776 shortly after her third child was born. It is reasonable to assume that Elizabeth's parents took over the care of John and his sister (also named Elizabeth) whilst John's father was serving in the army with George Washington. Nathaniel Chapman later married Lucy Cooley of Longmeadow, Massachusetts, with whom he had ten more children. Large families were the norm in that era when fathers needed sons to help in the fields, and mothers needed daughters to assist with the never-ending household duties.

Not much is known of John's early life. Legend has it that Nathaniel Chapman apprenticed his son to a Mr. Crawford, a neighbor who had apple orchards, and it may have been from Crawford that John acquired his initial skill as a nurseryman. With time, John developed his own nursery proficiencies.

It is not known *exactly* when John left New England. Round about 1792, when John was about eighteen, he decided to go west. There are stories of him practicing his arboricultural craft in the Wilkes-Barre area of Pennsylvania, along the Susquehanna. Those tales are rooted in truth. There is even a persistent rumor of Johnny residing in Pittsburgh in 1794 at the time of the Whiskey Rebellion. Perhaps there is a grain of truth in that old story. I know not for certain.

What I know is that John did make his way into western Pennsylvania around the period of the Whiskey Insurrection. It occurs to me that, since Pittsburgh was considered the "Gateway to the West," it is likely that John encountered many settlers there who shared with him their hankerings for the freedom the frontier offered, their yearnings for "elbow room" and the opportunity to own the land they worked. Though the frontier proffered opportunity, it also held many challenges– like putting food on the family table year round.

John realized the need for supplying seeds and seedling apple trees. The homestead law required each settler to plant fifty apple trees the first year on the new land. Apples, as already stated, were a practical food for early settlers.

Sometime in the late 1790s (most definitely by 1800), Chapman started collecting apple seeds from cider presses in western Pennsylvania– and thus began his apple-seeding mission.

Readers, the man whom History has christened "Johnny Appleseed" was a practical nurseryman, not a random/unsystematic "scatterer of seeds" as many folks erroneously believe.

John stayed ahead of the settler movement to start many nurseries throughout the Midwest, planting the seeds that he brought from the cider mills in Pennsylvania. I have read in some sources that John Chapman was from Pennsylvania, but that simply is not true. His original, cider-press seeds came from Pennsylvania.

Johnny continued westward, planting a series of apple orchards from the Alleghenies to central Ohio and beyond; and from then on, he sold or gave away thousands of seedlings to hopeful, adventurous pioneers. These acres of apple orchards would become a living memorial to John Chapman's missionary zeal– and to his dream.

Actually, these acres were more like nurseries than orchards. Chapman put up fences around them to protect the apples from wildlife and livestock; then he left the nurseries in the care of a neighbor who sold the young trees on shares. John would return every year or two to tend his nurseries.

Johnny's managers were asked to sell the trees on credit if buyers did not have the coin to pay, and he more-than-willingly accepted barter, such as clothing, cornmeal, whatever he could use in his life of a happy wanderer. But not all who wander are lost, and John Chapman was definitely not lost. I can't state in a literal sense that he was never lost. I reckon he may have been "bewildered" for a spell now and again in deep wilderness, but he most assuredly had his bare feet planted on a well-lighted path. He knew in which direction he was going, and he was fully cognizant of his purpose and his end. Johnny's barter-method of doing business was, in that era, rather common; however, he was unusual in remaining a wanderer his entire adult life. And it is significant to note here that Chapman never pressed anyone for payment.

A gentle, kind man, Johnny slept outdoors much of the time and walked barefoot in every season and in all sorts of weather. It is even said that he made his drinking water from snow by melting it with his feet. Another old yarn spun was this one: Once when Johnny fell asleep and a rattlesnake attempted to sink its fangs into his foot, the snake was foiled, because the skin on John's feet was as thick and tough as an elephant's hide. There just might have been some truth to that tale!

One of the few things we know for certain is that Chapman was a friend to everyone he encountered. Indians, settlers, animals– every living creature was drawn and took a shine to Johnny Appleseed. He walked alone without gun or knife. He felled no trees, and he harmed no animals. However, allow me to clarify my statement, "He felled no trees." That is a basically true declaration except for the fact that Johnny did work some in western Pennsylvania, helping farmers to clear their lands. He did that to raise capital to purchase land for his nurseries once he was in Ohio.

The Appleseed legend is chock-full of stories of Johnny romping with bears and communicating with all sorts of wilderness creatures as well as domestic animals. In fact, his religious beliefs contributed greatly to his deep respect and love for animals. If he came across a sick critter in the wilds, he was usually successful in healing it, after which he turned it loose. If he learned of a horse that was neglected or abused, he would purchase it, nurse it back to health, and then give it to a needy person, after extracting a promise to treat the horse humanely. Once asked why he should bother to heal the sick horse of a stranger, he answered: "Because I can."

As touched on above, John was completely in harmony with nature and the Native Americans, and his vast knowledge of medicinal herbs was the result of his respect for and friendship with the Indians to whom he gave saplings. It should be noted that, in addition to apples, Johnny planted many healing herbs, and despite his eccentric appearance, he was regarded by Indian and frontier farmer alike as a healer and even a saintly figure. His love for his fellow man rendered him a peacemaker between the settlers and the Indians.

John Chapman's distinctive characteristics combined to create the Johnny Appleseed legend of a primitive, natural man, cheerful and generous to a fault, who was at home in the wilderness. He lived simply, *quite* simply, in fact. Slept and ate outdoors, berries and apples mostly, though I believe he did fish when he was alone in the wilds. It is known that, now and again, he did accept lodging as payment for his young trees, so there were times he did eat the usual pioneer fare when he slept under a settler's roof.

Indeed, Johnny did look like a mountain man with his long hair and bearded, weathered face, his tattered clothing (sometimes fashioned from old sacks) and his bare feet. Even in the most inclement weather, he went about barefoot. He never took more belongings with him on his treks than he could tote lightly on his back or across a shoulder. And I do not believe I would be exaggerating when I state that Johnny Appleseed was one of the least materialistic persons who ever walked this earth.

It has been said of John that he wore his cooking pot, a tin pan, on his head as a hat! That is what "they" say, though I was skeptical of that cartoon characterization about our Mr. Appleseed. I used to think it more likely that the headgear he sported, of John's own design, *resembled* a cooking pot. The headgear was pot-like in appearance with a long beak much like a modern-day ball cap that shielded Appleseed's eyes from the sun's glare and the rain.

Conversely, there are historians, such as Joe D. Besecker, Director of the Johnny Appleseed Education Center and Museum at Urbana University, who says he has proof in the museum's archives that Johnny did, at times, sport his cooking pot on his head. After learning this, I have come to be a true believer of the cooking-pot-hat story. As I thought, Johnny did invent his unique headgear, and he wore his pot-hat for a number of reasons: for protection from the elements, to keep his hands free, and to store/protect valuable papers in inclement weather.

Among other references to the cooking-pot hat, the document in the Johnny Appleseed Educational Center and Museum archives was penned by a relative of John Henry Cook, who was a member of the Swedenborgian congregation in Cincinnati where Johnny often visited. Johnny and Cook habitually sat in the same pew when Johnny attended church there.

Cook's relative wrote: "He [Johnny] often wore a pyramid of three hats. The first was only a brim [what we would today call a 'visor']. Next came the cooking pot and surmounting all was a hat with a crown. The sum total was, if extremely odd, rather ingenious. It enabled [Johnny] to carry not only the kettle but his treasure of sacred literature [that was] sandwiched between the pot and the crown of the uppermost hat. The books were kept dry, and his hands were left free to deal with seed bags and tools."

As I said, John traveled light- his Bible, his provisions, planting tools, and sacks of apple seeds among the few belongings he toted on his journeys, the tools and seeds in a shoulder bag or backpack.

For your information: The Johnny Appleseed Educational Center and Museum, sponsored by the Johnny Appleseed Society and Urbana University, and located on the campus of Urbana University, Urbana, Ohio, seeks to promote the ideals by which Johnny Appleseed chose to live.

This interesting facility holds the largest collection of memorabilia and written information about the life of John "Appleseed" Chapman known to exist in the world. Special items on display at the museum include a cider press (circa 1850) that was used by John James to process apples from trees planted by Johnny Appleseed; commemorative plates from Johnny Appleseed festivals; wood and bark from original trees planted by Johnny Appleseed in Ohio and Indiana; as well as photographs of a variety of monuments and markers dedicated to Johnny Appleseed. Other exhibits include a collection of the countless publications penned about Chapman/Appleseed's life and legend.

In an interesting and informative discussion with Joe Besecker, Director of the Johnny Appleseed Educational Center and Musuem and the Johnny Appleseed Society, he made an inspirational statement about Appleseed/Chapman, I would like to share with you. "Johnny Appleseed is a wonderful role model for children due to the ideals that guided him. He taught by example to be of service to others, to practice charity, and that all living things have value. These are ideals we should all follow in our lives."

A colorful aspect of the JAEC&M is this: In 1999, seedlings from the last known living apple tree planted by Johnny Appleseed were transplanted to the museum's courtyard, a living testimony to Johnny Appleseed's everlasting contributions to agricultural stewardship. By the bye, that last known living Johnny Appleseed tree simply refuses to die. It has been struck by lightning several times and blown over by raging winds, but it just keeps regenerating itself. Think about that, readers. It's as though Johnny does not want to be forgotten- or more appropriately, he does not want his teachings or his work to be forgotten.

Trees have played an important role in the history of our nation. Take a moment sometime and research famous American trees and their stories. You'll be glad you did.

To return now to our main focus: Johnny's thin, wiry frame was always scantly clothed in the worst of the bartered garments he received for his young apple trees, because it was his habit to give away the better of the clothes to those in need. *And John continually came across someone in need.*

A fact that most people do not know about John Chapman is that he was, in addition to an American pioneer nurseryman, a missionary for the Church of the New Jerusalem, also known as the Swedenborgian Church, so named because it embraces the theological doctrines found in the writings/teachings of Emanuel Swedenborg, an eighteenth-century scientist, philosopher, and spiritual explorer.

John never married, and there is a strong belief that his heart had been wounded in love. A few stories survive concerning Appleseed and romance. In his *Historical Collections of Ohio*, Henry Howe stated that Johnny had been a frequent visitor to Perrysville, Ohio, where he is remembered as being a "constant snuff customer, with beautiful teeth." (I wonder how he managed that! Perhaps the apples he ate cleaned his teeth.) Apparently, John was smitten with Perrysville resident Nancy Tennehill. When Johnny went to Miss Tennehill's home to propose marriage to her, to his chagrin, he discovered that he was a day too late. "She had accepted a prior proposal."

Another tale relates that Johnny had loved deeply a lady whose love proved false to him. Yet another entertains the notion that John befriended a poor, orphaned young woman with no one to care for her. He took her under wing by sending her off to school with the intention of grooming her for his wife. However, as it was whispered to have turned out, when she was about sixteen, he called unexpectedly at the school to pay her a visit. There, at the institution's reception area, he found her sitting next to a young swain, her hand in his, listening to her "lover's" idle chatter. It was said the girl broke John's heart. Those stories connected to his lost loves I tend to view with a grain of salt, for as a follower of Swedenborgian, Chapman believed he would meet his angel-wife or wives in Heaven. And so, he was celibate here on Earth.

Appleseed himself liked to tell stories, especially to the children he met in his travels. Devoted to the Bible, he ofttimes quoted from it or from the teachings of Emanuel Swedenborg. From time to time, after reciting the Swedenborgian gospel, he would tear out a page or two from his Swedenborgian literature, leaving text behind with his adult listeners to read and ponder. Then, the next time he came through the area, he would trade pages, so that those folks had something new to read. Thus, in essence, Johnny Appleseed was the first lending librarian of the Midwest!

During the War of 1812, Johnny traversed northern Ohio alerting settlers of British movements and positions near Detroit, at the same time warning them of possible Indian raids. Years later, in 1871, in *Harper's New Monthly Magazine,* an article entitled "Johnny Appleseed, a Pioneer Hero" officially christened John Chapman with his legendary soubriquet.

Johnny made several trips back east during his life, both to visit his sister Elizabeth and to replenish his Swedenborgian literature. During those journeys, he would visit his many orchards, as stated previously, once or twice per year, to tend his trees and collect his earnings.

In spite of his shabby appearance, Chapman/Appleseed owned over 1,200 acres of land, not all of which were planted. Some of the tracts he did nothing with. Perhaps he intended to later cultivate them, or he may have just invested some of his profits in land. We don't really know.

We do know he had money, but he used it for charity and to further his work rather than for his own comforts. Remember, Johnny gave away many sapling apple trees to needy settler families as well as to Native Americans.

The harsh, subsistent lifestyle that John led we can attribute to his faith. He devoutly believed that the more he endured in this world the less he would have to suffer and the greater would be his rewards and happiness in the hereafter. Therefore, he submitted himself to every privation with cheerfulness and content, believing that in so doing, he was securing snug and joyful quarters in Heaven.

Notwithstanding the hardships and exposure Johnny Appleseed endured, he lived seventy winters, an advanced age for his era. There is some controversy and vagueness surrounding his death and burial, but the following seems to be the most accepted version: Whilst tending to one of his orchards in Indiana, he fell ill with congestion and a high fever that led him to seek help at the cabin of a neighbor. His passing was rather sudden and is recounted as "winter plague," probably pneumonia, due, some said, to exposure. However, this author believes that it was simply "his time," for it has been widely quoted that this man of the wilds was never sickly.

The amicable fellow went peacefully, enveloped in sleep, on a late-winter or early-spring night in 1845, on the St. Joseph River near Fort Wayne, Indiana. The neighbor (whose surname may have been Worth) took up Johnny's ever-present Bible to read a passage over his grave.

The actual grave has been lost to history, due to development of the area. However, a few miles north of Fort Wayne, Indiana, near to where Chapman is known to have expired, is a large memorial and park, the Johnny Appleseed Memorial Park, located on the St. Joseph River, that features apple orchards and an annual Johnny Appleseed Festival.

Today, over two centuries after his birth, we remember John Chapman as a kindhearted, eccentric man who so loved his apple trees that he wanted our young nation to share his sentiments along with the healthful apple benefits. Many of his trees were carried further west by the courageous pioneers in covered wagons.

Descendants of Johnny Appleseed's original tree plantings still exist. In my home county of Fayette, I have been told that apple trees in the Kentuck Knob area are descendants of those of the great man's. Beyond doubt, Johnny planted trees throughout the Ohio River Valley of southwestern Pennsylvania.

Yet today, people here in the Keystone State and throughout the Midwest can point to a tree on or near their property and proudly announce that it is a Johnny Appleseed tree.

When I think of autumn, I think of apples, and when I think of apples, I always think of Johnny Appleseed. Another autumn thought is for my mother's delicious apple crisp. I'd like to share the recipe with you, dear readers, in memory of my dear mother, Jennie Bell Hanlon:

Jennie's Autumn Apple Crisp

Peel and slice 4 <u>tart</u> apples into a 9x9 glass, butter-greased baking dish.
Sweeten the apples with a tad of cane sugar, not much.
Add about 3 tablespoons butter (not margarine).
Sprinkle with cinnamon to taste.
Sift 3/4 cup natural cane sugar and 1 cup flour, one teaspoon baking powder, and 1/4 teaspoon salt into mixing bowl.
Add 4 tablespoons butter (not margarine).
Crumble as for pie crust.
Add 1 beaten egg.
Mix well.
Spread mixture evenly atop apples in glass baking dish.
Sprinkle with cinnamon to taste.
Add a little over 1/3 cup of shelled, broken walnuts.
Bake at 375 degrees for 30-35 minutes.
Serves 4 or 5. Dish up warm topped with a scoop of cinnamon or vanilla ice cream. Personally, I prefer just the plain apple crisp with a good cup of coffee or an ice-cold glass of milk or Silk. If you are drinking Silk, remember to shake it well before pouring.

Among pioneer families, apples were a favorite, because they could be stored for a lengthy period of time, and because they were versatile. The oldest cookbooks and household books include recipes and instructions for drying apples for winter. Applesauce and apple butter were both made in large iron kettles and sometimes cooked outdoors.

Apples were made into jellies, stewed, baked, fried, sauced, and juiced, and made into a favorite pioneer beverage- applejack brandy. Apples were also used in pies- and lo! The pioneers loved their pies- tarts, dumplings, and cobblers. And, I ask you, what is more American than apple pie? Try it with a generous slice of good cheddar rather than an ice cream topper.

In my husband's family- the Lincolns/ descendants of our great President- recipes for both fried green tomatoes and fried green apples have survived. However, the fried green apples that Abraham Lincoln enjoyed were not unripe (as the fried green tomatoes). One should *never* use unripe fruit for cooking or eating. The "green" here refers to variety of apples, such as the Granny Smith, that are a perfect choice for frying. Here is the recipe.

Abraham Lincoln's Fried Green Apples

Ingredients:
2 tablespoons butter (not margarine)
1 cup sugar (can use natural cane sugar)
Cinnamon to taste
3 to 4 green, crisp apples, like Granny Smiths, (peeled or unpeeled) & sliced

Melt butter in a skillet over medium heat.
On a gas stove or over a fire, keep skillet near but not on the flames.
Drop in sliced green apples.
Sprinkle with sugar and cinnamon to taste.
Cook slowly, stirring occasionally until apples are browned and tender.
Enjoy!

Pennsylvania apples are great for snacking! Try these delicious, healthful snack ideas: Spread peanut butter on apple slices. Make a cheesy smile by melting a piece of cheese on an apple slice. Freeze applesauce, then whip it in the blender for an apple "slush."

Applesauce makes a great topping. Spoon it over hot oatmeal (or any hot cereal), ice cream, frozen yogurt, or mix it in granola for a sweet crunch.

Here's a great idea: Try substituting thinly sliced apple in place of jelly on your next peanut-butter sandwich. Thin, crisp apple slices are delightful on a grilled cheese sandwich too. Mix chopped apples and peanut butter for a spread on celery sticks; they will satisfy that urge to crunch on something while watching TV. Or team fresh sliced apples with low-fat cheese and your favorite crackers.

Here are some fun facts about Pennsylvania apples: Apples contain no fat, no cholesterol, and no sodium- and they are only about 80 calories apiece. Apples are an excellent source of fiber. Remember that old saying? An apple a day keeps the doctor away. It could well be true! Apples contain boron, a mineral that helps children's bodies use calcium and keeps brain function active and alert.

Pennsylvania grows approximately eleven million bushels of apples each year. October is National Apple Month.

The apple appears throughout history as a symbol of love. Cut an apple in half (across the center) and you will discover a cached-away star!

Eating a fresh, crisp apple will cleanse your mouth of more than 95% of the bacteria that cause tooth decay- smart way to top off lunch when away from home and your toothbrush. Two famous apple orchardists from the gilded pages of history are George Washington and Thomas Jefferson.

Eat an apple everyday, save the seeds, and, in the Johnny Appleseed tradition, plant a few apple trees of your own! What could be more American?

I will conclude this Chronicle with the wisdom of American author, naturalist and transcendentalist Henry David Thoreau: "Surely the apple is the noblest of fruits."

"Valley Forge, the Legend, Lore and Mystery"

"I was riding ... near to the Valley-Forge, where the army lay during the war of ye Revolution. ... It was a most distressing time of ye war, and all were for giving up the ship but that great and good man. ... I heard a plaintive sound ... I tied my horse to a sapling ... went quietly into the woods and to my astonishment, I saw the great George Washington on his knees alone, with his sword on one side and his cocked hat on the other. He was at prayer to ... God ... beseeching [Him] to interpose with His Divine aid ... ."
-From the diary of Rev. Nathaniel Randolph Snowden (in the reverend's own handwriting), an ordained Presbyterian minister and graduate of Princeton University and Dickinson College as told to him by the witness to Washington's prayer at Valley Forge, his Quaker friend Isaac Potts.
-The original <u>Diary and Remembrances</u> of Rev. Snowden are the property of the Historical Society of Pennsylvania.

It was the week before Christmas, December 19, 1777. Snow was swirling in a savage north wind, and beneath the gloomy grey skies, George Washington's ragtag army- representing the hopes and strength of the new nation- trudged wearily over the wintry Pennsylvania countryside, up the narrow sloping Gulph Road, a rutted dirt trace that would lead them to their winter headquarters- to the forested plateau and forbidding high bluffs known locally as "the Valley-Forge."

Behind the marchers, some as young as twelve, others as old as sixty, lay a landscape of defeat. At Brandywine Creek then at Germantown, the motley force that called itself the Continental Army of the United States of America had valiantly waged battle with George III's superior red-coated battalions- and lost.

As these wearied men and boys tramped along the Gulph Road, I can imagine that, like all soldiers throughout the ages, the thoughts of many turned to home with the doleful prospect of being away from loved ones for an unknown spell.

Before the advent of the opposing armies into the great vale, Valley Forge was a peaceful place, its hills forested with mighty oak, chestnut, and sporadic hickory trees, its underbrush laced with vines and ferns, tangled and guarded with briars and thorns. Now, some of those trees would serve the sentinels who would watch for any sign of that superior, not-too-distant enemy.

By the end of that snowy December 19, the shivering Continentals had completed their march up the Gulph Road to the site of what would be their winter camp. Here, thick woods, dense with ancient oaks five feet in circumference, surrounded the elongated plateau on which the bedraggled army was to bivouac. Hither and yon were patches of farmland, long since harvested of their rye, corn, or wheat. A scattering of houses completed the upland landscape. Looming over the plateau was a steep-sided hill christened

Mount Joy by William Penn nearly a century before. Behind it, on the opposite side of Valley Creek, was another crag, this one with a more apropos name- Mount Misery.

All in all, Valley Forge's high terrain made it a good choice for a winter encampment. The mountains, the creek, the Schuylkill River to the north, were natural defenses; and the slope to the plateau Washington promptly ordered fortified with redoubts and trenches that would guarantee reasonable security against a British attack.

Modern visitors to Valley Forge will see, along the Outer and Inner lines, the remains of the redoubts and trenches dug by Washington's stalwart soldiers in 1777-78.

Valley Forge's stately Pennsylvania Columns form a gateway to the area where the Pennsylvania soldiers were encamped in their huts.

Despite their recent two defeats, one has to admire Washington's men for their enduring spirit. Moreover, George Washington's army was an integrated army, the likes of which the nation would not see again for over two centuries. Filling the ranks were troops from all thirteen original colonies, from different ethnic backgrounds, and from different religions. For instance, Roman Catholics and Jews, though representing a small portion of the Colonial population during the Revolutionary War era, aggressively supported the patriot cause out of a keen desire to defend both homeland *and* religious freedom. These Colonial newcomers, like their immigrant counterparts years into the future, differed in religion only. In every other aspect, they were Americans and staunch patriots. Marching beside the Scotch-Irish, Irish, German, Welsh, French, Austrian, Dutch, and Polish soldiers were Native Americans (scouts and enlistees), and former Negro slaves for whom freedom shone with intense promise on the horizon.

I am proud to report that at Valley Forge there were more Pennsylvania soldiers than any other group. Two-thirds of the Pennsylvania troops were foreign-born, many of them Scots and Irish who had no love for the English, tough Gaels who had left the poverty and servitude of their homelands behind to find meaning and purpose in America- and their souls in the Cause of the Revolution. They had fought the British at home before taking up arms against the *Sassenach* (an uncomplimentary Celtic word for the English) in America. And with those strong-minded Celts, who it is said possess long memories, words like *freedom* and *destiny* loomed large.

All Washington's troops held different motivation for enlistment, though blessings of freedom and liberty topped those lists. To own the land they worked, be equal to their neighbors, and rid of the heavy, relentless boot of England on their necks- this was worth the suffering. This was worth fighting and dying for! Irrespective of the diversity therein, they all ate, slept, and fought side by side.

Yes, Washington's army was a marvel. The average age was eighteen, mayhap nineteen, farmers mostly, but as I said, they came from all walks of life, a hodgepodge of races, ethnicities, and religious persuasions.

Across the autumn countryside, they had marched and countermarched until they were so dazed with fatigue, their eyes and brains no longer focused. Many were barefoot. Washington made the comment that "... you might have tracked the army from White Marsh to Valley Forge by the blood of their feet."

The term "ragtag army" was a fitting moniker, for many of the men did, indeed, resemble ragamuffins. So many pairs of feet, wrapped in filthy, bloody rags, left those legendary crimson footprints in the snow that historic winter. In many cases, black frostbitten toes protruded from the foot rags, a dreadful, fearsome sight.

Though full uniforms clothed some, what had been summer uniforms hung on the gaunt bodies of others in filthy tatters. Blankets were an unheard-of luxury, with those possessing one sharing it with comrades. *This army traveled light.*

Each man had few possessions, the most important, of course, his musket (by far the most popular weapon) and a cartouche or cartridge box. If he had neither, the infantryman carried a powder horn, hunting bag, and bullet pouch. His knapsack or haversack held his extra clothing (if he were fortunate enough to have any), the rare blanket, a plate and spoon, a knife of some sort, perhaps a fork, and a small cup. Canteens were shared among many, and six to eight men shared cooking utensils. Rations had diminished to virtually nothing. *So terrible were those patriot sacrifices in quest for freedom!*

Yet, despite it all, as these near-starved Sons of Liberty bent into that icy December wind, they held fast to their dream, to the fact that they still had their leader and their great Cause of Liberty and Independence. Last but not least, they still had their will to fight again another day- and win.

When General Washington rejoined the army, the subsequent day of its arrival at Valley Forge (December 20, 1777), he pitched his marquee tent for himself and his aides rather than taking shelter in one of the nearby houses. He wanted to show his troops that he was willing to share in their suffering.

Today a stone marker near Valley Forge's Artillery Park designates the spot where Washington pitched his large tent.

Not all his officers followed suit, ferreting out, as some did, outlying farmhouses for their quarter; but since Washington desperately needed the full and unwavering support of his officers, he did not interfere with their choices.

The series of maneuvers and engagements that led Washington to the Valley Forge encampment had begun in late August (1777) when Sir William Howe, commander-in-chief of British forces in North America, landed approximately 17,000 of His Majesty's finest troops- a well-equipped, veteran army- at the upper end of Chesapeake Bay- his objective to take Philadelphia, the patriot capital.

Washington had positioned his 12,000-man army to defend the city. However, Howe's skillful tactics led to the British victory at Brandywine and the flight of the Continental Congress to Lancaster then to York (Pennsylvania), where Congress reestablished the capital. The British occupation of Philadelphia began on September 26, followed by the American defeat on October 4 at Germantown.

This author wants to drive home a vital point that though Washington's army was a varied collection of ragtag soldiers, they fought with spirit and determination and were often on the offensive whilst campaigning against superior numbers of professional soldiers. By the end of 1776, a series of reverses made it ap-

Vintage photograph of "Washington's" marquee tent at Valley Forge

parent that an army based on the militia-type system of short enlistments could not compete against the highly trained, well-equipped British, not to mention their hired mercenary cohorts, the Hessians– who were armed not only with their guns but with their reputations.

Though they had just lost two key battles as well as Philadelphia to the British, the Continentals emerged from these fights with the experience of hardened military personnel. They only needed additional training to bring them to their full fighting potential.

With winter setting in, General Washington had needed a place to rest and train his men. Hence, he chose Valley Forge for its location, about twenty miles northwest of Philadelphia, on the west side of the Schuylkill. The site was far enough away from the British-held capital to greatly lessen the threat of surprise attacks. The high ground, combined with the Schuylkill River, rendered the winter encampment easily defensible. To attack Valley Forge, the British would have had to charge uphill. As I said, it was an all-round excellent choice.

Named for an iron forge on Valley Creek, the area was near enough to the Philadelphia-ensconced enemy to keep pressure on the British, keep "Lobsterback" raiding and foraging parties out of the interior of Pennsylvania, stop outlying farmers and millers from selling supplies to the British in Philadelphia for hard cash, and subdue the considerable Loyalist sentiment in Bucks and Chester counties, though the number of Tories– the willing eyes and ears of the British– was far less in Pennsylvania than it was in New York and New Jersey. Washington was prone to say that New York and New Jersey were full of spies and Tories!

Armies often withdrew to fixed camps as wintry weather approached. Moving an army, horses, wagons and artillery over ice and deep snow made large-scale winter operations virtually impossible in that long-past era.

As the trudging rank and file passed into the area that would serve as their winter headquarters, their misery was redoubled by thoughts of their royal victors in the Philadelphia capital, feasting and drinking at its numerous taverns, enjoying the comforts of feather beds and cheery hearth fires in its abundance of stately houses. On top of their recent two defeats, that must have been devastatingly hard to swallow. Though these skeletal men were most assuredly hungry as well as exhausted, they were not what we might call "downtrodden"– and they were not licked yet!

British Commander-in-Chief Sir William Howe consoled himself with the ardent belief that Washington's "bobtail rebels" would disintegrate and disperse during the cold winter months, making his conquest easy in the spring. It was not the first nor would it be the last time Howe would underestimate the resourcefulness– and the pluck– of his adversary. And it would not be the last time Washington would use British cockiness to his army's advantage.

The fact that the Continental Army's spirits were undefeated is, according to the Valley Forge National Historical Park, attested to by an anonymous observer who recounted his visit to Washington's 1777 winter encampment in the New Jersey *Gazette* on Christmas Day of that historic year: "I have just returned from spending a few days with the army. I found them employed in building little huts for their winter quarters. It was natural to expect that they wished for more comfortable accommodations, after the hardships of a most severe campaign; but I could discover nothing like a sigh of discontent at their situation. ... On the contrary, my ears were agreeably struck every evening, in riding through the camp, with a variety of military and patriotic songs, and every countenance I saw wore the appearance of cheerfulness or satisfaction."

Washington himself would later remark: "To see the men without clothes to cover their nakedness, without blankets to lie upon, without shoes ... without a house or hut to cover them until those could be built, and submitting without a murmur, is a proof of patience and obedience which, in my opinion, can scarcely be paralleled."

When the Chevalier de Pontgibaud arrived at Valley Forge in December 1777, as he would pen in his memoirs after the war, "... I came in sight of the camp. My imagination had pictured an army with uniforms, the glitter of arms, standards, etc., in short, military pomp of all sorts. Instead of the imposing spectacle I expected, I saw, grouped together or standing alone, a few [of what looked like] militiamen, poorly clad, and for the most part without shoes or boots, many of them badly armed ... ."

To draw again from Valley Forge National Historical Park, "Army records and several eyewitness accounts speak of a skilled and capable force in charge of its own destiny."

Despite Washington's ever-present fear of mutiny, no real disaffection occurred. The men not only accepted their tragic plight with a sense of duty, they did so with a sense of humor. Readers, we owe this to Washington's ability to lead and inspire men!

As soon as he arrived at the winter encampment, Washington galvanized the men into action, locating supplies and cooking meals of their own concoctions, constructing log huts, even fashioning makeshift clothing and gear. The beloved and respected general offered a reward to anyone who could design a durable pair of shoes from tree bark. He also promised a reward of twelve dollars to "the party in each regiment who finished their hut in the quickest and most workmanlike manner."

When the soldiers were assigned to guard duty, fellow comrades in arms pooled their clothing resources together to loan to the sentries. In their stockingless feet, the guards often stood on their hats for protection from the wet, cold snow.

Within days of the army's arrival, the snow was six inches deep. Washington intensified his order to his men to build a log encampment to protect them from winter's fury. Hurry became the order of the day, and it was a cruel race with time to get the huts erected before the barefoot, half-naked soldiers froze to death. Unfortunately, the work went slowly, for it was complicated by the men's sheer exhaustion as well as lack of clothing and boots or shoes- and by a lack of tools- axes, saws, nails and such- not to mention the primary problem, the lack of food.

Roofing the little huts turned out to be a major problem. Splitting slabs to serve as shingles was hard, tedious work. Washington offered a hundred dollars to anyone who came up with a solution. It was a prize that went uncollected. Some men used branches from the felled trees for roofing; others used sod; and many cut canvas strips from their tents, which ruined those precious summer shelters.

On Christmas Day, the snow began to fall steadily with promise of deep accumulation. The men were cold and frightfully hungry, and along with the rest of the pitiful army, the horses were starving. The heavy snow forced Washington to abandon his marquee tent and move into a small stone house owned by Quaker Isaac Potts, one of the original owners of the forge that lent the valley its name. The current tenant, the widow Mrs. Deborah Hewes, agreed to rent the house to Washington, and he immediately took over one of the upstairs bedrooms, along with a downstairs room for his office.

In his desire to become better acquainted with the field officers of the day, Washington took to inviting them to sup with him every afternoon at three o'clock at his headquarters. When it became quickly obvious that the small house could not handle the situation, the general ordered a log dining cabin built to relieve the cramped condition. And it was here that Washington provided Christmas dinner for his aides, including General de Kalb and the Marquis de Lafayette. Though the meal was spartan and unadorned, consisting of mutton, potatoes and cabbage washed down with water, it was liberally seasoned with hope.

After the meal, Washington retired to his office, where he renewed his vigorous campaign to awaken a Congress he strongly felt did not trust him to his army's desperate plight.

Nevertheless, orders had been issued that the rank and file, at least on Christmas Day, would have as pleasant a day as their makeshift quarter and scanty fare permitted. Each man received his allotted ration along with a gill of whiskey or rum.

Now let us focus on Valley Forge's legendary log huts. To get the building underway, the men were immediately divided into squads of twelve, every unit setting about constructing its own hut. Each shelter was to be of the following dimensions: "fourteen by sixteen [feet] ... with roofs made with logs." Each hut was to have a fireplace.

Officer huts were to form a line in the rear of the troops' huts, though some of the officers, as mentioned earlier, boarded at nearby farmhouses. While Washington did not forbid this, it is also true that his anger mounted when he witnessed the carelessness and indifference of a few of his officers to the needs of their men, and he berated those officers severely for neglecting to daily oversee the men's necessities.

Between December 21 and early January, haste was the watchword as shelter construction became the top priority. Valley Forge evolved into a hive of activity, with the sounds of shouted orders, good-natured blather, axes, hammers and saws slicing the sharp, cold atmosphere, the scent of wood smoke drifting on the frigid air. On January 3, 1778, General Nathanael Greene penned a missive to his brother Jacob that included these words, "We are all going into log huts- a sweeter life after a most fatiguing campaign."

I cannot conceive of it being at all "sweet." Imagine sharing a space slightly larger than the average bedroom with eleven other adults- and for six long months! Greene would later write: "God grant we may never be brought to such a wretched condition again."

Under the direction of military engineers, approximately 2,000 log shelters went up, in parallel lines along intended military avenues, based on Washington's plan for construction. However, many men used their own Yankee ingenuity to build the tiny log cabins, and as a result, there were many variations in the size and shape of the shelters.

Bunks lined both sides of each hut's interior with a fireplace in the rear of each. Near the end of January, most of the men were living in huts (as opposed to the tents that had sheltered them to start). The troops then set to constructing miles of trenches, five earthen forts (redoubts), and a bridge over the Schuylkill.

Albeit Valley Forge was a winter of suffering, this was not a new experience to Washington's army. Valley Forge was more like "suffering as usual," for privation was a constant companion in the Continental Army throughout the entire course of the Revolutionary War.

Washington became defiant as Congress, through indifference and inexperience, ignored repeated requests for food, clothing, shoes, boots, and other necessities for the soldiers, a condition that persisted throughout the long, protracted war. (I use the word "protracted" in regard to the Revolutionary War, for it lasted over eight years. America would not be involved in so long a war until Vietnam.)

The Commander-in-Chief's problems worsened as Congress adamantly refused to recruit a regular army. This short-sighted policy meant that General Washington had to recruit a new army each year while confronting a powerful enemy. Later, Congress finally recognized the futility- the peril- of this situation.

Beginning in 1777, to put the Continental Army on terra firma, the Continental Congress allowed Washington to recruit soldiers for three years or even the duration of the war. In return for such arduous service, Congress offered land bounties and monetary bonuses. So please note, readers, that the men who answered the clarion call to arms from 1777 formed the bulk of a standing army that fought for the rest of the war. Washington's army's Valley Forge experience brought about this all-important enlistment change- among other significant military improvements.

Contrary to popular belief, disease, not the cold or starvation, was the camp's true scourge, *that* and the confounded dampness- the bone-chilling dampness that was Valley Forge.

Hundreds of horses did starve to death, and for the army too, starvation was a mortal enemy. Supplies did arrive at Valley Forge, though only in dribs and drabs; and there was often a string of up to six days at a time with barely a mouthful of food per man.

An estimated 34,000 pounds of meat and over 160 barrels of flour per day were needed to feed this army. Shortages were particularly acute in December and February; however, Washington nearly always had problems getting supplies to his troops. Though the good Pennsylvania farmers from the interior ensured that the army did not completely starve, and the soldiers frequently foraged for food in the forests and the farm fields, their stomachs constantly rumbled as critical shortages plagued them.

You can imagine how tired the poor men got of what they termed "firecakes," a tasteless mixture of flour and water cooked over the fires in their huts. I must state here that it was Washington's outstanding leadership, his constant concern for his men, that prevented mass desertion and the complete disintegration of his army. You can't toss Hope into a frying pan and eat it, but at Valley Forge, Hope was the staple for the duration.

Despite worsening weather in February, Army records reveal that about two-thirds of the nearly 2,000 men who perished at Valley Forge succumbed during the warmer months of March, April and May, when the cold had subsided and supplies were more plentiful. The real killers were influenza, pneumonia, typhus, typhoid, and dysentery- infectious filth and fever that swept devastatingly through the encampment.

The huts provided greater comfort than the tents used by the men when on campaign, but after months of housing unwashed men and food waste, these cramped quarters fostered discomfort and disease- what the men called "putrid fever, the itch, diarrhea, and 'rheumatiz.' "

Punishment for sanitation infringements was always severe, and some might even say *harsh* by spring; however, the death toll would have been much higher but for the strict camp sanitation regulations, as well as the dedicated army surgeons, the valiant women who nursed the soldiers, and a smallpox inoculation program that Washington had insisted upon.

It is important to discuss, at this point in our tale, the role the Oneida Indians played at Valley Forge and in the Revolutionary War in general. Having fought bravely in the 1777 campaigns of Oriskany and Saratoga, the Oneida Nation became known in American history as the "First Allies."

Only the Oneida and the Tuscarora of the once-mighty, six-nation Iroquois Confederation sided with the Americans during the Revolution. Their Iroquois brothers fought with the British, and it was, for the Iroquois, a brother-against-brother struggle. In fact, it was the Revolutionary War that fractured and finished the Iroquois Confederacy. Never again would it wield the power it once had. With American's bid for Independence, the Iroquois Confederation was no more.

Consistent with Oneida oral tradition, an Oneida woman named Polly Cooper walked more than 400 arduous miles from her home in Central New York to Valley Forge in the cruel winter of 1777-78 to help feed George Washington's starving troops. Along with several other Oneidas, Polly hauled 600 barrels of corn to feed the hungry American soldiers. The corn they brought was white corn and different from the yellow version that is prepared simply. By contrast, the white corn requires extended preparation before it can be eaten. However, Washington's soldiers were so desperate for food when Polly Cooper and her fellow Oneidas arrived, they attempted to eat the corn uncooked. The Indians forcibly stopped the ravenous men, knowing that if they ate the raw white corn in its dried state, it would swell in their stomachs and literally kill them. Polly showed the soldiers how to cook the corn, taking them, step by step, through the preparation process. The compassionate woman stayed on, after the other Oneidas departed for their homeland, to continue to help the needy troops.

After the war, the army attempted to reward Polly Cooper for her valiant service, but she refused any recompense, stating that it was her duty to help her friends in their time of hardships. She did, however, accept a token of appreciation from Martha Washington- an elegant shawl and bonnet. The shawl has been handed down through the long years by descendants of Polly Cooper.

In 1777, the Continental Congress recognized the Oneida contribution to the Revolutionary War, stating: "We have experienced your love, strong as the mighty oak, and your fidelity, unchangeable as truth. You have kept fast hold of the ancient covenant-chain and preserved it free from rust and decay ... bright as silver. Brave men ... you stood forth, in the cause of your friends, and ventured your lives in our battles. While the sun and moon continue to give light to the world, we shall love and respect you. As our trusty friends, we shall protect you, and shall at all times consider your welfare as our own."

Washington's pleas to Congress, describing the ragged condition of his soldiers brought little to no help. And it is indeed fortunate that there came no British attack while he was encamped at Valley Forge. It is doubtful his men would have survived a full-out attack, yet, as Washington always observed, his men were loyal fighters.

Many officers' wives joined the army during the winter encampments. It should be noted that George Washington did not go home to Mount Vernon, for what we would today term "R and R," throughout the entire Revolution; therefore, Martha joined him at eight winter encampments in the course of the long war.

Mrs. Washington arrived at Valley Forge in early February and remained until 8 June. Whilst there, Martha supervised the military household at Washington's Headquarters, including the servants and slaves she brought with her. She planned meals for up to thirty people daily, entertained the officers' wives, and acted as hostess when congressmen, French delegates, and other dignitaries came to meet with her husband and his staff.

During the winters of the Revolution when Martha Washington joined her husband, she responded, time after time, to the exultant cheers of "Lady Washington" from his men. Upon her arrival at Valley Forge, she noted immediately that this was the worst of the camp conditions she had thus far witnessed. Since she had been in correspondence with her husband, she knew to bring as many supplies from their home at Mount Vernon as her carriages could hold. In addition to food stuffs, she brought wool, cloth, sewing materials, and home medicines. Delayed at Brandywine Creek, due to a heavy snowfall and despairingly poor road conditions, she hired a large local sleigh to take her and her company of slaves, as well as the provisions, to her husband's camp, and they pushed off in the near-blinding snowstorm.

Before her arrival, camp morale had taken a turn downward. Her presence not only lifted her husband's spirits, the general's lady lifted the overall morale of the entire encampment. When her sleigh pulled into the area, she was greeted with adulations of "God bless Lady Washington!" "God bless you, good lady!"

In addition to her duties mentioned above, Martha wasted no time organizing the women of the camp into a relief squad. They sewed shirts and knitted stockings for the men as quickly as possible. They laundered and mended the torn garments the soldiers were already wearing, beginning with the most needy. This must have been an overwhelming task, considering the number of men bivouacked at Valley Forge, for all were in dire need of warm clothing. High-ranking officers had fared better since several of them took lodging with local farmers. Some, however– including Washington's artillery commander, the ever-laudable Henry Knox– later moved into huts to be closer to their men.

Frostbite was a major concern. Those who had to have limbs amputated due to this condition did so without the use of pain medication– there simply wasn't any. The pitiful screams of the amputees during such crude operations were horrific, and needless to say, many of those victims died from shock as well as infection. Through it all, Martha and her ladies did their best to comfort and care for the suffering.

Often was Lady Washington seen entering the various huts to console and reassure the men. According to *Valley Forge: Pinnacle of Courage* by John W. Jackson, a woman who would later become "Mrs. Westlake," and who accompanied Martha on her errands of mercy, would, in future years, write about the incident of a dying sergeant whose young wife was with him: "This case seemed to especially touch the heart of the good lady [Washington], and after she had given [the sergeant] some wholesome food she had prepared with her own hands, she knelt down by his straw pallet and prayed earnestly for him and his wife ... ."

It had been hard work to fight the well-equipped, well-trained British and their ferocious Hessian allies; it had been hard work to build the huts and dig the fortifications; and for some of those poor men at Valley Forge, it was even harder work to die.

Martha knew the importance of social activities to lift the army's morale. She had arrived in camp before her husband's forty-sixth birthday and, with her own hands, baked a small cake for the occasion that he shared with his officers; whilst outside his headquarters, a group of his soldiers serenaded the beloved general.

As often as possible, Martha arranged gatherings and activities for the men. Singing was always encouraged; and food, meager as it was, was always prepared for these occasions. Entertainment at Valley Forge took many forms. The officers liked to play cricket, known also as "wicket," and on at least one occasion, they were joined by Washington himself.

Several plays were staged, including Joseph Addison's *Cato* that played to a packed audience, as the saying goes. The play, with its theme of individual liberty versus government tyranny, was a literary inspiration for the American Revolution. Patrick Henry's famous ultimatum "Give me liberty or give me death," as well as Nathan Hale's valediction "I regret that I have but one life to lose for my country" are both shades of dialogue from the popular *Cato*.

Historians' best estimation is that 200 to 400 women were encamped with the army at Valley Forge during the severe winter of 1777-1778. These ladies known as "camp followers" joined the ranks of the army for basically three reasons: With their husbands gone, they had no source of income; those on farms could not run their farms alone. In addition, women were safer traveling with the army than in a community where all the men had gone off to war, and they could care for loved ones in the army who were sick or wounded. If you are wondering why women did not receive money from their husband's military pay, let me put it to you succinctly: Washington's war chest was almost always empty.

Enduring the same conditions as the soldiers, camp followers served invaluably as nurses, seamstresses and laundresses for the army, making soap by mixing ashes from campfires with fat from cooked meat, boiling the laundry in cast-iron kettles and scrubbing it clean on wooden scrub boards. Since it was difficult to dry wet clothes in icy weather, the women tried to limit their cold-season laundering to every few weeks. When the men were engaged in training or fighting, the women were depended upon to guard the camp and to help protect the baggage wagons and other military matériel. And though camp followers were non-combatants, their close proximity to the fighting often rendered them combatants.

The most famous of the women at Valley Forge were, in addition to Martha Washington, the vivacious wife of Major General Nathanael Greene, Catherine "Caty" Greene; Brigadier General William Alexander Lord Stirling's wife and daughter, Lady and Kitty Sterling; the beautiful Lucy Knox, wife of Washington's artillery commander Brigadier General Henry Knox; and Rebecca Biddle.

Rebecca was the wife of Colonel Clement Biddle, who was one of the first to take an active part in the Revolution. The Biddles were peace-loving Quakers, but that did not stop either from doing what they believed to be right and just during the Revolutionary War. Mrs. Biddle gave up the comforts of home to join the army with her husband, and with the most cheerful of dispositions did this high-minded woman undertake all of the lingering war's inconveniences, hardships and losses. Her attachment to George and Martha Washington continued throughout her life, and often were the Biddles honored guests at the Washingtons' table in Philadelphia when, after the war, Washington served there as the new nation's first President.

Rebecca survived her husband by many years, living upwards of seventy, a long life in that short-lived era. It is said that she ever loved to dwell on the notable display of Providence's guiding hand in our contest with the mother country; and whenever allusion was made to the Revolutionary War, it was a source of delight to her children to hear her "fight her battles o'er and yet again."

Catherine Littlefield Greene, known to family and friends as "Caty," left her two children (named for George and Martha Washington) with family in Rhode Island to travel to Valley Forge in February 1778. Caty had not seen her husband Major General Nathanael Greene since the previous summer. During his absence, she had been studying French, and how she enjoyed speaking her new language with the Marquis de Lafayette and the other French officers in camp at Valley Forge! Mrs. Greene was one of the few American women who spoke French. Caty was also very pretty and quite the coquette. One would think that would have bothered her husband Nathanael, who was several years older than she. It did not. On the contrary, he seemed to enjoy the obvious fact that other men found his wife attractive.

Caty's flirtatious ways did not, however, endear her to the other ladies at Valley Forge, though Martha Washington was fond of the young woman. Other than the occasional small moue of annoyance on Caty's rosy mouth, the charming coquette seemed rather oblivious to the jealousies of the majority of Valley Forge's women folk.

When spring's arrival brought the joyful celebration (May 6, 1778) of the French Alliance- most unwelcome news to the British- Caty was privileged to ride in a carriage with Mrs. Washington during a procession that preceded the *feu de joie*. This was a grand military display of skill and force executed on the Grand Parade grounds where the Continental Army had drilled and trained under Von Steuben. During the celebration, Washington shared a toast with each of his brigade commanders. After which, with Martha's approval, Caty enjoyed dance after dizzying dance with George Washington, who, it has oft been said, relished the company of the ladies.

One of the most famous legends of Valley Forge is that Washington took to his knees there to pray for his country. This author believes it is not just legend but fact, though I leave the belief of this story to each of you, dear readers.

There have been a number of artists who have executed renderings of Washington at prayer at Valley Forge. Several of those paintings depict him on his knees in the snow. Others show him kneeling on the grass of a glade in the deep woods. Back in the 1920s and 1930s, a guide in the Valley Forge area conducted tours during which he would point out the "exact spot upon which the General kneeled in prayer."

When I visited Valley Forge, the gracious supervisory ranger took me on a private tour of Washington's Headquarters (since while I was there, it had just undergone a thorough renovation and was not yet open to the public). He pointed out a portion of land, in the vicinity of Washington's HQ, being converted back to an orchard, as it had been when Washington and his troops occupied Valley Forge. That is the site where the Park believes Washington knelt in the snow to pray.

We know for certain that Washington offered a day of thanksgiving and supplication to his Maker for all of the troops on numerous occasions throughout the course of the war. We know that Washington was a believer and that he did pray openly. We know that he prayed at Valley Forge openly, and I for one accept the eyewitness accounts that survive that he prayed privately at Valley Forge.

Some historians have discounted Washington's prayer at Valley Forge, because eyewitness accounts, uncovered over the years, differ from one another. Why should these descriptions have to match exactly to reveal to us that Washington prayed alone at Valley Forge? Could not he have been discovered on his knees in solitude at different times, in different places? Why not beside his horse in its stall, as well as in the woods in the snow? Surely there is sufficient evidence that Washington was a spiritual person with a strong faith in God. He once stated with fervor, "It is impossible to rightly govern a nation without God and the Bible." Surely there is sufficient evidence to satisfy both the layman and the historian that Washington prayed; thus, why wouldn't he have sought seclusion for his own private communion with his God– and especially in times of peril and crisis?

The most eminent of the witnesses of Washington's private prayer at Valley Forge was Isaac Potts, a Quaker, who owned and operated (at Valley Forge) a grist mill that ground the grain carried by local farmers to Washington's army. Potts saw Washington alone on his knees in the snowy woods at prayer. Later, the devote Quaker related what he had witnessed to his friend and neighbor, Reverend Nathaniel Randolph Snowden, an ordained Presbyterian minister and graduate of Princeton University and Dickinson College.

Reverend Snowden recorded the account in his diary in his own hand: "I knew personally the celebrated Quaker Potts who saw Gen'l Washington alone in the woods at prayer. I got it from himself, myself: 'I was riding with him (Mr. Potts) ... near to the Valley Forge, where the army lay during the war of ye Revolution. ... It was a most distressing time of ye war, and all were for giving up the ship but that great and good man [Washington]. ... I heard a plaintive sound ... . I tied my horse to a sapling ... went quietly into the woods and to my astonishment, I saw the great George Washington on his knees alone, with his sword on one side and his cocked hat on the other. He was at prayer to ... God ... beseeching [Him] to interpose with His Divine aid. ... Such a prayer I never heard from the lips of man. I left him alone praying. ... I went home and told my wife. ... We never thought a man c'd [sic] be a soldier and a Christian, but if there is one in the world, it is Washington ... .'"

On a clear December night at Valley Forge, the tall, impressive figure of General George Washington stood on a stony, snow-covered ridge, surveying the encampment. The winter wind cut cruelly through his long field coat; however, it was his men about whom he worried. He had never expected this war to be easy; war was never easy, and throughout history, the price of freedom had always been dear.

But that night, as he stood gazing down at the snow-blanketed camp, his thoughts were especially heavy. He was anxious over his men who lacked warm clothes, even blankets. In the bitter cold, many were barefoot; several were sick, and all were hungry.

The snow crunched under his boots as he walked through the camp, his collar raised to ward off the damnable biting wind. Muttering a curse, he ducked his chin deeper into his collar. Of a sudden, in one of the crude huts, he caught sight of a soldier huddled over a makeshift tree-trunk table, where a candle glowed in the otherwise darkness. The general stood near the doorway in silence as the soldier lifted the lit taper to light a second candle, all the while speaking softly. Washington drew closer, but still he could not understand the strange words the soldier was uttering. In a moment, he cleared his throat.

"General Washington!" the soldier cried, surprised by the sudden appearance of his commander-in-chief, as he drew himself to attention, the revered name bringing the others, from the hut's dim interior, to their feet.

Washington told them to rest at ease, after which he remarked on the severity of the cold that night, his comment sparking a story from the candle-lighting soldier about the winters in his homeland of Poland, where the laws too were cold– and bitter to swallow. He went on to explain that if he were lighting a Hanukkah candle there, it would have to be in secret.

"Hanukkah?" asked the general. And the soldier related to him the story of Hanukkah, of how over two thousand years before, the people of Israel were not permitted to pray to their God, concluding with the statement that *he* could not follow his beliefs in his homeland either, and that was why he had come to America. To that, Washington mused, "The fight for liberty is an ancient one ... it is a noble cause- *the* cause of mankind."

"That it is," the soldier replied. "All those years ago, the people of Israel would not give up, though their force was small, and they were greatly outnumbered."

The general gave a quick nod, his blue eyes narrowing, for he knew such an enemy who left only two choices- battle or ignominious submission. George Washington knew well this desperate plight. His army had learned that when a soldier retreats before an invader in his own land, he leaves a little of himself behind- every bloody step of the way. Those retreats are thus limited and conditioned by death, and they create a point of no return.

"Wars ... causes are not won or lost solely on strength in the field." Breaking into Washington's thoughts, the soldier went on with his Hanukkah tale of victory over oppression, relating the miracle (at the rededication of the Temple of Jerusalem after its defilement by Antiochus of Syria) of the Hanukkah oil- enough only for one day, though it burned eight days in the temple.

The general's harried features softened with a smile. "Miracles are still possible."

"Indeed, the world would be a wretched place without them." The soldier returned the smile with his response that echoed in the hearts of the others, bringing a chorus of "Ayes" from the recesses of the shadowy hut.

"So it would," Washington pronounced with finality. "So it would." Then after a pensive moment, he said, his voice louder, "Carry on then."

As he continued on his rounds that frigid winter night at Valley Forge, the general's step was lighter. Later, when again he passed the Jewish soldier's hut, the Hanukkah candles were still burning.

The following December, George Washington was dining at the home of Michael Hart, a Jewish merchant in Easton, Pennsylvania. It was the middle of Hanukkah. When Hart started to explain the holiday to the general, Washington told him how he knew of the story of the Festival of Lights, how he had learned it from a Jewish soldier at Valley Forge. Hart's stepdaughter Louisa committed the occasion to her diary, and it subsequently made its way into Rabbi I. Harold Sharfman's book *Jews on the Frontier*.

This author read about it in the beautifully illustrated *Hanukkah at Valley Forge* by Stephen Krensky, illustrated by Greg Harlin. To quote Krensky, "The story is based on facts, though it must be accepted on faith. Certainly it fits with the curiosity and reactions Washington displayed on later occasions." In that spirit, I, like author Krensky, borrowed Washington's language from excerpts of his own writings "in the hope of echoing [the Father of our Country's] real voice."

In the *National Tribune*, Volume 4, Number 12, December 1880, an article appeared giving an account of a vision experienced by George Washington at Valley Forge. The story has been published several times as told by Anthony Sherman who supposedly was at Valley Forge during the winter of 1777-78.

According to Sherman, to whom a pale and somewhat shaken Washington had recounted his mystical experience shortly after it happened, Washington's vision was that of an angel who revealed to the Father of our Country scenes of the birth, progress and destiny of the United States of America.

The angel showed Washington three great perils to come upon the Republic against which America will prevail, the most fearful being the third; but even in this greatest conflict, the whole world united shall *not* prevail against America- *the last great hope of mankind.*

I am not stating for certain, readers, that George Washington experienced this vision. Only Washington himself could verify that. But it is a compelling story, and especially in light of today's perils, a most thought-provoking as well as a *comforting* one.

I have said it before, but some things are worth repeating: In times of crisis, the heroes of our great nation reach across the span of centuries- through history- to comfort us. The past *always* speaks to us- *if we listen.*

The most important consequence of the Valley Forge experience for Washington's soldiers was the army's maturation into a more professional force. This was the result of the strict and intense training of a former Prussian army officer. Baron Friedrich Wilhelm Augustus von Steuben, with Prussia on his tongue but freedom in his heart, arrived in camp in February 1778, bearing a letter of introduction from none other than Benjamin

Franklin, whom he had met (and keenly impressed) in Paris.

Valley Forge's impressive statue of Von Steuben on the parade grounds where he trained Washington's Continental Army

There has been much ado about whether or not von Steuben was, in fact, a baron. I shan't waste time and space arguing for or against, since Washington himself could have cared less. The fact is that von Steuben got things done. Washington believed that *discipline* was the soul of the army, that it made small numbers formidable. Straightaway, he assigned the Prussian godsend the duties of Acting Inspector General, giving him the great task of developing and carrying out a practical training program.

For one thing, Washington was ever concerned with the health of the army. Washington knew that the encampment had to be regularly policed to ensure a clean area. Men were to relieve themselves only in the dug latrines (there and then called "vaults"); however, in the freezing cold, this was often ignored- until the baron's arrival.

On March 13, two months after his initial directive, Washington issued orders to clean up the entire camp, including burying the carcasses of dead horses and offal. The necessaries/latrines/vaults were covered up, and new ones dug. Orders were adamant- this was to be a *weekly* task. A clean camp would improve sinking morale as well as health and discipline.

Long before the baron's arrival on the scene there was a constant vigilance. Situated where they overlooked the roads and the open areas, sentries stood guard day and night, though, I am certain, this was sheer misery during the freezing winter months.

Often sentries were posted in tall trees, where a crude shelter had been constructed for what protection against the elements it could provide. Observing any British troop movements or local farmers attempting to carry produce into Philadelphia for the enjoyment of the Redcoats there, a sentry quickly relayed these observations to other sentries and/or to his unit.

How did sentries usually relay a message? Gunfire or lanterns might be your initial responses; but keep in mind that these could easily be detected by the enemy. It is strongly believed that the men used the frontier ranger/Native American method of imitating the wild turkey and other wildlife to send prearranged messages.

Von Steuben's strenuous dawn-to-dusk training program turned Washington's army into a proficient war machine. Though he did not incorporate full European methods of training the spirited Americans, he did improve the army's lack of discipline- the most difficult, I am certain, aspect of his huge undertaking. The exacting Prussian inspired a "relish for the trade [craft/profession] of soldiering" that infused the American troops with a new sense of purpose, helping to sustain them through the many trials and tribulations as they held tenaciously to their vital task- that of securing America's Independence.

In the manual von Steuben penned for this new American army, the most remarkable theme was love. You did not read the word incorrectly. I said *love*: love of the soldier for his fellow soldiers, love of the officer for his men, love of country and love of this new nation's ideals. Steuben obviously intuited that a people's army, a force of citizen soldiers fighting for freedom from oppression, would be motivated most powerfully not by fear *but by its more powerful opposite*; as he put it: "Love and confidence"- love of their cause, confidence in their commander-in-chief and their officers, and confidence in themselves.

The Prussian knew that the genius of this new nation called the "United States of

America" was not to be compared with that of Prussia, Austria, France, or even the mother country of England. "They ordered their soldiers, 'Do this! Do that!'" he wrote. "But I am obliged to say, 'This is the *reason* you ought to do that,' and then the soldier does it."

Motivating soldiers through affection and idealism had significant practical advantages. With less danger of desertion, Washington's army could be broken into the smaller units necessary for guerrilla fighting. It also encouraged, as discussed elsewhere, longer enlistments. During inspections, von Steuben or his instructors would ask each man for his term of enlistment. When the term was limited, he would continue on with his usual inspection, but when a soldier exclaimed, "For [the length of] the war!" he or his subordinate would execute a sweeping low bow, raise his three-cornered hat and declare, "You, sir, are a gentleman. I am happy to make acquaintance with you!"

A soldier and a gentleman? Ah now, this too was a new concept for a new kind of military- for a new kind of nation.

Irrespective of the newness of the army and the nation, foreign officers were an essential component of Washington's Continental Army. They provided military skills that the Americans lacked. Some, including von Steuben, the Marquis de Lafayette and the Baron de Kalb, came as volunteers.

Like von Steuben and Lafayette, de Kalb quickly proved himself to Washington, and Congress commissioned him a major general. Lafayette was given command of a division of Virginia light troops in December 1777. Later he would take charge of additional units. And lest I neglect to mention: It was a French engineer, Louis Lebèque de Presle Duportail, who designed the layout of the Valley Forge encampment.

Another fact I must not overlook is that throughout the winter and early spring, men were frequently "on command," leaving camp on a variety of assignments. Units were formed to forage for food and other supplies; others were granted furloughs for hardship situations and such (though within a short time, Washington was forced to deny all hardship requests for leave), and some were sent home for another reason- to recruit from their home areas new enlistees.

With the spring came those new recruits, who arrived almost daily. Von Steuben "whipped" them into shape, and when the Continental Army marched out of Valley Forge, they were well schooled in the art of war.

Washington and Lafayette reviewing the troops *at Valley Forge*. Painting by Dunsmore.
Courtesy Library of Congress, Prints and Photographs Division, Washington, DC

Nathanael Greene accepted the appointment as Quarter Master General and began to correct the cursed problems with supplies. Morale improved continuously as confidence grew. The ragtag collection of individuals who had been christened by the British "Rabble in Arms" and who had trudged exhausted into Valley Forge in December 1777, marched smartly out (exactly six months later) in June of 1778 as a cohesive fighting force- confident and ready to do battle.

Washington had known from the outset that it would take a professional army to defeat England. Three years into the Revolution, the persistent man finally convinced Congress to purchase better supplies for his army, and short-term enlistments no longer were one of his greatest headaches.

Washington and his soldiers had come through yet another tribulation, and they emerged victorious. Valley Forge was a victory not of powder and lead but of iron will. The spirit of Valley Forge would remain with George Washington's Continental Army for the duration of the war. *And, readers, this was the army that would continue over the next five years to the supreme American victory at Yorktown.*

On June 19, 1778, the British abandoned Philadelphia, heading back to New York City. Washington and his ready-to-fight army immediately swung out after General Sir Henry Clinton's cocky British force, determined to engage them in a good, all-out fight. The ordered ranks, martial appearance, revived *esprit de corps*, and fighting skill of the American soldiers clearly displayed the great transformation that had occurred amidst the cold, the sickness, and the countless hardships that was Valley Forge.

The showdown- the hot, hard-fought battle at Monmouth, New Jersey- resulted in a draw. But irrespective of what conventional history books report, the Battle of Monmouth- one of the largest battles of the American Revolution and the last major battle of the north- was, for the Americans, a major victory of the spirit. They had overcome the severe winter at the Forge, trained hard and showed the British at Monmouth what they were made of!

On that bloody battleground, the Continental Army met the British in open field and forced them to retreat under cover of darkness- like frightened specters in the night.

British casualties at Monmouth were two or three times greater than those of the American troops, and it was at that ferocious battle where the roar of cannon was the much-needed roar of hope that swelled American hearts throughout the infant nation!

In the heat and smoke of Monmouth, a group of valiant American women made a permanent place for themselves on the blood-smeared pages of the American Revolution. History has christened them the "Molly Pitchers" because they hauled water to cool men and cannons during the intense heat and humidity of the battle.

One Connecticut soldier later wrote for Posterity's sake what he witnessed: "A [seven-month pregnant] woman whose husband belonged to the artillery attended with her husband at the piece [cannon] the whole time [of the battle]. While in the act of reaching for a cartridge and having one of her feet as far [from] the other as she could step, a cannon-shot from the enemy passed directly between her legs without doing any other damage than carrying away the lower part of her petticoat. Looking at it with apparent unconcern, she continued her occupation."

The lady's name was Mary Hays, wife of William Hays, a gunner in Washington's Pennsylvania artillery regiment. After the war, the Hays settled in Carlisle, Pennsylvania, where, after outliving two husbands, Mary Hays McCauley passed away in 1832. She is buried in Carlisle. Readers will enjoy segments on the Molly Pitchers in *County Chronicles I* and *II* of my Pennsylvania history series.

By summer, Washington could rightly claim that the war was going well. In truth, Valley Forge was not the darkest hour of the American Revolution. Rather, it was a place where an already accomplished force of determined men- and women- stood their ground, honed the craft of war, and thwarted one of the major hot-and-heavy British offensives of the Revolution.

And then, as though under the guiding Hand of the Almighty- as many believed it was- Washington's army went proudly forth to win America's courageous bid for Independence.

Perhaps the best-known place associated with the American Revolution, Valley Forge is located in beautiful Montgomery County (though the park grounds spread over three counties, Montgomery, Chester, and Schuylkill). Here, established in 1893, was Pennsylvania's first state park.

In 1976- America's bicentennial year- the site was transferred to the National Park System as Valley Forge National Historical Park. From its park beginnings, the mission of Valley Forge has been to commemorate both the sacrifices and the considerable accomplishments of the Continental Army. Today, the National Park service provides various programs, tours, and other interpretive activities to help visitors understand and appreciate the dramatic story Valley Forge has to tell. There is no entrance fee.

Park grounds are open daily, year-round, 6 a.m. to 10 p.m. Please note, however, that Valley Forge is closed Thanksgiving, Christmas, and New Year's Day. Washington's Headquarters, the eighteenth-century stone edifice that was rented to the general during his winter encampment at Valley Forge, is open daily (except for the holidays mentioned above) 9 a.m. to 5 p.m.

Built in 1770, Washington's Headquarters underwent a comprehensive repair and renovation program in 2008-2009, reopening in late spring 2009. Think about this: During the history-making winter of 1777-78, the

American Revolution was run from this little farmhouse!

The memories of Washington's soldiers at Valley Forge live on, where supernatural impressions have been burned into the very atmosphere. People have claimed to hear the cries of disembodied voices in the ever-present wind. Others have reported the shuffle of weary men marching into camp starlit nights to the haunting sounds of fifes and the slow, measured toll of a phantom drum. Some have even witnessed floating apparitions– mist-soldiers like figures of cloud– entering the log huts in the dark of night. Legends whisper of ghostly campfires and spectral sentries espied on lonely hillsides stormy nights, eternally duty-bound and silhouetted against a sky rent by jagged bolts of lightning. Like a ghost's chill breath, gusts of wintry wind shriek off those bare hills to snatch at a phantom rider's cloak– billowing it out behind him like the shadowy wings of Death. Or so it is said.

Because the traditional Valley Forge story includes images of men freezing and starving to death, visitors to the site might expect thousands of revolutionary graves. One area acknowledged as a camp burial ground was south of Route 23 near the Valley Forge sites now known as Varnum's and Huntington's quarters, where a lone headstone distinct with the initials "JW" appears to stand sentinel among who-knows-how-many-other unmarked graves. Another supposed burial ground was within the arc made by Outer Line Drive as it winds downhill from Wayne's Woods.

Both these areas were duly honored with monuments; and in 1901, the National Society of the Daughters of the American Revolution raised a shaft near the lonely headstone that, by this point in time, had been identified with John Waterman. The DAR dedication was/is to all the soldiers "who sleep in Valley Forge." The Valley Forge chapter of the DAR, in 1911, erected a second monument to the dead below the hill surmounted by Wayne's Woods. It has always been the sentiment that digging new graves to create a cemetery at Valley Forge might disturb the unknown resting places of those who expired at the encampment.

However, modern studies of eighteenth-century documents reveal few references to burials at Valley Forge, since many soldiers who became ill in camp were sent to outlying hospitals the army had set up in surrounding towns. Archaeological investigations in 2000 turned up no graves though many offal pits, where soldiers would have been ordered to bury bones and refuse from the livestock slaughtered for their rations.

The archeologists at Valley Forge were eager to do an investigation beneath the surface, to go below the grassy meadows and leaf-littered forest floors to uncover what they could of the legendary winter camp where Washington's army became a well-disciplined fighting force. What had these men left behind?

I should mention for my readers that the huts at Valley Forge today are all re-creations, replicated in the twentieth and twenty-first centuries. All the original huts were removed shortly after Washington's troops left Valley Forge, either pulled apart by local farmers who wanted to reuse the wood, or they simply rotted away. In fact, according to the Park, when Washington visited the area fifteen years after the war, he noted that all the huts were gone, and he was content that the signs of war had been obliterated.

Valley Forge was the only one of his army's winter encampments that George Washington ever revisited.

Two of Valley Forge's recreated huts

Funding, as well as three professional archeologists from the Valley Forge Center of Cultural Resources, along with a team of volunteers, ranging in age from ten to eighty, brought this long-awaited archaeological event to fruition over the spring and summer of

2000. Some of the volunteers had participated in digs before; others had not. Several gave of their time the entire summer; some spent a week on the project. Unlike Washington's troops' frigid experience, those folks had a hot, sweaty time of it.

Fragments of pottery and shards of glass revealed that officers (or their wives) brought from home high-quality dinnerware for their use at Valley Forge. Unearthed too were such things as a pair of ornate cufflinks and a civilian button, a gunflint, musket balls, and a hammer from a musket.

Areas where they believed graves might be were left undisturbed. The graves and ghosts of Valley Forge remain to this day one of the park's compelling mysteries.

Personally, I have not experienced an actual sighting at this historic locale. I have, however, sensed the unyielding spirit of the valiant men who were encamped here. Like Gettysburg and other hallowed grounds throughout our nation, there is a sacred essence that permeates Valley Forge. Visitors who stroll amid the replicated log huts, or walk among the massed cannon in Artillery Park will surely sense it.

Time-travelers who step into the hushed hallway at Washington's Headquarters, where the rooms are arranged as though waiting for the general to send his next dispatch, will verily feel the great man's essence.

To know that the Father of our Country walked over those same plank floors, to stand in George and Martha's Valley-Forge bedchamber, to stand at a window in Washington's HQ office and lose yourself in reverie, gazing out at the landscape as he surely must have done; to ponder the nearby stone edifice where Washington's two favorite steeds, Nelson and Blueskin, were stabled. Ah, there are no words I can conjure to describe how I felt. *Special moments in time last forever.*

By the way, both Washington's faithful warhorses the steady-under-fire Nelson and the fiery Blueskin lived to be fine old "gentlemen," retiring in luxury at Mount Vernon. 'Twas a well-deserved reward, for they had safely carried the general many a mile during the long Revolutionary War.

I visited Valley Forge in the winter and again in the spring. There were two good reasons for that. First and foremost, I wanted to see it as Washington and his men had seen it. And I wanted to go when most other people don't.

The Continental Army's bloody footprints in the Pennsylvania snow take on greater meaning when a chill wind is whipping round your own bundled-up self. Not that you are really

Washington's artillery commander General Henry Knox's cannon at Valley Forge's Artillery Park

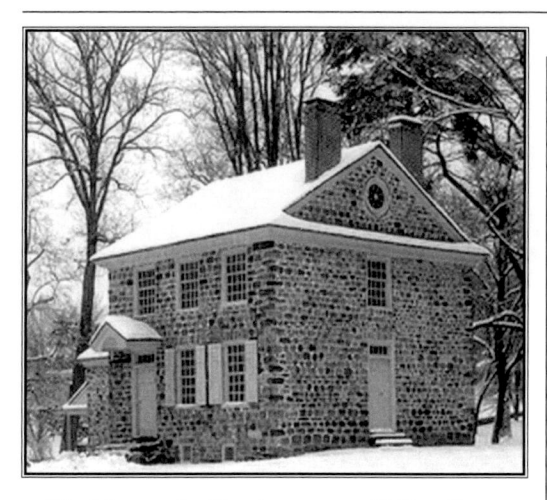

Washington's Headquarters, Valley Forge National Historical Park

forced to pull up the collar of your winter coat and tighten the wool scarf wrapped round your neck. With summer's hordes gone, off-season visitors can comfortably motor along the park roads, find ample parking in the small lots along the driving tour's major stops, and take in the sights at their own leisurely pace, absorbing the cold and conjured Washington-and-his-army imagery in tolerable doses.

Winter and spring visitors can take their time peering into the reconstructed soldiers' log huts; stand for a timeless time at the cannons pointed in the direction where the British forces were ensconced in not-too-distant Philadelphia; and relish the eighteenth-century ambience of Washington's Headquarters, where they will have the costumed docents and their store of historical knowledge all to themselves.

The furniture in Washington's Headquarters is not original though true to the period. The small upstairs bedchamber is where George and Martha slept. Downstairs, other officers slept wall-to-wall across the wooden floors. Slaves who accompanied Martha from Mount Vernon shared duties with cooks and other servants.

The Park's Welcome Center offers a helpful orientation with displays, artifacts, and a brief film. Their free brochure includes a useful map. Available too are (highly recommended) CDs to play in your car, or cell-phone tours, narrations that shape your ten-mile, self-guided drive-through tour.

With trees bare, views are open, affording appealing landscapes that Washington's scouts, looking for a proper winter camp, would have seen. In fact, trees in leaf are not even authentic. Washington's army of 12,000 made short order of what trees were there, using the wood for fuel and hut building. In reverie, visitors will gaze out at those defendable high ridges that surround the gentle valley broken only by Valley Creek and the Schuylkill River.

Across snow-blanketed Valley Forge, I conjured those crimson footprints as Washington's army entered the area that bitter-cold December in 1777. Gazing out over the frosty landscape, I imaged those exhausted men in their tattered uniforms, marching, nonetheless, to the steady beat of drums and the hopeful lilt of fifes. How *did* they do it? Each and every time I think about Valley Forge, I ask myself that question. How did they survive it? How did they emerge so strong and determined? It is nearly overwhelming to stand and ponder their fortitude, their bravery, and their strong sense of purpose of a winter's day at Valley Forge– *nearly overwhelming.*

Magnificent equestrian statue of General "Mad" Anthony Wayne, one of Washington's most stalwart officers, near Valley Forge's Wayne's Woods. Wayne is gazing in the direction of his home, nearby Waynesboro, PA.

County Chronicles

An Episcopal parish, Washington's Memorial Chapel at Valley Forge is a majestic gothic monument to George Washington and the American patriots.

Today, a hush has fallen over the valley, devoid long since of soldiers. Now, well-fattened deer roam the Park. Visitors will see them no matter when they visit. The deer are plentiful and quite lovely to watch. How thrilled the Continental Army would have been to see their great numbers during that miserable winter of 1777-1778! Then, the hungry soldiers scarfed up every deer they could ferret out for miles around.

Modern joggers, hikers and picnickers, as well as history enthusiasts enjoy Valley Forge's serene environment. I never realized how *beautiful* this historic site is. Hauntingly beautiful, Valley Forge has always held a curious power. It holds different energies than I experienced at Gettysburg.

One of the most important locations in our nation's history, Valley Forge is often referred to as the birthplace of the American Army. The site is a heartfelt reminder of the resilience of the great American spirit- of a moment in time when the great cause of Liberty and American Independence hung on a peg of destiny. And more than anything else, Valley Forge is symbolic of American perseverance and dedication to what we firmly believe is right.

At Valley Forge, I felt the birth of the American spirit.

And though I was not privileged to see the famed ghostly campfires or specter sentries silhouetted against the grey winter sky, the ghosts of Valley Forge did speak to me. There, carried upon the mystical wind, their voices reach across the span of more than two centuries to whisper, to people from all corners of the world, a single, all-powerful word- *Freedom!*

Dedicated in 1917, Valley Forge's Memorial Arch commemorates the "patience and fidelity" of the soldiers who wintered here in 1777-78. It is located at the high point of historic Gulph Road, where Washington's weary army tramped into Valley Forge.

"HAUNTED PENNSYLVANIA: TILLIE PIERCE, WHAT A GIRL SAW AND HEARD"

"The horrors of war are fully known only to those who have seen and heard them. It was my lot to see and hear only part- but it was sufficient."
- Matilda "Tillie" Pierce

"Matilda 'Tillie' Pierce was only fifteen at the time of the great Battle of Gettysburg. What she witnessed, what was burned in her memory and heart lasted a lifetime. In 1888, Mrs. Matilda (Pierce) Alleman published her account, <u>At Gettysburg: Or What a Girl Saw and Heard of the Battle, a True Narrative</u>. Her writings of those dramatic three days became an immediate best seller, rendering Tillie the civilian voice of the battle that changed the tide of the American Civil War."
- Ceane O'Hanlon-Lincoln

The deep-feeling young lady's name was Matilda Pierce, though, from the time she was a baby, everyone called her "Tillie." Born on March 11, 1848, in Gettysburg, Adams County, Pennsylvania, Tillie would call Gettysburg her home until after her marriage several years later.

Tillie's mother, Margaret, whose maiden name was McCurdy, was of Irish extraction. Tillie's father, James, a butcher by profession and a well-known entrepreneur in the area, was of German descent with a drop or two of English blood.

The youngest member of her family, Tillie had two brothers, William and James, and a sister Margaret known to one and all as "Maggie." At the time of the Battle of Gettysburg, William was in the 15th Pennsylvania Cavalry, James in the Pennsylvania Reserves. Both would survive the war, James unscathed. Though William would receive a minor wound in a skirmish in Tennessee, he would fully recover to rejoin his unit shortly thereafter.

When Tillie was four, James (Senior) built, onto the rear of the family's stately brick dwelling, a wooden addition that served as his butcher shop. He also owned the Dobbin House and stable, both of which he rented out. The family was quite comfortable, and I suppose we could say they were of upper middle-class in socio-economic standing.

During the Battle of Gettysburg, July 1 to July 3, 1863, Tillie was only fifteen, but she was possessed of a keen wit and a deep compassion for her fellow man. Patriotism too ranked high among the girl's many qualities. She was a comely lass with thick chestnut hair, piercing blue eyes, and a trim, slender figure.

Tillie witnessed several incidents preceding the battle and some of the opening day's fighting from her home at the corner of Baltimore and Breckinridge streets. Later that same day, Tillie left the house with Hettie Schriver and her two children for what they believed was the safety of Hettie's parents' outlying farm, the Jacob Weikert Farm, on Taneytown Road.

Little did they realize that they would be placing themselves in the maelstrom of the ongoing battle- within a few hundred yards of Little Round Top.

Tillie served as a volunteer nurse at the Weikert Farm, only to return home to administer to wounded in her own house.

The eye-witness account of a young girl during the three days of this pivotal, hard-fought battle is most certainly a worthy preservation among the volumes of our nation's literature. Tillie's tale is related with marked truthfulness, with honesty and clarity of expression and vivid depiction. This valiant young woman *lived* the great battle, passed through the riveting scenes she described, and beheld the suffering of the men, both Blue and Grey, to whom she endeavored to give succor.

Tillie begins her book with the humble words: "[It is not] my desire to be classed among the heroines of that period that these lines are written; but simply to show what many a patriotic and loyal girl would have done if surrounded by similar circumstances. In truth, the history of those days contains numerous instances in which America's daughters, loyal to their country and flag, have experienced, suffered and sacrificed, far more than did the present writer ... ."

Though she did not portray herself as such, Tillie Pierce was, in every sense of the word, a true heroine, and her story cannot fail to appeal to every red-blooded American, both young and old.

Within the book's introduction, Tillie stated that one of the reasons she had taken pen in hand to commit her story to paper was to leave behind a legacy for her own offspring as well as for posterity.

I am certain that she fully realized the heart-felt thanks, in response to her heroism and kindness, that sprang forth from the "boys in blue," for who more than a dying soldier can appreciate the deep sympathy and kindness of a stranger when those dear to him are so far away!

What follows is Tillie Pierce's gripping story as meticulously pieced together as I can present it to you, dear readers, drawing from interviews with the present owners of the Tillie Pierce House, church records, old newspaper articles, and Tillie's own account of what she saw and heard during the great Battle of Gettysburg.

~ ~ ~

Mistress Pierce begins her fascinating recollections by reminding readers that prior to the battle that would change the tide of the Civil War, the small town of Gettysburg, located near Pennsylvania's south-central border, was virtually unknown to anyone save the people who resided in the area and those connected to the Lutheran College and Theological Seminary there located. Prior to the events leading up to the great battle, Gettysburg was a sleepy little hamlet with a peaceful, tranquil kind of ambiance.

If ever you've visited there, you are no doubt familiar with the pale grey mists common to the mountains west of Gettysburg, where it is said phantom columns of blue and grey yet move through the peculiar haze and fog via the network of roads and byways along the Pennsylvania-Maryland border.

To the end of her life, Tillie held a strong attachment for her very special birthplace, to its hallowed grounds, though she relocated, after her marriage, to another region of the Commonwealth. I discovered in my research that this sentimental girl was rather more educated than the average woman of her era, having graduated, beyond grammar school, from the Young Ladies' Seminary, located, at the time of the battle, at the corner of Gettysburg's High and Washington streets.

Time could not efface Tillie's layered Gettysburg memories. They remained ensconced within the deepest regions of her heart. Often did she recall the fond scenes of her childhood, of lazy summer days when she and her family picnicked on the huge boulders at Devil's Den, of the "lovely groves on and around Culp's Hill, where [their] merry peals of laughter mingled with the sweet warbling sound of birds. What pleasant times were ours," she wrote, "as we went berrying along the quiet, [grassy] lane that leads from the town to that now memorable hill ... ."

Little did Tillie Pierce dream that, within a few years, from those cherished scenes of home, "the engines of war would ... belch forth their missiles of destruction; that through those sylvan aisles would reverberate the clash of arms, the roar of musketry, and the [boom] of cannon ..." to be followed by the shrieks and groans of the wounded and dying.

Little could she have imagined that those verdant hills and valleys with their scattered picturesque farms "teaming with rich harvest" would "soon be strewn with the mangled bodies of America's brothers," a copious assemblage for the "grim monster Death." Such, Mistress Pierce recounted, was the haunting swift transition from her girlhood to womanhood.

"The horrors of war are fully known only to those who have seen and heard them. It was my lot to see and hear only part, but," she tells us, "it was sufficient."

One of the things that Tillie penned for posterity is that the good people of Gettysburg, during the terrible struggle of brother against brother, conducted themselves courageously with the highest degree of patriotism and compassion for those who fought there. She reiterates how, long before the battle, military units were mustered at Gettysburg.

It should be remembered that Gettysburg and Adams County had, at the time of the battle, its full quota of men in the Union ranks, and the blood of its sons was spilled on nearly every field of engagement.

Tillie comments respectfully on the heroics of old John L. Burns, who, past seventy, took his antiquated weapon into the fray, the only civilian to participate on the battlefield. She mentions too that a neighbor, Jennie Wade, was killed whilst baking bread for the soldiers at her sister's home on Baltimore Street. (For both John Burns' and Jennie Wade's thrilling stories, see *County Chronicles Volume IV.*)

Though Jennie Wade was the only civilian to be killed during the battle, others were killed in its wake, several, including children, from unexploded shells.

One of the things I discovered from Tillie's account is that many Gettysburg families- her own among them- who had taken in wounded Union soldiers, concealed those helpless men from the enemy, within what became Confederate lines, during the battle.

Tillie surmised correctly that "many a Union soldier would have gone to Libby or the infamous Andersonville Confederate prison camps had it not been for the loyalty and bravery of the local citizenry. And she reminds us that "to all was presented the opportunity of caring for the wounded and dying after the battle ... nobly and [freely] did they administer the tender and loving acts of charity ... in their own homes as well as upon the field of battle and in the [numerous hospitals round about.]"

Bad news spurs a fast steed; and on more than one occasion prior to the battle, rumors had flown rampant through the border town of Gettysburg that the Rebels were about to make a raid. Always in the past they had proven false- until 26 June 1863 when Confederate General Jubal A. Early's force briefly occupied the town. Then, the chilling words of warning resounded through the streets- "The Rebels are coming! The Rebels are coming!"- that caused Gettysburg "hearts to throb with fear and trembling. To many of us," Tillie related, "such a visit meant destruction of home, property and perhaps life."

When the cry of alarm reached Tillie's ears, she was in literary class at the girls' school she attended (at the corner of High and Washington streets). Rushing out the door to the front portico, the students and their teacher beheld, in the direction of Seminary Ridge, a dense grey mass moving steadily (and with what was perceived as sinister purpose) toward the town.

For an extended moment, no one moved, so frozen- as in the most petrifying of nightmares- were they with dread. Then Tillie's teacher, Mrs. Eyster, pronounced in a stentorian voice: "Children, run home as quickly as you can!"

Though some of the girls likely did not reach home before the grey horde was in the Gettysburg streets, Tillie did make it to her front door, when, looking up Baltimore Street, she caught sight of several Confederates on horseback. Scrambling inside, she slammed the door and hastened to the parlor, where she peered with bated breath through the slats of the closed shutters out to the street.

"What a horrible sight!" she exclaims for future generations to hear. The Rebels, in her description, were anything but "cavaliers of the old South." Clad in near-rags, covered with road dust and layered grime, "riding wildly, pell-mell down the hill toward [her] home," they came, "shouting ... cursing, brandishing their revolvers, and firing left and right."

It must have been terribly frightening for this young woman, as, I am certain, it was for so many others in those bloody, uncertain times. And I am convinced that the question hovering in everyone's mind that late-June day in Gettysburg was "What were the Confederates planning to do to the town and its people?"

Since the rumor had been rife of their coming, the local merchants and bankers had transferred their monies to safety. However, to the enemy, the stores with their variety of wares were fair game; and as alluded to above, the Rebels needed and wanted everything they could carry off, and they took whatever suited them– food, shoes, boots, hats and other items of clothing, as well as liquor.

Horses had been shepherded out of the town to prevent their capture by the Confederates, Tillie remembered, "out toward the Baltimore Pike as far as the cemetery." There they were to be kept until the boys responsible for them received a message that it was safe to return.

In the charge of a hired boy, Tillie's father had sent their own horse out of harm's way... or so they believed.

The young woman was much attached to the animal, "for she was gentle and ... pretty." It was verily sad for Miss Pierce when the Rebels overtook the hired boy and commandeered the well-cared-for mare. Later, when the family caught sight of the poor creature being ridden hard through the streets of the town, "she was nearly lame and could hardly get along." However, no amount of pleading to the Rebel aboard or to his superiors could win her back. "That was the last we saw of her, and I felt that I had been robbed of a dear friend," Tillie confided in her book.

As an animal lover, whose own horse was a dear family member for many years, I can well imagine the crippling feeling of not knowing the fate of a beloved pet.

That evening, when the Rebel raiders were ready to take their leave, they ran all the railroad cars out to the railway bridge just east of the town, set the bridge and the cars afire and tore up the tracks. When the "Johnnys" departed Gettysburg that late-June day, there was nary a horseshoe left in the town. From there, the grey swarm headed for York, a thriving Pennsylvania community about twenty-five miles to the northeast.

I should mention that several days before, citizen volunteers of the area, including old John Burns, felled timber upon the mountain west of the town for the purpose of obstructing the passes against Rebel invasion. As it turned out, whatever obstructions the citizen-unit put in the way of the enemy, it was little more than a nuisance for the Confederate Army.

Another faction of Confederates was spotted early in the day on June 30, 1863. They were moving fast at a long trot toward Gettysburg via the Chambersburg Pike. Stopping briefly on Seminary Ridge, less than a mile west of town, this unit, led by Confederate General J. J. Pettigrew, did a hasty about-face, wisely departing the area in the same direction whence they had come. Needless to say, the harried Gettysburg townsfolk were both relieved and surprised. The reason for the swift retreat, in a word, was *Buford*; i.e., Union Brigadier General John Buford.

Just before noon on June 30, a great clattering of Union cavalry streamed into the town. When Buford and his blue-coated force rode into Gettysburg, the grateful citizenry came out to cheer them. To the young, impressionable Tillie Pierce, who had never seen so many soldiers at any one time, this was, in her own words, "a novel and grand sight." She learned afterwards that Buford's cavalry numbered about 6,000.

As it was when the Confederates had come into the area a few days earlier, Tillie was at school. Along with her teacher and the other girls, she dashed outside to see Buford's large force canter by. On a whim, Tillie's sister began singing the popular song *Our Union Forever* with the other girls joining in with gusto. The blue-clad men, almost immediately noting the patriotic gesture, rewarded the girls with tipping of hats, bright smiles, and hearty cheers.

Though the presence of so many Union troops was comforting, this, coupled with the events of the previous few days, warned the people of Gettysburg that "some great military event was coming pretty close ... ." Little did they realize, then, what a significant event would be unfolding in and about their formerly peaceful little town.

Early on the morrow (the first day of the three-day struggle that would change the complexion of the entire war) Tillie witnessed, passing near her home, another long line of cavalry, after which wagon after wagon rolled by, as she and her sister stood on the street watching, all the while singing the stirring patriotic songs that were popular in that long-past era.

Around 9:30 that morning, she began to hear cannon fire, faint was the sound at first, a low dim booming that might have passed for summer thunder, then steadily louder, until finally, she could see "great clouds of smoke rising beyond Seminary Ridge." The great battle had begun.

People tried not to listen to it, tried to talk, to carry on their daily lives as if the Rebels were not there, though always they listened and watched intently.

Sometime close to noon, Hettie Schriver, a neighbor, called to say that she was leaving her house to go to her father's (Jacob Weikert's) farm on the Taneytown Road, at the eastern slope of the Round Top. Since Mr. Schriver was away in the army, the frightened woman said that in light of the goings-on, she did not feel safe in the house with only her two children, seven-year-old Sadie and five-year-old Mollie.

The twenty-seven-year-old Hettie was a cousin on Tillie's mother's side of the family. She pleaded for Tillie to be permitted to accompany her. Matilda's parents did not have to be convinced that it was dangerous to remain in Gettysburg, and they readily consented to allow Tillie, their youngest daughter, to go.

The (first day's) battle was nearing full crescendo when the Schrivers and Tillie set out on foot about one in the heat and humidity of that historic July 1 afternoon. The most direct route to the Taneytown Road was through the Evergreen Cemetery. As the little party passed along Cemetery Ridge, they noted that Union forces were positioning there a number of cannons. Straightaway, the soldiers warned the two frightened women (each holding a little girl by the hand) that they were in grave danger. Waving their arms and calling to them– desperately trying to be heard above shot and shell and the shouted orders of the officers– the soldiers managed to get the message across: The civilians had better make haste; the Rebels were expected to begin shelling in their direction momentarily. Not responding with words, Tillie, Hettie, and the two little girls took to their heels, running as fast as their legs could carry them.

Looking back over her shoulder, Tillie could see and hear the cacophony of battle: "... troops moving hither and thither ... smoke arising from the fields ... shells bursting in the air, together with the [horrific] din rising and falling in mighty undulations." As they kept moving, as speedily as they could, in the direction of Hettie's parents' farm, the sights and sounds of the furious battle filled Tillie's soul, in her own words, "with the greatest apprehensions."

Finally reaching the Taneytown Road, they continued on toward Weikert's when they were overtaken by an ambulance wagon carrying a dead Union officer. Tillie learned later that it was the body of General Reynolds, who had been killed earlier that day.

The road was so muddy, they were forced to halt their progress. It was at this point, beside a small house (which would soon become General Mead's headquarters) that they were told by yet another Union soldier that they were in terrible danger. Hailing a passing military wagon, the soldier insisted Tillie and her party be given a ride to their destination, now not too far distant. And what a ride it was!

Over the deeply rutted, muddy road, they bumped, thumped, rocked and rolled until, at last, they reached Jacob Weikert's neat, well-tended farm, the buildings gleaming white in the hot glare of the afternoon sun.

No sooner had they received a welcome from Hettie's parents and younger sister, when Union artillery rumbled past as though the Devil himself was on their tails, the horses being urged on with shouts and whip in the direction of the raging battle. Within seconds of their passing, a Confederate shell hit the caisson, sending one of the artillerymen flying high into the super-charged atmosphere. Several minutes later, Union soldiers staggered out of the thick, acrid smoke with wounded they carried to the Weikert farmhouse. Tillie remembered with especial horror that one man, his eyes blown out, was scorched pitch-black.

As the hot, humid day wore on, thirsty Union soldiers continuously arrived at the farm to drink from the spring on the north side of the house. It did not take Tillie long to realize that she could be of some help. Locating a bucket, she hastened to the stream, and for hours, until the spring was empty, she carried water to the parched men.

With the wounded came the frightening news that the North might be routed and lose the battle. More and more, the number of wounded increased, "some limping, some with ... heads and arms in bandages, some crawling, others ... on stretchers or brought in ambulances ... it was a truly pitiable gathering."

Before night drew a curtain over the battlefield, Jacob Weikert's barn was overflowing with wounded, "with the shattered and dying heroes" of the first day's death struggle at a small Pennsylvania border town called Gettysburg.

After the spring was emptied, Tillie began filling her bucket from the pump on the opposite side of the house, continuing with her mission of mercy until well after dark, when she finally sought repose inside.

Later, with Beckie Weikert (Hettie's younger sister who resided with their parents on the farm), Tillie went out to see about the wounded in the barn, stopping abruptly at the entrance and nearly stumbling backward. There, she and Beckie collided with the most gruesome sight. Crowded side by side across every inch of the barn floor, lay bleeding men, some with hideous wounds, groaning, crying, writhing, many of them dying, whilst attendants sought to relieve their pain as best they could. "So overcome by the sad and awful spectacle," the girls turned on their heels and dashed back to the house, weeping hysterically.

Be that as it was, under the guidance of the older women/nurses, Tillie was able to get control of her young self and soon after pitched in to help as best she could with the wounded.

Day two of the great battle dawned even hotter as the relentless July sun rose over the Gettysburg battlefield. At one point during the day, Tillie discovered that one of the passing officers to whom she offered a cool drink from her bucket was General Meade, the Union commander. Not long afterward, another group of high-ranking officers stopped at the farm to ask if they might use the roof of the house to make observations.

Up through a trapdoor they sprang, and taking out their field glasses, they took in the furious panorama about them. In spite of the distance, she could hear the hubbub of voices, shouting and calling, and she could feel the fever-pitch of the battle. By and by, the men asked Tillie if she cared to have a look. "The country for miles around seemed to be filled with troops, artillery moving here and there as fast as they could go; long lines of infantry forming into position; officers on horseback galloping to and fro! It was [at once] a grand and awful spectacle. ..."

The fighting that afternoon became so intense- accompanied by heavy cannonading from the two Round Tops at the rear of the house- some of the soldiers suggested strongly that Tillie and the Weikerts run for their very lives across the fields to the east, to a farmhouse about a half-mile distant.

En route, Tillie caught sudden sight of what looked like a "sheet of lightning" in the direction of the town. Her immediate thought was that Gettysburg was aflame. Panic lay just beneath the surface, and flinging aside her manners, she took firm hold of the sleeve of a passing soldier, verbalizing her fear to him. As Tillie would say years later when she took up her pen to write about her experiences, "... More bent on mischief than sympathy, [he] answered: 'Yes, that is Gettysburg and all the people in it.' "

Running across that field, stumbling and weeping from despair and worry about her family, she arrived at the neighboring farmhouse at wits' end. Seeing her distress, a kind soldier asked what had happened to bring about her terror-stricken state. Choking back tears, Tillie poured out what she had seen and heard, ending with the fact that her parents and sister were in the town. It relieved her panic somewhat when several of the men informed her that in rules of war, helpless, innocent civilians were always permitted to leave a place before destruction. The soldiers also assuaged her fear that Gettysburg was not burning. However, their additional news was not as welcome.

Shells shot from the Round Tops were sure to fall with direct hits on the farm where Tillie and the Weikerts now stood, attempting to catch their breaths and calm their fears. Shells should pass over the Weikert place they were told. They must go back whence they came- and fast!

For sometime now, the cannonade had increased in intensity, making it difficult for Tillie and the Weikerts even to speak to one another nose-to-nose. During their frenzied flight back to the Weikert farm, shelling was such that "occasionally a shell [came] flying over Round Top [to] explode high in the air overhead. It seemed as though the heavens were sending forth peal upon peal of terrible thunder ... while at the same time, the very earth beneath [their] feet [fairly] trembled ... ."

Late in the afternoon of that second day of the battle, Tillie caught a fragment of conversation between the Union soldiers milling about the house that there would be "... hell to pay if the Rebs broke through to the Taneytown Road." Not long after, another bit of snatched dialogue revealed that the Pennsylvania Reserves were on their way into the fight. Tillie's brother James was in the First Regiment of the Reserves. Anxious to see whether the unit would indeed be along, she set her bucket down and hurried to the south side of the house. There, looking in the direction of Little Round Top, she saw a grey mass moving rapidly toward the Weikert farm. Of a sudden, she heard the faint sound of fifes and drums coming from the opposite side of the barn, followed by the shouts of the

Union soldiers in the area: "Here come the Pennsylvania Reserves!"

Running to see for herself, she saw the acclaimed unit, coming fast at the double-quick, between the Weikert barn and Little Round Top- firing as they charged, the roar of their battle cry on their lips.

The valiant assault of the Pennsylvania Reserves that Tillie witnessed lasted but a flash on this page of history, for the Rebels were soon routed. Nonetheless, the number of wounded coming to the Weikert place that day and night was appalling. Mangled, bleeding men lay all about the interior and exterior of the house. The yards, orchards, outbuildings and barn were so crowded, "the scene," Tillie tells us, "had become terrible beyond description."

Mistress Pierce continuously made herself useful, in whatever way she could, assisting the blood-covered surgeons and nurses. Since Tillie's father was a butcher by trade, I cannot help but think that the gore-splattered surgeon's aprons reminded her of her father's attire at his shop.

That night the teenage girl was so exhausted she slept the sleep of the dead- who lay in horrifying numbers on the grounds all about.

The morn of the third and final day of the battle- as a young nation waited in anxious anticipation- the fighting became so intense around the Weikert place that a rider in cavalry blue, coming toward them at the gallop and reining in so abruptly that his mount nearly sat on its haunches, shouted to the family and Tillie that they *must* vacate, for they would soon be in the midst of flying bullets, shot and shell the likes of which they could never fathom. The officer informed them that one of the soldiers would drive them to a place of relative safety. Then, a quick touch to his slouch hat, and he was off again at a gallop.

A quarter of an hour later, making haste to get into a wagon for a speedy departure, Tillie, whose nerves had been stretched to the near breaking point, gave a loud shriek and dived for the floor of their escape buggy as a shell came screeching through the trees directly overhead, exploding loudly. Unable to restrain himself, the soldier at the reins laughed, saying to the effect, "My child, it's the one you don't hear that'll kill you." Feeling a mite sheepish, Tillie sat up, attempting to recover her dignity. "Sound logic, that," she returned, a nervous smile twitching at the corners of her lips.

En route to safety, between Taneytown Road and the Baltimore Pike, the horse-drawn wagon passed through a section of woods, where, not long before, Union and Confederate cavalry had clashed. Here, Tillie noted many Rebel prisoners: "There [seemed to be] a whole field [of] them. Their appearance was very rough, and they seemed completely tired out."

Beyond the pike, they found the Lightner farm full of refugees who had fled their homes to get clear of the fighting. Isaac Lightner, an Adams County sheriff and farmer, had built his graceful, Federal-style brick farmhouse and his barn circa 1862, about a year before. Tillie and her party remained at Lightner's until late afternoon, when, with the roar of battle subsided, they started wearily back for the Weikert place, the silence in the battle's aftermath an eerie stillness heavy with dread and looming fears.

As Tillie rode in the bumpy wagon to her neighbor's parents' farm, she shrank back against the rough seat in horror. All along their route, they were met with hideous sights, sights that registered in the core of her being forever. Everywhere, "fences were thrown down ... knapsacks ... and other articles lay scattered [all about]. The whole country seemed filled with desolation. ... Upon reaching the [Weikert's farm], [she was] aghast ... the approaches were [so] crowded with wounded, dying and dead ... the air ... filled with moanings and groanings." As they passed on toward the house, they were compelled to place their steps carefully so that they "might not tread on the ... bodies."

Tillie stepped over wounded and dead men, men who lay still with open eyes that stared unblinkingly at nothing, some with hands that in death still clutched to bellies where dried blood had glued torn uniforms to wounds, over men whose beards were stiff with red-brown blood, over half-dead men whose parched, cracked lips parted as they rasped out the gut-wrenching cry, "Water!"

When Tillie and the others entered the house, they hardly knew which way to turn, for it too was overflowing with wounded. Nevertheless, their hands were needed, and they all pitched in, tearing bandages, dressing and wrapping wounds.

Amputation benches had been set up about the place; and through one of the windows, Tillie stared in disbelief at the grisly pile of amputated limbs- higher than the portion of fence that remained to the south of the farmhouse. Upon first glance, she recoiled, clapping her hand to her mouth and struggling against the powerful urge to vomit.

In Gettysburg, there would never again be an afternoon as long as that one- or as hot. Or as full of evil, unrelenting flies. They swarmed relentlessly around the wounded, tormenting them piteously. Everywhere- *everywhere*- was blood, dirty bandages, groans, and screamed curses of pain as the women and the surgeons hurried about, attending the bleeding men. The smell of blood, sweat, unwashed bodies, and excrement rose up in waves in the heat, nauseating her until the fetid stench nearly overwhelmed her.

The house was an oven, and Tillie's sweat-drenched clothes never dried but became wetter and stickier as the hours crept by. Perspiration ran down her face and her body in streams as she went about her duties, mostly in answer to the heart-tugging cries "Water! For God's sake, water, please!"

With the twilight came the welcome news that the Rebels had been licked- but at an awful sacrifice. That night the wind howled and shrieked whilst torrents of rain pelted the area, accompanied by loud claps of lightning and the terrible roar of thunder. A night so violent seemed filled with portents and beset with the banshees from the tales told by her Irish mother.

The day after the Battle of Gettysburg was the Fourth of July. After the wild and raucous storm had pounded the blood of the fallen into the battlefield for all time, America's eighty-seventh birthday dawned misty, as though the elements themselves were tearful. Like loyal Americans everywhere, the Gettysburg folk offered many a prayer of thanksgiving for the pivotal Union victory, though the significance of the battle was not fully realized until later.

"But oh! The horror and desolation that remained," Tillie breathed with keen sentiment into her book. "The general destruction; the suffering; the dead; the homes that nevermore would be cheered; the heart-broken widows; the innocent, helpless orphans! Only those who have seen these things can ever realize what they mean."

After getting word to her parents that she was safe, Tillie stayed on at the Weikert place until July 7, continuing to assist the surgeons and nurses with the many wounded. On that day, she, Hettie and the two Schriver children set out before noon- on foot across the fields for Gettysburg and home. The mud made it impossible to travel the roads.

As the little party gingerly made its way across the body-littered terrain, "... the stench rising from the carnage was most sickening. In addition to the dead men, their tunic buttons popped by their bloating bodies, dead horses, swollen to nearly twice their size, lay in all directions. "Stains of blood frequently met [their] gaze, and ... army accoutrements of all kinds covered the ground."

When Tillie entered her house, her parents and sister, at first glance, did not even recognize her, so covered was she in sweat, dirt and mud, and so completely disheveled was her appearance. She wore the same dress she had on when she left home a week earlier, for no one at the Weikert place was her size, "... not that they would have had time to think of such a thing," she added. Her light chestnut hair was dirty and tangled and her face drawn and haggard from the scenes and the trials through which she had passed. "Mother," she said in a hoarse whisper, when her mother appeared in the hall.

For a long moment, Mrs. Pierce stared at the disheveled girl, then the weeping woman ran to her, clasping her daughter in her outstretched arms. "My dear child, is that you! How happy I am to have you home again without any harm having befallen you!"

For several days afterward, Tillie and her family exchanged stories about what had happened to and around them the past few days. Tillie's father had had a couple of narrow escapes with Confederates on the streets, and he rounded up a few Rebel deserters he encountered in the town, turning them over to Union soldiers shortly after. Later, he discovered, to his extreme surprise, that the musket (retrieved from the pavement), with which he had herded the deserters along, was empty!

Upon her return home, Tillie helped her mother nurse the five sick and wounded Union soldiers in their house. The courageous family had hidden the poor, suffering fellows, at their own peril, from marauding Confederate search parties.

It may be of interest to my readers that in July 1888, exactly twenty-five years later, one of those men the Pierces had nursed back to health returned to pay his respects. By that point in time, Tillie's mother and sister were departed, but Tillie's father, then in his eighty-third year, greeted the returning vet and shook his hand. The former soldier was Corporal Michael O'Brien of the 143rd Pennsylvania Volunteers, who had been mustered in his hometown at Wilkes-Barre.

About a month after the battle, Tillie began a nursing stint at nearby Camp Letterman, where she served valiantly until the following November.

Once the largest field hospital ever built in North America, Camp Letterman, east of Gettysburg on the York Pike, spread over the George Wolf farm. In close proximity to the road as well as the railroad, Camp Letterman was strategically situated. Supplies arrived regularly, and recovering patients were sent by rail to permanent hospitals in Baltimore, Philadelphia, and Washington, DC.

I must comment on the efficiency of this place. After the July 1-3 (1863) Battle of Gettysburg, Letterman was ready to operate by mid-July, equipped with a small army of surgeons, nurses, quartermaster, cooks, and supply clerks, in addition to camp guards to look after supplies and the wounded Confederate prisoners.

Matilda "Tillie" Pierce shortly before her marriage in 1872

In September 1872, Matilda "Tillie" Pierce married attorney Horace Alleman at Gettysburg's Lutheran Church of Christ (that had also served as a hospital after the battle). The couple settled in Selinsgrove, Snyder County, Pennsylvania. Their union would produce three children. When Selinsgrove was ravaged by a fire, the ever-compassionate Tillie immediately set about raising money for the restoration of her adopted hometown.

In 1888, Mrs. Matilda (Pierce) Alleman published her first-hand account of the great battle, *At Gettysburg: Or What a Girl Saw and Heard of the Battle, a True Narrative*. Her book (from which I have quoted throughout this Chronicle) immediately became a best seller, seeing seven subsequent printings.

After enjoying many years of domestic bliss, Matilda "Tillie" Pierce Alleman succumbed to cancer in 1914 at the age of sixty-six. She is buried beside her husband Horace at Trinity Lutheran Cemetery at Selinsgrove, Pennsylvania.

I read Tillie's story after it was recommended to me by a dear friend and fellow author, Patty Wilson, a respected paranormal expert whose works I have often cited. Patty suggested that I make yet another visit to Gettysburg to stay at Tillie Pierce's house, in fact, to sleep in her very bedroom, feasible, since today the house is a lovely Bed and Breakfast. The first question I put to Patty, in light of the fact that Gettysburg is one of the most haunted sites in the entire world, was "Is the Tillie Pierce House haunted?" Her concise answer was "Yes."

Our mutual friend, Mark Nesbitt, a former Gettysburg park ranger and author of the compelling *Ghosts of Gettysburg* series, had recently conducted paranormal tests at the Tillie Pierce House, where his EVP equipment picked up some interesting recordings. EVP/electronic voice phenomenon records audio frequencies that animals can hear but humans cannot. When Mark asked James Pierce, Tillie's long-departed father, if he would like to speak with him again, the EVP picked up the clear, succinct response: "Yes, sir."

Mark then asked, "Mr. Pierce, are you worried about Tillie?" The EVP picked up the same male other-world voice that informed Mark that Tillie was "in the cellar."

EVP is really amazing because the human ear does not hear anything at the time the question is asked by the researcher at a haunted site; accordingly, the paranormal investigator will pause after each question, leaving space on the recorder for an answer. Later, when the recording is played back, answers will often issue forth from the machine- sometimes very surprising answers.

For those of you with a computer, YouTube has several Mark Nesbitt and Tillie Pierce House recordings. Of course, I also encourage you to visit the official sites of both the Tillie Pierce House and Mark Nesbitt's Original Ghosts of Gettysburg Tours.

I was anxious to stay overnight in Tillie Pierce's actual bedchamber. Thus, I booked into the Tillie Pierce House in October 2008. And I was in no way disappointed.

Gettysburg's Tillie Pierce House, built in 1829, is one of Baltimore Street's oldest and most historic buildings. Its location placed it in the thick of the action during the Battle of Gettysburg. As the fighting advanced through the town, a Confederate line was established on Baltimore Street almost directly to the fore of the house. As the struggle continued, both Blue and Grey made use of the house, and it became a makeshift hospital during and after the battle.

At this writing, Leslie and Keith Grandstaff are the proud owners of the house where the fifteen-year-old Tillie Pierce lived during the momentous Civil War battle. And I must relate that these fine people, historians in their own right, have done a meticulous job of restoring this remarkable house with nineteenth-century furnishings and hangings, period artwork and paint colors. In a word, the Grandstaffs are *purists*. To quote Keith, "The house has been renovated even down to the proper color of the mortar between the exterior brickwork. The house deserved [authenticity] ... and so do our guests."

I cannot say enough about the ambience of this historic Gettysburg landmark, or of the graciousness of our hosts. The Grandstaffs are the *perfect* hosts, and I highly recommend

The meticulously restored Tillie Pierce House Bed and Breakfast, 303 Baltimore Street, Gettysburg, PA

anyone who has a penchant for history, or who simply wishes to be pampered, to embark on a time-travel sojourn at the Tillie Pierce House. Though the integrity of the house has been meticulously preserved, special attention has been given to modern amenities and guest comforts. The climate-controlled guest rooms all have private baths with new plumbing. At Tillie's, it's the best of Victoriana and modern-day luxury!

Proudly posted on the right front façade of the building, along with a Historic Civil War Building plaque, is the 2008 Historic Preservation Award presented to the Grandstaffs by Historic Gettysburg-Adams County. HGAC is a non-profit organization formed in 1975 to spearhead and coordinate efforts to preserve, restore and interpret the county's historic heritage and encourage appreciation by the general public.

The Tillie Pierce B&B's cheery dining room

This memorable Bed and Breakfast offers several exciting packages, including a thrilling Hallowe'en weekend event, a Thanksgiving weekend package, and a nostalgic Civil War Christmas.

A nice feature the proprietors added in 2009 is a female reenactor who plays the role of Tillie Pierce to the hilt. Dressed in period clothing, she interacts with the guests in the first person, never stepping out of character.

For more information and to have all your queries answered, telephone the proprietors at: 866-585-1863 or 717-337-1733 or email them: TilliePierceH301@aol.com. You may also write to them at: Tillie Pierce House Bed and Breakfast, 303 Baltimore Street, Gettysburg, PA 17325.

Gettysburg hosts many fine restaurants. Here, I will mention those I've tried. Cashtown Inn, approximately eight miles west of Gettysburg and about which I wrote in *CC IV*, offers delicious meals that will please the most discriminating connoisseur. I suggest reservations.

Dobbin House, at 89 Steinwehr Avenue in Gettysburg, was built in 1776, four score and seven years before the Civil War, by Reverend Alexander Dobbin for his family. Born in Ireland, Reverend Dobbin was an early pioneer who helped to settle and develop the area. Later in time, Dobbin House became part of the Underground Railroad. The property was owned and rented out during the Civil War by Tillie Pierce's father James, a successful Gettysburg entrepreneur.

Today, Dobbin House is as fine an eatery as one could hope to discover anywhere. There are several dining rooms. For casual dining, Dobbin's Springhouse Tavern, downstairs, is cosy and romantic with two glowing fireplaces and rustically beautiful furnishings and surroundings. You won't be disappointed in the fare; anything on the menu is sure to please.

Upstairs, the Alexander Dobbin dining rooms are absolutely breathtaking where candlelit elegance, superior food, and gracious service bring back the sights, sounds and tastes of the true Colonial period. The portions are generous, so come hungry. And do sample the Adams County apple cider. Hot or chilled, it is the best in the nation!

Adams County is famous for its apples- and rightly so. You will discover in the Gettysburg area apple cider, apple jack, apple fritters, apple dumplings, apple sauce, apple butters, apple pies, apple crisp, and dozens of other apple delights.

I know you are especially curious about the hauntings at the Tillie Pierce House; so without further ado, let us begin that segment of our discussion.

Can ghost stories and history coexist? In and about Gettysburg, most folks think the paranormal and history are opposite sides of the same coin. After all, history is learned and passed down through the ages via both artifacts and stories.

Did I encounter Tillie's ghost whilst occupying her bed chamber? In all honesty, I did not. However, the entire Tillie Pierce House possesses an essence of something unworldly. I felt nothing dark or sinister; rather I sensed the presence of more than one entity who, I believe, simply love the house and remain, therefore, protective of it.

Tillie Pierce's charming bedchamber

My good friend and travel companion, Arlene Zimmerman, who makes history-related treks with me when my husband cannot, related that she had passed a very restful night– as did I. In fact, I can state for the record that I experienced a soothing, tranquil feeling in Tillie's room, reflective of her comforting, compassionate nature. And, from the moment I set foot in the house, I felt energized.

After a lengthy discussion with Leslie Grandstaff, I learned that guests have experienced the strong scent of flowers within the house's downstairs walls. This I attribute to the fact that Tillie and her sister had gathered large bouquets of flowers to hand to the passing Union soldiers when General John Buford's men rode through the streets of Gettysburg.

The girls gathered the flowers the previous evening, intending to hand them to and/or toss them at the passing mounted warriors. However, on the morrow, excited shouts that Union cavalry was coming toward the town at a canter sent the breakfasting girls flying from the table to the streets. They later realized that in their haste they had left the flowers behind. When they arrived back home, a sweet floral scent greeted them at the front door, for, there in the parlor, was the table-full of flowers they had so carefully picked for their blue-clad heroes.

Over Leslie Grandstaff's delicious breakfast the morning after my night in Tillie's bedchamber, I was conversing with a couple from Connecticut, when the woman remarked that neither her cell phone nor their camera would work during their walk the previous afternoon through portions of the battlefield. She then stated that someone had told her this was a common occurrence at Gettysburg.

I responded that my camera gave my husband and me troubles at Devil's Den a few years ago, and that my cell phone refused to operate on the porch at nearby Cashtown Inn, which was used as Confederate General A. P. Hill's headquarters prior to the battle, and from whence Confederate General John D. Imboden's seventeen-mile-long "wagon train of misery" carried wounded and dying after the battle. Imboden penned later that he had not fully realized the horrors of war until Cashtown. [See "Haunted Pennsylvania," *County Chronicles Volume IV.*]

Indeed, unexplained dead ... i.e. *drained* batteries and electronic equipment refusing to operate correctly is common to the Gettysburg area.

One of the things I did during this particular trip to Gettysburg was to experience Mark Nesbitt's *Ghosts of Gettysburg*, which, by the bye, is just across the side street, Breckenridge Street, from the Tillie Pierce House on Baltimore. We chose the popular Baltimore-Street tour that begins in the *GoG*'s courtyard, where disembodied voices have been recorded with EVP equipment, and where a little boy named "Robbie" has been actually sighted more than a century after his passing. In fact, more than one paranormal expert has reported the presence of phantom children at Mark Nesbitt's *Ghosts of Gettysburg* headquarters– very playful children, I might add.

Nesbitt's ghost tours are the best and the most authentic, and this is not just my opinion but the feedback from several people in-the-know, including many locals. A former National Park Service Ranger, resident of Gettysburg for over three decades, and author of, at this writing, fifteen books, historian Nesbitt collected documented ghost stories of unexplainable sightings, entity activity, and strange echoes from another time whilst living in historic houses on the battlefield and in the town. His tour guides are well-versed on the- and again let me reiterate- *documented* ghostly happenings they relate- no made-up tales, no fiction here- and every guide is attired in period Civil War clothing. Each escort carries an old-fashioned, lighted lantern, as he or she leads a group of ghost-seekers through the historic Gettysburg byways. I loved watching the various, candle-lighted tours passing through the streets! The period clothing, the lighted lanterns, the true stories all serve to whisk those on the tours back through the long tunnel of time to another era, the era of the war that tested our young nation, purged it of the evil of slavery, and preserved the Union.

To quote from Mark Nesbitt's *Ghosts of Gettysburg* brochure: "Of all the forlorn, countless souls awash in time, none reach out to us more than those of the dead at Gettysburg. They were young men mostly, caught up and cruelly thrown down again in the great, hot, whirl of mortal combat ... their presence on earth silenced forever by death." Or perhaps not ... .

I won't spoil your *GoG* experience by repeating the tales told to me that memorable night, but I will share with you something new I learned. Since, after the battle, the stench of the thousands of dead bodies, including those of hundreds of horses and mules, was so dreadful in Gettysburg that hot, long-past July, the people there took to smearing peppermint oil or vanilla under their nostrils when they had to step outdoors. (It took from July to November to bury all the dead.) Ladies often saturated their handkerchiefs with peppermint oil to hold over their noses when they were forced to venture outdoors. To this day, people have been known to detect a ghostly whiff of peppermint or vanilla as they walk Baltimore Street.

Those readers with computers can go online to Mark's site to have most of their questions answered in regard to tour times, prices, and reservations. Go to: www.ghostsofgettysburg.com, or you can telephone: 717-337-0445. The original *Ghosts of Gettysburg* candlelight walking tours are headquartered in a haunted house at the corner of Breckenridge and Baltimore streets.

Dating back to 1834, the *GoG* headquarters, the former Andrew Woods house, was occupied by Confederate soldiers who established a barricade, to the fore of the dwelling, across Baltimore Street. Rebel sharpshooters used the second-floor balcony windows to fire at Union soldiers on Cemetery Hill. Several paranormal occurrences transpired within the house during the historical restoration Nesbitt undertook upon purchasing the building for his tour center. You may learn of those events in Mark Nesbitt's books, *Ghosts of Gettysburg IV* and *VI*. In addition, you could book the *GoG*'s Baltimore Street tour and learn of those happenings- *perhaps firsthand*- for yourself.

Mark Nesbitt's famous <u>Ghosts of Gettysburg</u> headquarters, corner of Breckenridge and Baltimore streets, Gettysburg, PA

Another thing I want to relate, dear readers, is something that happened to me on the battlefield. My travel companion and I hired a licensed battlefield guide to take us over the sites of the Gettysburg campaign. Our escort was a "gentleman of the old school" as well as a very learned man named John Winkelman. I had never hired a private tour guide before this, but I highly recommend it to my readers. The entire tour- related for clarity in the order that the events unfolded- took over three hours. John drove his car, and we not only passed through those hallowed grounds, we made constant stops where John reinforced his discussions with maps and pictures of the commanders involved in the action. He included- to my delight- many human-interest stories, and his knowledge of the battle and its protagonists is commendable.

Our proprietors at the Tillie Pierce House had made all the arrangements for the tour for us, and I learned more in those three hours from our personal guide about the Battle of Gettysburg than ever I had from lectures or books.

When we arrived at the woods on Seminary Ridge, I experienced a deep feeling of sorrow and dread. Tears filled my eyes as a suffocating heaviness gathered in my chest.

On the third day of the pivotal Battle of Gettysburg, whilst R. E. Lee's artillery attempted to knock out the Union battery on the opposite ridge, here was the spot where General George E. Pickett's Virginians awaited their fate in what would become a disastrous, uphill charge across an open field into the face of a re-energized Union battery. These were sons, husbands, fathers- men who *knew* they had a good chance- a very good chance- of being blown to bits within the next few minutes.

While they waited, some of them played cards, others read from the Bible; still others made peace with their God before what they were certain would be a bloodbath.

Finally, after two hours of ear-shattering cannon fire, barked orders called weary men to their feet to form their brigades, line after grey line. Out from the trees and under the broiling sun, they waited to advance.

Intensified by high humidity, the heat was oppressive, and with the lingering cannon smoke, coupled with the weightiness of the charge ahead of them, it was difficult to breathe. For the first time that afternoon, there were elongated moments of silence, lulls of an eerie stillness that in the heavy, smoky atmosphere seemed, somehow, unreal. It was as if the young nation held its breath and waited- waited for one of the bloodiest pages of American history to unfold.

Finally, the order carried over the cannon-quieted scene. Some of the Confederates muttered a quick last prayer, others turned to exchange a final look with a friend, still others fixed their gazes to their front, perhaps trying to envision, in their mind's eye, a glimpse of home, or a beloved's face. They weren't so different from their blue-vested enemy, filled as they were with an aching desire for home.

Approximately 12,500 grey-clad men in nine infantry brigades, stretching over a mile-wide front, moved forward then- to their rendezvous with Destiny and into the raucous realm of military history. *Across the open fields they marched- for over a mile- under the murderous fire of revitalized Union artillery and rifles.*

I want to give you an idea of what those Confederates faced, marching as they did into the Federal big guns, not to mention the blitz of thousands of rifles. Cannon are set according to range. Typically, at long range, artillery would use solid shot and shell, then as the range decreased to 500 yards or less, artillerymen switched to deadly canister, tins packed with two dozen or so iron balls.

Let us talk for a moment about canister, i.e. the encased shot for close-range artillery fire. As mentioned above, at roughly 500 yards, canister is utilized; sometimes double and triple canister, as was launched against Pickett's Charge. The simplest way I can explain this is to have you imagine a huge, sawed-off shot-gun blast. Those men hit in the front lines of that ill-fated charge were disintegrated — *a resultant red spray*. And readers, I tell you no lie when I say that I sensed the fear along with the tremendous sadness and dread of those poor men who awaited their bloody fate that day at Seminary Ridge. *I felt their forebodings- and I shall never forget that weight upon my heart. Never.*

I also experienced a ponderous sensation at the spot where Robert E. Lee's artillery commander Porter Alexander orchestrated the Confederate cannon fire on the Union big guns. No small wonder. Alexander's young shoulders bore the weight of the ultimate decision that third and final day of the Battle of Gettysburg. The decision to make the Confederate charge across that open field depended on whether or not Alexander succeeded in knocking out the Union battery.

In addition to the feelings described above, I experienced difficulty breathing, and that I attributed to the thick, acrid smoke that hung over the field that final day of the battle. As a "sensitive," or more particularly, an "empath," I was receiving residue of the powerful energies that remain on Gettysburg's hallowed grounds.

For those who may not know, I will endeavor to explain the word "empath," as I have come to understand it. An empath is a born intuitive capable of sensing emotion, both past and present. I have a tendency to pick up strong emotions and/or memories that linger

PENNSYLVANIA HISTORIES

The sacred, hallowed grounds of Gettysburg

near people, places, and things, some memories perhaps better ignored, or even forgotten. I have only recently come to grips with this extrasensory perception. It is too bad I didn't understand it sooner; it would have saved me from internalizing a lot of emotional turmoil growing up, much of which wasn't even my own. I don't mean to imply here that being an empath translates *superhuman*, though, in a way, it is *extra*human. I have come to realize, with time and experience, that empaths possess an amazing gift that helps us traverse the rougher waters of life, an additional sense of understanding of the world, of events, and, most importantly, of people.

In any case, can *you* imagine how the young Tillie Pierce felt, witnessing first-hand so much of the bloodbath that was the great Civil War clash at Gettysburg? Or, even more significantly, how the men and boys, both Blue and Grey, felt who participated in one of our nation's most momentous battles?

Our tour guide also related to us the stirring tale of Sallie, the brindle bullterrier mascot of the 11th Pennsylvania, of her loyal, heroic behavior during the Battle of Gettysburg- but that, dear readers, is a whole other Chronicle!

Tillie Pierce photos courtesy the Tillie Pierce House, Gettysburg, PA
Other Gettysburg photos by Arlene Zimmerman, Chicago, IL, formerly of Connellsville, PA

"The Story of the 11th Pennsylvania's Sallie"

"Sallie was a true hero."– The 11th Pennsylvania Infantry

Sallie was the canine mascot of the 11th Pennsylvania Infantry during the dark days of the American Civil War. I discovered her heart-wrenching tale during an October 2008 excursion to Gettysburg. I am happy to share it with you.

The original 11th Pennsylvania Volunteer Infantry, Company K, was recruited in Latrobe, Westmoreland County, on 26 April 1861 for a three-month enlistment period in response to President Abraham Lincoln's call to arms at the outbreak of the conflict. When Lincoln called for 75,000 volunteers, Pennsylvania promptly answered. Thus, the "Old Eleventh" became what was known as a "First Defender" unit in the sacred cause to save the Union.

If you wonder why the enlistment period was for a mere three months, it is because– on *both* sides– people believed the war would be over in a matter of weeks.

Straightaway, the 11th Pennsylvania was sent to Camp Wayne in West Chester, Chester County, Pennsylvania, for training and organization.

Assigned to the Army of the Shenandoah, the regiment earned its most famous moniker the "Bloody Eleventh," after its baptism by fire at the Battle of Falling Waters, where the Pennsylvanians defeated an enemy force under the formidable Stonewall Jackson.

The men of the 11th re-enlisted at Youngstown, Westmoreland County, Pennsylvania. Then they were off for re-organization at Camp Curtin in Harrisburg, whence they continued their meritorious service in such engagements as the Second Battle of Bull Run, Antietam, Chancellorsville, Gettysburg, the Siege of Petersburg, and on to the war's end in April 1865 at Appomattox.

On the first day of July 1865, the seasoned veterans of the 11th were mustered out of service after the Civil War came to its sanguinary conclusion.

The 11th's most notable commander was Colonel Richard Coulter, a lawyer from Greensburg and a Mexican War veteran. His distinguished war record earned him a promotion to brevet brigadier general by August of 1864, and it should be noted that Coulter ended the war as a major general.

However, it is not my intent in this Chronicle to spotlight either General Coulter or his fine men, though I must comment that this unit was known far and wide for its valor under fire. Rather, this discussion's focus will be on a four-legged hero.

Always in history when men have marched off to war, chances are that an animal talisman went with them. The loyalty and bravery of wartime animal mascots inspired the men and earned their true love and affection. Respected wartime pets were also a reminder of beloved pets left behind at home. Too, the act of nurturing a mascot relieved the boredom in camp, as well as the stress and tensions associated with war.

During the first month of the Civil War, in April 1861, when the newly formed 11th Pennsylvania volunteers were training at the fairgrounds in West Chester, a civilian sauntered into camp, carrying a small wicker basket. He presented it to one of the officers, First Lieutenant– soon to be Captain– William R. Terry. The lieutenant reached inside the basket and, with a smile, withdrew from the blanket therein a pug-nosed, brindle bull terrier. The female puppy was scarcely four weeks old. When set upon the ground, she toddled unsteadily on her little legs, winning the hearts of the men in the unit immediately.

She was cute, so the soldiers named her after one of the local beauties in the West Chester area. In the weeks that followed, Sallie, who had been taken from her mother far too soon, happily discovered that she now had a family of hundreds of uniformed men. Each could be counted on to scratch her ears, rub her tummy, give her a pat, or a morsel of food. Sallie, or Sal, as some of the fellows took to calling her, quickly became the "official" mascot of the 11th Pennsylvania Infantry Regiment.

The little terrier rapidly developed a unique personality. Clean in her habits, well-trained and eager to please, Sallie was even-tempered and ultra-affectionate with the soldiers in the unit. Yet, she exhibited a strong distaste for civilians and strangers. It soon became a standing joke that Sallie had a dislike for Rebels, Democrats, and women. (Remember, readers, that the newly formed Republican Party had its first President, Abraham Lincoln, in the White House at the time of the Civil War; through the war and its aftermath/ Reconstruction, through a good portion of the next century, the "Solid South" translated "Democrats.")

Another noteworthy thing about Sallie was that she carried herself with pride and dignity. Her bearing was almost what we might call "regal." During encampments, she slept by or in the captain's tent- after strolling through the entire area, making her own kind of camp inspection. She quickly learned the bugle and drum rolls. At reveille, she was the first one out of quarters to attend roll call. At drills, she stuck close to a particular soldier and pranced alongside him throughout the entire exercise. At dress-parade, she took up a prominent position beside the proud regimental colors. Sallie was something to behold!

Growing up with the men of the regiment, Sallie became a comrade-in-arms, sharing the marches, the hardships, the extremes of weather, even the dangers of war.

Her first major battle came in 1862 at Cedar Mountain. She dynamically entered the fray with the men, steadfastly remaining close to the 11th Pennsylvania's colors throughout the engagement. In fact, she remained in close proximity to the flag bearer in each action, at bloody Antietam, Fredericksburg, and Chancellorsville. In the heat of the battles in which Sallie participated, she would race around the front line, barking ferociously, snarling and flashing her teeth at the grey and butternut-clad enemy.

I suppose no one thought to send the little dog to the rear during a fight, for she was the regiment's spirit- *their inspiration*. I seriously doubt she would have stayed in the rear anyway. Sallie had a stubborn streak, and in regard to staying out of a fight, I don't think any amount of training would have yielded the desired result. What's that old saying? "There's no nourishment gnawin' on a dry bone." For all her loving ways, Sallie could be a scrapper; that much is for certain.

A story survives that, during the intensity of one particular battle, when a panicked soldier of the 11th tried to skulk away, the bull terrier sunk her formidable teeth into his leg, forcing him back into the fight.

In a review of the Union Army in the spring of 1863 at Falmouth, Virginia, Sallie splendidly marched with her prancing feet in step beneath the colors and alongside the parading men of the 11th Pennsylvania. An extremely tall man in the very center of the review stand caught sight of the little dog. Immediately, a twinkle sparked in his dark eyes, and he raised his stovepipe hat in salute. In that manner did President Abraham Lincoln pay special acknowledgment to the Old Eleventh's canine mascot.

In the summer of that same year, Sallie made the long march from Virginia to Gettysburg, Pennsylvania, with her regiment. During the first day's fighting of the pivotal three-day battle, when the Union line collapsed, the 11th Pennsylvania was driven back from its original position on Oak Ridge and into the streets of the town. The men of the unit staggered through Gettysburg to Cemetery Hill, where they reformed and counted their losses. Among the missing was Sallie.

In the confusion and smoke of the battle or the retreat, Sallie had become lost. Three days later, when medical and burial details moved onto the battlefield, a captain of the 12th Massachusetts, Benjamin F. Cook, discovered the courageous dog. Tired, hungry and thirsty, Sallie had wandered out to where her brave comrades had fought and died, somehow managing to find her way back to the 11th Pennsylvania's original position on Oak Ridge. There, she kept a stalwart vigil of the wounded, licking their injuries and guarding the dead of her unit, so that no Confederate could rob or disturb the bodies.

By that point, poor Sallie was half-dead herself, so weak was she from malnutrition and want of water in the heat and humidity of those historic three days. Be that as it may, neither hunger nor thirst had swayed the little dog from what she considered her duty, to lend what comfort she could to her wounded compatriots, and to steadfastly guard the Bloody Eleventh's fallen. Whatever else I could tell you about Sallie, she was ever-lastingly duty-bound.

How she escaped harm in the core of such ferocious fighting and shelling was a miracle. Needless to say, Sallie's return was met with welcoming cries of glee and open arms. When the men heard what she had done, there was nary a dry eye in their midsts. With especial care, the 11th nursed Sallie back to health, doubling the affection and attention she had received prior to the great Battle of Gettysburg. Sallie was not only a mascot- now *she was a hero.*

Recovering quickly, Sallie remained, of course, with her regiment, continuing to share in the dangers and duties faced by her multiple masters. The subsequent May, at the Battle of Spotsylvania, the canine soldier received a neck wound, and thereafter, the beloved dog bore a "red badge of courage."

In the Petersburg lines throughout the long night of February 4-5, 1865, Sallie's mournful cries awakened the sleeping encampment. The enemy was about!

In the morning, the 11th Pennsylvania made a concerted attack at Hatcher's Run, Virginia. Men in the second wave were advancing under heavy fire when they caught sight of Sallie, lying still and unmoving, on the battlefield. In her usual position in the front lines next to the unit's colors, she had been shot through the head and killed instantly.

Such were the intense feelings of the men of the regiment toward their brave and loyal comrade, weeping soldiers of the 11th Pennsylvania buried Sallie on the field where she had fallen- despite heavy enemy fire. It was only fitting.

Two months after Sallie was killed, the long, drawn-out war ended. When all was said and done, four officers and 177 enlisted men of the Old Eleventh's ranks succumbed to disease. Twelve officers and 224 enlistees were killed or mortally wounded making the Bloody Eleventh's casualty total 417- in addition to one small, brindle-colored dog named Sallie.

During her all-too-short life, Sallie bore four or five litters. The puppies were always adopted, many of them sent by the men of the regiment back home to their families.

There is a touching epilogue to Sal's story. In 1890, surviving veterans of the 11th Pennsylvania Infantry dedicated a monument to their regiment on the hallowed Gettysburg battlefield. It is located off Doubleday Avenue on Oak Ridge in the National Military Park. From a distance, the memorial looks pretty much like other regimental shrines: a bronze statue of a defiant soldier atop a tall, ornate granite pedestal. This one depicts a full-size 11th Pennsylvania infantryman overlooking the rolling fields where Iverson's North Carolin-

The heroic Sallie guarding the dead and wounded from her unit at Gettysburg. Note the money next to her likeness. Though there is no official policy, park personnel collect the coins left at the 11th Pennsylvania's/Sallie's memorial to turn in at the visitors' center for upkeep of the hallowed battlefield. I have also read that the change collected goes to the local animal shelter.
I like to think the doggie treats and dog biscuits left at Sallie's likeness are awarded to her in Heaven.

ians made their fateful charge. But get out of your vehicle and move closer. You will then see that this memorial possesses a unique addition near the bottom of the pedestal.

On a ledge of the monument's base, is the bronze likeness of a bull terrier. It is none other than Sallie, who, her head on her paws, appears as she must have looked those three days on Oak Ridge, Gettysburg, in July 1863.

"In all likelihood," said distinguished history professor and author James Robertson, Jr. several years ago in a radio broadcast, *The Little Mascot*, "she is keeping watch through eternity over the spirits of soldiers with whom she shared an undying love."

"The Salient Spring of Rachel Carson"

"If I had influence with the good fairy who is supposed to preside over the christening of all children, I should ask that her gift to each child in the world be a sense of wonder so indestructible it would last throughout life."

"The human race is challenged more than ever before to demonstrate our mastery- not over nature but of ourselves."

"Those who contemplate the beauty of the earth find reserves of strength that will endure as long as life lasts."
- Rachel Carson

"There was once a town in the heart of America where all life seemed to live in harmony with its surroundings. ... Then a strange blight crept over the area and everything began to change. Some evil spell had settled on the community. ... No witchcraft, no enemy action had silenced the rebirth of new life in this stricken world. The people had done it themselves."

Thus began the classic book that launched the great environmental movement- *Silent Spring* by the incomparable Rachel Carson. In her masterpiece, and later in testimony before a congressional committee, Carson asserted that one of the most basic human rights must surely be the "right of the citizen to be secure in his own home against the intrusion of poisons applied by other persons."

Through ignorance, greed, and downright negligence, government had allowed "poisonous and biologically potent chemicals" to fall "indiscriminately into the hands of persons largely or wholly ignorant of their potentials for harm." Rachel Carson awakened both the government and the public with the alarming evidence of environmental damage from the widespread use of the chemical DDT and other long-lasting agricultural pesticides. Suffering and literally dying of cancer, it was an extremely brave thing for this remarkable lady to have done. She wrote to a close friend at the outset of the project that she would never again be able to enjoy birdsong when, in her above fable for tomorrow, no birds would sing. "There would be no peace for me, if I kept silent," she avowed.

In 1962, the multi-million-dollar chemical industry was not about to let a former government editor- a woman- to undermine public confidence in its products. The CEOs of the chemical companies called the author of *Silent Spring* a hysterical woman, a romantic spinster who kept cats and was therefore clearly suspect. They even labeled Carson a Communist!

Looking back from today's perspective, it is hard to believe Rachel Carson's messages in *Silent Spring* could have generated such angry rebuttal and response. The answer, of course, was money, i.e. the loss of income for the chemical pesticide companies.

When asked why she did not defend her book more vigorously, Carson answered, "Let the course of events provide the answers."

Our greatest historian, Time, has proven that Rachel Carson was as much prophet as writer and scientist.

Her final book was a landmark event, for *Silent Spring* stimulated the growth of the environmental movement. After the book caught the attention of President John F. Kennedy, federal and state investigations were launched into the validity of Carson's claims.

"The history of life on earth has been a history of interaction between living things and their surroundings," Rachel told us in her chartbuster book. Rarely does a single book alter the course of history, but Rachel Carson's *Silent Spring* did exactly that. The clamor that resulted from the book's publication in 1962 forced the banning of DDT and spurred revolutionary changes in the laws affecting our air, land, and water.

Rachel Carson's passionate concern for the environment- indeed for the continuation of life as we know it on our planet- reverberated powerfully throughout the world. Carson had no illusions about what the book could accomplish. When the manuscript was nearly finished, she penned in a missive to her closest friend, "It would be unrealistic to believe that one book could bring a complete change."

If Rachel Carson failed at anything, it was to anticipate the enormous and enduring impact of *Silent Spring,* which became one of the most influential books of the last hundred years.

In 1999, Carson was selected by *Life* magazine as one of the 100 most important Americans of the twentieth century.

Unfortunately, Rachel did not live to see anything but the immediate outcome of her work, and though she was dying of cancer when her blockbuster book debuted, she held to her sense of humor. When queried about what she ate, she answered, "Chlorinated hydrocarbons [the stuff of DDT, subject to biological magnification through the food chain], just like everyone else does."

Silent Spring is, without question, one of the milestone books of the twentieth century. Since its release in September 1962, it has never been out-of-print.

~ ~ ~

A quiet, somewhat solitary child, Rachel Carson's early life did not indicate that she was the type of individual to take on the mantle of a crusader. Born on May 27, 1907, in Springdale, a river community just north of Pittsburgh in Allegheny County, Rachel Louise Carson was a determined child who decided quite young that she would be a writer. Early on, she found that she enjoyed expressing herself on paper.

Rachel was also a child of the woods, who took great pleasure in nature's wonders. The wild creatures were her friends. She understood them, communicated with them, and delighted in each of them. Both these lifelong passions Rachel always attributed to her mother's influence.

In the Carson's small, four-room house in its country setting, Mrs. Carson cooked the family's meals on a wood-burning stove; and like many homes in the early 1900s, the Carson place had no gas or electricity, and no running water. Oil lamps and candles were the family's light source, and their only heat came from the kitchen stove and the fireplace in the parlor.

The family kept chickens, a milk cow, a few pigs, and some rabbits. They grew their own vegetables, and their apple orchard supplied them with an abundance of crisp, healthful apples. There was always a big bowl of rosy apples from the orchard in the center of the Carson table.

The child Rachel spent a great deal of time alone with her mother, Maria McLean Carson. Rachel's father, Robert, worked at a variety of jobs, selling insurance or working for the local power company, jobs that kept him away from home much of the time. Rachel's much-older brother Robert and sister Marian, more like uncle and aunt, were often busy with school, friends, and hobbies that took them away from the house, and there were no other youngsters near the Carson home with whom she could play. Though she was not an only child, all her life, Rachel remembered herself as a solitary child.

Before she married, Rachel's mother had been a teacher. In those long-past days, married women were not permitted to teach school, so Maria had been forced to give up the calling at which she excelled. However, everything in life happens for a reason, and Maria's intense love of teaching was showered on her youngest child, who possessed a curious mind and a keen intelligence. From the time Rachel was a year old, she and her mother spent long periods of time outdoors, roaming the sixty-five-acre farm- exploring the woods, meadows, springs, and the river, naming and discussing the flowers, birds, woodland creatures, and insects.

Rachel Carson would faithfully follow her mother's example. As a scientist, she often collected live specimens for study, especially sea creatures. Never did she toss them away when her work was finished; rather, she kept the fish, clams, crabs and such alive in a bucket of seawater, returning them to their natural habitat as soon as she could.

"Close your eyes," Maria Carson frequently instructed the child Rachel. "Listen carefully." In this fashion the future scientist and author learned to appreciate the lovely sounds of nature- birdsong, whirring insects, whispering breezes, rustling leaves, the rippling river, and the babbling streams.

Maria encouraged reading, and her protégée, who learned to read exceptionally early, required no prodding. Maria subscribed to a juvenile magazine entitled *St. Nicholas* that published work by children, giving them right of membership. Each month the periodical held competitions for the best poems, essays, stories, and puzzles. In addition to its status as a "child's playground," the beautifully illustrated magazine was wholly educational. Moreover, no other children's publication of the era provided nature study and the values of examining and analyzing nature more comprehensively than the *St. Nicholas*. In addition to her mother's teachings, the magazine would greatly illuminate Carson's path in life.

Rachel was an unusually pretty child with the bonnie blue eyes and fair complexion common to her Scotch-Irish heritage. There was a softness in her eyes that people always remembered. Her dark hair glowed auburn; and all her life, she exhibited an elfin quality that was charming.

Her sweet nature coupled with her enthusiastic desire to learn made Rachel her mother's favorite. Maria completely dedicated herself to her youngest offspring, and by the time the little girl began school, she was far ahead of the other students.

Along with a basketful of wishes, Rachel Carson sent her first submission to the *St. Nicholas* League contest in the spring of 1918. The piece was "A Battle in the Clouds," a World War I story that reflected the influence of Rachel's brother Robert, who had enlisted in the Army Air Service in the fall of 1917. In one of his letters from the front, Robert recounted the tragic death of a Canadian flying instructor who had been killed in combat in France. In her entry to the *St. Nicholas*, Rachel retold the heroic tale in her own words.

Like all new writers, little Rachel waited with ill-concealed anxiety for the results of her submission. Finally, when the September 1918 issue of the magazine emerged from the Carson's mailbox, she was thrilled to discover that, not only was "A Battle in the Clouds" published by the *St. Nicholas* League, it had been awarded a silver badge for excellence in prose.

Nothing succeeds like success; thus, Rachel immediately entered a second story, also in a World War I setting. This account appeared in the January 1919 edition. A third story followed the very next month, and this one, "A Message to the Front," earned the young author a gold badge. After a fourth entry escalated Rachel to the lofty status of "Honor Member," in addition to a cash reward, she was convinced she could become what she dreamed- a published writer and even a famous author.

Rachel's final story for the *St. Nicholas*, "My Favorite Recreation," appeared in July of 1922. The theme of the swan song was nature. It was prophetic as well as pure Rachel Carson. Here, Rachel tells of going bird-watching in the Pennsylvania hills with her dog, equipped with a boxed lunch, canteen, notebook, and camera. Throughout her life, Rachel liked to say that she became a professional writer at age eleven.

Actually, Rachel had written her first "book" when she was in second grade. The homemade book was filled with little stories and poems about animals, birds, fish, and insects. On every page was a drawing, each a good rendering, to illustrate her words. Rachel had been so proud of the manuscript, she presented it to her father as a birthday gift.

From grade school upward, Rachel's report cards bore a rank of A's with the occasional B. There were, however, from the outset of her school years, many absences. Rachel's mother, Maria, protective of her favored child, and not wanting the youngster to walk the half mile through deep snowdrifts, kept her home when harsh winter weather howled at their door, or outbreaks of whooping cough, diphtheria, measles, mumps, or other contagious diseases plagued the school.

In all truth, Maria's one-on-one tutoring was likely superior to the classroom, for Rachel continued to excel with each passing school year.

Rachel's mother looked stern, with her dark hair pulled severely back from her somber face into a tight bun and her no-nonsense spectacles perched on the end of her nose. But she taught her inquisitive little daughter with love and gentleness.

Rachel especially loved her mother's nature talks. Cold winter evenings before the cosy fireplace, with her mother's voice spinning stories or reading aloud, Rachel loved to snuggle deeply into the overstuffed chair and watch the glow from the oil lamp shimmer and dance on the big conch shell atop the mantel. Then she would dream of the sea.

While her two grownup siblings went about their lives, Rachel and Maria developed a close bond that would last a lifetime. Always an avid reader, Rachel, to her mother's joy, immersed herself in books, with nature and animals claiming equal amounts of her time. When her father wheeled the buggy out of the barn and hitched up the horses, she would plead to go along to town so she could visit the library. Library visits were brimming with excitement. Choosing the books was nearly as delightful as reading them and discovering all the wonders their turning pages held.

In 1923, Rachel's parents sent her to Parnassus for her final two years of high school, a town a couple of miles north across the river, not far from New Kensington. The studious young girl rode the trolley to and from school, where she enjoyed competing in sports as well as winning high academic achievement.

Rachel Louise Carson graduated first in her class from Parnassus in May 1925 just a few days before her eighteenth birthday. The yearbook editors created a little poem for each of the departing seniors. As valedictorian, Rachel's was quite apropos:

Rachel's like the mid-day sun
Always very bright
Never stops her studying
'Til she gets it right.

The only college Rachel's mother Maria considered for her was the Pennsylvania College for Women. Then as now, this institution for higher learning, known today as Chatham University, was an elite private school in Pittsburgh.

PCW had an excellent academic reputation, and it was located a mere sixteen miles from the Carson home in Springdale.

Parnassus' star graduate won admission to PCW easily and was awarded an annual $100 tuition scholarship, but it was not nearly enough. Maria, however, refused to permit Rachel to apply for a campus job to supplement her expenses. She insisted that her daughter's constitution was too frail, and that she should devote all her time to her studies.

To solve the college dilemma, the Carsons planned to borrow money from the bank and sell off lots of their property to help meet PCW's $800 room-and-board fee. Though the plan was a good one, Rachel's father Robert set the price of his lots too high, and as a result, land sales yielded only a small portion of the amount needed for Rachel's tuition and expenses.

Not to be thwarted, Maria increased her piano-student roster, sold chickens, eggs and apples, even her family's lovely heirloom china. Be that as it may, there was still barely enough to send Rachel to college properly dressed; and the girl would have absolutely no spending money.

Take into account, readers, that the Carsons had always lived a simple life with no extras; hence, totally mindful of her mother's sacrifices, Rachel was content to wear the handmade, serviceable clothes Maria made for her scanty college wardrobe, and to do without pocket money.

It must have been at once exciting and sad for Rachel to leave the Carson homestead for Pittsburgh, difficult to say goodbye to her beloved canine companions and to her secret woodland paths and hideaways.

I wonder what thoughts skipped through her head as she and her mother climbed into the Model T Ford her father had borrowed to carry her off to college. One thought I know must have coursed through her mind as they drove south to the big city and the PCW campus: Rachel was fiercely determined to become a writer, the best writer who ever took pen in hand– a writer whose work would make a difference!

I wonder too what the young, college-bound Rachel would have thought had she known that one day, a bridge, the Ninth Street Bridge spanning the Allegheny River in downtown Pittsburgh, would be named for her, as well as a national wildlife refuge along the rocky coast of Maine.

When Rachel Carson entered PCW, she did so with determination and well-defined goals. Hers, in fact, was an unusual sense of purpose and drive, and from the outset of her college career, she applied herself with gusto.

Irrespective of college and escalating studies, never did her love affair with nature wane. Rather, her passion for the outdoors steadily intensified, as reflected in her college themes that possessed her ever-fresh delight in discovery. Perhaps her intimacy with nature, animals and birds was a substitute for the more conventional relationships, from childhood through adolescence, that she never experienced. Geniuses are, I think, rather solitary individuals, and Rachel Carson was no exception.

Resolute in absorbing as much knowledge as she could– to become all that she could– this exceptional young woman had a vision, perhaps not yet uttered, but nonetheless, a vision of a special calling that waited just around the next corner.

The enchanting PCW campus extended over ten wooded acres atop Murray Hill overlooking Pittsburgh's mansion-lined Fifth Avenue in the east-end neighborhood known as Shadyside. Another aspect that Maria Carson liked about her choice of college for her daughter was that the school, founded by well-to-do Presbyterian congregations in Shadyside, was a Christian institution.

The campus and original manse had once been the sumptuous home of George A. Berry, a wealthy entrepreneur, who sold the property and the three-storey, brick, Gothic-style mansion to the college. Berry Hall, as it was known, had been reputed to be the largest private residence in Allegheny County. Its vast reception area, dining room, and spacious parlors on the ground floor housed the president's offices, faculty quarters, and general classrooms. The other two levels were used as dormitory rooms.

With its added dormitories, such as Dilworth Hall and Woodland Hall, the scenic hilltop campus emerged a serene yet impressive site of academic pursuits.

At PCW, Carson was never "one of the girls." Rachel was unique and set-apart, and it was not totally due to her homemade clothes and her lack of spending money. There were other girls on campus on scholarship. Miss Carson had, as I said, *purpose*, and her values were mature beyond her years. Despite her plain, serviceable attire, she carried herself with a visible air of independence and intellectual self-confidence that was often misread by her fellow students. The majority of the girls, who did not take the time to find out differently, translated Rachel's reserve as arrogance.

Rachel did not attempt to alter the situation.

When she arrived at PCW, her otherwise pretty face, neck and shoulders were marred by severe acne; and her thick, dark hair, chin-length during most of her college years, was the oily type that required daily shampooing, which Rachel often neglected. The studious Miss Carson seemed indifferent to her physical appearance, since her mother had never attached any importance to outward beauty. However, she was young with the potential to be attractive and popular in addition to academically successful, and surely she suffered inwardly because of her isolation.

There was another reason that Rachel did not establish many close friendships at college, and this was due to her mother's frequent visits. Maria Carson came up to the campus nearly every weekend, remaining all day Saturday. When Mrs. Carson did not make the trip to PCW, Rachel caught the train home for the weekend. According to leading biographer Linda Lear in her compelling *Rachel Carson,* the stern-faced, white-haired Maria, habitually draped in black from head-to-toe, exchanged no small talk with anyone, took no interest in anyone but her Rachel, and was a "formidable presence in any freshman dorm."

Maria Carson usually came armed with a basketful of treatments for Rachel's persistent acne, as well as home-baked cookies. One of Rachel's former classmates remembered that the pair would sit on Rachel's bed and talk for hours, "eating cookies without ever thinking to offer them to anyone else."

If the young Rachel ever harbored any resentment or embarrassment in regard to her mother's constant visits, she never exhibited it outwardly. Well aware of all her mother's sacrifices so that she could attend college, Rachel likely saw no reason why her mother ought not to share in campus pleasures.

In addition to her close bond with her mother, two other things remained constant in Rachel's life, and those were her love of writing and her love of nature. In her very first college theme for English composition, she described herself, in an essay entitled "Who I Am and Why I Came to PCW," as "... a girl of eighteen years, a Presbyterian, Scotch-Irish by ancestry, and a graduate of a small, but first-class high school." Listing the pastimes she enjoyed most, she wrote further that she was "intensely fond of anything pertaining to the outdoors and athletics." She expressed with ardor that her real love was nature. "I love all the beautiful things of nature, and the wild creatures are my friends."

Rachel participated in sports during her college years, working her way up to goalkeeper on the field hockey team and playing basketball as an eager substitute. Small and petite in build, but scrappy and courageous in mettle, I can conjure an image of her in the required uniform- baggy blue serge bloomers, black silk stockings, and high, white tennis shoes.

Rarely did she attend any of the school's social functions, preferring to stay in her room and study. The activity she most enjoyed was a solitary one. Often would she slip over to the Carnegie Museum of Natural History to study the animal and bird exhibits.

The one college requirement outside the classroom that met with Rachel's (and her mother's) full approval was compulsory church attendance Sundays. At first, she attended service at the East Liberty Presbyterian Church. Later, at her roommate's introduction, she went frequently to service at the Calvary Episcopal Church, so impressed was she with the architectural beauty of the towering, grey-stone gothic structure.

Since Rachel had entered college intent on becoming a writer, her major was English. Thus, it is no surprise that the professor whose opinion mattered the most to her was Miss Grace Croff. In her mid-thirties, Professor Croff taught freshman composition. Rachel Carson quickly became her favorite student, and the two spent a good deal of time together, sipping tea whilst discussing literature, writing, music, and art. This did not surprise me, for Rachel's best friend had always been her mother, and the girl had never had any close friends her own age. Croff was the advisor to the student newspaper, *The Arrow*, as well as to its occasional literary supplement, *The Englicode*, and she encouraged Rachel to join both the subsequent year.

At the end of her first year at PCW, Rachel had good reason to be proud of herself. Her grades were excellent; in fact, she finished her freshman year as one of ten students selected for "freshman honor." She had a mentor who told her she had the potential to be a great writer, and she had broken through some of her social barriers to be recognized as a capable, enthusiastic athlete. Freshman year hadn't been all roses, but Rachel's summer back at the Carson homestead would prove a great deal thornier.

The Springdale house was terribly crowded that summer. Her brother Robert had moved back home with his wife and baby, and to make the situation worse, sister Marian had left her husband to move in with her two toddlers. When Rachel came home from college, Robert and his family (since he could not afford separate housing) were forced to pitch a large tent in the backyard, though they took their meals inside the tiny house.

Rachel spent the entire summer helping her mother and babysitting her three small nieces. To say that the household was chaotic would be an understatement.

Maria Carson had never approved of Robert's marriage to a Roman Catholic, and she and Meredith were openly hostile to one another. The long, hot nights were filled with the loud quarreling between Robert and Meredith. Their baby was teething and fussy, and Marian's little girls were routinely boisterous. Recovering from a bout with appendicitis, Marian could not help much with the work load. Most of the work was accomplished by Maria and Rachel, a state of affairs that would persist for years to come.

Fortunately, Rachel found solitude in the surrounding woods. She took long tramps into the familiar hills above the Allegheny, where she could find temporary escape reading or writing stories or poetry. At summer's end, she was more than ready to return to college. She would have Miss Croff again for composition, and in order to fulfill her one-year science requirement, she would be taking biology.

Introductory biology was taught by Miss Mary Scott Skinker. She was beautiful, elegant, highly intelligent, possessed of high standards- and she would change Rachel Carson's life forever. Immediately cognizant of Carson's exceptional ability, as well as the breadth of her knowledge of nature, Professor Skinker took her under her capable wing.

Rachel's biology class participation was notable, as was the depth of her curiosity and her enchantment with the course. Skinker's biology class kindled Carson's brilliant mind. She rapidly discovered that biology was yet another way to unlock the secrets of nature.

However, this discovery soon presented a quandary that tormented Rachel. Should she switch majors? Her love of writing and her love of nature were equal. What should she do?

It was a question that plagued her throughout most of her sophomore year at PCW. Neither English Professor Croff nor biology Proffessor Skinker ever suggested to Rachel that perhaps, with her poet's gift for language, she could find a way to *combine* science and literature.

The dilemma of her major was solved when Miss Croff assigned the class to read "Locksley Hall," a poem by Alfred Lord Tennyson. Outside her dorm window, a Pennsylvania thunderstorm was raging in all its fury. Rain pelted the window; lightning flashed across the sky, and thunder boomed and rumbled, the fierceness of the storm rocking the rafters of the old Victorian mansion Berry Hall. As a banshee wind whistled and hissed through the leaded, diamond-paned window, Rachel read aloud the lines:

Cramming all the blast before it, in its breast a thunderbold.
Let it fall on Locksley Hall, with rain or hail, or fire or snow;
For the might wind arises, roaring seaward, and I go.

Evoking the poem's final verse years later, Rachel wrote: "... that line spoke to something within me, seeming to tell me that my own path led to the sea- which then I had never seen- and that my own destiny was somehow linked with the sea."

It was then that Rachel Carson took the first giant step toward her great calling. She continued to major in English, but began a minor in science. It was a prophetic beginning to a luminous career ahead. She had always wanted to see the great oceans of the world. How elated Rachel would have been that storm-swept night to know that, indeed, "roaring seaward" she would go!

As her sophomore year progressed, Rachel became more and more haunted by a career choice. She was in college on a scholarship because she and her mother had planned all these long years for her to become a writer, an accepted career for a woman during the 1920s. Comparatively, few women gravitated toward science in those days. Translated: few women could support themselves in the ranks of science. Teaching in women's colleges, as Mary Scott Skinker was doing, was perhaps an option, but teachers made next to nothing in that era, and Rachel knew she would need to make enough to support her family. Her father never made much money, nor did her brother Robert. The Carsons were always short of cash, and now, with the homestead crowded with dependents ... . Rachel was acutely aware of the financial implications of changing her major, and even more importantly, of jeopardizing her mother's dreams of having a famous author for a daughter.

Despite the above, Professor Mary Scott Skinker was a powerful mentor and role model. By the dawn of 1928, Rachel had made up her mind to change her major to biology. Despite comments from classmates that she had made a foolish decision, she decided to immerse herself in science, and she was hoping to go right on for her master's.

Come April of that year, Rachel applied for graduate standing in zoology at Johns Hopkins University. If accepted, she expected to complete her master's degree in two years. Of course, in Rachel Carson's case, getting accepted was only half the battle. She would also need substantial scholarship assistance.

That summer she waited, with bated breath, to hear from Johns Hopkins while she filled her time helping her mother, reading, exploring, and writing eager letters to Professor Skinker, who was at the Marine Biological Laboratory in Woods Hole, Massachusetts, on the southwestern tip of Cape Cod. Skinker penned such enthusiastic missives about her study there that Rachel responded: "It must be a biologist's paradise!" Carson vowed that one day she would also study at the MBL. It was a promise she would keep to herself.

Senior year at Pennsylvania College for Women proved somewhat a discontented one for Rachel. Both her mentors, Professor Croff and Professor Skinker, were missing from the school's faculty on leaves of absence. Rachel had known Professor Skinker was taking time off from her teaching duties, but when she returned to campus in the fall and learned that her other mentor was also taking a sabbatical, it resulted in a lonely time for Carson, who, unlike many of the girls, was not a social butterfly.

At the end of December 1928, Rachel reapplied to Johns Hopkins. Finally, in mid-April 1929, the news for which she had been so anxiously waiting arrived. Johns Hopkins offered Carson a full tuition scholarship for her first year of graduate work. It was a burden lifted from the shoulders of both Rachel and her mother.

Maria Carson was so proud of her daughter that she immediately contacted the local newspaper to print the news: "The scholarship awarded by Johns Hopkins University is one of seven offered to applicants of high scholastic standing who have given evidence of their ability to carry on independent research. The honor of this award is seldom conferred upon women." The cost of tuition having been accomplished, the Carsons now had to overcome the next challenge- how to finance Rachel's living expenses in Baltimore.

Rachel's father Robert had never been able to sell more than a handful of his Springdale lots; and now, with the Depression worsening every day, the value of his land was ever depreciating. In order to meet their debt at PCW, Rachel's parents had signed over, as collateral against their obligation, two large contiguous lots to the college. If the Carsons could find no buyers for the land, Rachel would begin making payments of $1,600 in the fall of 1930. Despite all her hard work and superior intelligence, it would be *years* before Rachel Carson would be financially independent.

Now, her mind was on finishing her undergraduate work, which was fast coming to an end. But the best news of all was that Rachel had won a seat for the summer at the prestigious Marine Biological Laboratory at Woods Hole, where she would be a "beginning investigator" for eight consecutive weeks. Amidst all the money worries, this was a dream come true!

How often as a little girl in Springdale had she climbed on a chair to reach the large, creamy conch shell tinged with pink her mother kept on the heavy beam above the fireplace. Pressing it to her ear, she had envisioned images of the distant, vast sea. For most folks living far from an ocean, a conch is just a lovely curio. But to Rachel, it had always meant so much more. Even as a small child, she had entertained an intense fascination for the sea. As she would later write, "I dreamed of it and *longed* to see it ... ."

When she had read the MBL acceptance letter, the line from "Locksley Hall" came rushing back in a wave of joy to engulf her, "... roaring seaward, and I go"!

The stage was now set for her destiny with the sea- as a respected scientist and a profound and prolific writer. Little did she know that one day she would share the magic of the sea with millions of readers around the world!

Rachel Carson graduated *cum laude* from Pennsylvania College for Women on June 10, 1929. The entire Carson clan attended the graduation exercises. The sixty-year-old Maria Carson watched her daughter flip the tassel on her cap, deeming, with pride and satisfaction, her countless sacrifices worthwhile.

After graduation that June, before leaving for Woods Hole, Rachel was back home in Springdale. Her beloved woods were still there, but while she had been away, changes had occurred to the river and the air about the old homestead. Once-clear streams were now yellowed by sulfur, and its rotten-egg stench assaulted her nostrils as she stood on the Carson land and looked out over the smoky horizon.

Sulfur was a by-product of a local coal and coke company that supplied coal to Duquesne Light's new local power station. Duquesne had become the Pittsburgh area's largest supplier of electrical power. In the opposite direction was the newly expanded West Penn Power Company. The two power plants, within two miles of one another, stood on opposite sides of Springdale like two giant bookends, squeezing the town between them. As Rachel's blue eyes traveled across the horizon, her gaze no longer took in the pristine farms and fields of her childhood. Now, she looked upon the dark, looming smokestacks of the power plants. Other than being separated from her mother for the summer, Rachel had no sadness about leaving Springdale- and the image of industrial pollution would be seared into her heart and memory forever.

Baltimore, Maryland, and not Woods Hole, was Rachel's first stop that significant summer. She wanted to scout about for a room for the fall in addition to acquainting herself with the sprawling Johns Hopkins campus, after which she was to meet with her mentor Professor Mary Scott Skinker at nearby Luray, Virginia. There, Skinker's family had a vacation spot in the mountains, where a sprinkling of cabins had been aptly christened "Skyland."

At the finish of a long, hot journey, begun on a bus and ending on horseback, the two women finally met on the wooded path leading to the Skinker cabin. Rachel was enchanted with the place- the storybook log residence, the myriad of woodland creatures, and the wild, rustic beauty of the Shenandoah Valley.

Now affectionate friends, rather than teacher-student, the pair enjoyed horseback riding, hiking- the views about Skyland were breathtaking- and talking evenings before the companionable glow of an open fire. Their discussions were mostly about Rachel's future as a scientist. It must have been rewarding for Rachel Carson to have her former idol now a close friend and confidante.

It was at Woods Hole, Massachusetts, on Cape Cod, where Rachel's future books on sea life were sown. At the Marine Biological Laboratory's library, an eager-to-learn Carson discovered a spectrum of scientific journals from around the world. Rare books, new books, an endless array of tomes about the sea provided what astute biographer Linda Lear referred to as a "feast for [Rachel's] imagination and an endless source for her curiosity." Needless to say, Carson spent long hours in that library, in addition to glorious exploration and lab work.

She discovered that she especially liked to walk along the shore at low tide, looking at the tide pools. She was continuously finding new organisms clinging to the seaweed or cached away among the rocks. Rachel had dreamed about visiting and studying the ocean for so long, her first summer at Woods Hole was like a dream, carrying on its fragrant sea breath an almost magical quality.

So utterly captivated was she by the sounds, the sights, and smells of the ocean, Rachel often wandered off by herself, pausing occasionally to stare out into the beckoning open arms of the sea. She loved the soft sea fogs that, with mystical splendor, rolled over Woods Hole from the endless reaches of the water. The sheer beauty and power of what she saw sometimes moved her to tears. "Someday," she promised herself, "I will live close to the ocean."

If Carson had come to Woods Hole with doubts that she could become a scientist of worth, she boarded the train for Pittsburgh and home that fall secure in the knowledge that she would succeed. It was not really "goodbye" that she whispered to Woods Hole and the rolling, ever-changing sea. She knew in her heart of hearts that she would return.

Her classes at Johns Hopkins were scheduled to begin in two weeks; but first, Rachel wanted time to spend with her mother. There was ever so much to relate to her!

On the way to Johns Hopkins, a more confident Carson made a stop at the United States Bureau of Fisheries in Washington, DC. She wanted to ferret out just what she should study to land a job as a biologist. She discovered that her best opportunity might be a government job; however, she was told frankly that never had the Bureau hired a woman scientist. Be that as it may, Rachel Carson made an impression on Elmer Higgins, the gentleman with whom she had spoken. Higgins told her to come back and see him after she had completed her master's.

Once the budding scientist was immersed in her studies, she found she very much liked Baltimore. There was only one hitch. Rachel missed her mother's moral support and encouragement. Since she and Maria dreaded being away from one another for long periods, and Rachel could not afford to travel back and forth to Springdale, or even to telephone home, it was decided that the family should relocate to Baltimore. There were more job possibilities there, and having her mother with her to keep house and fix meals would leave Rachel more time for her studies. Maria Carson had always been her daughter's sounding board when she had papers to prepare, and Mrs. Carson often typed Rachel's work for her. It was an arrangement Rachel would choose, over and yet again.

Finally, after nine months apart, the longest the two would ever be separated throughout the course of both their lifetimes, Rachel and Maria were reunited. Rachel had found a house to rent outside of Baltimore, out on the Old Philadelphia Road. The fact that it was in a rural community and located but two miles from Chesapeake Bay pleased Rachel to no end. To boot, the house was larger than the one at the old homestead, and it had indoor plumbing, something the Springdale home never had. Neither place had central heating, but there was a big open fireplace.

As is often the case in life, matters took longer than Rachel had anticipated due, in large part, to the Depression. Rachel's father had affairs to settle, and her brother was engrossed in trying to rent the Springdale house. Rachel's mother arrived in Baltimore in January 1930, the rest of the family by spring.

At the end of her first year, Rachel was leaning toward the possibility of a teaching career with plans to go directly on for her doctorate in zoology. Again, as it had always been, money was the snag, and with an increase in the tuition at Johns Hopkins, her only option was to get a part-time job and become a part-time student.

That summer Rachel worked as a teaching assistant, which sounds a lot more important than it actually was. She washed laboratory glassware, cleaned tables, and set up lab equipment for each class. The job brought in some money, desperately needed money, and she welcomed it. At the same time, she was learning as much as she could- always was she learning.

Brother Robert found part-time work as a radio repairman; and once, when a customer could not pay in cash, he paid with something else. That night, Robert brought home a mother Persian with its three tiny, mewing kittens. Though the child Rachel had always been partial to dogs on the Springdale farm, this episode opened the door for a lifelong passion for cats. She would talk to them or write about them as though they were human, and throughout her extraordinary life, she developed a feeling that their soft, warm, purry companionship was crucial to her work. Far into the wee hours, the Persians began taking turns lying on her manuscripts. Years into the future, during the period when she was writing *The Edge of the Sea*, she replied to a letter from the Cat Welfare Association: "I have always found that a cat has a truly great capacity for friendship. He asks only that we respect his personal rights and his individuality; in return, he gives his devotion, understanding, and companionship. Cats are extremely sensitive to the joys and sorrows of their human friends ... ."

Another of Rachel's jobs while working towards her master's was as a teaching assistant in Johns Hopkins biology department. Simultaneously, she worked as a lab assistant to one of her professors, adding a third job as a part-time assistant in the zoology department at the University of Maryland. The Maryland job meant a thirty-five-mile bus trip each way, that took precious hours out of her busy week, but she needed all the jobs to secure that master's, and Carson was determined not to give up.

Over three decades later, a male classmate remembered how hard Rachel Carson had worked getting her master's degree. "We used to feel sorry for Rachel," he said, "and we told her so. In those days, we didn't think a woman was up to being a scientist. And we certainly didn't think a woman could work three jobs, go to classes and keep up with the work load, commute back and forth, get top grades- and survive."

Carson did more than survive. Earning excellent marks, she received her master's degree in zoology in the spring of 1932. However, the years of strife were far from over.

For the next three years, Rachel struggled to earn a living at part-time jobs, all the while applying for full-time employment as a scientist. Things were no easier for Rachel Carson in the 1930s than they had been for her mother Maria forty years earlier.

The Great Depression continued to slam against the Carson family like a great battering ram. Rachel's brother Robert and sister Marian were both divorced. Robert, Jr., who earned a little money repairing radios, resided off and on with the family. Marian and her two children had moved in. Rachel's father contributed a small pension, but Rachel was the family's main support.

In 1935, Rachel's father died, and the Carson household was plunged into sorrow as well as desperation. Mr. Carson's pension and odd jobs had helped the family keep body and soul together. His passing called for a bold move. Memory rang a bell with Elmer Higgins' invitation, and squaring her thin shoulders, Rachel went to see him.

In Higgins' office complex, scientists were writing radio shows about fish for public broadcasting. Most of them could not write a single passage without using heavy scientific jargon that was difficult for laymen to comprehend. Higgins already knew Rachel was a highly intelligent scientist with a master's; nonetheless, he had one question for her: "Can you write?"

Rachel landed the job for $19.25 a week.

Still, the radio-script writing was only part-time work. Rachel *had* to find full-time employment. When the next US Government Civil Service examination was given, Carson took it. She was the only woman applicant, and she received the highest test score. Now, she was hired as a biologist working for the United States Fish and Wildlife Service, then called the Bureau of Fisheries.

Elmer Higgins asked to have Rachel placed in his office. When she reported for work her first day on the job, Higgins welcomed her warmly, explaining in detail her various duties. As Fate would have it, she would not be working so much as a biologist as she would as a writer. Some things are just destined.

Rachel's new position bolstered her family's income, and before long, she would even be eligible for a small length-of-service increase. She enjoyed her work and was often challenged by it. Research for her writing assignments required her to consult with experts in several fields of fishery biology, and I can imagine she was learning a great deal as she was researching and writing these government articles.

Carson once described the milieu of her one-window office at the Bureau "... like working at the bottom of a well." Though she missed spending a lot of time outdoors, she was grateful for the work and happy to be writing again– she really had no idea how much she had missed it– and she liked her fellow employees.

At noontime, when they ate together, laughter filled the lunchroom, spilling out into the halls. Though Rachel was cool and reserved in public, she exhibited a warm humor to close friends, and she used her pleasantries at the office as the catalyst to keep herself and the others writing at their best.

Now that Rachel supplied her family with a steady income, their financial problem was solved, though, as usual, there was never money for extras. Conversely, another family tragedy was on the horizon as Death stood ready to wrap its dark cloak around Rachel's sister Marian.

In late January 1937, Marian succumbed to pneumonia a few days following her fortieth birthday. Marian's daughters, twelve and eleven, were virtual orphans, since their father had never contributed anything to the girls' nurture or support. There was no other option for Rachel and her seventy-year-old mother but to take over the complete charge of Marian's daughters. Robert, who had moved out, was no help financially, though he did do physical work for his mother from time to time.

The roles Rachel and her mother chose for themselves were the familiar ones. Rachel would continue as the breadwinner, Maria as cook and housekeeper. If she bore resentment of the financial responsibilities her family continuously heaped upon her, Rachel never exhibited it.

Despite the loss of her independence, lessons were not lost on this astute lady. She had observed from childhood that a woman should not depend totally upon a man. Her father had never been a good provider, though he tried. Her brother Robert certainly was not, nor could he always be counted upon. Rachel had witnessed, early on, his failed marriage. She had also watched the once-beautiful, vivacious Marian struggle to find domestic happiness and saw that her sister was often a victim of a man's negative behavior. Rachel Carson observed the precarious nature of marriage and failed choices. Those lessons stayed with her all her life. She never married.

Even after a raise in salary in 1939, there was never enough money. Rachel decided to move her family to a more affordable rented house in Silver Spring, Maryland. It was a quieter residence on Flower Avenue, where her mother could enjoy a small truck garden, and where Rachel's bedroom spread over the entire second floor. Maria and the girls had their bedrooms on the ground floor. Here, Rachel could work undisturbed.

To supplement her income, Rachel began to write and sell articles on nature to the local newspapers. She had developed the habit of working, when the house slept, late into the night. Like most writers, her creative process required solitude. The Persians, however, kept her company during her late-night endeavors. Years later, she remembered: "Buzzie ... used to sleep on my writing table, on the litter of notes and manuscript sheets. On two of these pages I had made sketches, first of his little head drooping with sleepiness, then of him after he had settled down comfortably for a nap."

Carson was a meticulous writer, preferring to revise paragraph by paragraph, sentence by sentence, before she continued on to the next segment. Cognizant of the impact of word flow and rhythm to create atmosphere, she often read long passages out loud to herself (and the cats) before she asked her mother to read them aloud to her. Days, Maria typed the revised pages, placing them carefully on Rachel's upstairs desk, so they would be waiting for her when she returned from the office.

Rachel was devoting a great deal of her time these days "fleshing out" an article she had titled "Undersea" into a book. Elmer Higgins had told her it was simply too good to remain an article. A modest person, she was bold enough to choose as the subject for her first major work nothing less than the sea itself.

Carson's submitted outline to Simon and Schuster was accepted, and the publishing house rewarded her with an advance of $250.

Every night the light in her top-floor bedroom glowed till her head dropped, and she could not write another word. Then, she would stand and stretch, smiling that the cats had long since fallen into deep, peaceful sleep.

Rachel Carson's first book, *Under the Sea-Wind*, introduced readers to the sea by relating the stories of the sea creatures that inhabit the world's great oceans. What makes Rachel Carson's writings so special is the spiritual and physical bond she felt with those creatures, her understanding and identification with them.

She wrote for the general public, avoiding technical language. Her relationship with scientific writing would always be that she understood it but opted not to use it. Rachel was quite properly furious (though always polite) with editors who undertook to rewrite selections from her works. She never permitted any editor to take what she called "liberties with [her] text."

After three laborious years, the book was ready to send to the publisher, who expected sales to be good. When it was released in November 1941, it sold for $3 a copy, par during that era for its size and genre.

Rachel presented her mother with the first copy off the press, who, upon opening it, wept at the succinct, heartfelt dedication: "To my mother." The second copy she gave to Elmer Higgins, inscribed, "To Mr. Higgins, who started it all. Rachel L. Carson, November 1, 1941."

Now came the game that writers detest- waiting- for the critics and the sales.

"Skillfully written as to read like fiction, but in fact a scientifically accurate account of life in the ocean and along the ocean shore" was the jubilant *New York Times* review of *Under the Sea-Wind*. However, another kind of wind was stirring. In truth, the winds of war had long been howling. *Under the Sea-Wind* and the thirty-four-year-old Rachel Carson would have to wait for those exalted book sales.

Less than a month after her book made it to the shelves, the Japanese attacked Pearl Harbor. Though her reviews were all good, few people were reading *Sea-Wind*. America was at war.

Under the Sea-Wind's scanty sales were depressing for Rachel who commented to a friend: "Don't ever write a book. It doesn't pay as well as a single well-placed magazine article." Timing was the only thing wrong with *Sea-Wind*. At that point in history, America had no time for reading much of anything except the glaring headlines in the newspapers.

Rachel Carson, author and biologist, circa 1944
Courtesy the US Fish and Wildlife Service

World War II kept Rachel at the Fish and Wildlife Service (the new name for the Bureau of Fisheries) exceptionally busy. All through the war years, the department was a hive of activity. For one thing, battleships and submarines constantly needed to know more about ocean depths and currents.

As the war progressed, and the atom bomb was dropped on Japanese cities, scientists, including and especially Rachel Carson, discovered that life on Earth would not necessarily go on irrespective of what man did. It was a discovery that left Carson apprehensive to say the least.

At thirty-seven, Rachel was petite with a trim figure and, according to friends, "exceptionally good legs." Throughout her life, she liked plain food and ate and drank but little. Her thick, dark auburn hair she wore brushed back from her temples and held with combs allowing her widow's peak to accentuate the pretty heart shape of her face. Despite her tiny frame, Rachel was strong, physically fit, and well coordinated.

By 1945, Rachel Carson had journeyed to a place of specific purpose in her life. She had learned how to combine her two great passions, writing and science, and she had developed the confidence in her abilities to express her inner visions in regard to nature.

It was in 1945 when she first began researching the new pesticide DDT. The wise, perceptive woman knew, in her own words, that this was "something that [affected] everybody."

The government had used the pesticide to combat lice and insect-borne diseases during the war, but chemical screening for the "safety of the stuff" had barely begun. Little did Carson realize when she began her research where this investigation would eventually lead her.

During the postwar years, mother Carson was still able to act as cook and housekeeper, and though her two nieces were still residing with them in Silver Spring, they were out of school with at least part-time jobs. Rachel had a car now, and a little freedom, though not much, since her work demanded the bulk of her time.

By this point in her life, Carson was doing a good deal of freelance writing that took her to new and exciting places and introduced her to experts in the various scientific fields about which she focused. She cherished the advice of these specialists and authorities as well as their sometimes unexpected friendships. And more significantly, Rachel Carson realized that if she ever wanted any kind of independence at all, free from her government job, the only way out was to publish herself out. Rachel loved her job, but it afforded her little time to do her own writing, to do what she called the "real work of [her] life."

At the beginning of the summer of 1946, after saving up a year's leave for a month's vacation in Maine, Carson, after ten years in government service, packed her old, faded green jalopy, and she, her mother, and the cats headed north- to her destiny.

At Maine's Boothbay Harbor, Rachel Carson discovered an area that she grasped immediately to her heart. She was not the first writer to be captured by Maine's breathtaking beauty of unspoiled rocky coasts and cathedral forests of stately pine and spruce, but few have captured the nuances of land, sky and sea with the keen intellect and artistry of Rachel Carson. She knew at first sight, tears glistening in her eyes, that she would make this rustically beautiful region of America a significant part of her life and writings forever after.

In an essay Rachel wrote during this period, she cautioned the public against the plunder of minerals, topsoil, and lumber. As a child of industrial Pennsylvania, with the principles of ecology embedded in her essence from childhood, along with firsthand knowledge of how human activities can foul nature, Carson cited overfishing, unregulated hunting of waterfowl, and excessive damming of rivers where fish spawn.

She stressed the negative impact of the culture of American abundance: "Because it is more comfortable to believe in pleasant things, most of us continue today to believe that in our country there will always be plenty. ... This is the comfortable dream of the average American. But it is a fallacious dream ... a dangerous dream. ... Only so long as we are vigilant to cherish and safeguard ... against waste, against over exploitation and against destruction will our country continue strong and free."

In 1946, Maria Carson underwent serious intestinal surgery. Now came Rachel's turn to care for her mother. It was difficult juggling two jobs, taking over the household chores and the cooking, as well as caring for the recovering Maria. As so often happens in life, it never rains but it pours. Rachel's brother also had to have surgery, and to top it all off, Maria and Rachel's beloved cat Kito passed away.

By January 1948, Rachel had developed a painful case of the shingles, and though she made a fairly quick recovery, the condition, including surgery of her own, put her further behind at her office and with her own freelance writing.

Through all her trials and tribulations, however, Carson had bravely decided to pen a new book. First, due to the failure of *Under the Sea-Wind*'s commercial success, she sought to find a new publisher and did so with Oxford University Press. Matters were progressing nicely when Rachel received the soul-shattering news that her old mentor, Mary Scott Skinker, was dying of cancer.

Borrowing the money for the plane trip to Chicago, Rachel left as soon as she could. It must have been devastating for her. Her former teacher turned friend had enduringly infused Rachel Carson's consciousness with *ecology*- a word Carson would introduce to the American public. In fact, *ecology* and the *environment* would become household words through Carson's readable works.

Rachel stayed with Skinker as long as the latter was alert. Mary had always cultivated Rachel's abilities, supported her ambitions, encouraged her, and gave her the necessary confidence to realize her dreams. She had kindled the flame in Carson's soul to become a scientist. And she had fired the young Carson's imagination as to where those hopes and dreams could lead. In truth, Rachel dearly loved Mary, and her passing in December of 1948 left a deep void. She returned home bereft of her dearest friend.

What Carson missed most was not a lover or husband in her life but an emotional intimacy with someone who understood her- understood the loneliness of her creative calling and could nurture and support that vision, that intense sense of mission or quest that was hers alone. Mary Scott Skinker had given Rachel that for so many years. For a while, at least, the void would be somewhat filled by her new literary agent Marie Rodell.

In 1950, Rachel Carson had been with the Fish and Wildlife Service for nearly fourteen years. By this time, she had assembled an impressive network of scientific colleagues and experts who encouraged her oceanographic research and her beautifully crafted and scientifically accurate explanations of the natural world.

In September of that year, she had to have another tumor removed from the same breast where an earlier, smaller cyst had been removed in 1946. Both times she was told there was no sign of malignancy. After a brief recuperation period, Rachel was up and running off to do more seashore research. Her agent, editor, and publisher were relieved. Needless to say, so was Rachel. The doctor's report was what she had wanted to hear, and as a result, she did not seek a second opinion.

Before Christmas of 1950, Rachel and Marie's beloved silver Persian cat passed away. Tippy was the last of the original brood of Carson Persians, and both women felt the loss with intensity. Cats, however, would continue to be a special part of Rachel's life.

Just three short weeks after Rachel's second book *The Sea Around Us* debuted in mid-1951, it entered the *New York Times* "Best Seller List" in fifth place. It remained on the List for eighty-six weeks, winning, among other prestigious honors, the National Book Award.

The book's success led to the republication of her first work *Under the Sea-Wind*, which also became a best seller. It must have been sweet satisfaction to witness the exuberant reception of her once-neglected first book.

Fan mail came pouring in. "Kin this be me!" Carson joked to a friend. In order to get an autograph, one bold reader tapped on the hairdryer under which Rachel sat at the beauty shop; and sometimes, fans rapped on the door of her hotel room mornings before she was even dressed. That sort of thing was, I am certain, for this very private person, more than a bit disconcerting.

In 1951, few people had ever heard of the word *ecology*, but Rachel wrote so clearly and so beautifully that readers reported that the writing was like poetry. This is what made Carson's books so effective. She answered that "if there is poetry in my book[s], it [is only] because no one could write truthfully about the sea and leave out the poetry."

Rachel immediately put her mother in charge of the deluge of fan mail. Emotionally and practically, Maria Carson was still indispensable to her daughter.

Speaking invitations were another constant those days. However, the shy, reticent Rachel, uncomfortable with the thought of addressing large audiences, turned down most of the engagements, preferring autograph sessions in the various bookstores. At one college speaking engagement, Carson looked so unhappy that a friend asked her if she was all right, to which she responded, "The truth is I'm much more at home barefoot in the sand ... ."

All in all, she was beginning to feel like the Mad Hatter, running in all directions at once. Turning down speaking engagements was not entirely due to shyness. If she had accepted, in her own words, "... all of these invitations ... they would absolutely wreck the writing program I am now laying out." And there would not have been future Rachel Carson books for the public to enjoy.

Despite it all, Carson did accept a few select speaking invitations, and it was at this time that she began to fine-tune her environmental philosophy and to speak openly about it. In an article penned for *This Week Magazine*, she touched again on the theme of gaining strength of spirit from the beauty and mystery of the natural world. "In the darker hours of life," she revealed that she had drawn on her rich memories, garnered from Earth's treasure chest of beauty, for comfort and release from tension. She advocated that it was from this store of nature reminiscences where she had found the calmness during the war years to face a world in turmoil, racked as it was with hate and violence.

Now that she was becoming famous, people were often surprised to discover, upon meeting her, that Rachel Carson was "not a big woman." She wasn't tall, and she did not bulk large. She was petite, slim, and feminine, with a soft, calm voice. She rarely wore jewelry, dressing conservatively but neatly. She still wore her dark auburn hair brushed back from her face, and she kept her nails meticulously manicured and polished. Her legs were still shapely, and she enjoyed wearing high heels when the occasion called for it. And all her life, she entertained a penchant for hats. Hats, I have come to note, do not flatter everyone, but they did compliment the mysterious Miss Carson.

Acclaims and awards were not the only good things that came out of her first two bestsellers. For the first time in her life, Rachel Carson began experiencing a measure of financial security. Her mother's health and seemingly hers had improved, and Rachel had even added a new research assistant to her household, a handsome little feline she christened Muffin, who turned out to be an unusually good traveler.

Spring of 1952 seemed to Rachel the right time to take her leave of the Fish and Wildlife Service for the freedom to dedicate to her own literary endeavors. On June 3, 1952, her resignation went into effect. Her reason for resigning simply stated was "To devote my time to writing."

Though she had enjoyed her work at the bureau, the freedom she now felt lifted her on wings of ecstasy. There was another reason for her bliss: Carson had decided to build her dream cottage on a rocky shore of the Maine coast near Boothbay Harbor, where the atmosphere seemed to glow opal. She would name her cliff-side castle-in-the-sky "Silverledges." Life was good, and it held promise.

In July 1953, Rachel met her new neighbors- the Freemans, Dorothy and Stanley. They shared common denominators, including an intense love and respect for nature, cats, and the care of an elderly mother. Dorothy was a companion who could fully sympathize. The bond that Carson made with the Freemans, especially with Dorothy, would be lifelong and as deep as the love they both held for the sea. With Dorothy, Rachel had the delightful feeling of being understood. To love is ofttimes easy, but to *understand* ... ah now, that is rare!

Rachel, who had a strong hand in designing her dream cottage on the tract of land she had purchased, spent the first few weeks just getting settled in with her mother and Muffin. That first summer she did not get round to doing much writing due to all her exploring. There were, of course, the ever-beckoning tide pools complete with sea creatures; and there stood on one side of her property a lush forest of evergreens through which splashes of sunlight fell like pools of golden wine. The woods were alive with birds of virtually every variety, and her front yard was a bevy of wildflowers and sweet-smelling balsam firs. This was a place where magic could be spun!

Several times a day, accompanied by either Dorothy or her mother, or offtimes alone, Rachel eagerly descended the stairway she had built from the cottage to the shore, where she could watch loons and seals, and sometimes even the majesty of a whale. From her desk in her office/den, she could gaze out the wide expanse of window to both the woods and the endless ocean. It was, indeed, a long-awaited dream come true- and Rachel was happier than she had ever been in her life.

The only sad event that first full summer at the cottage was the untimely death of Muffin that occurred shortly after Rachel and Maria had arrived in Maine. Rachel's new-found friend and kindred spirit Dorothy Freeman understood the loss and shared the sadness.

When they met and sealed their abiding friendship, Dorothy, at fifty-five, was nine years older than Rachel, though they looked about the same age. In tune with the sea all her life, Dorothy Freeman was the perfect muse and confidante for Rachel Carson. In addition to other shared penchants, both women loved writing, though Dorothy's took the form of elegantly crafted epistles. It began when her son, Stanley, Jr., had gone off to college; thence, Dorothy developed her letter writing into an art.

In their lifetimes, Rachel and Dorothy would exchange many expressive letters. So often in those countless missives, the pair wrote of something, as the letters passed in the post, in the exact same way. They took to calling this "stardust." Their most treasured letters were the ones they exchanged at the end of each year, to be savored before bed Christmas Eve.

If Rachel Carson had ever felt loneliness at never having fallen in love, or, with the exception of Mary Scott Skinker, of never having a confidante, she no longer felt that. Now, in addition to her mother and the cats, she had Dorothy in her life. Rachel, who had always been reticent, reluctant to display her heart on her sleeve, began to show affection and, like Dorothy, to use endearments.

Fish and Wildlife artist Bob Hines, who had illustrated her *Edge of the Sea,* was a close friend as well as a kindred spirit, but there had been no romance between them. Rachel always said she never had the time for dating or for marriage. In truth, as more than one friend pointed out, with caring for an elderly mother and nieces, Rachel had a lot more family responsibilities than many married people.

Après Dorothy, she seemed more open as well as more affectionate. In a speech she made in 1954, Rachel voiced: "I am not afraid of being thought a sentimentalist when I stand here ... and tell you that I believe natural beauty has a necessary place in the spiritual development of any individual or ... society. I believe that whenever we substitute something man-made and artificial for a natural feature of the earth, we have retarded some part of man's spiritual growth."

She concluded that presentation with the inspiring words: "The more clearly we can focus our attention on the wonders and realities of the universe about us, the less taste we shall have for destruction."

Rachel's greatest fear was that man, intoxicated by his own power, was dangerously going further and further into the destruction of his world- and himself.

After completing another bestseller, *The Edge of the Sea,* Carson welcomed 1955 with a mélange of fatigue and anticipation. She was a bit weary of deadlines, and consequently was not in her usual all-fired hurry to get started on another book ... just yet. A summer in Maine at the cottage with her mother, Jeffie the cat, and Dorothy nearby with whom she could share her love of the sea (without the pressure of a new book) called to her with the irresistible pull of a mermaid's song. How delightful it would all be! Such freedom! Rachel could hardly contain herself.

That autumn, when *The Edge of the Sea* made its appearance, she surprised the Freemans with its special dedication: "To Dorothy and Stanley Freeman who have gone down with me into the low-tide world and have felt its beauty and its mystery."

Deeply touched, the Freemans responded by giving Rachel a gold and diamond brooch fashioned in the adorable shape of a seashell. She would wear it first against the forest-green taffeta of her evening dress at the book's debut in New York City.

With *Edge of the Sea*, Carson had crossed an important threshold, she was now not only an acclaimed literary success- she was an honored and respected scientist.

Yet again with the joy came sorrow, for Rachel's elderly mother's health began to seriously decline. Rachel was taking as good a care of Maria now as Maria had always done for her.

I must comment here on Carson's July 1956 article for the *Woman's Home Companion,* "Help Your Child to Wonder." While her niece Marjie and grandnephew Roger Christy were staying with them at the cottage, Rachel had fun with little Roger, selecting which adventures to include in the piece and making the most of a child's delight in discovery.

In one of the most brilliant passages of that work, Carson wrote: "A child's world is fresh and new and beautiful, full of wonder and excitement. It is our misfortune that for most of us that clear-eyed vision, that true instinct for what is beautiful and awe-inspiring, is dimmed and even lost before we reach adulthood. If I had influence with the good fairy who is supposed to preside over the christening of all children, I should ask that her gift to each child in the world be a sense of wonder so indestructible that it would last through life, as an unfailing antidote against the boredom and disenchantments of later years, the sterile preoccupation with things that are artificial, the alienation from the sources of our strength."

It is no small wonder that this article would later be expanded into a book for generations of parents and children to delight over.

Early in 1957, sickness swept through Rachel's family. Her niece Marjie and Mrs. Carson contracted pneumonia, while Rachel fought a terrible bout with the flu. Rachel and her mother finally cast off their illnesses, but Marjie died. Suddenly, fifty-year-old Rachel had a lively five-year-old boy to care for full time, in addition to her near-ninety-year-old mother. It had become harder than ever to find the necessary time and solitude to write.

In Maine, when the Freeman's grandchildren came to visit, they'd always run over to Rachel's to play with Roger. Carson would lead them all down the steps from her house to the ocean, where they would enjoy themselves exploring. She'd patiently answer all their questions, never tiring to explain. In Carson's cottage living room, a microscope always stood at the ready for close inspection of the sea creatures they found; and before anyone could have snacks, they had to carefully cart the sea's residents back down to the water, putting each animal right back where they had discovered it. Rachel wasn't big on rules, but that was one rule she always enforced.

Though Rachel loved Roger and gave him a great deal of herself, the writer in her soon became restless. She needed a new project with a fresh direction. The idea arrived in a letter from a friend who wrote to Carson to recount the devastation wrought upon insects and particularly bird life in her private bird sanctuary north of Cape Cod by an aerial spraying of the insecticide DDT and fuel oil for mosquito control. Could Rachel do something about this? It was terrible, and she went on to describe the horrible deaths of her robins.

In the 1950s, chemical companies had carte blanche to sell nearly any kind of poison to kill bugs, weeds, mold, and other pests. Literally tons of these pesticides were used without any intervention or control. Several scientists were already concerned about what these poisons were doing to animals, to the soils, to the seas ... to people. Among those concerned, Rachel Carson believed that human beings were being put at risk by the use of these dangerous chemicals. Actually, Carson had been interested in the role of poisons in the environment since 1938. She decided, at first, to pen an article. But this was just too big for one article- *far too big*.

In the midst of her pesticide research, in the fall of 1958, Rachel's beloved mother passed away after suffering a severe stroke. Several days later, Carson composed a letter to her dearest friend Dorothy Freeman, describing Maria's passing: "During that last agonizing night, I sat most of the time by the bed with my hand ... holding Mamma's." Occasionally Rachel slipped away to look out of the picture window at the lacy tangle of tall, black trees against the deep purple sky with its bright dusting of stars. "Orion," she wrote, "stood in all his glory just above the horizon of our woods, and several other stars blazed more highly than I can remember ever seeing them. ... I told Roger about the stars just before Grandma left us, and he said, 'Maybe they were the lights of the angels, coming to take her to heaven.'"

Maria Carson, who had shaped Rachel's life, left her daughter a lifelong interest in nature and conservation. It was a rich legacy.

Though her mother's death also left a deep void, it sharpened Rachel's sense of mission, of carrying on the quest of their shared vision. In truth, Maria's passing gave Carson a renewed measure of energy for her work. She dived into the research, spending weeks upon weeks working in chemistry, physiology and genetics, more and more convinced that she was pursuing the right course in finding wildlife damage, threats to the environment and severe dangers to human health. She was finding, for example, connections between pesticides and the physiological changes that signaled the onset of cancer.

It was tough going. Rachel Carson, who had always done meticulous research, double and triple checking facts, in addition to going directly to the experts on each of the topics found in her books, now was even more concerned with "getting it right." She knew the insecticide companies would have experts of their own, and especially would they be ready to debunk a woman's research. She was determined that her book, in her own words, "had to be built on an unshakable foundation."

At the beginning of 1960, Rachel was fully in command of her harvested material. She had drafted separate chapters on birds and wildlife, water, and soil; in addition, there were two chapters dealing with cancer. She had also made a good beginning with the difficult chapter on cell biology and genetic mutation. Moreover, she had garnered several allies on the project, and thus far, felt encouraged by her progress. Albeit it was slow, it was also steady. And many of her alliances with fellow scientists and experts brought her new and lasting friendships.

Roger was content with school, and the pair was constantly discovering new interests they could share. And there was, of course, Dorothy's steadfast friendship and encouragement.

Though Carson was increasingly convinced that she was right in the matter of these poisons, her slow pace was daunting- so often did she remind herself that slow and steady win the race- however, there was an upside to that. Her measured steps gave her the reassurance that the case she was building on the dangers of uncontrolled pesticides would be able to stand up against the onslaught of criticism that would surely come. She knew the powerful insecticide companies would fight her, and she figured the Department of Agriculture would back them up.

At that time, the publicity about DDT was voluminous and overwhelmingly positive. DDT had the advantages of being inexpensive and easy to make. She had a good idea what she was in for, but somebody had to warn the world that one day, if things did not change, there would come a silent spring. And that somebody had to be both a scientist and a writer.

Readers, Rachel Carson was not well when she began the vast undertaking of *Silent Spring*. Sadly, one illness after another plagued her- painful arthritis, flu, an agonizing stomach ulcer, various infections in her knees, an eye infection, a heart condition, along with the cancer that would finally claim her life. And there were times when she questioned if sharing the truth was worth the battle she knew she would face upon the book's release. She hated the limelight, and this project would force her into the brightest glare of attention, but she was so certain that she was right. She knew, beyond the shadow of a doubt, that she *had* to write the book. What she began to worry about most was if she would have *time* to complete it.

So that she could do effective research and writing- so that the book would indeed "be built on an unshakable foundation"- she kept the project a secret. She was (in regard to her physical health) no longer strong, but her book had to be as strong as it could be before her enemies learned about it.

In actuality, the pesticide danger was worse than anyone knew. In the innocent age of the 1950s, people trusted that the government would protect them from any danger. Rachel Carson was discovering that was not true. To quote from *Silent Spring*: "To the question 'But doesn't the government protect us from such things?' The answer is 'Only to a limited extent.'" (Consider that Carson would deliver to the public *Silent Spring* soon after the tranquilizer thalidomide was revealed to cause birth defects.)

It was not that the government did not care, they were simply not informed.

Early in 1962, *Silent Spring* was finished. Rachel Carson had done what few authors have been able to do- she tied the diverse facets of information about pesticide abuse and ubiquitous exposure, biological and environmental impact into one story that was wholly readable and understandable by a public not steeped in science.

After over four years, the article no one would publish had matured into an informative book. Would it suffice as a warning in time to save life on earth? Rachel wanted to hear what the editors thought at this point. With apprehension, she sent the manuscript off to her publisher as well as *New Yorker* magazine. Then she waited.

Within a week, she received a late-night telephone call from William Shawn, editor of The *New Yorker*. He had just read her book, and with emotion, he told her that he simply could not wait until morning to call her. Though he told Carson that the book was a "brilliant achievement," adding that she had made it "literature, full of beauty and loveliness and depth of feeling," he was at once horrified by what he had learned from *Silent Spring*. How could this have happened! And what, in God's name, could be done about it?

That was exactly the reaction Carson had waited to hear. She knew now that all the years of research, writing, triple checking of facts, interviews with experts, rewriting, and dogged perseverance would bring the results for which she had labored. She picked up her cat and walked into her study, dropping down into their favorite chair with a deep, audible sigh. Jeffie began to purr loudly, and with his warm, rough tongue against her cheek, he told her that he quite understood. Whether she had time left or not, she knew then and there that her work might have a chance, a good chance, to make a difference. *After all, what are we here for but to make a difference?* After a few pensive moments, she got up and put on a favorite classical record, sank back down into the chair, and cried into Jeffie's thick fur. Her tears were tears of relief.

Though Rachel had always seemed to believe her medical prognosis was good, the surgery she had endured (to remove malignant breast tumors, her lymph nodes on her left side, as well as a good portion of the pectoral muscle on that side) had been brutal. But she had soldiered on with the book, working in bed on a lap desk during her recovery. Even through radiation treatments, she had always maintained a constant desire to get back to the book. Always fearing she was nearing the end, she had pushed herself hard.

Tragically, the cancer continued to painfully spread. Now as she fought *for* her life, the fight *of* her life manifested itself before her as a formidable enemy.

Although Carson had been careful not to mention any trade names, she and her publisher knew there would be a basis for legal action on the claim that her book hurt product sales. They were legally armed, but I don't think that either Rachel or her publisher was psychologically prepared for the storm her book was about to unleash.

Shortly before the release of *Silent Spring* in 1962, the Book-of-the Month Club in their *News* bulletin announced to their members that *Spring* would be the October selection. About that same time, President John F. Kennedy was asked by one of the reporters present at his regular press conference if he had considered asking the Department of Agriculture to take a closer look at the growing concern among scientists regarding the dangerous long-range side effects from the widespread use of DDT. The President answered in the affirmative- that due to Miss Carson's book, they were already looking into the matter.

After Thanksgiving, Carson's long-awaited television interview with Eric Sevareid for *CBS Reports* was taped. This must have been exhausting for Rachel; however, she appeared on camera as a very knowledgeable woman, and one with great integrity. Sevareid was deeply impressed with Carson's logic and eloquence, as well as her quiet, self-assured presence.

Silent Spring became an instant bestseller, remaining on the *New York Times*' List for thirty-one weeks. The book's advance release in the *New Yorker* magazine resulted in a myriad of newspaper editorials. By December, 100,000 copies of *Silent Spring* had already been sold, and more than forty bills in various state legislatures had been introduced to govern the regulation of pesticide use.

The 1962 holiday season, that should have been a time of celebration for Rachel Carson, saw her braving ice storms and blizzards to get to and from the Washington clinic from her Maryland home for treatments. Rather than joy, there was instead intense nausea.

In addition to battling for her life, Carson had to face early on the ferocious industry-led attacks. She was called a Communist, an alarmist, a nut, an eccentric, a hysterical woman, even a crazy woman. After all, she kept cats; she was a nature writer, a mystic of sorts. She had to be crazy! And how dare a *woman* reveal the sins of a male-dominated industry! How dare her!

Rachel had expected the onslaught to be fierce, and it was. Many of those who attacked her book had not read it carefully or did not care to report on it accurately. Some had not even bothered to scan it.

Despite the hoopla, I liked the Carson wisdom used by *Life* magazine after its statement that Rachel was "unmarried but not a feminist." Here, Carson was quoted as saying, "I am not interested in things done by women or by men but in things done by people."

Among her other ailments, Rachel began experiencing attacks of angina. She was given several doses of nitroglycerin. Her doctor ordered: a hospital bed to elevate her head at night, minimal walking, no stairs, and no housework. Especially was he adamant that there be no more travel or public speaking until the attacks were under control.

By the middle of March 1963, the angina attacks were tamed, but Rachel's deepest fear was the potential collapse of her vertebrae from the cancer that had spread to her bones. So grave was her concern, that she was willing to try experimental, even controversial, drugs.

At the end of March, Rachel received word that "The Silent Spring of Rachel Carson," the *CBS Reports* television program was scheduled to air on April 3rd.

By this juncture, the pesticide industry's efforts to discredit her and her ideas were gaining in strength. With Eric Sevareid narrating, the show opened with the acknowledgment that a pesticide problem did exist. The all-important question Sevareid probed was "How serious of a problem is this?"

From the outset, Carson's position was made clear to the millions of Americans watching their television sets. "In spite of her view that present pesticide safeguards are inadequate, Miss Carson does not advocate discontinuing the use of pesticides immediately. Instead, she proposes a gradual shift to other methods of pest control."

Seen by viewers in her wood-paneled study, wearing a tailored suit and a simple necklace, Rachel, seated in her office chair, spoke calmly and clearly about what she had set out to accomplish- and why. She appeared at ease and natural as she spoke. "We've heard the benefits of pesticides. We have heard a great deal about their safety, but very little about the hazards, very little about the failures, the inefficiencies, and yet the public was being asked to accept these chemicals, was being asked to acquiesce in their use, and did not have the whole picture, so I set about to remedy the balance there."

Early on in her book, Carson quoted French biologist and philosopher Jean Rostand: *"The obligation to endure gives us the right to know."*

During the show, Rachel read passages from six different chapters of *Silent Spring* in her unhurried, deliberate manner. The readings presented viewers with examples of the pesticide use and abuse. Never did Carson become agitated or authoritarian. Rather, she clearly stated the facts as she believed them to be. As a result, she came across as a dignified, respectful, concerned scientist whose sole goal was to alert the innocent/naive public to a very significant and dangerous problem.

As soon as the show concluded, Rachel's telephone rang with calls from friends congratulating her. CBS Television was immediately deluged with hundreds of letters praising the show. At the same time, the United States Department of Agriculture, the Public Health Service, and the Food and Drug Administration were inundated with angry missives that protested the use of such chemicals with lack of scientific evidence about the long-term effects of what they were doing. Carson herself received a myriad of letters. All in all, Rachel was pleased with the show and called the producer to tell him so.

Most gratifying of all was that the show lit a fire under the government.

President Kennedy appointed a committee to study pesticides. Rachel's literary agent Marie Rodell drove her to Capitol Hill to meet with the committee and testify before the United States Congress. Rachel's testimony took about forty-five minutes, during which time she established the context of the contamination of the physical environment of water, soil, air, vegetation, animals, and humans, and its many sources.

Her concern was the evidence of pesticide pollution that had developed over the past year, emphasizing its wide dispersal from the point of application- a new kind of fallout. Carson drew two major conclusions: that aerial spraying of pesticides should be brought under strict control and should be reduced to a minimum strength needed to accomplish the essential objectives and that a "strong and unremitting effort should be made to reduce the use of pesticides that leave long-lasting residues, and ultimately to eliminate them."

Carson also left Congress with several recommendations. The most important was "the right of the citizen to be secure in his own home against the intrusion of poisons applied by other persons. I speak not as a lawyer," she said, "but as a biologist and as a human being, but I strongly feel that this is or should be one of the basic human rights. I am afraid, however, that it has little or no existence in practice."

Secretary of the Interior Stewart L. Udall said, "Rachel Carson alerted us to the subtle dangers of an Age of Poisons. She made us realize that we had allowed our fascination with chemicals to override our wisdom in their use."

Those who heard Carson speak that historic morning on Capitol Hill did not see an "eccentric, crazy woman" in the witness chair. They saw an accomplished scientist, an expert on chemical pesticides, a brilliant writer and speaker. But first and foremost, they saw a woman of conscience. *Rachel Carson's witness had been equal to her vision.*

Rachel looked tired and pale during the autumn of her life. Those were busy months, and most attributed her heavy schedule to the way she looked. Close friends, including Dorothy Freeman, however, knew the truth. For Rachel Carson, time was fast running out.

In May 1963, President Kennedy's Science Advisory Committee released a forty-three page report that called for limits on the use of pesticides. It was a good beginning.

Rachel spent the summer in Maine at her cottage. One afternoon late in the season, she and Dorothy Freeman were sitting at the top of the rocky cliff near Rachel's home. They talked, listened to the sounds of the sea below them and enjoyed the flight of monarch butterflies heading south for the winter.

As the butterflies pirouetted along the cliff's edge, Rachel and Dorothy pondered over how many would make it back. The pair realized without sadness that most would not live to return. That was simply how it was.

Later that day Rachel penned a poignant note to her good friend, stating what "those fluttering bits of life taught me this morning." Carson related that she had found a "deep happiness" in the knowledge that "it is a natural and not unhappy thing that a life comes to its end."

Each passing day became more and more bittersweet for Rachel. Her mobility was severely compromised with each week, until, by the autumn of 1963, every step was a torturous effort, and leaving her beloved cottage in Maine to return to her Maryland home was especially heart wrenching that fall.

Public attacks on *Silent Spring* had begun to diminish after President Kennedy's Advisory Science Committee agreed with Rachel's findings, and Carson had by now abundant evidence of the influence of her ideas and the enduring value of her work. "Can anyone believe it is possible to lay down such a barrage of poisons on the surface of the earth without making it unfit for all life? They should not be called insecticides but biocides," Rachel had succinctly told the committee.

Carson's words bring to mind something Albert Schweitzer once said, "Man can hardly even recognize the devils of his own creation."

Keep in mind, readers, that DDT was not a selective poison, targeting just certain insects. Bald eagle shells, for instance, became so thin due to DDT that there was a great risk of breakage before the eaglets could hatch. Bald eagles, America's national emblem, have taken a long time to make a strong comeback, and it is just at this writing that they have.

On December 3rd, among other prestigious awards and accolades, Rachel received the Audubon Medal, presented to her for distinguished service to conservation.

Sitting next to Carson at the Audubon affair was Margaret Owings, whose background was as nearly opposite Rachel's as anyone's could be. Growing up the daughter of one of California's most esteemed conservationists, Owings had always known wealth and privilege; however, she and Carson were kindred spirits.

Owings' impassioned efforts to rescue the mountain lion from extinction made her spiritual kin to Carson. With her special "sight," Margaret Owings saw that evening what many others did not- that Rachel Carson was dying. Spontaneously, she confided in Rachel about a time in her life when she had found great comfort in reading *The Sea Around Us*. Moved to tears, Rachel confided that she was deeply concerned over who would take up her work when she was gone. Owings grasped Rachel's thin, fragile hand and promised her that she for one would continue the fight.

When Rachel returned home, she had to deal with the death of another of her longtime companions. Though the weather had turned foul, she constantly ran her elderly cat Jeffie to and from the animal hospital for treatments.

Taking up her pen, she wrote Dorothy: "My heart is so burdened about Jeffie that I need to talk to you. He is slipping so fast that I feel he will surely have left us by Christmas. You know that deep in my heart I feel I ought to be willing and even thankful to let him go while I am still here to care for him. But it is so very hard to think of doing without him. His little life has been so intertwined with mine all these ten years."

That night, Rachel sat up late in her bedroom with Jeffie, stroking him and talking to him until he crawled under her bed to be alone. In the morning, after Roger left for school, Jeffie died. Rachel gently placed him in his basket with his favorite toy and supervised his burial, with the aid of her handyman, under the stately pine trees just outside her study. They had been through so much together; Jeffie's was an especially difficult "goodbye."

During her next visit to the doctor, Rachel was told that she was "something of a miracle." He added that patients in her condition did not survive more than five years. She fully understood what he was telling her: "Don't expect too much more time."

Death did not take a holiday, as the saying goes, for next it claimed Stanley Freeman, Dorothy's husband, who passed away in mid-January 1964. As sick and in pain as Rachel was, she had to go to her dear friend.

In March of that year Carson entered the Cleveland Clinic. The cancer had entered her liver, and though her heart condition made any type of surgery risky, doctors decided to go forward with an implanted radioactive treatment. At first, it looked like the end, but gradually her condition stabilized. Rachel, to whom each day had always been precious, was clinging tenaciously to life.

At some point Rachel told Dorothy that she had experienced, either during the surgery or immediately after it, an out-of-body experience, in which she described herself surrounded by a brilliant, shimmering white light. Buoyant and free of all pain and suffering, lifted by the light, she had felt herself floating above her physical body. "Don't ever be afraid to die," she said. "It is beautiful."

Rachel Carson did not live long enough to see DDT banned. That would not come until 1972. Just before sunset on April 14, 1964, Rachel Carson passed away, of heart disease and cancer, in her home in Silver Spring, Maryland. She was fifty-six years old. Her agent Marie Rodell broke the news of her death in New York, stating for the press that "Miss Carson had cancer for some years," and that "she had been aware of her illness."

That summer, Dorothy did as Rachel had requested. She scattered her beloved friend's ashes along Maine's rocky coast of the Sheepscot, near the cliff-side cottage she had christened "Silverledges."

A *New York Times* editor wrote of Carson's passing: "She was a biologist, not a crusader, but the power of her knowledge and the beauty of her language combined to make Rachel Carson one of the most influential women of our time."

Senator Abraham Ribicoff, who had been an honorary pallbearer at Carson's funeral service at the Washington National Cathedral, opened the hearings the afternoon of her death with a tribute to her, "Today we mourn a great lady," he pronounced. "All mankind is in her debt."

The great American author Albert Pine once said, "What we do for ourselves dies with us. What we do for others and the world remains and is immortal."

America read *Silent Spring,* and wisely, heeding Rachel's warning, the country began to turn away from wholesale toxic pollution.

To give you an example of wholesale toxic pollution, allow me to draw from Carson's book, citing the gypsy moth. The Long Island area was included within the gypsy moth spraying in 1957. This region consists mainly of heavily populated towns and suburbs with bordering salt marsh. The gypsy moth is a forest insect, certainly not an inhabitant of cities, nor does it live in meadows, cultivated fields, gardens, or marshes. Nevertheless, planes hired by the United States Department of Agriculture and the New York Department of Agriculture and Markets showered DDT down on the entire area.

They sprayed truck gardens and dairy farms, fish ponds and salt marshes. They sprayed suburbia, including children at play and commuters awaiting trains at railway stations. Flowers, trees and shrubs were ruined. Birds, fish, and useful insects were killed by the indiscriminate poison. At Setauket, a fine quarter horse that drank from a water trough in a field the planes had sprayed died a horrible death.

The contamination of milk and farm produce in the course of the gypsy moth spraying came as an unpleasant surprise to many people- since DDT accumulates in the fatty tissues of animals and humans.

As for the wholesale poisoning of "weeds," honeybees and wild bees depend heavily on "weeds," such as goldenrod, mustard, and dandelions, for pollen that serves as the food for their young. No small wonder that the honey bee is endangered nowadays!

After its American introduction, *Silent Spring* was published in dozens of other countries and in several languages. No matter in what language it was printed, the message was crystal clear: *We must be more careful about what we do to the Earth.*

Around the world, new laws were passed regarding pesticides. Rachel Carson's pen had been a virtual pen against poisons!

"These insecticides," Carson wrote in her history-changing *Silent Spring,* "are not selective poisons; they do not single out the one species of which we desire to be rid. Each of them is used for the simple reason that it is a deadly poison. It therefore poisons all life with which it comes in contact: the cat beloved of some family, the farmer's cattle, the rabbit in the field, the horned lark out of the sky. These creatures are innocent of any harm to man. Indeed, by their very existence they and their fellows make his life more pleasant. Yet he rewards them with a death that is not only sudden but horrible."

Rachel went on to describe these horrible deaths, the meadowlark that's muscular coordination was such that it could not fly or stand, but continued to beat its wings while lying on its side, its beak open as it laboriously sucked for air. Even more pitiful was the mute testimony of the dead ground squirrels that "exhibited a characteristic attitude in death. The back was bowed ... the forelegs with the toes ... tightly clenched [and] drawn close to the thorax. The little head and neck were outstretched, and the mouth often contained dirt, suggesting that the dying animal had been biting at the ground.

"By acquiescing in an act that can cause such suffering to a living creature, who among us is not diminished as a human being? The question is," Rachel had asked earlier in that same chapter, "whether any civilization can wage relentless war on life without destroying itself, and without losing the right to be called civilized."

Even after her death in 1964, Rachel Carson's awards and honors continued. In 1980, President Jimmy Carter posthumously awarded her the Presidential Award of Freedom, the highest civilian honor of our nation, accepted on her behalf by her adopted son/grandnephew Roger Christie. The medal was inscribed in part, "... she created a tide of environmental consciousness that has not ebbed."

The subsequent year, the United States Post Office in Springdale, Pennsylvania, Rachel's hometown, issued the Rachel Carson Stamp graced with her likeness.

Six years after Carson's death, the United States Environmental Protection Agency began operation on 2 December 1970, charged with protecting human health and with safeguarding the natural environment: air, water, and land.

However, in spite of the progress made, we are yet poisoning the air and water and eroding the biosphere, albeit less so than if Rachel Carson had not written her books. There are still far too many people who do not believe that what we do to nature we do to ourselves. "Man," Carson said, "is a part of nature, and his war against nature is ... a war against himself."

Though the silent spring of Rachel Carson is long past, the great lady's work continues to echo down the tunnel of time into the future: example, "Go green."

Far ahead of her time, Carson prompted society to rethink its relationship to the natural world, and half a century later, her writings still stand among the finest in conservation. *Thus was the salient spring of Rachel Carson.*

Just as Carson's work required sacrifice, the struggle to keep our planet safe is far from over. "The 'control of nature,' " Rachel reminded us, "is a phrase conceived in arrogance, born of the Neanderthal age of biology and ... the convenience of man. "The human race," she said, "is challenged more than ever before to demonstrate our mastery- not over nature but of ourselves."

I will conclude this Chronicle, dear readers, with my favorite Rachel Carson quotes: "In contemplating the exceeding beauty of this earth, I found calmness and courage." "The more clearly we can focus our attention on the wonders and realities of the universe about us, the less taste we shall have for destruction ...

That is what I wanted to say."

"MASSY HARBISON, TERROR ON THE FRONTIER"

"Mr. Closier came near to the shore and saw my haggard and dejected situation. He exclaimed, 'Who in the name of God are you?' This man was one of my nearest neighbors before I was taken; yet in six days, I was so much altered he did not know me, either by my voice or my countenance."
- Massy Harbison, 1825, from her memoirs, <u>A Narrative of the Sufferings of Massy Harbison from Indian Barbarity</u>

Massy Harbison's story captivated me the first time I heard it, a true tale of terror on the frontier in the aftermath of the American Revolution.

In 1792, the long struggle for Independence was over; but for those settlers on the western Pennsylvania frontier, the bloodshed had not yet ended. Encouraged by the British to ever-more treachery, the Indians continued their raids on the scattered, outlying farms in the Ohio River Valley.

The half-century of eternal vigilance would come to a furious halt with General "Mad" Anthony Wayne's defeat of a confederation of Native Americans at Fallen Timbers, Ohio/Indian country, in 1794. (See "Haunted Pennsylvania," in *County Chronicles III*.) However, when our story opens in late May of 1792, that long-awaited day was still very much in the future.

Massy Harbison, whose unusual *prénom* was likely taken from the Bible as "Massa" and corrupted, in the frontier way of speaking, to "Massy" (also "Massey," though I have seen it too as "Mary" and "Mercy"), was born on March 18, 1770, in Somerset, New Jersey. Her maiden name was White. Massy's father Edward had been a soldier of the Revolution, contributing to the Great Cause with the fervent love of Liberty embedded in his Scotch-Irish heart.

In New Jersey during the course of the protracted war, the child Massy, with eye and ear, had been witness, on more than one occasion, to what those staunch American patriots had sacrificed for freedom. At the battles of Long Island, Trenton, and Monmouth, in her own words, later related in her memoirs, she "heard the roar of the cannon and the din of war."

During the Battle of Springfield, she witnessed the bloody vista as Westfield patriots helped defeat the British that memorable day. Massy had been at school when the battle commenced, whereupon the children were excused to go immediately home; but she, along with several of the other youngsters, ascended a steep hill that commanded a panoramic view of the field of engagement. There, they could hear the shouted commands of the officers and see the movements of the troops– that is, until the thick smoke engulfed the scene.

Before I get into the core of Massy's spellbinding story, let me give you an idea of the mettle of this woman and the Scotch-Irish in general.

They were a pugnacious race, God-fearing, hard-working and harder drinking, music-loving, free-spirited, resolute and persevering. In Northern Ireland's Ulster, their men outnumbered the women; and thus, they married many of the native Irish, blending the captivating ways of the fun-loving, adventurous Irish with the tenacity and obstinacy of the Scots.

A handsome people, the Scotch-Irish were lithe yet strong and robust, many of them tall for their era. Their language had developed into a tongue that wove and spun a mixture of English cockney, musical Irish brogue and Scottish burr, and into their common speech had crept many colorful phrases still used today. One such phrase that leaps to mind, common to my neck of Penn's Woods, is "redd up," meaning "to set in order" or "tidy up."

Like the Native Americans, the Scotch-Irish were born of a matriarchal society, family-oriented but cruel and unforgiving to their enemies. Like the Irish, this race of pioneers had come to America with an inbred hatred for the English. They had fought the British long and hard at home; and so, during America's bid for Independence, they were invaluable to Washington's army.

The hardships of the New World tested their mettle, physically and spiritually, but they were a match for this wild country and its even wilder natives. The wily English took immediate note that the Indians and the "wild Irish and Scots" (especially the Highlanders) shared many common denominators, among them the war dance.

The Indians too took immediate notice of this particular race of Whites, whom they counted as *formidable* enemies. The Irish and the Scotch-Irish- the Celts- were a race to be reckoned with. To be sure, they possessed what came to be known as "grit," exhibiting unyielding courage in the face of adversity and danger. The English never defeated them at home, and they made a lasting and prominent place for themselves in America- giving us our Daniel Boones and Davy Crocketts, our Patrick Henrys, Lewis and Clarks, our Stephen Fosters, our Robert E. Lees, Ulysses S. Grants, and an impressive list of our Presidents.

To return to our main focus: After the Revolutionary War, in 1783, Massy's family moved from New Jersey with a land grant to the western frontier of Pennsylvania, on the Monongahela, to a "place then called Redstone-Fort, where Brownsville now stands."

A comely lass, Massy was petite in stature and build, with lustrous, red-brown hair and that peculiar shade of eyes that almost seems to match auburn hair. Her face was more striking than it was beautiful, with the fair skin and the high cheekbones prominent to Celts, and a cleft chin.

Massy White lived in her father's cabin until she took a husband, John Harbison, in 1787.

Her father vehemently disapproved of her choice of mate. However, Massy was a feisty one with a mind of her own; and though she and her father locked horns over the matter, in the end, her choosing of a husband was hers and hers alone.

After two years with no chance of reconciliation from her father, Massy and John relocated to the "head waters of Chartiers Creek," where they made a pleasant home for themselves, living quite comfortably until Indian trouble erupted in the spring of 1791.

Albeit peace had been restored between England and America, the Indians who had sided with the British were not content to bury the warhawk.

As mentioned above, the British kept them pretty well stirred up against the Americans; and in Massy's words, "They had not sufficiently bathed the murderous [tomahawk] in the blood of the Americans, hence they continued to exercise toward them the most wanton acts of barbarity ... ."

As I have stated in previous volumes of my *County Chronicles*, Native Americans conducted *total* warfare. To borrow again from Massy's account, "... cruelties were inflicted upon prisoners of different ages and sexes, and [suffice it to say] that the scalping knife and tomahawk were the mildest instruments of death ... in many cases, torture by fire and other execrable means were used."

On March 18, 1791, a raiding party attacked the cabin of Thomas Dick on the Allegheny, taking the husband and wife prisoner and killing and scalping a young man who boarded with them. The couple were each adopted by their captors and resided with the Indians for a period of about four years. I might remind my readers that Native Americans treated adopted captives like blood kin.

Thomas Dick and wife would be freed in 1795, along with several hundred other captives, resultant to "Mad" Anthony Wayne's victory over the Natives and the subsequent Treaty of Greenville.

On the dark, moonless night of March 22, 1791, a small raiding party entered the cabin of Abraham Russ, who lived about two miles above the mouth of Bull Creek, approximately twenty-three miles northeast of Pittsburgh.

Leaving their rifles at the door- a well-known token of friendship on the frontier- they asked to sup at the Russ table. Their request was granted, after which, one of the warriors got up from the table to position himself in an aggressive posture in front of the door, preventing escape, whilst the rest of their numbers commenced to tomahawk the family. Once the grisly deed was done, the raiding party plundered what they wanted from the barn and cabin, before firing the buildings with the dead inside.

During the massacre, Mrs. Dary, daughter of old Mrs. Russ, endured the hideous sight of the simultaneous slaying of her elderly mother and her eighteen-month-old baby, as an Indian viciously swung the child by the feet, dashing its brains out against the head of the grandmother.

Horrified and galvanized by fear, the Dary woman ran for the door, just as another Indian brought his tomahawk down on her head. However, she averted the blow as best she could with her raised arm, and as a result, the hawk missed her scalp, slicing painfully through her cheek. With the adrenalin-charged strength of two men, she then yanked the clapboard cabin door clean off the hinges to make her escape, clearing a passage for her three daughters, who, shrieking in terror, dashed after their mother. While the warriors were busy killing the men, a couple more of the women ran, screaming, from the blood-spattered cabin with their "young'uns."

The escaping women and children rushed as fast as their legs could carry them to the river, where their screams were heard by a neighbor and relative, Levi Johnson, who crossed at his own peril to rescue the lot of them by means of his canoe.

Another Russ family member, a teenage boy, who had experienced a chillingly sinister sensation during the time the Indians were supping, quietly slipped out of the cabin. Then, as if the fiends of hell were after him, he took to his heels beyond the cabin's clearing to the adjacent woods, frantically pushing and ducking his way through the thick underbrush and low-hanging branches to cache himself in the recess of a fallen tree. Pulling leaves and other forest debris over his hiding place, he remained there, hardly daring to breathe.

Rigid with fear beneath that veil of foliage, the frightened boy lay as still as humanly possible, whilst the Indians passed right next to him, searching for those who had escaped. Above him, in the darkness, the flickering flaming torches the painted war party carried rendered them even more terrifying. However, God must have been watching over him that dreadful night. He survived the murderous affair, though for the rest of his life- and he lived another forty years- he suffered from nightmares and often awoke screaming.

Evil tidings take wing fast. 'Tis a marvel and a mystery how quickly messages of warning sprouted wings and ranged the vast countryside in those long-past days. Through the cold, frosty night, word of the incident traveled swiftly to the outlying farms, reaching the ears of Massy and John Harbison and seven or eight other families before midnight. Immediately, Massy readied the children whilst her husband packed what they could carry with them. Ah, the limitless penetration of a whisper! For all a frontier parent had to mouth softly was the word "Indian," and the pioneer children of that dark and bloody era knew what to do and not do. In less than an hour's time, they had set out on the approximate seven-mile journey for the large cabin of James Paul on Pine Run (as per the instructions of the express/ranger who had tapped on their cabin door, warning them of the imminent danger).

Churning with nerves, the seven-month pregnant Massy mounted a horse, after which her husband put the youngest child in her arms. He then tied the four-year-old behind her so he would not fall off.

Readers, imagine, if you can, that flight through the dark woods. Every sound, every rustle of limb or leaf, must have been petrifying for the little family as they made their perilous way to the relative safety of the nearest neighbor's.

By first light, they had arrived at the Paul retreat, where between seventy to eighty women and children had gathered. No sooner had the Harbisons dismounted when all the men, with the exception of four, set out after the raiding party. Massy stood and watched till they were out of sight. Her heart had quieted, but not her mind, and in her husband's absence, her thoughts tortured her.

The posse lit out first to the scene of the massacre, whence the horrific smell of the burning flesh nearly overwhelmed several of them. I did not find in my research the details of what the men did at the Russ place, but in all liklihood they buried the remains and pronounced words from the Holy Scriptures over the graves. That would have been a given, unless, of course, there would have been signs that the Indians were still in the area, though this was highly unlikely since war parties hit and quit with the speed of a panther.

At that point, it was decided among the group that they proceed about a mile down the Kiskiminetas (a river that runs into the Allegheny), where they began the construction of a large blockhouse. I might mention here that often a blockhouse was referred to as a "station." Christened "Reed's Station" (a logical name since a Reed owned the property), the building of the fortress-like edifice took a couple of weeks. As soon as the structure was up, the assembled neighbors at the Paul place removed to the blockhouse, where they remained till the advent of winter. The cold and snow of winter brought blessed relief from the eternal vigilance on the frontier. Indians typically did not make war in the cold season.

A word about the design of a blockhouse, in the event you have missed or forgotten previous discussions: A combination dwelling-fortress, a blockhouse was an easily defended structure of heavy timbers– in essence, a projecting upper cabin atop a stout lower cabin with all sides loopholed for gunfire. The reason for the projecting upper level was to prevent enemies from rushing the blockhouse's lower portion. Those inside the upper level could shoot down at attackers bent on forcing their way into the door below.

Frontier blockhouses were constructed over or near a stream, and central to outlying, scattered farms and cabins. Often surrounded by a palisade, many blockhouses were stockaded forts. Since siege was something Native Americans seldom utilized in warfare, the frontier blockhouse was an excellent means of defense against attack, and rarely, if ever, did they capitulate.

In late-summer of that year 1791, from the above-mentioned Reed's Blockhouse, Massy's husband John set out for six month's service in a locally mustered corps to join forces with General Arthur St. Clair's ill-fated punitive campaign to take the war to the Indians. As the force advanced to the Indian settlements along the Wabash River (about fifty miles from present-day Fort Wayne, Indiana), they were routed, on November 4– out-generaled in the fight by a tribal confederation led by Miami Chief Little Turtle and Shawnee Chief Blue Jacket.

That the campaign was led by a general who had proven himself in battle never actually lent confidence to St. Clair's men. Rather, there was, from the outset, a feeling of gloom and foreboding that followed the doomed troops into the clash.

St. Clair's bloodstained page of history marks the greatest thrashing of the US Army (though St. Clair's force did contain militia) by Native Americans. St. Clair's losses totaled more than either Major General Edward Braddock's losses in 1755 or General George Armstrong Custer's future defeat by the Plains Indians in 1876.

Massy's wounded husband John Harbison, who had fought like a wild boar in the fray, returned to her and their three children at Reed's Station on Christmas Eve. John was one of the few lucky survivors of that campaign, though I can well imagine that for the reminder of his life on this earth, he suffered many a nightmare, his dreams beset with the wild yelps of the painted terror he had faced on the "northwestern" frontier.

After his recovery, John was engaged again as a "spy," i.e. a ranger/express, whose sole purpose it was to look for Indian signs, spy on the Indians in their distant camps or villages, watch and report on any and all Indian movements, as well as track raiding parties to recover captives whenever possible.

In the spring of 1792, the Harbison family was living in a small log cabin constructed for safety only about 200 yards from Reed's Blockhouse. It was while John was absent from the cabin that disaster befell his twenty-two-year-old wife Massy and their young sons.

"Vicissitude," Massy would state later in her memoirs penned in 1825, "is the characteristic feature of the present life." Every human is subject in a greater or less degree to trials and tribulations, so that "every heart knoweth its own bitterness ... yet it is all too evident that there are those of us," that valiant frontier goodwife declared, "who are called to pass through ... [trials] that are infinitely more severe than others."

Upon her husband's departure into the woods, on May 22, 1792, Massy Harbison was about to endure suffering of an almost "overwhelming magnitude."

To anchor you, readers, on the Pennsylvania county map located on *County Chronicles'* end papers, Massy's ordeal unfolded between the far northwestern corner of Westmoreland County, in an area now called the River Forest Golf Club, and the section of Butler County known historically as Kearns Crossing, above what is now the city of Butler, where routes 422, 38, and 68 converge.

Because of repeated ranger reports of "no Indian signs," most of the families who had been crowded together for the past year in the blockhouse had scattered to their outlying farms to again take up the cultivation of their fields. Harbison, thinking his family safe so close- in fact, within view- of the blockhouse, left for duty with an untroubled mind that fatal morn of 22 May.

A few days before, on May 15, a band of rangers had stopped at the Harbison cabin to seek supper and overnight lodging. Massy had requested that one of the men escort her to the spring and springhouse, so she could put together a suitable meal. While she and her ranger escort were at the spring, they heard a distinct sound issuing from the dark, not-too-distant woods, like the bleating of a fawn, or perhaps a lost lamb.

The noise alarmed both her and the ranger; and they hastened back to the cabin, he behind her, guarding her back, his Pennsylvania Rifle pointed at that section of forest. Whether this was a signal, a warning of the cruelties through which she was to pass, we know not.

Though nothing out of the ordinary occurred that night, alone in the cabin with her young children upon the rangers' departure, the sound lingered in Massy Harbison's Celtic soul- lingered like a shadowy portent through the subsequent hours of darkness.

Several days passed without incident until, during the evening of 21 May, two other rangers stopped at the house for refreshment and a place by the fire till morning. At daybreak, the reveille horn sounded at the nearby blockhouse, and the men rose and went out.

Awake but still abed, Massy noticed that the cabin door was ajar. She wanted to get up to close and latch the door, but with her babe at her breast, she decided to get him back to sleep before rising. However, she accidentally fell asleep herself.

There would come a day in the future when the scouts would relate to her that when they returned to the cabin, they had found her sleeping peacefully and thus quietly secured the door before leaving to return to duty. She would also learn that the door after her abduction bore the appearance of having been forced open.

I must pause here in our tale to state for my readers that Massy was about seven months pregnant at the time of her abduction, albeit she was still nursing baby John who had been born the previous May. The child she was carrying, James, would survive the traumatic episode to be born that July.

In the twilight state between sleep and wakefulness, Massy remembered having her feet tugged hard, as someone roughly yanked her out of bed. Her eyes flew open to see the cabin crowded with Indians, their garishly painted appearance taking her breath, as though one of them had hit her hard in the gut. As in the most terrifying of dreams, for a few moments at least, she was stricken helpless and unable to move as peril gripped her heart.

Some of the invaders were painted completely red, others black- an indication those warriors meant to either take lives or be killed themselves. Some had grotesque symbols painted over their faces, lending demoniacal expression to their features.

At once cognizant of her dire situation, the young woman, attired only in the petticoat in which she had slept, jumped up, tearing herself free of her momentary paralysis, and clutching her baby in one arm, grabbed with the other for her clothing from a peg on the wall. One of the Indians jerked the article from her grasp and with a threatening sound, pushed her toward the door that now stood wide open. Again, Massy thrust out her hand for a piece of her clothing, and once more she was roughly shoved toward the cabin entrance.

At the same time she was struggling to get hold of something to cover herself, a couple of the other warriors were engaged in pulling the two older boys from their beds. The remainder busied themselves with the barbarous plunder of the family's possessions, beginning with the two feather beds, which they dragged to the door and emptied, filling the single room with a blizzard of soft, white down.

With wild whoops, the raiding party seemed to delight in the total destruction of the cabin's interior; and what they could not carry, they smashed, shattered, or slashed to shreds with their scalping knives.

Still clutching her year-old baby, Massy grasped the hand of the nearest boy, the five-year-old, and while the Indians yelped with joy through their devastation, she dashed with those two children outside.

There, she caught sight of one of the soldiers, whose surname was Wolf, exiting the blockhouse for the spring to fetch water, completely unaware of the danger he was in. Straightaway, she noted that three of the Indians were attempting to skulk between Wolf and the fortress. Impulsively, she let out a loud

County Chronicles

The Eastern Woodland Indians painted themselves with images at once breathtakingly beautiful and terrifying. Some of those expressions had universal meaning; others were known only to the wearer. In this powerful Robert Griffing painting, we are privileged to view two warriors whose paint reflects the most basic expressions of all— <u>Life and Death</u>.

scream, warning the soldier in the nick of time. Wheeling round, he made a mad bolt for safety, with seven or eight of the warriors firing at his retreating back. Though one of the shots hit Wolf in the arm, breaking it, he was miraculously able to make it inside the blockhouse's log walls.

As soon as Massy had sounded the alarm, one of the Indians rushed up to her, a wild trio of yowls bursting from his throat as he brandished his warhawk as though to brutally snuff out her life on the spot. This pioneer woman flinched not, but rather met with valor what she believed to be the savage face of Death.

At that, a second warrior sprinted forth, and putting his hand to her mouth, signaled her to immediate silence. Nearly simultaneously, a third member of the painted enemy advanced with raised tomahawk and a bloodcurdling yell. This one would surely have bashed in her skull, when, to Massy's surprise, the first of the trio averted the blow, and in the brave young woman's own words, "claimed [her] as his squaw." In the ensuing course of events, this would prove her salvation.

Hearing the sharp reports of the guns, the commissary and his aide, who slept in the storehouse near the station, stepped outside to see what was amiss. Quickly taking in the situation, the commissary darted for the fortress with his aide close behind him.

The Indians, however, had spotted them, and firing a rain of bullets after them, shot off a fragment of the commissary's scalp and succeeded in bringing down the aide, just outside the storehouse door, with two bullets to his middle.

Missing a bit of his hair, the commissary managed to dive inside the station, as the Indians, sending up a chain of wild yelps and shrieks (called "scalphulloes" by those who had the misfortune of experiencing them) descended on the aide's body with their scalping knives in hand. However, to their intense displeasure, the heavy firing, coming now at a steady pace from the blockhouse's loopholes, prevented "their diabolical purpose" from coming to pass and resulted in a chorus of howls from the attackers.

While all this was going on, Massy had thought out a plan. She mistakenly reckoned that if she could divert the Indians' full attention to the blockhouse, she might have a chance of escaping to an underground tunnel leading to a cave she knew was close by, near the run.

I could not find in my research any particulars about this "subterranean rock," as she called it, but I know that often local militia dug from a fort or blockhouse a tunnel that came out somewhere in the nearby woods, so that if a courier had to make an escape from the fortress to run for needed manpower/firepower, he could get away undetected, rather than from the fortress itself, whence he would be sure to be seen.

At any rate, Massy began talking to the Indians around her (some of whom she had discovered spoke English) about the strength of the stronghold. She told them there were at least forty men inside, all excellent marksmen. This information prompted those with her to call back the warriors who were firing at the blockhouse. Then, flogging her with their whipping sticks to hurry her (and two of her children) along, they hastily made their retreat. To her chagrin, all she had succeeded in doing was quickening her fate, in Massy's language, "at the hands of the savages."

However, as this author is prone to say, everything happens for a reason. The reason here was for the preservation of Reed's Station and those souls inside, for unbeknownst to Massy, the men inside had loaded the last of their ammunition. The remainder of their powder, in the storehouse, was dangerously inaccessible to them.

Massy (with her infant) and her five-year-old boy, wide-eyed and watchful, were herded along, while her three-year-old stood at the cabin door, screaming loudly for her. When an Indian attempted to drag him out, the fiery toddler, though he cried for his mama, let the painted warrior know, in no uncertain terms, he was *not* about to go with him. The child dashed back inside and plopped himself down stubbornly in front of the fireplace. When the Indian again grabbed him, the wee boy put up a fight, screaming, kicking, and biting for all he was worth, until the Indian's patience was wholly spent.

Raiding parties with captives moved fast; there was no time for this, and unfortunately, the captors were unwilling to leave the youngster behind. The Indian whose patience he had drained forcibly took the tot by his feet and dashed out his brains against the doorsill of the cabin. The painted foe then scalped and stabbed the boy, leaving his lifeless little body in a pool of gore.

Massy let out a heartrending scream, feeling a faintness come over her she had never before experienced in her life, so horrified was she by what she had just witnessed. One of the enemy hit her a terrific blow, sending her to her knees, as all the while, she held fast to the infant in her arms. Jerking her roughly to her feet, the Indians marched her forward. Massy Harbison's fate was now cast into the uncertain, howling winds of the times.

At the top of the nearest bluff, the raiding party paused to divide the plunder, and it was at this point when Massy took stock of their strength, finding the force to number thirty-two, including two white men dressed and painted as Indians. Senecas and Munsees she determined they were, several of whom could speak English, and Massy recognized a couple of the warriors who had stopped at the settlement in the past to have their trade weapons repaired by her husband.

As discussed in an earlier volume, Indians often carried trade guns that were made up of parts they brought in to local gunsmiths for piecing together.

From there, the party with the woman, her babe and five-year-old son moved along at a good clip toward her uncle John Currie's place, where the Indians confiscated his horses, putting Massy on one with two Indian guards afoot, one on each side of her horse, and her son on another with a warrior behind him on that horse's broad back. Then they started off in the direction of the mouth of a tributary of the Allegheny, the Kiskiminetas (near Freeport at Schenley, about twenty-five miles northeast of Pittsburgh), whilst the others in the party set out towards Puckety (present-day New Kensington area).

Before long, Massy's group came to a precariously steep bank of the river. Seeing immediately that the grade was far too dangerous to descend on horseback, in opposition to her guards, she flung herself off her mount.

After a verbal exchange that included angry gestures from both factions, the Indians gave up attempting to get the feisty woman back on the horse. They then led her mount down the slippery bank to the river.

However, the horse that Massy's son was riding fell, whinnying and screaming in terror as it plunged, rolling over and over again, down the steep, rocky slope, with the child and his Indian guardian falling off the frightened animal from behind. It seemed that both man and beast must slide down to where the slope ended. The warrior rolled, but the youngster tumbled head-over-heels to the bottom, appearing, at the river bank, only to be bruised and covered with mud and debris rather than seriously injured.

Here, an Indian took firm hold of the crying boy, while the others uncovered bark canoes they had secreted at the water's edge. Massy tells us in her account of her captivity, "They attempted in vain to make the horses take the river. After trying for some time to effect this, they left the [unwilling steeds] behind ... ."

With their captives, the Indians then pushed off in one of the canoes for the island (Todd's Island) on the Allegheny River, between the Kiskiminetas and the Buffaloe (Buffalo Creek near the present-day borough of Freeport).

As soon as they landed, Massy Harbison was made to witness the second murder of one of her sons. Her five-year-old, still upset over the violent death of his little brother, and who yet was sobbing and cranky over the injuries he had sustained in the fall down the rocky cliff, became the next victim to the already blood-stained warhawk.

The Indians gruffly shoved Massy forward so that she would not hinder the violent deed, as another pulled his weapon from the belt at his side and tomahawked then scalped the complaining youngster.

Up ahead, Massy stood where the harsh hands had pushed her, pausing for a moment to catch her breath. Something made her look back. Turning quickly and beholding that further "scene of inhuman butchery," the poor woman fell to the ground, her babe's tiny hands entangled in her hair, in a dead faint, as she related later, for how long, she did not know.

When she did open her eyes, the first thing she remembered seeing was the fresh, dripping scalp of her son dangling from the hands of one of the painted foe. It was too much to bear, and she immediately sank back down to the ground, as darkness mercifully overtook her once again.

Two of the Indians beat her with sticks. She groaned but did not get up, murmuring the words that the Indians knew were magic, because they had heard them before and seen the effect they had on other white captives: "The Lord is my shepherd; I shall not want ... for Thou art with me. Thy rod and Thy staff they comfort me ... in the presence of mine enemies ... ." She looked up at those enemies, and pride and gumption were in the tilt of the chin, endurance in the set of the bruised mouth.

This time her wakefulness was met with a rain of severe blows and gruff Native words, as the Indians essayed to get her to her feet and moving again- stumbling onward to the river, where they plunged her beneath the frigid water to physically revive her, for 'twas Massy's body that was damaged, not her spirit. This having the desired effect, they pressed on, cognizant, I am certain, that a rescue party might well be pursuing them.

Crossing the breadth of the island, they forced the distraught woman into the water to wade over to the "Indian side" of the river. As the water lapped at her breasts, she was able, with the assistance of her captors- and holding her baby high above the cold, rapid current- to arrive safely on the opposite bank. "From thence," Massy tells us, they "proceeded forth with rapidity," passing through the Buffalo(e) Creek area where they came upon a waterfall, never stopping to rest or wet their parched lips with even a sip from the clear, bubbling brook.

At this point in the nightmare, Massy had taken all she could take, and she had pretty much made up her mind to provoke her captors into killing her too. She stopped dead in her tracks, and ripping from her shoulder the large powder horn they had forced her to carry, she threw it to the ground. Tightly shutting her eyes and still clutching her baby, she expected to feel the wrath of the warhawk against her skull.

To her surprise, the Indians did not kill her. Rather, there was an ugly rumbling among them as they cursed her again in their strange, guttural tongue, picked up the powder horn, and roughly flung it anew over her shoulder with an angry gesture to walk on.

Obviously, these fellows were not familiar with the grit of a Celtic woman! For the second time, Massy tore the leather strap from her shoulder and pitched the powder horn to the ground, sticking her cleft chin out at them in even more defiance. Not to be disobeyed, the Indian picked up the horn and, jerking her by the arm, hung it once more on her shoulder, giving her a shove that nearly caused her to fall forward on her face.

The hot blood of her Highland ancestors boiled in her veins, and now Massy was as furious as her Indian opponent. Yanking the powder horn off for a third trial, she drew back and hurled the thing as far as she could. Over the rocks it sailed, as the angry warrior dashed after it, drawing the one who had claimed her as his squaw to her side with a look of obvious admiration. "Well done!" he shouted in clear English. "Good squaw! Let the lazy son of a b— carry it himself!"

The contest over who would carry the powder horn had ended with Massy the victor, and she would later thank a gracious God for sparing her life. From this point, the one who sought to make her his squaw walked behind her rather than in the lead, to protect her, she assumed, from the rage of her antagonist.

The party trekked on until dark, when they finally rested for the night at what is historically known as Kearns Crossing (the convergence of routes 422, 38, and 68) above what is now Butler.

With hands secured behind her, Massy was forced to pass the night between her captors. She was given nothing to eat and nary a drop of water to drink, this to weaken and subdue her as a captive.

To calm your thoughts, readers, Indians did not rape women. The Iroquois were a matriarchal society, and rape would have been a sacrilege. But can you imagine how Mrs. Harbison must have felt, how heavy her heart that first night as she lay on a bed of leaves between those who had so brutally murdered her children?

In fact, Massy makes a plea in her little book to "... think ... what I endured; and hence now you are enduring the sweet repose and the comforts of a peaceful and well replenished habitation, sympathize with me ... as one, who was a pioneer in the work of cultivation and civilization." 'Twas then, that first night in captivity, when Massy made up her mind to escape.

The hours passed slowly, and finally she fell into an exhausted but fitful sleep, dreaming of her escape and her safe arrival among her own kind in Pittsburgh.

In the morning, one of the Indians went back along the way they had come to see if any Whites were pursuing them. In the absence of her protector, the more violent of the pair- a cunning, menacing figure to be sure- took out her son's scalp, the dried blood clinging to the hair and skin as he inspected it with deliberate scrutiny. Producing from his pack a hoop, he proceeded to stretch the trophy over it, the Native way of preserving a scalp.

Massy drew in her breath. For the remainder of her days, the image of her young son's scalp was engraved upon her memory as though etched there by needles of fire.

Nonetheless, her initial feeling of horror was quickly replaced with an even stronger sentiment of revenge that rose up hotly from the deep well of her soul. At once, her eyes narrowed to slits of dark, turbulent waters as her anger lent her strength, effacing her fears, and she felt she could fight the very Devil himself. She clenched her teeth and waited, waited for her chance.

Engaged in his grisly work, the Indian was unaware that his captive was attempting to lift his tomahawk from his belt. Closer and closer crept her tingling fingers. So close were they, she could almost feel the cold weight of the weapon in her callused hands. She had nearly succeeded in securing the hawk- then to deliver the fatal blow- when, in his peripheral vision, her nemesis caught sight of the movement, painfully grasping her hand and cursing her for a "Yaaawn-kee (Yankee)."

There is an old saying, "If looks could kill... ." If indeed they could, Massy Harbison would not have survived to write her story for Posterity's sake! In her own words: "... the looks of the Indian were terrific to the extreme; and these, I apprehend, were only an index to his heart."

By this time, the warrior who had gone out to check their trail for pursuers had now returned, and the more vicious of the two left the camp to take his place. It seemed no one was yet following them.

Massy's guard then began questioning her about the strength of the Whites in the area where she had been taken, their numbers, weaponry, and such. With exaggerated bragging, he concluded the conversation, as proper Native oratory demanded, with his triumphs the preceding autumn in St. Clair's defeat.

This author is thinking that it must have taken a good deal of restraint for Massy not to have responded to those boasts.

Satisfied with his rhetoric, the Indian then opened the satchel that contained his share of the plunder taken from her cabin. He quickly found the little leather purse in which she had kept the family's coin. In it she had cached ten dollars in silver and half a guinea in gold. How that must have irked this thrifty pioneer woman to see her family's life savings in the hands of one of her children's murderers!

That day, Massy's captors saw fit to share with her some dried venison, "about the bulk of an egg." But owing to the blows she had sustained, she was not able to chew the cured meat, though she did break it up into tiny pieces for the baby. Later, as she lay stiffly between her captors under the stars, the second night of her captivity, she prophetically dreamed again of her triumphant return to Pittsburgh.

In the morning, after one of her guards left to check and watch the trail, the other, though he appeared to be awake, did not rise from the makeshift bed of leaves. Rather, he seemed to want yet for sleep. Massy opened her eyes to see a flock of birds above the camp, and their song, at least in her mind, was a song of escape. Immediately, she closed her eyes and feigned snoring, as though she were in a deep slumber. This was the day- in her heart she knew it.

As soon as she was certain that the remaining Indian had fallen back to sleep, she quietly got up, and though she yearned to slay this killer of her children, she thought better of it. She would have had to put the baby down, to free both her hands, and do the job effectively. That, she feared, would cause the babe to cry and sound the alarm. Thus, she contented herself with gingerly taking from a pillowcase of plunder from her home, a clean petticoat, a child's frock, and a handkerchief, pulled more or less at random from the case. With that, she stealthily took her leave of the campsite, the sun being about a half-hour high.

Eventually, she came to the creek she had crossed with the Indians. She followed it downstream, over briars, thorn bushes, and sharp rocks, with feet and legs bare, until what she believed to be about two in the afternoon. Cleverly, she traveled northwest rather than southeast, from whence she had come- to deceive her captors- over rocks and through water as much as possible, rendering tracking more difficult. Once she covered a good distance, she changed direction, coming upon Connoquenessing Creek.

I am certain this stalwart woman thanked God that she had learned the tricks and techniques of survival first from her father and later from her ranger husband. A child of the forest, Massy had an excellent chance of making good her escape!

At this point in her arduous journey, Massy ascended a hill to give herself a good lookout to spot the enemy if they came for her. Then she sat down to rest and wait for the North Star to make its appearance in the night sky. She wanted to make certain that the direction she was now traveling was correct.

This, however, was not a restful stop, for her legs and feet throbbed with pain from the offending briars and thorns, and she and the baby had nothing to eat, though they were snug enough in their blanket of leaves.

Twilight fell with sinister shadows sweeping beneath the silent pines, ever-deepening shadows that reached dusky fingers toward her.

The night wind rose and began its moan. In the strange owl-light, the tall pines along the creek, so warmly green in the sunshine, were dark now against the horizon, an impenetrable row of black giants veiling the moving water at their feet. Massy sighed and scanned the star-lit sky. Once she located the North Star, she eventually fell asleep, lulled by the soothing sound of the creek.

At first light, that heartening flock of birds stirred her to life. It was the fourth day of her ordeal. She was in constant pain, hungry, tired, heartsick, near-naked and chilled, but not yet defeated.

That whole day was devoid of incident as she continued without pause to make her steady way to what she believed was the direction of the Allegheny River. That evening, unfortunately, it began to rain, more like a descending mist than an actual shower. To keep warm and relatively dry during the night, Massy began to prepare a makeshift shelter for herself and the baby. Experiencing a problem gathering enough leaves for their bed, she decided to lay the child down, but as soon as she did, he began to cry, and she was forced to scoop him up and put him immediately to her breast.

Suddenly, with the sixth sense of a Celt, she froze, holding her breath and listening hard. Just as she had perceived, her ears picked up the sound of footfalls coming toward them from the exact direction whence she had come. Massy knew she had to have left footprints in the soft earth. But this woman was possessed of another sense- and her strong will would not permit a second captivity!

Looking quickly around for a hiding place, she spied a fallen tree and quickly cached herself, babe in arms, into its thick tangle of limbs and leaves. Sorely thankful for the leafy camouflage as well as the cover of darkness, she intently listened for her pursuer, praying the baby would not cry again.

Within moments, one of her captors appeared, stopping at the very spot where the babe had let out his wail. The Indian was so

Here we see Too Quiet, *another painting by Pennsylvania artist Robert Griffing. The Eastern Woodland warrior's accoutrements of war, after years of hunting and fighting, had reduced to the barest essentials- breechclout, leggings, and moccasins, in addition to his weapons, by the era of Massy Harbison's story, a scalping knife, a warhawk, and a rifle.*

The Indian used his face and body as a canvas for tattoos and paint that played a significant role in the psychological warfare at which he excelled.

The model for this rendering was (then-reënactor) H. John Heinz IV, son of the late Pennsylvania senator. When his mother, Teresa Heinz, learned that Griffing had done the painting, she purchased it and donated it to the Heinz Foundation, Pittsburgh.

Griffing images courtesy the artist and Paramount Press, Inc. Robert Griffing's art and the books embracing his artistry can be purchased through Paramount Press, Inc. at www.paramountpress.com or by telephoning 1-800-647-2901.

close to where Massy and her child now lay, she feared she would be betrayed by the loud pounding of her own heart. By the grace of God, the baby, now fed, out of the chilling drizzle and warmed by her body, had fallen fast asleep.

For an endless time, the lone Indian stood there in the forest, his sharp ears pricked, with every dragging minute, for the sound of a baby's cry. Massy tells us in her account that "he stood and listened with nearly the stillness of death for two hours."

My feeling, and it is only that, is that it was less. Perhaps it seemed like two whole hours to her. All the same, the time passed with agonizing slowness, as she continued to lay as motionless as she could, barely daring to breathe, praying she would not sneeze under the leaves and dusty forest debris, and that the child would continue to sleep.

After what must have felt like an eternity, there came upon the night's breath the distant hooting of an owl. The Indian who had nearly come upon them let go, unexpectedly, a loud, bloodcurdling yell that struck terror in the very marrow of Massy's bones. With another couple of savage yelps, the warrior hastened away to join his companions. It was a miracle the baby did not awaken screaming!

At this point, Massy believed it completely unsafe to remain where she was, should the Indian lead a tracking party back there, with the aid of daylight, to conduct a thorough search for her. And she knew from her ranger husband and the terrifying tales others who had suffered captivity told that if she were caught now, her fate would be horrific beyond measure.

From this brave woman's own telling, it was especially difficult for her to move from that warm spot that awful night, so exhausted and drained was she. However, her will was strong, and with tremendous resolve and purpose, she pulled herself to her bleeding, swollen feet and pushed on for the duration of the night. It had grown cold and ominously still. So many times did she pause and listen. The night seemed to her too still, though once she thought she heard the distant, lonesome bark of a coyote ... if indeed it was a coyote.

Never having lost track of time and date, Massy calculated that the fifth day of her ordeal was Saturday, 26 May. Exhausted, starved, and utterly wretched, she resumed her arduous journey after a brief rest; and that day, she came to what she believed was Pine Creek that emptied into the Allegheny some four or five miles above Pittsburgh. Here, she crossed, and on the opposite side soon discovered in the woods a path that she began to follow, thinking it would lead to a White cabin or settlement.

Within minutes, and with alarm, she discovered two sets of moccasin tracks on the path, freshly made, and headed in the same direction she was taking. With quick insight, the pioneer woman realized that she would likely see them before they spotted her; and perhaps, moccasin prints aside, the footprints were those of white men. She pressed on, hoping against hope the tracks did belong to allies.

After two or three miles, she came to the men's abandoned camp. Their fire was warm and smoldering, and she could tell by the look of things that it had been a hunters' camp. Again alarm sparked within her soul, and she decided to quit the path.

No sooner had she made this decision when a trio of deer came crashing through the trees and brush toward her at full speed, glancing back, as they ran, at their pursuing hunters.

Massy turned her head in that direction in time to see the flash of a gun. Echoing loudly, the sharp report was followed by the baying and barking of dogs. The canine trackers dashed after the deer, past where Massy hid crouched behind a large log. When she placed a hand on the ground for the leverage to rise- that she might get a look at the hunters- she espied a family of rattlesnakes, the largest coiled and ready to sink venomous fangs into her face. It was that close!

Once again, by the grace of Providence, she escaped danger. Because of it, though, she missed catching even a glimpse of the hunters, and still did not know if they were White or Red, friend or foe!

For the remainder of that day, Massy followed the stream (Squaw Run) with nothing of any significance befalling her except for the numbing dampness, the gnawing hunger, and the threat of exhaustion ready to halt her efforts to return home. For most of the day, it poured a miserable, soaking rain. As she moved along, her teeth chattered, and she shivered in her thin, wet, sleeveless garment, thinking she could never remember being so cold, the term "chilled to the bone" taking on a most poignant meaning.

That night when she stopped for rest, she leaned her body back against a huge, old tree, and hung her head forward, the baby in the shelter of her lap, the wet landing on her and not so much on the child. Soaked to the skin, she felt weak, flushed and feverish. Longingly, her thoughts drifted back home to the family cabin- and to her warm cosy bed, a flotsam of inviting memories. Oh for sleep, peaceful, blessed sleep! Of a sudden, the silence was pierced by the scream of a wildcat ... or was it an Indian signaling to his companions? She waited for a timeless time crouched amidst some underbrush, but no one revealed himself from the dark tangle of woods surrounding her.

Sometime during the night, she was awakened from restless slumber by the soughing of the wind, a wind that presaged storm. Caught in the thick boughs of the old tree, it whipped the branches overhead into a sudden frenzy. The wind smelled of rain and something else ... spring and new life. Massy closed her eyes again, listening to the sound of that wind as it whispered through the leaves.

In the old countries of Scotland and Ireland, wind listening was an ancient form of divination. On a windy day, those who wished to learn the future would go deep into a forest, alone, where they would not be disturbed. Then, selecting a patch of woods where the trees were especially leafy, they would lie down upon the earth, relax and close their eyes, feeling Earth Mother beneath them. There, they would listen intensely as the wind rustled through the branches above them, listen to capture the voices that held messages from far beyond the conscious mind. As a true Celt, Massy had never feared wind listening. She did not fear it now, as the voices, the Old Ones, rose unbidden to tell her she would make it home, that she would, indeed, survive- if she stayed the course as the Celtic warrior-woman they knew her to be.

She lifted her face, expecting to see and feel the beginnings of the storm. Instead, through the lacy network of limbs, she saw only a moonless expanse of velvet-black sky sprinkled with countless twinkling stars. Then she slept.

By her faithful calculations, daylight brought the Sabbath. It was the sixth day of her nightmare now, and it took every last ounce of perseverance to pull herself to her mangled feet and continue her trek homeward. That Sunday morning, she had not gone far, when she came upon another path on which she discovered cattle had traveled not long past. Surely this trace would lead to white people!

With luck riding high on her aching shoulders, she pushed on. After following the forest path for about a mile, she came upon a cabin and was dejected beyond words to discover it empty. Despair filled her, and she felt had it not been for the child, she would lie down in the abandoned cabin and die. Her gloom was abruptly interrupted by the unmistakable sound of a cow bell. Seized with renewed hope, she moved as fast as her damaged legs and feet would carry her down to the river bank, oblivious to the pain, to anything but rescue.

On the opposite shore, she immediately spied the fort at Six Mile Island (near what is currently the Fox Chapel Yacht Club; Pittsburgh area) and at the water's edge- three white men. Oh, to have finally arrived back to civilization! There are no words to describe the feeling of elation she must have felt!

With the last reserve of energy she possessed, Massy called out with a voice that was both croaky and tremulous, realizing how strange it was to hear sound coming from her own throat.

She quickly realized, with sinking heart, that the men were wary of coming across the water to fetch her, since Indians often used captives as decoys to lure would-be rescuers into their clutches. "Go back up the bank a ways, and let us see if the Injuns are usin' you t' trick us!" one of them shouted to her.

Massy closed her eyes and asked for Divine intervention, then, cupping her hands around her cracked lips, she yelled as loudly as she could that her feet were so torn up, she could not take another step. Again and again she called to the men, pleading for all she was worth to get them to believe that she was acting alone and desperately in need of their help. She called out that she had been taken captive Tuesday last on the Allegheny and that she had made her escape from the Indians with her year-old babe.

At last, one of the trio made the decision to cross for her, and getting into his canoe, he glided across the water, whilst his two companions stood on the bank, watchful, their loaded rifles aimed to fire.

The man in the canoe was James Closier, and when he put in on the opposite shore before the haggard, gaunt woman covered with mud and blood, her filthy, ragged clothing barely covering her bruised, sunburned body, her dirty, tangled mane of hair akin to the most frightening of banshees, he blurted, "Who in the name of God are you!"

Massy cocked her head, answering with surprise, "Mr. Closier, it is Massy Harbison, your nearest neighbor ... don't you recognize me?"

He most assuredly did not. So much was her appearance altered in the past six days that he did not know her either by voice or countenance.

Once they had landed on the fort side, those inside came pouring down to the river to see the pitiful woman. Now that she felt safe, Massy found that she was surprisingly unable to move. With soft words delivered on the familiar lilt of a Scot's tongue, a kind woman pried the baby from her; and the next thing she knew she was being carried to the Carter home, a cabin that stood near the fort.

Through the entire nightmarish event, Massy Harbison had never shed one tear. Now, for the first time, the tears flowed copiously, almost uncontrollably. Then, at long last, she began to keen.

Inside the warm cabin, the fire, the aroma of the cooking victuals, the press of the folks around her nearly caused the poor woman to faint. A few of the ladies scurried about to lay a feast before the starving creature, and but for the intervention of Major McCulley who commanded the soldiers at the fort, and who entered the cabin at that express moment, a large plate of food would have been set before her. However, the major told the assembly that would be the worst possible thing for the deprived woman, that they must restore her to health with small quantities of food at a time, beginning simply with beef stock.

A couple of the goodwives began to extract the myriad of thorns from Massy's mangled feet. How excruciating that must have been, for some of them had gone completely through and had to be pulled out from the tops of each foot. Massy recounted in her memoirs that "Mr. Felix Negley stood by and added up the thorns" taken from her feet and legs. Negley counted 150, though many more were extracted later.

The flesh hung in shreds from Massy's legs and feet, and per her own account, the "wounds were not healed for a considerable time." It was a little over two weeks before she could stand to put weight on her feet to take even a couple of steps.

What's more, since she had been attired only in a petticoat, nearly her entire body was painfully raw from exposure and sunburn. The garment that she had drawn from the pillowcase before her escape, remember, was also a petticoat, since that was all that was available to her amongst the Indians' plunder.

Soon after her arrival at the fort, two rangers came in, John Thompson and James Amberson. She soon learned that it was *their* moccasin tracks she had followed on the forest trail. Thompson and Amberson, with the fleetness of the deer they had been tracking, carried the tale of Massy's escape through the settlements, first to Coe's Station, then to Reed's Blockhouse, where the news reached Massy's husband John Harbison.

That same evening, word reached Pittsburgh, whence a young man employed by the office of magistrates came to fetch Massy to testify so that her "deposition might be published to the American people."

Since Massy was unable to walk, she was taken by canoe to Pittsburgh and carried to the office of John Wilkins, Esquire, where she gave testimony of her ordeal. The account of her captivity was printed in several newspapers around the country and in Volume I of *Loudon's Indian Narratives* (originally printed in two volumes in 1808 and 1811).

Several years later, Massy Harbison's personal narrative was published.

The news of Mrs. Harbison's capture and the murder of her children spread across the frontier like wildfire. The entire area around Pittsburgh became immediately alarmed and watchful for a twenty to thirty-mile radius. In outlying cabins, Pennsylvania Rifles were at the ready, and no one ventured away from cabin or blockhouse without a loaded weapon. Children, taught from babyhood what to do and not do when the word "Indian" left the lips of their parents, were prevented from venturing outside stout log walls.

Massy was able to describe the location, on Todd's Island, where the Indians had killed her five-year-old son. Scouts found the mangled body and buried it, nine days dead.

Massy and John Harbison continued to live in several cabins along the western Pennsylvania frontier, moving from the Chartiers Creek area to Buffalo Creek to Puckety Creek then Bull Creek, finally settling on the Little Buffalo Creek, Butler County, in the area called "Mount Joy."

The Harbisons had lost all their household items to the Indian raiders, and it was slow acquiring everything they needed to be comfortable again. Massy had to work hard during those years, cooking and doing laundry for the men in the various blockhouses, but with time, they did make a cosy home at Mount Joy. Massy and her family resided at that site for sixteen years.

According to *Flood Tides Along the Allegheny* published in 1941 by Francis R. Harbison, a descendant, the (Mt. Joy) cabin windows were devoid of glass but rather fashioned of a greased paper that let in some light but all too much cold in winter. When Jack Frost blew his frigid breath round the homestead, castoff apparel or animal skins covered the greased paper. The cabin floor was laid with thick logs hewn flat on one side, as was the loft floor, reachable via a ladder constructed of split saplings.

The Harbison's crude furniture was fashioned from the trees of the surrounding forest, including a long table of split slabs hewn smooth as glass on the upper side with rustic legs cut from smaller trees. Three-legged stools stood along each side of the table and at each end. These were quite sturdy and serviceable for many years.

Tableware was simple and sparse, wooden mostly, though the Harbisons, like other pioneer families, did own a few special pewter items. Cooking was done in iron pots over the cabin's open fireplace that took up most of one wall. The food Massy set upon the table for her husband and what grew to be a large family was simple but healthful.

The wilderness supplied their meat, for game was abundant; and the streams gave forth a bountiful supply of fish. In the warm season, wild berries were plentiful, and autumn's gift was nuts, to eat and to provide the dyes for homespun garments.

Like other pioneer women, Massy Harbison's work was never done. Except for the Sabbath, each day was chore-filled from dawn to dusk- cooking, baking, milking, washing, sewing, making soap or butter, looking after sick children or livestock. Such was life on the western Pennsylvania frontier.

In each of my *County Chronicle* volumes, I have endeavored to open a window to the past- and the hearts of my readers- to illustrate the heroism and savagery in both the White and the Native peoples.

We are fortunate to have this brave pioneer woman's personal account of what she endured on the frontier at the hands of the Indians. And know, readers, that hers and most of the first-hand accounts of Indian captives were dictated to a magistrate or some official, with hand to Bible, and in those days, folks were deeply religious. That was an era when a person's word meant something. Their stories that survive are true accounts.

Natives and settlers alike struggled not only for possession of the precious land but for *a way of life*. This land was *home* to the Indian, and he revered it like his mother. But when a frontier farmer stood on the land he worked, and he gazed out across his furrowed fields toward the horizon- all he could see was the future. I reckon there was a good reason for that. The frontier was wild and sublime, a thing of wonder, of mystery; beyond all else the very essence of which gripped the heart of a man- Red or White- to unleash his daring spirit.

For over half a century (1754-1795), it was a bloody struggle for dominance in the great Ohio River Valley. By the time Massy's story unfolded, the Native Americans- those displaced Americans who saw their lands being taken and their way of life crumbling before the inevitable White advance- had already experienced *layered* injustices, numerous broken treaties and swindles, as well as cruel White-perpetrated incidents that equaled Massy's torturous ordeal. As high a regard as Indians hold courage, they believed in avenging wrongs; not to have done so would have been against what they held true in their hearts.

In history, as in life, there are rights and wrongs on each side of a conflict, good and evil in every race of man. What is always tragic in history is that the good often suffer for the wrongs of the wicked.

The Treaty of Greenville in 1795 was the beginning of a new era- for the West and the entire nation. As for the Indians, their hearts would be ever-more heavy with sadness, as more and more treaties would be broken and more and more of their lands would be taken from them. For the Native Americans, this new era was the beginning of the end.

Massy Harbison was a nurturing and loving mother, raising a total of ten of the thirteen children to whom she gave life. Two boys had been killed by the Indians, and another died later in infancy. Massy passed away at the age of sixty-seven on December 9, 1837. Her grave is located in the new Freeport Cemetery.

Her husband John, stricken with wanderlust, wanted in their later years to sell the Mount Joy land and move westward, but Massy did not want to leave her children, most of whom resided in the Little Buffalo Creek area of Butler County. She always considered that region her home.

Massy Harbison in the autumn of her remarkable life

John's strong wanderlust ruptured all bonds, and in 1822, he left home supposedly to visit their daughter in Kentucky. It is believed he died in the vicinity of Cincinnati and is buried on an unknown site.

Before John's exit, he and Massy actually ended their marriage (a rare thing in those long-past days), and he gave their Mount Joy home to their son William. Bear in mind that in Massy's time women did not own property.

Perhaps, since Massy had seen the face of terror and met it with courage, afterward she never really feared anything again. And perhaps that lack of fear combined with her strong will got her into trouble within the bonds of her marriage. Men, in her era, believed that women should be wholly obedient creatures, even that there was something unnatural about a woman who wasn't ever afraid. And, after her ordeal, Massy was not afraid of much of anything– or anyone.

In 1825, the stalwart woman dictated an account of her harrowing experience, *A Narrative of the Sufferings of Massy Harbison from Indian Barbarity*. She then peddled the book from house to house, using the proceeds to support herself in her old age.

This author cannot say how much education Massy would have accumulated in her youth, but it could not have been much, certainly not past the grammar-school level. The language of her dictated account is not the language of a frontier woman; thus, we may assume that much of the language was that of Robert Scott, Esquire, to whom she communicated her story, and who gave it his seal of authenticity.

Massy and her younger children had stayed on at Mount Joy with the Harbison homestead's then-owner, her son William. However, William later sold the property and moved to New Castle, leaving Massy and her dependents penniless and homeless. William had asked his mother and the younger children to accompany him, but Massy would not leave the Buffalo Creek Area.

Never again having a home of her own, Massy Harbison spent the last years of her life moving from child to child, visiting her children and grandchildren. Her final sojourn was with her son Benjamin at his cabin in Freeport, where the three counties of Westmoreland, Butler, and Armstrong converge.

Today a historic marker designates the spot where this cabin sat on the corner of what is now Fourth Street and Mulberry Place, at this writing, the parking lot for Freeport Elementary School.

For more information about Massy Harbison, visit Drenda Gostkowski's web site at www.saxonburglocalhistory.com. Readers may email: drenda225@consolidated.net, or telephone her at 724-816-4913.

A learned and respected authority on Massy Harbison, Drenda Gostkowski is available for lectures. In 2005, she edited and republished Massy's 1825 book. For sale in a number of places as well as from the historian herself, the 2005 edition includes addendum with photographs, maps, and historic references uncovered by Gostkowski during her meticulous research.

"LOUISA MAY ALCOTT'S MAGIC INKSTAND"

"We all have our own life to pursue, our own kind of dream to be weaving, and we all have the power to make wishes come true- as long as we keep believing."

"Far away there in the sunshine are my highest aspirations. ... I can look up and see their beauty, believe in them, and try to follow where they lead."

"I'd have a stable full of Arabian steeds, rooms piled with books, and I'd write out of a magic inkstand, so that my works should be ... famous."
- Louisa May Alcott

Born on November 29, 1832, Louisa May Alcott was the second of four daughters of noted Transcendentalist Amos Bronson Alcott and Abigail May Alcott. In keeping with the fashion of the day, Louisa May's mother bestowed her maiden name on her daughters.

Though of New England parentage, Louisa, who shared her father's birthday, was born in Germantown, now part of Philadelphia. Germantown, by the bye, is one of Philadelphia's oldest settlements.

The Alcott family moved to Boston about 1835, where Louisa's father established an experimental institution called the Temple School. There, he joined the Transcendental Club, an intellectual circle.

Growing up in the Boston and rural Concord, Massachusetts area, Louisa was enveloped by one of the most noteworthy intellectual and literary movements of the first half of the nineteenth century- *Transcendentalism*, a philosophy that asserts the primacy of the spiritual and transcendental over the material and empirical. Simple translation: They believed the spiritual life transcends the material.

This New England coterie of writers and thinkers that originated in the 1830s fundamentally believed that people are born good, that they possess a power called intuition, and that they come closer to God through nature.

"Surely, dear father," Louisa told Bronson Alcott in the fall of 1855, "some good angel or elf dropped a talisman in your cradle that gave you force to walk [through] life in quiet sunshine whilst others groped in the dark."

Certainly, Louisa's father was idealistic, if impractical, about such matters as the support of his family. He taught in Connecticut, Pennsylvania, and Massachusetts, introducing art, music, physical education, and nature studies to his classes in an era when these subjects were not taught. Many parents did not understand this innovative man's ideals and methods of education, and thus withdrew their children from his schools, which is why the Alcotts moved so often.

Louisa's mother Abigail always believed in her visionary husband in spite of his eccentricities. In truth, we could go so far as to say that Abigail believed in Bronson even when it seemed the entire rest of the world did not. She wrote in her journal that she could never live without him.

Like her husband, she keenly felt the injustices of the world and worked ardently for various causes, helping the poor, working for women's rights, temperance, and abolition. Duty and charity were the principles that governed her life. To her children, Abigail was a saint, the "most splendid mother in the world!" Throughout her life, she devoted herself to her four daughters, continually encouraging their talents and providing them with practical rules by which to live.

Most of Bronson Alcott's fellowship of kindred spirits- Ralph Waldo Emerson, Henry David (originally David Henry) Thoreau, Margaret Fuller, and Nathaniel Hawthorne- were members of "The Club" in addition to being the leaders of an emerging *American* literature.

How fascinating must have been Louisa's visits, as a youngster, to Thoreau's cabin on Walden Pond, Ralph Waldo Emerson's library, and theatricals in the barn at Hillside (later Hawthorne's Wayside)! Though throughout her childhood and early adulthood she shared her family's poverty (i.e. their lack of *material* wealth), how fortunate for this future author to have tramped through the Concord woods with Thoreau, listening to his fanciful tales of woodland faeries! This author cannot help but further exclaim that coming of age rubbing shoulders with Thoreau, Emerson, and Hawthorne must have been infinitely inspirational!

Emerson was an advocate of the great Secret, also known as the Law of Attraction, the directive that like attracts like. He wrote "... the moment you decide that what you know is more important than what you have been taught to believe, you will have shifted gears in your quest for abundance. Success comes from within, not from without. The Secret," he said, "is the answer to all that has been, all that is, and all that will ever be."

Louisa often ventured into Emerson's remarkable library in search of new books- and wisdom. From the time she could read, she was a voracious reader, for books were always an integral part of her family's life. Reading was never a chore for this creative youngster but a thoroughly enjoyable pastime. To Louisa, the selection of each book was just as much of an adventure as the reading of the book, followed by the equally pleasurable discussion of the experience of each read with family and friends.

Like her character "Jo March" in her future bestseller *Little Women*, Louisa was a tomboy. "No boy could be my friend," she claimed, "till I had beaten him in a race."

And: "No girl if she refused to climb trees [and] leap fences ... ."

Louisa May Alcott's uncle, Samuel Joseph May (her mother's brother), a Unitarian minister and fellow member of the Transcendental Club, was one of the greatest social and educational reformers of the nineteenth century. He advocated and organized for fair rights for workers, women's rights, temperance, penal reform, education reform, better treatment of Native Americans, and abolition of slavery. Because he was so far ahead of mainstream acceptance of the policies for which he fought, he was often at odds with his ministerial colleagues, church members, and the public at large.

Absorbed by Utopian and educational experiments, Louisa's father, as previously mentioned, never really provided well for his family. It was a good thing he had a generous brother-in-law. Samuel May was second only to Ralph Waldo Emerson in his financial and sympathetic support of the Alcott family. Bronson Alcott admiringly dubbed May the "Lord's chore boy" for his unrelenting pursuit of human rights.

Louisa May Alcott would grow up to become both a staunch abolitionist and a purposeful feminist. Prior to the Civil War, the family would harbor a fugitive slave at Orchard House, their most permanent residence.

In 1840, after several setbacks with her father's school, Louisa's family moved to a cottage on two acres along the Sudbury River in Concord. There would be other moves. About three years hence, there was a brief interval with Bronson Alcott's Utopian Fruitlands Community. After its collapse, the family rented rooms, and finally relocated to a country estate in Concord they christened Orchard House (which we'll touch on presently) purchased with Louisa's mother's inheritance and assistance from close family friend Emerson.

Louisa later described those early years of her exceptional life in a newspaper sketch entitled "Transcendental Wild Oats," afterward published in the volume *Silver Pitchers* (1876) that relates the atypical experiences of her family during their experiment in "plain living and high thinking" at Fruitlands.

Principally educated at home by her father, Louisa devoured, like a hungry wolf, a smorgasbord of literary works. Charles Dickens was her favorite author, but she also admired the medieval adventure epics and novels of Sir Walter Scott. John Bunyan's Christian allegory *Pilgrim's Progress* was a family favorite that her father read aloud annually. Another beloved book, of Louisa's especially, was Charlotte Brontë's *Jane Eyre*.

Each of those works influenced Louisa's writings, and I can image the Alcott family gathered round their lively dining room table mealtimes, discussing literature, nature, women's rights, and other social reforms.

Coming of age in such a literary environment prompted the young Louisa to build her own castles in the sky, no different, I am certain, from those dreams of her autobiographical character Jo March in *Little Women*: "I'd have a stable full of Arabian steeds, rooms piled with books, and I'd write out of a magic inkstand, so that my works should be ... famous. I want to do something splendid before I go into my castle- something heroic or wonderful that won't be forgotten after I'm dead. I don't know what, but I'm on the watch for it and mean to astonish you all someday. I think I shall write books and get rich and famous." Indeed, she did.

For Louisa, writing was an early passion, for she was possessed of a vivid imagination. I suppose we could say that her writing began at the age of seven with her diary. Always imaginative in their fun, the four Alcott sisters wrote plays as youngsters, acting them out in the dining room to the delight of family and friends who watched from the adjoining parlor. Sometimes, even the family cats had roles- in costumes- so it certainly should not surprise readers that Louisa's early works were inspired by the melodrama of the theatre- and the Alcott girls' productions were *melodramatic*, to say the least. Louisa always preferred to play the "lurid" roles in these plays, the "villains, ghosts, bandits, and disdainful [and/or wicked] queens."

It was especially delightful to craft these dramas on winter evenings when the tempest winds howled, heaping the garden and orchard with big, ghostly drifts. Louisa struggled heroically against the difficulties of affectionate dialogue in her "love scenes." Thus, the young dramatist preferred tales of bandits and pirates, for such blackguards did not converse lovingly. She favored tragedies of earls and countesses whose conversation she loved to pepper with scraps of French and Italian- and a dozen other subjects she didn't know much about.

I daresay Alcott did not storm the ramparts of success overnight. Like most authors, hers was not an easy road to fame. Her way was paved with hard work, hard times, poverty, disappointments, and even tragedy. Louisa's tale reminds me of an old Irish saying that "Hard times breed hard people."

Due to her family's poverty, she began work at an early age taking whatever job she could find- as a domestic helper, seamstress, governess, occasional teacher, and writer. Never forget, readers, that Louisa and her female contemporaries were confronting a society that offered little opportunity to women seeking employment. This girl, however, was *determined*, as is evident in the words she expressed at this juncture of her life: "I will make a battering-ram of my head and [thrust] my way through this rough and tumble world."

For all the trying times, it was not all heartbreak and drudgery. Mostly, there was love- of her family- that was exceptionally strong and binding.

Louisa's unique beauty was her affecting dark eyes coupled with the liveliness of her expression. She talked incessantly and with vivacity; consequently, her close friends and family referred to her, with warm affection, as a "chatterbox." Though, years later, she would finally be persuaded to marry off the autobiographical Jo in *Little Women*, Alcott herself never married.

Louisa's first published piece was a poem entitled "Sunlight" that was printed in *Peterson's Magazine* in September 1851 under the pseudonym Flora Fairfield. Louisa was then not yet nineteen. Her story, "The Rival Painters, a Tale of Rome" was published less than a year later in the May 1852 edition of *The Olive Branch*, a family magazine.

The young writer was thrilled to see her name in print and to receive, in the post for her contribution, the grand sum of five dollars. She had long ago met that somewhat elusive lady named "Inspiration." She'd just encountered that other ofttimes elusive sprite "Lady Luck" on her life's path, and she was now a published author.

Royal castles, long-cached-away secret legacies, and romance, woven artfully into rags-to-riches tales, echo throughout these early stories. She continued to see her poems and stories published in a variety of newspapers and magazines, and in December 1854, she saw her first book published. *Flower Fables* was an anthology of tranquil, nature-inspired fairytales told originally to the daughter of close family friend and neighbor Ralph Waldo Emerson.

By the late 1850s, Alcott was earning money writing for the more high-status newspapers, such as the *Saturday Evening Gazette*, and by the early 1860s, she was elated to be published in the era's most prestigious literary magazine, *The Atlantic Monthly*.

Because the public ate up this type of book and constantly hungered for more, Louisa soon began writing what she referred to as "blood and thunder" tales for Frank Leslie's newspapers. Leslie was a publisher of what were popularly known as "penny dreadfuls," low-priced accounts chock full of villains, vice, victims and vindication.

Like Jo March in *Little Women*, Louisa cast her fertile imagination abroad to Europe, where her counts and countesses, heiresses, gypsies, and banditti took her readers on a magic-carpet ride to the truly exotic.

Lesser-known of her works are the passionate, fiery novels and stories she penned behind the veil of the pseudonym A. M. Barnard. These tales, such as *Pauline's Passion and Punishment*, were known in the Victorian era as "potboilers." If the writings she had submitted to Frank Leslie were chock full of adventures, the thrills in her potboilers were "shock-full." Her character Jo March in her future bestseller *Little Women* publishes several such stories but ultimately rejects them after being told that "good young girls should [not] see such things."

Be that as it may, Louisa's protagonists are willful young girls, relentless in their pursuits and steadfast in their aims, which often include revenge on those who humiliated or thwarted them. Her young-maiden characters are regularly blessed with an abundance of friends, some in high places, and woe betide the scoundrel spreader-of-scandal who could not support words of accusation with proof! Alcott's potboilers achieved immediate commercial success and remain highly readable yet today.

During the Civil War, Louisa served as a nurse at the Union Hotel Hospital in Georgetown, DC. Her memories of this episode of her life, basically her revised letters home, later found their way into her nostalgic book *Hospital Sketches* that also achieved commercial rewards.

Whilst satisfying her desire to do something for the war effort, during her nursing stint, Louisa contracted typhoid fever. Unfortunately, she was affected for the rest of her life with mercury poisoning (since mercury never leaves the system), the result of repeated calomel treatments for the typhoid.

Louisa May Alcott

After the war, in 1866, Alcott's "Moods" premiered in a magazine serialization. This is a story about obsession, showcasing a woman who was not suited for the Victorian role of marriage.

"I like danger," the heroine Rosamond tells the diabolical Philip Tempest, in the rather shocking-for-its-era tale, before she discovers his true nature. The rogue Tempest relentlessly pursues the coquettish Rosamond across the broad continent of Europe in a long, fatal love chase. In 1867, *Moods* was published as Alcott's first novel, but the critics were not kind to it, and even Alcott's publisher considered it "too sensational." Alcott would later revise *Moods* in 1882.

Despite the critics, the proficient Louisa was proving that she could earn money from her writing, and the dream of becoming a famous and successful author was not only possible– it was waiting to joyfully greet her around the next corner.

As I said, Louisa's success was hard-earned. She worked ceaselessly, with nary a day off, and always with eye and ear alerted to what the public wanted to read. I think she knew there was something that was trying to speak through her. "I *have* to write," she once said. She could no sooner quit writing than quit breathing. She was born to it, just as she was born to succeed.

The same year of *Moods'* book debut (1867), Louisa became the editor of a children's magazine *Merry Museum*. But it would be her next venture that would make her famous.

Born under the pressure of financial need, the thirty-five-year-old Alcott succumbed to requests from her publisher to "write a girls' book." It is always good to write about what you know. Thus, Louisa took pen in hand and settled down to write a novel virtually about her own life with her three sisters.

An immediate commercial and critical success, *Little Women* made its first appearance in 1868. It has since been the basis for subsequent editions to this day. Actually, the original *Little Women* was published in two volumes, the second of which was entitled *Good Wives*.

When Alcott first began the project, she wrote in her journal, "I plod away, though I don't really enjoy this sort of thing. Never liked girls or knew many, except my sisters, but our queer plays and experiences may prove interesting, though I doubt it." How wrong she was!

Set in a quiet, rural Massachusetts setting, *Little Women* unfolds during the American Civil War. Meg, Jo, Beth, and Amy March are reared in genteel poverty by their loving mother Marmee, whilst their father serves in the Union army.

The March girls, though sisters, are each unique, and they entertain themselves by producing plays and a weekly newspaper. They befriend their wealthy neighbor's grandson, the leading male protagonist, who falls hopelessly in love with Jo. In the end, however, he becomes engaged to Amy abroad; whilst Jo, who has gone to New York City to write, marries a German professor and scholar, and together, they found a school for boys.

The natural characterizations of the March girls and Jo's non-traditional marriage are delightful reading. As you might suspect, the book mirrors the Alcott family's interest in Transcendentalism in addition to their keen beliefs in social reform, including women's rights.

Little Women not only made Alcott famous- it made her wealthy. Her childhood dream had come to pass! Louisa May Alcott was now a professional author, and one who could earn a good living from her pen. I love the L.M. Alcott quote I uncovered while engaged in the writing of this Chronicle: "Resolve to take Fate by the throat and shake a living out of her!" Amen.

Over the long years, *Little Women* has been filmed several times. I strongly suggest that anyone who has not read this wonderful classic do so, in addition to viewing the movie(s). The 1933 version starred Katherine Hepburn as Jo. The 1949 version starred Elizabeth Taylor, Janet Leigh, Mary Astor, June Allyson, and Margaret O'Brien, to mention a few of its stellar cast.

My personal favorite is the 1994 adaptation with Winona Ryder, Gabriel Byrne, and Susan Sarandon. The scenery in this holiday version is breathtakingly beautiful, especially the snow-blanketed winter scenes.

An Old-Fashioned Girl made its delightful entrance onto the American literary scene in 1870, followed by *Little Men* in 1871. Then came *Eight Cousins* (1875), *Rose in Bloom* (1876), *Under the Lilacs* (1878), and *Jo's Boys* (1882).

Louisa May Alcott not only realized her dream, she became one of the most celebrated authors of the nineteenth century. However, none other of her works matched the huge success of *Little Women*.

Little Men picked up and continued Jo's story with her professor husband, and reflected the educational ideals of Louisa May Alcott's father- that he was never able to communicate effectively in writing.

Little Women was written at Orchard House, the Alcott home in Concord. This, as I said, was the Alcott's most permanent, as well as most beloved, residence (1858-1877). Louisa's father christened the place "Orchard House" due to its apple orchards. Likely that facet of the estate appealed to Mr. Alcott who considered apples the most perfect food.

Orchard House purred with love and learning, and it was there, in her bedchamber between two large windows, on a half-moon-shaped shelf-desk built especially for her by her father, where Louisa May Alcott penned her classic novel. Her father also built a bookcase in her room, where she kept her favorite books- dear friends that she visited and revisited often.

Louisa always had a room of her own, due to her often turbulent emotions and her vivid, romantic imagination that demanded solitude for writing. Louisa's artist-sister May (*Little Women's* "Amy") painted a panel of calla lilies in the budding young author's room near her desk, and over the chamber's fireplace, she painted for her writer-sister the charming image of a wise, old owl.

Louisa set her *Little Women* in Orchard House, and since there have been very few changes to the place, walking through this house-museum today is "like walking through the book," an utterly enchanting experience, to say the least.

Louisa nursed her mother in that saintly lady's final years, writing all the while. When Louisa's sister May died of complications of childbirth, the dying woman assigned guardianship of her child to Louisa. The baby, named for her aunt, was also given the same nickname, "Lulu." The author also adopted her nephew, John Sewell Pratt, who later changed his surname to Alcott.

But a few words about Louisa's youngest sister May: While Louisa was forever the tomboy, May was ultra-feminine. Louisa had dramatic brunette coloring, and May was the blue-eyed, golden girl.

"She is so graceful and pretty and loves beauty so much," Louisa wrote of May in a letter to their sister Anna in 1854, "it is hard for her to be poor and wear other people's ugly things. I hope I shall see the dear child in silk and lace with plenty of pictures and 'bottles of cream,' Europe, and all the things she longs for."

Like Amy in *Little Women*, May had a true talent for drawing and painting. She studied art in Boston and dreamed of going to Europe. It was Louisa's success with *Little Women* in 1868 that finally got her there. May made three crossings, studying art in London, Paris, and Rome. Though the sisters were quite different from one another, Louisa and May shared an artistic nature that expressed itself in ambition, willfulness, and in a certain competitive spirit. When the Paris Salon accepted one of May's still-life paintings in 1877, she wrote in a telling missive, "Who would have imagined such good fortune and so strong proof that Lu does not monopolize the Alcott talent. Ha Ha, sister, this is the first feather plucked from your cap!"

In 1878, May married a Swiss businessman and musician, and the couple settled in Meudon, a charming, picturesque Paris environ, where they lived an idyllic life enveloped by music, art, and love- until her untimely and tragic death the following year, six weeks after her baby was born. May's death, a bolt from the blue, was a shock to the entire family.

To return to the core of our story, Louisa had been ill ever since her Civil War nursing experience. With time, however, she grew increasingly worse. She moved into Boston to be near her doctors, hired assistants to help her with the care of her niece, and wrote *Jo's Boys* that tidily details the fates of her most popular characters. It was in this final book in which Alcott incorporated her strongest feminist sentiments.

Prior to her passing in March 1888, as her father evermore hoped and wished, Louisa May Alcott had most certainly achieved her place in the "estimation of society."

Though *Moods* was published as Alcott's "first novel," in actuality, her first novel was written- penned in her own hand- in 1849, when she was but seventeen.

The Inheritance, which shares similarities with Alcott's best-known work, was unpublished until 1997. Whether the author herself ever attempted to have it published, we likely will never know. The one thing we do know is that she felt the work important enough to write and paste upon the cover of the handwritten manuscript, "My first novel ... ."

Passed down to Alcott's heirs, the manuscript was loaned to Orchard House, the Alcott family home in Concord, now a museum. The treasure remained there until 1974, when it was deposited at Harvard University, catalogued, stored in their archives, and virtually forgotten until "discovered" by researchers in the summer of 1988 and later published for the first time nearly a century and a half after the teenage Miss Alcott had set it aside.

I do not think I would be exaggerating to state that *The Inheritance* was the springboard for what became the truly remarkable career of an unforgettable author.

Though she is best known for her writings, Louisa May Alcott, lest we forget, was also a huge supporter of reform movements- antislavery, temperance, and women's rights, including suffrage.

Due to her worsening illness, Louisa eventually retired to a rest home. On March 4, 1888, she visited her beloved father on his death bed. A few hours after he expired, she returned to quietly pass away in her sleep on March 6- indeed, a providential conclusion, since father and daughter shared the same birthday, and were of the same mind and heart in regard to so many things, especially human rights.

"Love," the brilliant writer pronounced, "is the only thing we can carry with us when we go- and it makes the end so much easier."

A joint funeral was held, and both father and daughter were interred in the family plot at Sleepy Hollow Cemetery, Concord.

Hailed during her epoch as the "Children's Friend," Louisa May Alcott is today considered one of the great women of American letters. Her books about young people and for young people are her legacy, to be read and enjoyed for generations to come.

Was Ms. Alcott's inkstand truly magical? It certainly contained the right ingredients for producing magic. In keeping with the great *Secret* of life (a.k.a the "Law of Attraction" and the "Law of Love"), Ms. Alcott asked, believed, and received, manifesting her beautiful dreams into beautiful realities.

"We all have our own life to pursue," Louisa once penned from her magic inkstand, "our own kind of dream to be weaving, and we all have the power to make wishes come true- as long as we keep believing."

"ZANE GREY ... COWBOY SECRETS"

"The man has always lived in a land of make-believe."
- Dolly Grey in regard to her husband

Most of us live in a world filled with responsibilities, commitments, everyday tasks and chores. At least some of the time, we have our feet planted on terra firma- even those of us in the creative arts. Albeit authors of fiction explore a make-believe realm of life, Zane Grey, for a great deal of his existence, dwelled in the fantasy world of his books, his avocations, and his unconventional relationships. Grey was more than just a dreamer- he was the consummate dream weaver with the heart of a maverick.

In *County Chronicles III*, in the segment about Tom Mix, I mentioned in passing that Zane Grey too was Pennsylvania-born. Allow me to explain. Zane Grey was not *literally* born within the perimeters of Pennsylvania; however, he was *literary*-born of our great commonwealth, for it was in Lackawaxen, Pennsylvania, Pike County, where this prolific writer's career took root. His Pennsylvania years gave birth to the writer Zane Grey- to his genesis and his genius as an author.

Grey attended the University of Pennsylvania, met his wife in Pennsylvania, relinquished his dentistry career for a writing career in Pennsylvania, and was laid to rest in Pennsylvania. His intense love of nature flourished and matured amidst the rustic beauty of our Pennsylvania wilds.

All good stories are best spun from the beginning, so let us back up to that point.

The future rider of the purple sage was born Pearl Zane Gray on January 31, 1872, the fourth child to Lewis M. Gray, a dentist, and Alice "Allie" Josephine Zane Gray, in Zanesville, Ohio. The town was founded by a maternal ancestor, Ebenezer Zane, a Revolutionary War patriot. Zane's father would later change the family surname from "Gray" to "Grey"; and Zane would drop his feminine first name to go simply by "Zane," an appellation at once distinctive, masculine, and authorial sounding.

Pearl Gray was a wayward youth who, due to his feminine *prénom*, often engaged in fisticuffs. During these many fights, Pearl hurled himself into combat with such aggression and ferocity that his opponents always met with injuries. His father answered these violent brawls with severe beatings that never deterred Pearl's fighting but only served to fan the uncontrollable fire that burned within the youth.

Years later, Zane Grey recalled, "I had many a poignant acquaintance with the apple switch." Some of those beatings were harsh and what this author would call abusive.

Zane also recalled how he and some of his young pals constructed a pirate's hideout, and there he penned, on scraps of wallpaper, a short narrative entitled "Jim of the Cave." When his father discovered the children's retreat and Pearl's story, he angrily tossed his son's first writing endeavor into the hungry flames of the campfire and commenced to whip the boy more harshly than ever he had.

In truth, Lewis Gray was an irascible, antisocial man who could not abide in his son any deviation from what he perceived "correct" conduct. However, what he succeeded in creating was an equally irascible opponent. Years later, on the day that Lewis passed away, in July of 1905, Zane was living in Lackawaxen, Pennsylvania. The future best-selling author had begun a journal that day in which he described (much like a scene from one of his yet-to-come novels) an approaching thunderstorm:

"Dark and forbidding came the fast-scudding broken clouds." His second entry read: "My father died today."

On the morrow, Zane added: "My thoughts go back to the days I climbed the hills with my father when I was a lad eager and gay, with no thought of tomorrow, no understanding of the sadness of human life. And [now] he is gone, I shall never see him again. Somewhere in the darkness and silence, alone, stone-cold, he lies. If only I might have done more."

There is an old saying that one does not become the person he/she is destined to be until after his/her parents are gone. For Zane, it would take his father's death to end the force of his influence, though heredity's long arm always seemed to keep its firm grip on him.

Pearl's mother counterpoised the father's personality, for she was a sweet, gentle woman, loving, nurturing and understanding, who, I think, later in time strongly influenced his choice of wife.

To compensate for his inability to establish a bond with his father, Pearl found himself a father substitute. When the young loner discovered some local boys hurling rocks and taunting an old man for his raggedy appearance, he sprang to the elderly fellow's defense, resulting in one of his most violent fights. In their meeting that followed, Pearl fastened his gaze on the old man's "weary sad eyes" and mild, soft-spoken demeanor, a striking contrast from his father's "piercing gray eyes." The astute future writer had found a kindred spirit.

This significant figure in Pearl's life carried the unusual moniker of "Old Muddy Miser." Muddy loved to fish, and he heartily approved of Pearl's penchant for fishing- that was much more than a pastime to either of them. For Muddy Miser, fishing was a way of life.

Muddy also encouraged Pearl's writing. From his formative years spent with his free-spirited mentor, Pearl's lifelong avocation and vocation- as well as his offbeat ways- took firm root.

Muddy's old face was like a withered apple. He was bent and frail, ofttimes trembling, and his voice was like a wailing of the wind across the flatlands. Muddy spouted philosophically on the rewards of an unconventional life, advice that the lonely youngster took to the deepest reaches of his poetic soul. Pearl never asked Muddy about his past, figuring it was none of his business. Despite severe warnings by his father to steer clear of Miser- "If you don't learn to like work and study, that's where you'll wind up, like Old Muddy Miser"- Pearl spent approximately five influential years in the near-constant company of the unique old fellow. In essence, Muddy gave Pearl Gray a wondrous gift. He taught him to follow his heart and trust that he would "become somebody someday."

Although he was a dreamer, a condition that would follow him throughout his life, and not much of a student, Pearl was an avid reader who stoked his burning imagination with action-packed adventure stories, such as *Robinson Crusoe* and the *Leatherstocking Tales,* as well as all the dime novels with Buffalo Bill and Deadwood Dick he could devour. Little did he realize at the time how dominant these works would become in his future life as a best-selling author!

Another passion the naturally athletic youngster indulged and developed was baseball. In fact, after Lewis Gray's financial situation took a dive, baseball would hurl his son Pearl into college on a full scholarship, and it would take the wayward boy away from the domineering, negative reaches of his father.

Due to Lewis' failing dentistry business, Pearl dropped out of high school and began working with his father to help out at home. There was a hushed-up scandal entangled with Lewis' loss of business, a humiliation that either was related to a bad financial investment, a woman, or both. To this day, the details are veiled in secrecy, after which Mr. Gray altered the spelling of the family surname, changing it to "Grey." His severe monetary setback in 1889 and the resulting loss of business also prompted Lewis, out of sheer embarrassment, to relocate his family to Columbus, Ohio.

Pearl shed real tears as he looked out the rain-streaked window of the train that carried him and his family away from Zanesville. Utmost in his heart was his parting from Muddy Miser. He felt completely alone in the world, and that sadness nearly overwhelmed him. It also frightened him.

In Columbus, Lewis struggled to re-establish his dentistry practice, with his son Pearl's apathetic assistance. The teenage Pearl, who from his father had learned tooth extraction, made rural house calls as an unlicensed dentist- that is, until the state intervened, whilst his brother Romer helped out at home by driving a delivery wagon. Those were tough times at the Grey household, and Pearl took on a second job as a part-time usher in a movie theater. Summers, he played baseball for the Columbus Capitols with aspirations of becoming a major leaguer.

Through these rough years, baseball served as Pearl's outlet. In years to come, the author Zane Grey would always have his outlets! And as it was with nearly everything he did and would do in his life, Pearl played the sport with such gusto and innate talent, he was singled out by baseball scouts, receiving several college offers.

Both Pearl and his brother Romer were extremely athletic boys, enthusiastic baseball players, and skilled fishermen. Like his brother, Romer also attracted the attention of the scouts and went on to have a brief pro-baseball career. Pearl Grey chose a scholarship to the University of Pennsylvania.

By today's standards, his was a rather unheard-of award in light of the fact that young Pearl had not completed his high school education. Nevertheless, he had been apprenticed in dentistry by his father, which, back in Lewis' day, had been more a trade than a profession. Things had changed by the time Pearl came of age at the turn of the last century. Though, as a high school student, he had worked with hands-on experience and training alongside his dentist father, according to the law, he had to acquire a license to legally practice dentistry. But the years he had apprenticed with Lewis served him well, for Pearl Zane Grey was offered a full ride to the University of Pennsylvania's school of dentistry.

From its beginnings, one of the top schools of dentistry in the nation, Penn's School of Dental Medicine can boast a brilliant history of forging precedents, research, and patient care. It was a lucky break for Pearl Grey, and he grabbed it.

When he arrived at Penn, Pearl had to prove himself worthy of his scholarship before *officially* receiving it. He rose to the occasion by pitching against the Riverton ball club, pitching five no-run innings and hitting a double in the tenth that contributed to the Penn victory.

The Ivy League was highly competitive, creating an excellent training ground for future pro-baseball players. Pearl was an outstanding hitter as well as a skilled pitcher who relied on a sharply dropping curveball. Unfortunately, when the distance from the pitcher's mound to the plate was lengthened by ten feet in 1894 (primarily to reduce the dominance of Cy Young's pitching excellence), the effectiveness of the young Grey's "hurling" skills suffered, and he was re-positioned to the outfield. It mattered little. From the moment of his first proving game, the short, wiry baseball player remained a campus hero the duration of his Penn years, chiefly on the strength of his timely hitting.

During those college years, Pearl joined the Sigma Nu Fraternity. He was, however, an indifferent scholar, repeating the habit he had set during his earlier school years of achieving a minimum average. When not in class, Pearl spent his time at baseball, pool, and creative writing, especially poetry. His poetic nature and his teetotaling set him apart from his mates- a condition not unfamiliar to him.

His fundamentalist upbringing burned in his soul a lifelong distaste for alcohol and tobacco, but not for the temptations of the opposite sex, of which he had become tantalizingly aware early in his life, as a young boy. In high school, he had enjoyed his first crushes, parties and dances with flirting, stolen kisses and secret embraces. The thing is, Pearl Zane Grey was never just *fond* of anything in his life. He loved what he loved with a consuming passion, and from puberty, he developed a passion for women, becoming a devilish womanizer.

At sixteen, he had been arrested in a brothel; and during a summer college break, while playing baseball in Delphos, Ohio, Grey was charged with a paternity suit involving a belle of that city. He quietly settled out of court.

Pearl's father paid the $133.40 cost, and the young Casanova resumed playing baseball that summer in Delphos, managing to conceal the episode from Penn when he returned there in the fall. Pursuing a multitude of pretty maidens at a time served as a vent for the dark moods that plagued him for most of his life. Early on, women became a permanent passion.

Pearl debated whether to become a professional baseball player, a writer, or a dentist. Baseball and writing topped his short list, but dentistry, he unhappily concluded, could earn him a living. It was, he knew, the *practical* choice.

Remember, readers, that professional athletes in those long-past days did not command the lofty salaries they do today, and since a pro does not play ball for that many years, sports, in those days, was a *risky* career choice.

Pearl never welcomed the idea of practicing dentistry. In fact, the mere thought of doing that for the rest of his life cast him into a bottomless well of depression. Thus, he compromised with himself, planning to start out life as a dentist and write in his free time, with the hopes of becoming a professional writer and breaking out of the confines of a dental practice.

In the meantime, he played college baseball, even going on to play, for a few years, minor league ball with a team in Newark, New Jersey, as well as with the Orange Athletic Club. Meanwhile, Pearl's brother, Romer Carl "Reddy" Grey (known to family and friends as "R. C."), played baseball in the minor leagues and in one major league game, in 1903, for the Pittsburg(h) Pirates.

Pearl Zane Grey graduated from Penn on June 11, 1896, after which he played baseball, practicing his apathetic dentistry with a dentist in Newark, until he obtained the approval to practice in the state of New York by getting the required certification.

Three years after graduation, Grey established his own dental practice in New York City, under the name of Dr. Zane Grey. He would never again use the *prénom* Pearl ... that is, not openly.

He chose New York for its money-making opportunities, and because it was close to publishers. To offset the tedium of his work, he spent his evenings writing. These were, again for Zane, trying times, times of financial struggle, and he became increasingly indifferent to his practice. As he was a born outdoorsman and athlete, Grey was a natural writer, but his early literary endeavors were unnaturally stiff and grammatically weak. Whenever possible, he happily pulled on the baseball togs of the Orange Athletic Club, a lineup of former collegiate players, said to be one of the best amateur teams in the country.

During his years as a New York dentist, he longed to escape the noisy, dirty, crowded city and often took camping trips to Lackawaxen, Pennsylvania, with his brother R. C., who had now become a reluctant dentist himself.

The upper Delaware River area was a popular summer attraction for city dwellers. For Zane, it was merely a short ferry boat ride from New York City to Hoboken, after which he hopped the train, reading or napping for the hour's time it took to get to Lackawaxen.

It felt good to reconnect in this way with his brother. Camping out was not only therapeutic and enjoyable, it was affordable. The pair enjoyed fishing together in the sparkling, sun-splashed river, relaxing on its lush, wooded banks and soaking up the rustically beautiful Pennsylvania scenery and serenity.

R.C. and Zane were both cognizant of the fact that baseball was a young man's game, that their days as players were limited and fast dwindling. The Pennsylvania wilds- the fresh air, the spiritual uplift nature always provided him, and the escape from the work he did not like- soothed Zane like nothing else ever had; and it was here, whilst canoeing in Lackawaxen, where he met his future wife.

Lina Roth, better known as "Dolly," was but seventeen, a buxom brunette who was fetchingly bonnie, when they had a chance meeting at the Lackawaxen Railroad Station in the late summer of 1900. Dolly came from a family of physicians and was studying to be a schoolteacher when she first encountered the dashing Zane Grey.

The enamored couple had a passionate five-year courtship, intense, as you might suspect with Zane. They quarreled frequently, and he suffered bouts of depression, anger, and severe mood swings. In his words, penned years later, his moods were like "... a hyena lying in ambush- that is my black spell! I conquered one mood only to fall prey to the next ... I wandered about like a lost soul or a man who was conscious of imminent death."

I know what you must be thinking, readers, so I will attempt to respond to your reflection now. During his courtship with Dolly, Grey was still seeing previous girlfriends. He warned her frankly and with no bones about it: "... I love to be free. I cannot change my spots, Dolly. The ordinary man is satisfied with a moderate income, a home, wife, children, and all that ... but I am a million miles from being that kind of man, and no amount of trying will ever do any good." He thought he'd better add to that: "I shall never lose the spirit of my interest in women."

Though over the long years Dolly often doubted her power over Zane, she knew she could help to make him a great writer. "My ambition is for *you*," she wrote him during their courtship, "and I shall extend all my energy and all the power I possess to make you a great man."

Once they married in 1905, Dolly gave up her teaching career for the "higher ambition" of helping Zane realize his dreams, and they moved to a rustic farmhouse in Lackawaxen (that had been owned by the Delaware and Hudson Canal Company), with Grey's mother, sister and brother Ellsworth joining them after Zane's father Lewis' passing. Since the farmhouse was located on the point at the confluence of the Delaware and Lackawaxen rivers, Zane and Dolly christened it "Cottage Point."

The house was next door to Zane's brother "R.C."/Romer's residence, built by Romer in 1906. The Zane Greys moved into that house in 1912. Zane and Dolly purchased Romer's house in 1914, enlarging it in 1915 and 1916. This was the Lackawaxen house destined in future years to become the Zane Grey Museum.

Lina "Dolly" Roth Grey circa 1906
Courtesy the National Park Service

Grey happily gave up his dental practice to devote full time to his literary pursuits. Initially, Dolly's inheritance provided the financial cushion to make Zane's dream of becoming a successful author real.

Though he was thirty when he decided to become a professional writer and thirty-three when he married, Grey thought of himself as a *young* man, and he harbored intense longings for adventure and excitement. High on his list of distractions- as you must have guessed- was women. Zane ever relished the company of beautiful young women.

Over the next two decades, while his wife managed his career and reared their three children (Romer, Betty, and Loren), Grey often spent months away from his family, fishing, writing, and enjoying the company of his numerous mistresses.

Monogamy was totally against his orientation. He was often in love with more than one person at a time and in different ways. Jealous at first, Dolly came to look upon Zane's errant behavior with other women as a handicap rather than a choice he made. She may have had a valid point.

As soon as I read Grey biographer Thomas H. Pauly's very readable book *Zane Grey, His Life, His Adventures, His Women*, the word "bipolar" (though it was not mentioned) sprang to mind. Zane Grey's soaring highs and deep, dark lows, as well as other of his traits prompt me to speculate if he may have been afflicted with that or a similar disorder. Bear in mind that a century ago, such things were not discussed openly. Mind too, readers, this is only my query, *nothing more*. I wonder if Grey's behavior and his harem of mistresses were rooted more in some sort of disorder and/or insecurity than in sexual appetite. Insecurity seems to have been one of the demons that never stopped torturing Pearl Zane Gray/Grey.

Moreover, Zane's father, Lewis, had displayed the same type of highs and lows. So dark were his blue moods that his family no longer resided with him prior to his death in 1905. Perhaps whatever Zane's issues were, they were inherited.

This author always says no one is free who has ancestors, and as a chronicler of the past, I try never to judge the historical figures about whom I write. Most of us are neither lily-white nor sinister black but rather varying shades of grey- i.e. *human*. If, in his tangled life, Zane had an inherent "dis-ease"- a "chemical imbalance" is today's catch phrase- it is unfortunate there was next to nothing in his era to help him control it. But then, on the other hand, if he hadn't been possessed of his unique disposition, his ultra-free-spirited nature, would he have left behind such a rich legacy? Howbeit, he was lucky to have Dolly.

Dolly began, from their beginnings, to create the Zane Grey the reading public came to know. And *that*, I believe, coupled with her abundance of love for the man, is the reason she stayed with him irrespective of his womanizing. Dolly took it upon herself, in actuality from the time they had first met, to create the nation's best-selling/most popular author. She succeeded in doing just that, and in no way was she going to give that up- ever.

Zane Grey was largely Dolly's creation, and she enjoyed being Mrs. Zane Grey. After all, she had invested her money, her time, her talent, and most of all, her emotions in her husband. She put up with the women, and as a result, their marriage survived as an open marriage. In time, Dolly acted as mediator between Zane's mistresses when feelings were hurt, even patching up relationships between her husband and his women.

After a lengthy chat with Dorothy Moon, the historian at the Zane Grey Museum at Lackawaxen, I realized another reason for Dolly's compliance was a sign of the times in which the Greys lived. Dolly was reared as a Victorian woman; thus, divorce was out of the question. And lest we forget: Men in the lofty echelon to which Grey's success propelled him often took mistresses.

In addition to being Zane's wife, best friend, editor, business partner, business manager, and confidante, Dolly, though she was eleven years younger than her husband, frequently "mothered" him. She always said that Zane was her most difficult child. Men often choose wives who are like their mothers. Grey's tremendous success as a writer was a true case of "Behind every successful man there is a woman."

I have read that that woman is a *good* woman, a *great* woman, a *strong* woman- or *a woman who knows when to keep silent.* I can imagine that it was painfully difficult, throughout their enduring marriage, to hold her tongue, but the ever-patient Dolly did learn rather quickly to keep silent about those things she knew she could not change.

Throughout their life together, Zane valued Dolly's management of his career and their family, and he treasured her solid emotional support. Dolly was always there to assure Zane Grey the writer. She had good business sense, and her handling of all his contract negotiations with agents, publishers, and movie studios brought them an abundance of wealth. All his income, Grey split right down the middle with Dolly, with her share covering the household expenses.

She typed his hand-written manuscripts, edited them, and made countless suggestions to him about his work. Their considerable correspondence over the long years, most of which survives today, is clearly evidence of his abiding love for his Dolly, despite his countless indiscretions and personal emotional turmoil.

Besides keeping the snarling dogs of his emotions in check, the adventurous excursions with beautiful women provided inspiration for his novels. He mused through his pen: "I like to climb mountains with a girl, and picture her on mossy stones, in lichen-covered cliffs, or rugged trunk of twisted pine or oak ... . The flush of cheek, the flash of eye, the peal of real laughter, the waving of hair, the action, the reality, the charm- these I feel with all the power there is in me. ... *At the bottom of all the great stories lies the power of a woman.*"

With competitive feeling, when his first child was born (a son, whom he named Romer after his favorite brother), he wrote: "My boy was nine months old yesterday. He is beautiful, sturdy, unusually strong and active, a picture of health and wonderful life ... . Day by day, I learn wisdom from this baby, and something else I cannot name."

In 1918, the Greys relocated from Pennsylvania to California, spurred by the magnificent memories of their Western honeymoon that had started the Western-novel ball rolling.

In 1920, the couple purchased a prominent mansion in Altadena, on East Mariposa Street known locally as "Millionaires' Row." Majestically beautiful in the Mediterranean style, the sumptuous manse had been built in 1907 by Chicago business machine manufacturer Arthur Herbert Woodward as the first fireproof home ever constructed in Altadena. Woodward's wife Edith had survived a devastating (1903) fire that resulted in the concrete and steel-reinforced edifice.

Over the years, Grey's early stilted style improved immensely. His gradual achievement of more fluid, descriptive writing was the result of Dolly's proofing and stylistic corrections, as well as numerous writing guides– and the sheer amount of writing he did. It should be noted that, from the onset, vivid description was the strongest aspect of Zane Grey's writing, and as he noted in his diary, "A cunning writer will avail himself of images likely to be stored in the minds of his readers."

When his first magazine article, "A Day on the Delaware," a human-interest piece about a fishing expedition with his brother R. C. in Lackawaxen, was published in 1902, Grey was still practicing dentistry. When the story appeared in the May issue of *Recreation*, Zane was so thrilled, though he had reaped but ten bucks for the article, he offered reprints to his patients in his waiting room.

By that time, he had given up baseball, met Dolly, and discovered he had what it takes to become a published writer. In truth, he desperately needed a writing career to escape the harshness of his life and his nagging demons. "Realism," he said, "is death to me. I cannot stand life as it is."

After having read Owen Wister's great Western novel *The Virginian* and making note of its structure and style, Grey decided to try his hand at a full-length story. His first novel, *Betty Zane*, penned in 1903, dramatized the heroism of his ancestor who saved Fort Henry.

During the Revolutionary War, an Indian attack on September 12, 1782, had exhausted the fort's stock of gunpowder. The brave, sixteen-year-old Betty actually saved the day by running through a barrage of gunfire to return with a new supply.

Fort Henry was located in the Ohio River Valley, just over the Pennsylvania border, where the town of Wheeling, West Virginia, is now located.

After Indian sign had been discovered and the alarm had been raised, the inhabitants of the locality had hurriedly crowded into the adjacent Fort Henry, but they had not had the time to secure a supply of gun powder from the magazine in Colonel Ebenezer Zane's blockhouse some fifty yards distant.

Betty volunteered to fetch powder from her brother's cabin, and waving aside objections that a man could run faster, she uttered a valiant declaration that went something like this: "You have not one man to spare. A woman won't be missed in the fort's defense– 'tis better a maid than a man should die." Then she made a mad dash for her brother's cabin, much to the amazement of the now-attacking Indians, who reportedly shouted "Squaw! Squaw," and did not fire.

However, when she reappeared at the door of the log dwelling with a supply of gunpowder, they opened up with a deadly barrage, and though the bullets ripped through Betty's clothing, by a miracle of God, none struck her body, and she made it back inside the safety of Fort Henry with the saving powder.

Hunched over a table in his dingy dentist's office late at night, *Betty Zane* had been a torment to write over the fall and winter of 1902-03. When publishers rejected it, Zane sank into deep despair. Writing about his famous ancestors whose lives had been ever so much more eventful and satisfying than his own (then) *bleak* life, *Betty Zane* had been the unhappy dentist's escape.

Dolly and his brother helped him to shake off the darkness and self-publish the book with funds from either Dolly's inheritance or brother R.C.'s wealthy girlfriend Reba Smith.

The coal mines Reba's family owned in Blairsville, Pennsylvania, furnished her ample monies, and when R.C. married her, he never had to work again. Likely, it was Reba's money that funded the publishing of *Betty Zane,* because that Christmas Zane presented her with a special autographed copy. Thus, in a variety of ways, did Pennsylvania give birth to Zane Grey's first novel– *and to his extraordinary literary career.*

Before we continue on with Zane's zesty biographical sketch, let me say that his historical figure Betty Zane was in no way the conventional pioneer woman of her era. Betty was a colorful variant. Intent upon having her own way– and God help anyone who attempted to restrain her!– Zane's Betty was head-strong, bold and daring, a good shot and an accomplished rider, who liked to fish, and could skillfully maneuver her own canoe. Though she hailed from Philadelphia, the comely lass favored her life on the frontier because it allowed her to be the independent person she longed to be.

I am in accord with biographer Pauly's compelling account that states that much of Betty was patterned after Dolly, whom Zane was courting at the time he penned *Betty Zane.*

Dolly delighted in their Lackawaxen getaways, thrilling to the woods, the canoeing, even the fishing. From the start of their lasting relationship, the pair were not just lovers but companions- best friends- which was the heart of their success as a couple.

It had been Dolly's idea to honeymoon in the West, and her money financed the trip. That first-time Western experience awed Zane with its scenic splendor, and he endeavored to capture and file away in his writer's soul everything he saw, heard, felt ... and dreamed.

However, he knew he lacked experiences he would need to render his novels more credible; so after attending a lecture in New York in 1907 by C.T. "Buffalo" Jones, famed Western hunter and guide, Grey arranged for a mountain-lion hunt to the north rim of the Grand Canyon. Here began writers' habits that he employed for the rest of his career. He took along a camera, documenting his trips, capturing images, memories, and the veracity of his wild adventures. He also initiated the lifelong habit of taking copious notes- of scenery, experiences, the locals, even of local slang and dialogue.

This trip as well as the next proved perilous and arduous to the tenderfoot. Be that as it may, Grey learned from his rough compatriot adventurers, soon gaining a measure of confidence and the authenticity to write convincingly about the American West.

Zane Grey loved the West, I think, because it was much like himself with its irascible tempers, its scorching heat and parching thirst, its freezing blizzards and suddenly warming Chinooks. The West he experienced was wild, free, and untamable- like Zane Grey himself.

He wrote: "Surely, of all the gifts that have come to me from contact with the West, this one of sheer love of wildness, beauty, color grandeur, has been the greatest, the most significant for my work."

Through his wife Dolly, Zane had found the one mistress he would never grow tired of- the great American West.

Grey poured his skills and practical knowledge into *The Last of the Plainsmen* in 1909 that recorded the true life adventures of Buffalo Jones. He glowed with high hopes that the work would spark his career as a professional writer. Instead, it too was rejected several times, with the coup de grâce delivered by Harper and Brothers' editor Ripley Hitchcock in a devastating tête-à-tête declaration, "I do not see anything in this to convince me you can write either narrative or fiction."

Needless to say, Grey was beside himself, writing during that dark period in his journal, "I don't know which way to turn. I cannot decide what to write next. That which I desire to write does not seem to be what the editors want. ... I am full of stories and zeal and fire ... yet I am inhibited by doubt, by fear that my feeling for life is false."

The Last of the Plainsmen was later published by Outing, lifting a bit of Grey's gloom and providing some satisfaction. Fearful of attacking a Western novel, he spent the next several months writing magazine articles, as well as juvenile works.

In my opinion- and it is only that- Grey did not yet possess enough confidence in his own abilities as a writer. He took that editor's words to heart. With time, however, he would learn the great Secret of life: The real magic is believing in yourself. For others to accept his work and see merit in it, Grey would first have to believe in himself.

With the birth of his first child on the horizon, Zane began to feel a sense of urgency to produce his first Western novel. He took pen in hand and set about writing what *he* wanted to write, what burned inside him. Within four months, he completed *The Heritage of the Desert* (1910). With true grit then he faced that same editor who had told him he could not write.

Soon, *Heritage* was flying off the shelves to jumpstart Zane Grey's enduring career as an author of popular novels about the Old West and the behavior of men in its unforgiving elemental conditions.

Two years hence, Grey cranked out his most popular book, *Riders of the Purple Sage* (1912), the first of his books to make the best-seller list, that turned out to be an all-time bestseller and one of the most successful Western novels of all time.

Do you believe this one too was rejected by the foreboding editor Ripley Hitchcock? Despite that, by this time, Grey had acquired- thanks in large part to Dolly- that needed confidence in his work. He walked out of Hitchcock's office and hand-carried his manuscript directly to the publishing house's vice-president, who accepted it. After that, Harper and Brothers readily agreed to handle all Grey's works, for his name was fast becoming a household word.

As the productive writer began to churn out a book a year, Zane was paired with the best illustrators of his era. It didn't take long for other publishers to catch the Western-novel fever that had begun to sweep the nation. They set about finding a Zane Grey of their own, bringing to light the works of Max Brand (Frederick Faust) and Louis L'Amour (Louis Dearborn LaMoore) to name but two.

Another significant event took place that same year of 1912. Dolly gave birth to their child Betty. It was a difficult delivery, prompting Zane to write in his journal: "I left the room just before the child came, and it was at this time that [Dolly] had the severest pains. I crouched in my chair in the next room, and listened to the first real cries of mortal agony I ever heard. ... Powerless to help her I trembled there, suffering through that cry, realizing through it all what she really meant to me. ... 'It's a girl,' said the doctor. And then I knew. Elizabeth Zane Grey had been born to me. A Betty Zane!"

From 1918 to 1932, Grey was a regular contributor to *Outdoor Life*, becoming one of the magazine's first celebrity writers. In that popular publication, he began to concentrate on big-game fishing. With success now his, Zane had the money to indulge in his passions– fishing, adventure travel, and women. Time after time, he left his family behind to go deep-sea fishing, relax with his mistresses, and write.

Although he commented that "... the sea, from which all life springs, has been equally with the desert my teacher and religion," Grey was never able to summon a great sea novel from his fertile imagination.

Nonetheless, the sea did help to soothe his dark moods and reduce his nagging depressions; and like the desert, it bestowed on him another gift, the opportunity to harvest deep thoughts: "The lure of the sea is some strange magic that makes men love what they fear. The solitude of the desert is more intimate than that of the sea. Death on the shifting barren sands seems less insupportable to the imagination than death out on the boundless ocean, in the awful, windy emptiness. Man's bones yearn for dust."

Over his years as a best-selling author, Grey's habit was to spend part of the year traveling and living out his dreams in his adventures; whilst the remainder of the year, he wrote, using his adventures as the basis for the tales in his writings. Unlike some writers who can write productively everyday, Zane experienced dry spells that he learned to ride out, for he would also experience sudden bursts of creativity when he could dash off up to 100,000 words in a month.

Nearly everywhere he traveled, he encountered enthusiastic fans of his books, who warmly greeted him, asking for his autograph. His travels– and the people he met– were quite varied. He spent time on the Rogue River in Oregon, where he maintained a cabin he had constructed on an old mining claim he purchased. Other adventures carried him to Washington state and big-sky Wyoming. His jaunts to his cabin in the wilds of Arizona also nurtured and inspired him. He spent several weeks a year there, from 1923 to approximately 1930. That cabin burned to the ground in 1990. It has since been reconstructed.

During the 1930s, Grey continued to turn out his books, though the Great Depression hurt the publishing industry as it did just about every other business in America. His book sales fell off to some extent; but Zane fared the lean years better than most folks, for he had not owned any stocks, and of course, he continued to receive his royalty checks. Actually, nearly half of his film adaptations were executed during the decade of the 1930s.

From 1925 to his death in 1939, Grey traveled further and with longer absences away from his family. He had become keenly interested in exploring unspoiled lands, particularly the far-flung, remote islands of the South Pacific. His beloved Arizona was beginning to be overrun by tourists and speculators, prompting these words near the end of his life: "The so-called civilization of man and his works shall perish from the earth, while the shifting sands, the red looming walls, the purple sage, and the towering monuments, the cast brooding range show no perceptible change."

The more books Grey sold– and he sold a phenomenal number of his Westerns– the more the critics seemed to attack him. Heywood Broun once said in a particularly stinging critique of Grey's work that "... the substance of any two Zane Grey books could be written upon the back of a postage stamp."

Broun and a few others said that Grey's depictions of the West were too fanciful, too violent, and not faithful to the moral realities of the frontier, and that his characters were unrealistic and much larger-than-life.

That criticism seems to this author unfair. Grey's books were fictional accounts not histories of the West. In truth, Zane Grey relied on first-hand experience, careful and copious note-taking, as well as considerable research.

HARPER BOOKS

Zane Grey

has written a new novel that, in the three months since its publication, has found its way to more than a quarter of a million readers—a tribute to its author's wide popularity and the charm of this latest of his books. *The Man of the Forest*, is a fine achievement in the realm of pure romance; a book that in its subtle delineation of the kinship of nature recalls the work of W. H. Hudson. And it adds another volume to that glorious epic of the West which Mr. Grey has built up novel by novel.

THE MAN OF THE FOREST

is the story of a man and a women driven to take refuge in a hidden paradise of the Arizona Mountains, and of how in the shadow of its circling peaks and the deeper shadow of the danger that lurked behind them, these two found the eternal miracle of love.

"Over all hangs the enveloping beauty of Mr. Grey's word-pictures of the forest, mountain and desert. From beginning to end never does the feeling of suspense relax, never does the expected happen. . . . He is the born story-teller and he adds one more stone to his monument as a writer of fiction in this living tale of passion, avarice, revenge, and love among the Arizona deserts and mountains."—*New York Sun-Herald*

Richard Le Gallienne says:

"One hangs on the story as though one had never heard the like before, and loves and hates the characters. . . . 'Las Vegas' . . . is one of those characters that one would like to go on reading about as long as the author cares to write. . . . A book flooded with the golden loveliness of Arizona."

THE MAN OF THE FOREST
Illustrated.   Post 8vo.   Cloth. $1.90

HARPER & BROTHERS, *Publishers,* Established 1817, New York, N. Y.

Canadian Representative: The Musson Book Company, Ltd., corner East Dundas and Victoria Streets, Toronto, Ont.

He was a born storyteller. Overall, the enveloping beauty of his word-pictures of the forests, mountains, and deserts of the American West captivated millions of readers. Readers devoured his Westerns, and over the years, he developed an impressive following that turned his popularity into celebrity.

Unfortunately, despite his great popular and monetary success, the ultra-sensitive Grey read the reviews and took them continually to heart, the negative comments triggering sentiments of anger and self-doubt that led to those aforementioned dry/dark spells.

I have said this before, but some things are worth repeating: Belief in self is *magical*. Thoughts are magic wands– powerful enough to make anything happen– anything we choose. Or, as Henry Ford used to say, "Whether you think you can, or you think you can't– either way, you are right."

Once, after a particularly enflaming review, Grey flopped down and countered with an angry lengthy treatise entitled "My Answer to the Critics," in which he sharply defended his forthright intentions to produce great literature of the Old West, stating that *Westerners* knew that he was absolutely true to the settings of his romances. He suggested that the critics ask his readers what *they* think of his books.

Grey would have done better to focus on what he did want, not on what he didn't want. To draw on the wise council of Carl Jung, "What you resist persists." Translation: What you fight you get more of. Now, that's a law, and one that Grey never really learned. Sensibly, Zane heeded Dolly's good advice and did not publish the treatise, thereby avoiding an open negative tennis match with the critics.

In 1925, Grey's book *The Vanishing American*, first serialized in *The Ladies' Home Journal* in 1922, did fire up a heated debate. The Navajo hero is patterned after Jim Thorpe, about whom this author wrote in *County Chronicles Volume II*.

With his *Vanishing American*, Zane attempted to portray the constant struggle– against the corrupting influences of the Whites, both the White government and the missionaries– of the Navajo to preserve their traditions and culture and retain their identity and dignity. In doing this, Grey enraged various religious groups. The author contended, "I have studied the Navajo Indians for twelve years. I know their wrongs. The missionaries sent out there are almost everyone mean, vicious, weak, immoral, useless men."

I know Grey's opposition sounds harsh, but in all honesty, there were rights and wrongs on all sides of the Navajo-missionary-and-government issue, as there almost always are in most of life's contentions. When his editors and his publisher bucked at Zane's choice of words with his liberally tossed-off sarcasms, the thin-skinned author relented, taming his sentiments in order to see the book published. Zane would have been wise, on more than one occasion in his life, to heed this time-honored advice: Never attempt to substitute sarcasm for self-assurance. People almost always see through a pall of sarcastic smoke to the insecure person who disgorged it.

With the release of *The Vanishing American*, the book, Grey completed the most productive period of his writing career, having presented to the reading public nearly all his major themes, character types, and settings.

As it were, Zane Grey produced his best work early in his career, repeating himself later with formulaic writing rather than breaking new ground. His fans, however, were continuously thrilled with his efforts, eagerly anticipating each new book, even after his death.

It should be noted here that Grey's *Wanderer of the Wasteland* is his thinly disguised autobiography.

One of the first millionaire authors, Zane Grey was now earning considerably more than Babe Ruth, the eminent baseball star of the era. By 1920, the forty-seven-year-old, still-youthful Grey had climbed with firm footing to the top rung of his ladder of success, a beloved author who connected with millions of readers worldwide. During the mid and late 1920s, the sales of Grey's writings were superseded only by the Bible.

Know this, readers: Zane Grey was a major force in shaping the myths and legends of the Old West. And never forget what a *prolific* writer he was. It is estimated that he penned over nine million words during his writing career, authoring some ninety books, several published after his death. Critic approval or no, his total book sales exceeded forty million. From 1917 to 1926, Grey's books were among the top ten on the best-seller list nine times, requiring sales to exceed 100,000 copies with each book to get there.

After Grey's passing, his publisher had a stockpile of his manuscripts and thus continued to publish a new title per year until 1963.

During the decades of the 1940s, '50s and '60s, sales of Grey's books exploded. By the 1960s, the shelves of paperback galleries literally overflowed with Zane Grey Westerns. Pretty impressive, wouldn't you say?

Remember, Zane Grey's books were not all Westerns. He authored a couple of hunting books, several fishing books, about a half-dozen juvenile books, and even a couple of baseball works.

Erle Stanley Gardner, another prolific author and the genius of the *Perry Mason* series, once said of Zane Grey: "He had the knack of tying his characters into the land, and the land into the story. There were other ... writers who had fast and furious action, but Zane Grey was the one who could make the action not only convincing but inevitable, and somehow you got the impression that the bigness of the country generated a bigness of character."

Grey's association with Hollywood began when William Fox purchased the rights to *Riders of the Purple Sage* in 1916. At the time, Zane received $2,500. Zane Grey's rising star was harmonious with the ascending popularity of the art form known as "the movies."

Cowboy stars Bronco Billy Anderson (see in *County Chronicles'* premier volume "Lights, Camera, Action!"), William S. Hart, and Tom Mix (see in *CC IV* "Tom Mix, King of the Cowboys") all brought Zane Grey's characters to life on the Silver Screen. Later, legendary director John Ford would orchestrate the action from the pages of Grey's adventurous Western novels. In fact, one of the reasons the Grey family relocated from Pennsylvania (a place they would forever hold affectionately in their hearts) to California was to be nearer to the film industry and the Western settings he utilized in his writings, as well as to enable Grey to enjoy big-game fishing.

Grey formed his own motion picture company for a while, allowing him artistic control of his stories, i.e. faithfulness to his books. After seven films, he sold the company to Jesse Lasky (Famous Players), a founder (with Adolph Zukor) of Paramount Pictures. Subsequently, Paramount produced a number of films based on Grey's writings, hiring the author as an advisor. Many of these movies were shot on location in Monument Valley, Arizona, a favorite location described in his books.

Why don't I let Zane describe to you himself, from his *Tales of Lonely Trails*, his first sight of this wondrous place. "At length we turned into a long canyon with straight rugged red walls and a sandy floor with quite a perceptible ascent. It appeared endless. Far ahead I could see ... black storm-clouds; and by and bye began to hear the rumble of thunder.

"Darkness had overtaken us by the time we had reached the head of this canyon, and my first sight of Monument Valley came with a dazzling flash of lightning. It revealed a vast valley, a strange world of colossal shafts and buttes of rock, magnificently sculptured, standing isolated and aloof, dark, weird, lonely. When the ... lightning flared across the sky showing the monuments black against that strange horizon the effect was marvelously beautiful. I watched until the storm died away."

John Ford's movie classic *Stagecoach* (1939, the year of Zane's death) certainly attested to Grey's long-standing belief in the Valley's cinematic potential. Those of you readers who grew up during the 1950s with the myriad of television Westerns know Monument Valley, to be sure. Thus, was the powerful influence of Zane Grey.

Though he was initially enthralled with moving pictures, Grey gradually became disenchanted by the movies with the pirating of his work and the steady dilution of his tales and his characters. All told, nearly fifty of his novels were translated into over one hundred Western movies- the most by any Western author.

The movie version of his book *Western Union* (1941) opened shortly after his death. Directed by Fritz Lang and costarring Randolph Scott and Robert Young, it spearheaded a resurgence of Western movies during the decades of the 1940s and 1950s, including the classics works of director John Ford. *The Zane Grey Show* ran on the radio via the Mutual Broadcasting System for five months in the late 1940s, and *Zane Grey Theatre* had a successful five-year run with its 145 episodes during the early years of television, from 1956-1961. Still other works were born out of Grey's books. For instance, from his *Lone Star Ranger* emerged *The Lone Ranger*.

Many actors who rose to fame got their start as Zane Grey characters, such as Shirley Temple and Fay Wray, Wallace Beery, Gary Cooper, Buster Crabbe, William Powell, and the fore-mentioned Randolph Scott.

To cite two more of the film industry's top directors, Victor Fleming, who would later direct *Gone With the Wind*, and Henry Hathaway, who was destined to direct *True Grit*, both learned their craft on wild and wonderful Zane Grey movie sets.

Before his death of heart failure in 1939, Zane Grey indulged his fishing to the utmost, taking longer and more distant sojourns in search of new frontiers, on grander and grander yachts he purchased for himself– *Fisherman I* (1924) and *Fisherman II* (1931).

Grey had begun traveling to and writing about the South Pacific. He first sailed to New Zealand in 1926, catching large fish of great variety, including a mako shark that was a ferocious fighter.

With his exceptional fishing skills, Grey secured several world records, including a 1,040-pound blue marlin. He even invented the "teaser," a hookless bait that is used by fishermen yet today. Grey's many articles in international sporting magazines helped establish deep-sea sport fishing in various locals throughout the South Pacific, especially where he maintained fishing camps in New Zealand, Australia, and Tahiti.

The famous author's getaway home in Avalon, Catalina Island, California, is today the Zane Grey Pueblo Hotel. During his years on the Island, the avid, record-holding fisherman was a prominent member of Catalina's posh fishing organization, the Tuna Club.

In 1939, at the age of sixty-seven, Zane Grey, who had always appreciated new vistas, passed on to the final frontier, the result of a massive heart attack. He was interred at the Union Cemetery in Lackawaxen, Pike County, Pennsylvania, where the National Park Service maintains the Zane Grey Museum as part of the Upper Delaware Scenic and Recreational River.

Dolly, who passed away in 1957, is buried with her husband. They share the same headstone. Actually, after Zane died, he was cremated and his ashes kept by Dolly until her passing, after which she too was cremated. Their daughter Betty had their ashes interred together, in the same plot at Lackawaxen, in keeping with the couple's request.

Open seasonally, usually Memorial-Day weekend through Labor-Day weekend, the museum displays Grey's memorabilia, vintage photographs, and books in the rooms that served as his office and study. During Grey's occupancy, his work areas were colorfully decorated with a Navajo sand-painting and Hopi Kachina doll designs painted by Dolly Grey's cousin, Lillian Wilhelm, one of Zane's romantic liaisons.

I strongly suggest that before visiting (since there are weekends the museum is closed), you contact the Zane Grey Museum online or by telephoning them at 570-685-4871. Grey was forever enamored with the peaceful setting in Lackawaxen, just below the confluence of the Lackawaxen and Delaware rivers and just north of the Roebling Bridge, where the woodlands and rolling green lawns fall away to tranquil, rippling waters. He retained the Lackawaxen property after the family moved to California in 1918, and they returned to their Pennsylvania abode whenever they were on the East Coast.

In the summer of 1929, when he was in New York talking with editors, the fifty-seven-year-old Zane Grey made his last trip back to Pennsylvania to visit his Lackawaxen residence. He had not been there since 1922. It was a poignant visit, brimming with memories.

In a letter to Dolly that June, he penned in reference to their Lackawaxen home: "I was overcome with the beauty,

Zane Grey with koala bear and one of his mistresses during an Australian trip

the sadness, the loneliness, the desertedness of it. Oh, Dolly, the rooms are haunted! Those are our spirits there. ... I recalled everything. I felt the cold of the old cottage. I saw you in bed- I heard Romer's tiny wail; I heard the wind, the river. For the first time, I went into the room where my mother died. Something strange came over me there ... . The dust, the dirt, the decay, the ruin reproached me. Why have we not taken care of [this place]? [It is] a first and great part of our lives. Love, struggle, my work, our children- they all came to us here." The dampness and chill of the forsaken house caused Zane to move closer to the warm stove of memory. He thrilled- and he wept.

Grey's home in Altadena is listed on the National Register of Historic Places, and a lovely residential street, Zane Grey Terrace, in the scenic hillsides of Altadena, carries his name. There is another museum, the National Road Zane Grey Museum, on US Route 40, ten miles east of Zanesville, Ohio, the author's birthplace.

Certainly, Zane Grey did not invent the Western novel- other writers wrote about the West before him- but he profoundly influenced the genre's popularity. Grey's romantic stories spiraled out beyond the actual locales and the annals of history to render the American West *legendary*. Zane Grey's fantasies became the fantasies of the nation.

Baseball star, avid traveler, and chronicler of the Old West, millionaire, best-selling author, world-record-holding fisherman, Grey, for a great deal of his existence, dashed about wrapped in his unconventional relationships in the wishful-wistful-make-believe world of his books. Usually far from home on one of his lengthy adventures, most of the time fishing, his was a unique life, a diverse life of woven and interwoven dreams, significantly wilder and more untamed than the adventure stories he made famous.

Succinctly stated, Zane Grey lived the American boy's dream. His life is best summarized by a pithy comment from his ever-patient wife Dolly when she said, "The man has always lived in a land of make-believe."

Over the course of his incredible life, the eccentric, out-spoken Grey offended many people. Dolly was the one person who remained steadfastly loyal to him. From the beginning, she recognized his genius, and despite his long absences and his madcap ways, her love never waned.

When he drew his final breath, Dolly opened the copy of her husband's just-released novel *Western Union* that he had inscribed simply, "To Dolly from Zane." After a private, pensive moment, she smiled and taking up her pen, added, beneath his dedication, her final edit to his prose: "Gone fishin' on October 23, 1939."

Of that she had no doubt.

Zane Grey Lackawaxen photos courtesy the Library of Congress, Prints and Photographs Division

Zane Grey's Pennsylvania house, circa 1916, now the Zane Grey Museum, in Lackawaxen, Pike County, PA

Zane Grey's study in his Lackawaxen home

"It Might Have Been, the Story of Billy Conn"

"There has never been a fighter like Billy Conn, handsome as a movie star and tough as a junkyard dog. Conn threw combinations with the beauty and speed of later masters Sugar Ray Robinson and Muhammed Ali."
- Conn biographer Paul F. Kennedy

"Of all the sad words of tongue or pen, the saddest are these- it might have been."
- John Greenleaf Whittier

"Though Joe Louis' crown eluded him, Billy Conn was a sports hero whose place in boxing and sports history should never be forgotten."
- Ceane O'Hanlon-Lincoln

Once, in the smoky city of Pittsburgh, Allegheny County, Pennsylvania, there lived an Irish-American boxer named Billy Conn. Pittsburgh has always loved its Irish, and the people there loved Billy ... most of the time. But then again, seems like there are Irish everywhere, or, as Billy used to say, "wanna be's."

Like other pugs, Billy carried a couple of snappy monikers, "Sweet William" and the "Pittsburgh Kid." There would be another "Pittsburgh Kid" in the years to come, but Paul Spadafora would not be in the same class with Billy Conn.

This Chronicle is plucked from the heart of a gritty lad who came within six minutes of winning the richest crown in pugilism. In addition to revealing interviews with Billy Conn's son Tim, it is drawn from the brilliant writings of Conn biographers Andrew O'Toole, Paul F. Kennedy, and sportswriter Frank Deford. It's a good all-around story, readers, one you'll like even if you're not a boxing fan. And if you're a romantic like me, you'll *love* it. So pour yourself a nice cup of tea, and curl up in a comfortable spot.

Billy Conn was born 17 October 1917 in the Pittsburgh district of East Liberty that slides off the neighborhood's tongue as "S'liberty." First, last, and always, Billy was a Pittsburgher.

His father William, whose family originated in Belfast but had converted to Catholicism, labored as a steamfitter at the Westinghouse plant in East Pittsburgh. William had worked for a time as a policeman for the city. "Wild Bill," as he was known, was a tall, strapping Irishman with coal-black hair and a pencil-thin moustache. "He liked to drink and fight, fulfilling the Irish stereotype of the times," wrote biographer Paul F. Kennedy in his compelling *Billy Conn, the Pittsburgh Kid*. "But he worked hard ... supported his family, and he adored his kids."

The Conns are descended from a legendary *Ard Ri* (High King) of Ireland, "Conn of the Hundred Battles," who ruled over a big chunk of the Old Sod until his assassination about the year 157 by fifty of his enemies disguised as women.

The surname "Conn" is derived from the Gaelic word for "hound," the warrior-king having been named for the speed of greyhounds and the pugnacity of ferocious sea dogs. The "Hundred Battles" portion of his moniker emerged from the *Ard Ri*'s constant warring with other provincial kings, a common occurrence among the clans in Ireland's early history.

Monikers rolled readily down the great tunnel of time in clan Conn. Rather than call his father "Dad," or the Irish "*Da*," Billy called him "Westinghouse," after the elder Conn's place of employment. It was a habit Billy would keep throughout his life, fitting those he loved with illustrative nicknames.

He adored his mother, calling her "Maggie." Margaret's people had come from County Down, and she would carry the lilt of her native brogue on her tongue her whole life. Maggie was a beautiful woman, buxom, with the fine porcelain skin- white as snow with the bloom of the rose on her cheeks- the ladies of Eire are known for. Like a typical colleen, her hair was raven-black, her eyes a deep, midnight blue. Maggie had a fine voice, and Billy loved to hear her sing all the old songs: *Ireland Must Be Heaven*, *I'll Take You Home Again, Kathleen*, and *When Irish Eyes are Smiling*.

All his life Billy would say, "A boy's best friend is his mother." He meant it too. To her dying day, Maggie and her oldest son were best friends. It was obvious that Billy got his striking good looks from Maggie, his scrappiness from his *Da*.

Growing up, Billy heard the metallic, quasi-Scottish accent of his paternal *grandda* Joseph Conn from Northern Ireland's Belfast and the more musical brogue of the Emerald Isle from his mother and her family. However, Pittsburgh had its own dialect of English, and that became Billy's language.

This "Pittsburghese" was rooted in the dialect of the eighteenth-century Scotch-Irish settlers, who had come to western Pennsylvania from Northern Ireland. Like other Pittsburghers, Billy left the *hahse* (house) in *S'Liberty* (East Liberty), after he redd up (tidied up) his room. When he met his friends, he'd ask, "*Jeet yet?*" (Did you eat yet)? Then they all went *dahntahn* (downtown). And lest we forget to mention the expression unique to western Pennsylvania- *you'ons* (the bastardization of "you-ones"), the Pittsburgh-area plural of *you* that usually comes out sounding like *yins*.

Billy was far from stupid, but he never liked hitting the books. He was wild and so full of vim and vigor that it was, even for the strong-willed Sisters of Charity at the Catholic school he attended, a little like trying to catch stardust with a butterfly net. He was just fourteen when he quit school. His father knew no good would come from his boy wandering the tough East Liberty streets. What the kid needed, he figured, was a "lesson in reality."

Wild Bill collared his son and took him to the Westinghouse plant. "Without schooling, this is where you're goin' to end up," he pronounced in a tone as heavy as the pipes he toted at work and as gloomy as the smoky Pittsburgh sky. Years later, Billy would say that had "scared the hell out of [him]."

Pittsburgh was the "Steel City" back then. "Hell with the lid off," they called it. After the Civil War, steel was king in that "big small town" where three rivers meet. The skies over Pittsburgh were so black, the street lights seldom went off. That is no exaggeration. Winters were especially dismal when the air was bitter cold; the smoke hung over the city like a shroud, the ugly grey skies streaked black from the riverside mills.

The year Billy was born, two-thirds of Pittsburgh's population was made up of immigrants and their children. Immigrants came in droves to do the hardest, dirtiest labor. They came from Scotland and Ireland first, as well as from Germany, England and Wales; then from western, eastern, and southern Europe. In those days, the immigrants who came to Pittsburgh to work stayed among their own kind, and Pittsburgh became a city of neighborhoods. It still is today.

During the mid and late 1800s, there was steam power and Irish power, and by that I mean "muscle." All around the Pittsburgh area, in that pre-union era, wages were kept low because of the continual supply (due to the "Troubles" at home) of cheap labor from the old country. "Irishtowns," communities and neighborhoods, sprang up across our great commonwealth and our country at large, where traditions, beliefs, and values were passed on.

In Pittsburgh, the Irish settled on the North Side and in East Liberty, spreading rapidly all across town. The Germans settled on Troy Hill, the Italians in the Bloomfield section, the eastern Europeans on the South Side, the Jews on the Hill- the Hill District that is- that later took on a large African-American population, with many of the Jews shifting to Squirrel Hill.

At their labor and on the streets, these immigrants coughed and wheezed, wetting their parched throats in the Smoky City's countless saloons. In those days, the "Burgh" was a-shot-and-a-beer kind of place, where jobs could be had by those not afraid of hard work. And make no mistake about it; the Pittsburgh mills spelled w-o-r-k!

Another thing Billy Conn said years later was "People think you gotta be nuts to be a fighter. They're right; it is nuts, but it beats workin' in those mills."

Billy came from a family of scrappers, and I suppose we could say, to a certain extent, that he grew up fighting. Soon after he quit school, his father took him to Johnny Ray's gym. Tucked away above a noisy Irish pub on Penn Avenue, Ray's was a shabby one-room sports hall that, to quote Conn biographer Andrew O'Toole in his *Sweet William, the Life of Billy Conn*, "... gave birth to imaginings, improbable thoughts of fame and glory, riches that would keep the romantic from toiling in one of the Burgh's many mills."

Indeed, the visitor would've had to have been a romantic, for Johnny's place was no castle in the sky. Cigarette butts littered the filthy floor, and the air was thick with the ever-lingering smoke and the stench of stale sweat. The dream-weaver in Ray's gym would have had to have an exceptionally good imagination, for Johnny Ray's supplied no frills. A dusty ring, a couple of speed bags, and two or three heavier bags were the stuff of a fighter's dreams at Johnny's.

Ray, whose real name was Harry Pitler, was born in Pittsburgh's Hill District. He was Jewish, but an Irish handle had seemed to him more appropriate for a boxer (later turned trainer/manager); thus, he had taken and kept the name "Johnny Ray."

Wild Bill Conn feared his son might follow in his own untamed footsteps. Though Billy had never been one to start trouble, and in fact, had never had a brush with the law, his father was taking no chances. He offered Ray a dollar a week to keep his kid out of trouble with "Pittsburgh's finest." Too, he figured learning to use his fists would always come in handy.

A buck a week was nothing to sneeze at during the Great Depression. To Ray, an ex-fighter himself, it translated to "a couple of meals or four drinks." Johnny took Conn's offer, and one of the most colorful chapters in sports history began to unfold.

As it happened, Johnny Ray chose to do more than just keep Billy away from the "boys in blue." He decided to train his young protégé in the art of boxing. The old fighter saw something right off the proverbial bat in this dimple-faced, curly headed lad with the sparkling sapphire eyes and the endearing smile- an obvious aptitude for the sport of boxing.

Johnny noted early on that his young amateur boxers gave Billy a wide berth. When he asked them why, they told him in no uncertain terms. For Billy, each sparring session was a fight to the finish- he didn't know when to quit. They already knew it in S'Liberty, and they knew it on the Hill: Billy Conn could lick any kid in the Burgh's tough neighborhoods. Like I said, Billy never picked fights, but he'd give you one, if you pushed him. And you didn't have to push too hard. No one messed with Billy Conn.

From the outset, Billy and Johnny were inseparable, and from their friendship and later partnership, their familiarity produced yet another Billy-Conn-created nickname. Billy referred to Johnny as "Moonie," since the latter liked to drink. In truth, Moonie's drinking was more than a tall one at the end of a long day. His was a drinking problem that in the end would claim his life. But for now, Moonie and "Junior," as Johnny called Billy, were a team made in boxing heaven.

At the age of sixteen, on 28 June 1934, Conn made his first professional boxing appearance. The bout took place in Fairmont, West Virginia, against veteran twenty-one-year-old Dick Woodward. Billy lost on decision in the fourth round. His share of the modest $2.50 purse was two measly quarters that Ray slapped down in front of him with an expression that matched the winnings. "There ya are, Kid."

"Why fifty cents?" Billy voiced with objection.

"We gotta eat," Johnny replied flatly.

"Yeah," Billy agreed, "but how come I'm payin' outta my share?"

"That's simple," Ray emphasized with a lift of his wiry brows. "You're the one who lost."

Most of Conn's early fights were against older, more experienced opponents. Beginning his career as a welterweight, he fought against heavyweights. By the time he reached the age of twenty-one, Billy had defeated nine former or present world champions. Nearly a third of his fights were against title-holders, and though often outweighed and out-experienced, Conn never lost to a heavyweight- with the exception of one. But lest I get ahead of myself in our tale ... .

Slowly, as his profile increased, Billy became known as the "Baby-faced Assassin" or more commonly as the "Pittsburgh Kid" and "Sweet William." If his sparring partners and opponents didn't think so, the opposite sex thought of Billy as *sweet*. When he walked into a room or the arena, his tall, Adonis-like body, with muscles rippling, towered above his handlers. Then, every pair of female eyes in the place stalked him, bringing forth a chorus of "Ooohs" along with those barely audible, more wistful "Hmmms."

Conn was a Celtic god, a Celtic warrior- and he was sure pretty with his mop of jet-black hair that spilled boyishly over his forehead, those sparkling blue eyes fringed with long, inky lashes- bedroom eyes, they used to call them- chiseled face with its dimpled cheek, strong jaw, and dazzling white teeth. Boxers aren't usually this handsome. Billy resembled more a film star than a pug, but then again, Billy Conn was not the usual pug.

Conn gained national attention with his upset victories over middleweight champion Fred Apostoli at the overture of 1939. At that time, Apostoli was regarded as the best pound-for-pound fighter in the world; but in his New York debut at Madison Square Garden, Billy soundly beat him.

Sportswriters universally refer to the Garden as the "Mecca of Boxing." Reaching Madison Square has been the goal of every fighter since the place first opened its doors before the turn of the last century.

Conn beat Apostoli again just five weeks after their first match. As one reporter said, "It was a honey of a fight."

Billy returned to Pittsburgh a sports hero. "Apostoli is the best fighter I've ever met. But he's one of the dirtiest ... ."

Billy had that right. For one thing, Apostoli had chewed and stretched the thumbs of his gloves so that he could poke Billy in the eyes during the fight. Along with hooks and jabs, Billy often delivered dialogue to his opponents in the ring. In regard to the thumbs in his eyes, he had retorted to Apostoli that he should use those gloves to hitchhike back to San Francisco.

Conn's cheers, letters, and telegrams must have been exhilarating. "Here's a funny one," Billy exclaimed to reporters. Some girl in Orange, New Jersey, sent me a letter with her picture and a crushed flower. She said she wants me to say 'hello' to her on the radio. Imagine that!"

The press everywhere was intoxicated with Billy's charm, charisma, and quick wit. Snatching their pencils from behind their ears, they dashed off on their notepads just about everything he said. They wanted to know all about this plucky kid from Pittsburgh. Who was his favorite singer? "Bing Crosby." What was his favorite dish? "Corned beef and cabbage, what else?" What was his favorite song? "The same as Maggie's, *Ireland Must Be Heaven*."

After the Apostoli fights, Conn was on a roll. On 13 July 1939, he copped the Light-Heavyweight Championship from Melio Bettina. By this time, the Pittsburgh pretty boy had a myriad of supporters. Bettina wasn't pretty, but his leonine head was adorned with the glittering crown that Billy fancied for his own curly head. And in spite of the heat and humidity- the Garden was like an oven that night- Conn, with his usual gusto, went after it, dancing and jabbing and taking the sixth, seventh, eighth and ninth rounds easily. Make no mistake; Billy had style- and he had speed.

A revitalized Bettina moved in on Conn in the eleventh, scoring with a number of solid body blows. However, the onslaught ended when Billy tagged Melio with a powerful right. Though Bettina did not go down, he let both his hands drop, as all life seemed to drain from his short, compact body. Rather than move in for the kill, gentleman Conn backed off, allowing his opponent to recover.

The fourteenth was more of the same, with Billy taking the fight to Bettina. In the final round, Melio mustered what he had left for one last offensive. Still, Billy continued to return fire, and the decision was unanimous: "The winner and new Light-Heavyweight Champion of the World- Billy Conn!"

The dethroned champ did not think he had lost- "And shurrre n' wasn't th' fight close!" Even so, when the ref had raised Billy's sweaty right arm in triumph, nary a sound of protest rose from the Garden's packed house.

The question now on everyone's mind, including Conn's, was when he would fight the heavyweight champion Joe Louis. When the press put the query to him, Billy replied with fire in his eyes, "I'll fight 'em!"

He added that the time would be when Johnny said he'd be ready. After all, following Johnny's advice had won him his new title. The long hours working out in the two-bit gyms had paid off. Like the crooned-about Road to Tipperary, it had been a long, winding path for Junior and Moonie. And sometimes, like after the Apostoli and the Bettina fights- *it sure felt like long.*

The barnburner match with Joe Louis came on 18 June 1941, at the Polo Grounds, New York City, and it would be the fight for which Billy Conn would most be remembered throughout sports history.

Following the customary introductions of attending luminaries, the timekeeper sounded the bell thrice, the signal for the two fighters to be introduced. "The Heavyweight Champion of the World, from Detroit, Michigan, weighing 199 pounds and wearing red trunks, Joe Louis!" The "Brown Bomber" humbly received his due from the crowd.

Then: "From Pittsburgh, Pennsylvania, weighing 174 and wearing purple trunks, the very capable challenger, Billy Conn!" A roar greeted the underdog Conn, filling his very essence with the Celtic fire of his Irish ancestors- warriors all.

I might add here that Billy's weight was actually 169 and three-quarters, Joe's a hair next to 200. Conn's announcement weight of 174, fight-night and to the press, was with fight promoter Mike Jacobs' finger on the scale. Conn's weight was stated as such with protection of the bout's gate in mind. The fact that the boxing commission did not wish to present Conn and Louis with too much of a weight difference (for fear too many people would stay away if they knew the true weight disparity) translates "money." In regard to Billy, that weight difference translates, to me, as nothing short of "guts." According to Conn's son Tim, the weight difference never bothered Billy. He believed skill and technique mattered most.

Rhetoric aside, Conn was outweighed by thirty pounds, but was about four years younger than Louis. Billy grinned at the cheering crowd, while Joe sort of gazed downward, as if reviewing his strategy for keeping the crown secure on his head.

The crowd was still cheering as both men met at center-ring. "Let's have a good, clean fight. Now touch gloves and come out fighting," referee Eddie Joseph instructed, as the two champions touched gloves in the traditional pugs' handshake, locked eyes, then retreated to their respective corners to await the bell.

In Pittsburgh, everything had come to a screeching halt as citizens of the Burgh paused in their lives to listen to their radios. At the Conn's new home on Pittsburgh's Fifth Avenue, Maggie, who was sick in bed (due to terminal cancer), sent word downstairs to her family gathered round their set to "keep up the praying."

At the posh Waldorf in Manhattan, a gorgeous blonde anxiously paced the floor of her suite, nervously chatting with her chaperone-aunt, as they listened to the fight over the radio and waited for word from Billy from the Polo Grounds. At one point, the blonde bolted to the bathroom and turned the shower on full force so she would no longer hear the announcer's voice. Her name was Mary Louise, and she had entered Billy's life like a thunderbolt.

Before I continue with the first of the Louis-Conn fights, let me tell you about the boxer and the blonde. Mary Louise Smith was a stunning Irish-American lass, the daughter of Greenfield Jimmy Smith, a former baseball player, another of the Steel City's celebrated Irish. Though Jimmy himself was a sportsman, he was adamantly opposed to his daughter marrying anyone in the field of sports- especially a pug. However, from the moment Billy had set eyes on the beauty queen, who was several years his junior, he was captivated by her charms, falling madly in love. What can I say? "Mary Lou" was a knock-out!

Irrespective of what her father said, Miss Smith was a spitfire, and the enamored couple met, for dinners mostly, at hideaway places out of town, where no one would see them and tattle. It was all very innocent in those more-innocent times, and what they shared were hopes and dreams, promises, stolen kisses, and their song, *A Pretty Girl is Like a Melody*.

Their life together was almost like a song, for they never fell out of love. However, that historic June night in 1941, in the ring with Louis, Billy's reverie of Mary Louise, whom he had affectionately christened "Matt" (for the way her hair matted when it was wet), would prove disastrous for him.

The vivacious Miss Smith had turned eighteen, and the couple had just taken out a marriage license. For Billy, this fight for Joe Louis' crown was a daydream wedding present for Mary Louise as well as a final gift to his dying mother.

Did you ever hear the phrase "It's hard to beat a slugger"? Or "Never slug it out with a slugger"? Louis was the slugger's slugger, but Billy Conn out-boxed and out-slugged Joe Louis for the first twelve rounds, almost sending the champ to the canvas at the end of the twelfth.

To that point, Johnny's plan had produced for his fighter pure *magic*. Conn continuously moved backward and to Louis' left, a tactic that baffled Joe. Billy was finding his openings and scoring regularly with hooks and jabs. "Move!" Moonie shouted from their corner, and Junior did just that.

The eighth began an unbroken stretch of five glorious rounds for Conn when the retreating ceased, and the Pittsburgh Kid went on the attack, using everything in his arsenal- hooks, jabs, and overhand rights- that sent the Irish and Pittsburgh factions at the Polo Grounds virtually to the moon.

The Kid had come to symbolize the city of his birth, the heartbeat of America, despite its smoke and grime. Pittsburgh, like America, had endured a dozen years of the Great Depression; thus, its hero Billy Conn was a shining beacon of hope.

"I got him," Billy told his corner. "I got him."

To be sure, Louis had yet to run into anything like Billy. Not in all his title defenses, among all the true pugs or the bums, had there ever been anyone like Billy Conn.

Along with his punches, I'll remind you that Billy often delivered snappy dialogue to his opponents. "You're in a fight tonight, Joe," Billy told the champ as they met at center-ring to ignite the ninth.

"I know it," Louis answered tersely. The Kid was brash- *and he was good*.

To echo Billy's biographer Paul F. Kennedy: "Conn rooters were starting to believe it could really happen. At Forbes Field, in Irish enclaves in New York and around the nation, in the bars and humble homes of smoky Pittsburgh, they clutched beer mugs, rosary beads, and each other," as they

Billy and Mary Louise at the Jersey shore circa 1941 Billy Conn photos courtesy the Conn family collection

watched, blow for blow, what was turning out to be "one helluva good fight!"

In the tenth, Louis proved to the waiting world why he was such an admirable sportsman. At the sound of the bell, Joe came out like a bull. For one breathless moment, Billy slipped and went down, bringing a stereo gasp from the crowd. A true champion and a gentleman, Louis always wore his heavyweight belt with class. As Conn rose from the canvas, Joe took a step back, and rather than take advantage of Billy in that vulnerable attitude, he permitted him to regain his composure before he once again pressed his attack. Such was the incomparable Joe Louis.

All through the eleventh round, Conn demonstrated his mastery of the sport of boxing. Louis seemed to be tiring and, at times, even a bit confused.

With four rounds yet to go, Billy was surprised to discover how easy this bout was unfolding. On the opposite side of the ring, the champ sat with an almost dazed look as his corner encouraged him. The fight, however, was far from over.

During the twelfth, Billy delivered a full-armed left that knocked Joe backward onto his heels. Staggered, Louis dipped forward into a clinch. In the champ's embrace, Billy tried to put him down with an array of blows that were anything but "love taps."

The screaming fifty-five thousand fans at the Polo Grounds sprang to their feet. *I've got him*, thought Billy. *I've got him now*. But the signal to end the round sounded.

Saved by the bell, Joe was still standing after an onslaught of slams that would have put any other fighter to his knees. Take into account that thirty pound difference between these two men. Billy Conn was essentially a light-heavyweight, whereas Louis was a definite heavyweight.

When Billy returned to his corner, for the first time in his career, he listened with a deaf ear to what his men had to tell him. The bell rang for the thirteenth round. Billy put in his mouthpiece, looked Johnny in the eye and announced, "I'm gonna knock him out!"

Moonie could not believe his ears. He turned immediately white, and the word shot from his open mouth, "NO, Junior! Stick and move! Stick and move! Just keep movin'; play it safe!" Trouble was- *"playin'-it-safe"* was the one thing this brash Irisher did not know how to do.

Now don't misunderstand what I'm about to tell you. Billy stayed focused on his performance all through that first match with Louis. Since he had "hurt" Louis, his instinct was to go in for the kill. He just wasn't satisfied to win this all-important title-fight on points. Mark you, readers, Billy Conn was fearless, and he was all about "guts."

Before the bout, he had envisioned Mary Louise on his arm- the most beautiful couple in the world- as they promenaded down the street, any street in America, where people stopped to exclaim, "Look! There goes the man who knocked out Joe Louis!"

With a broad grin, Billy met (a recovered) Louis at mid-ring. The dancing had stopped as the two fighters circled each other like two cats- big, powerful cats, ready to pounce.

A minute into round thirteen, Billy moved in for the kill with a terrific combination, a dozen or more punches ferociously launched, most finding their mark. Still Joe remained standing like an unmovable force, his right cocked, waiting- patiently waiting- for the opening he knew he would get.

When it came, Billy was hitting Louis with a left to the body, then one to the head that allowed the champ the chance he had been waiting for. Bam! With lightning speed, Louis delivered a devastating right to Billy's head that visibly stunned him. Bewilderment instantly vanquished the confident look on Conn's face, as his knees buckled, and he fell back against the ropes with Joe in hot pursuit.

Now Louis opened up with a barrage of hard, fast blows, twenty at least. Billy desperately tried to protect himself, but little good it did against this all-out Joe Louis attack. A powerful right to the head followed by a blitz of body punches sapped whatever Conn had left, with the *pièce de résistance*, Louis' overhand right- straight to the jaw- shattering Billy's dream for all time.

As Conn lay sprawled on his back, Eddie Joseph picked up the count. At seven, Billy courageously attempted to reach his feet. On eight, he was, indeed, sitting up, though bleary-eyed. Nine saw him still in that punch-drunk position. **"Ten!"** Billy had just managed to stand with the wave of Joseph's hand counting him out. Two seconds remained in the thirteenth round.

If he had listened to Johnny, Billy Conn would have won that historic fight and the elusive heavyweight crown on points. He didn't know it at the time– but Billy had just vanquished the magic.

At the Conn home in Pittsburgh, all the women huddled round the radio were sobbing except the feisty eleven-year-old youngest, Peggy Ann, who took on the clamor of reporters outside. "If only he could have gotten up," she told the *Associated Press*. "But he'll get another chance, another match, and he'll beat Joe Louis then. I'll bet you!"

To the *Post-Gazette*, she stated, "I think Billy was wonderful! If only he had a few more seconds. But he'll get another chance ... and then you watch what happens!"

As the press boys scrawled their notes, Peggy raced off into the night, with her older sister calling at the door after her, "Don't you go fighting with anybody, no matter what they say!"

Meanwhile, back at the Polo Grounds, the tears had begun to roll down Billy's cheeks before he and Moonie reached the locker room. Standing with his fighter under the deluge of the shower, Johnny told him, "Go ahead, Kid, have a good one. Let it all out."

Sobbing, Conn poured out his apologies to the man who had taken him on his long journey. "I let you down ... I let you all down."

Within minutes, and with summoned Irish grit, Billy was ready to meet the reporters with his famous grin. "Sure. Sure, I'll beat him the next time," he said of Louis.

Across the way, the champion held court. "Billy Conn is a great fighter with a lot of heart," Louis pronounced graciously. "He was much faster than I was, and I had a hard time catching him ... and anyone who says Conn can't hit hard enough to hurt you doesn't know what he's talkin' about."

The reporters got off their comments too, and the newspapers had a field day. "Conn made the mistake of slugging it out with a slugger." "Too much courage. Too much Irish." All true, and reflective of what Billy himself said: "I guess it's the Irish in me ... I was going for the knockout. Maybe I had too much guts and not enough common sense."

My father used to say something like that to me when I acted impetuously, rushing in where angels fear to tread. "You feel too much and think too little! There's no doubt you're Irish!"

As foolish as it might have been, Billy had so wanted to earn the title by beating the champ and not just out-boxing him. He had wanted that for Maggie and for Mary Louise. My dad liked to say something else too: "Anyone can take a hit. The trick is in the getting up again."

Almost immediately, Billy made up his mind that if he got another chance at Louis, he would beat him. You have to admire his pluck.

At the Waldorf, the knock on Mary Louise's door finally came. She opened it to a tearful Billy, who fell into her arms, whispering into her hair. "I tried my best, Matt. Honest to God, I did."

So, the boxer and the blonde ran off and got married, and yes, they lived happily ever after. Billy would star (in 1941, right after he married his sweetheart) in a Hollywood film, *The Pittsburgh Kid*; and he and his bride would spend a portion of their honeymoon with a few of the Silver Screen's big names, fans of Billy's who had become friends, such as Barbara Stanwyck and her husband Robert Taylor, Bob Hope, and Frank Sinatra. But Hollywood didn't thrill the couple, and Billy and Mary Louise were happy to return to Pittsburgh.

The Pittsburgh Kid made its movie-circuit debut before the end of 1941. The money had been pretty good, but Billy always dubbed the picture a "real stinker," dusting it off and playing it, in years to come, for houseguests who over-stayed their welcome.

Closer to the moment and back in the Burgh, the newlyweds bought a beautiful brick home on Denniston Street in Squirrel Hill, not far from her family's place on Beechwood Boulevard.

Eventually, Mary Lou's father Jimmy relented and accepted his son-in-law as his daughter's choice of mate ... *eventually*. The couple had four children over the years, and the boxer never won a decision over the blonde.

Now I'll share with you something my mother used to say: "If a man treats his mother like gold, he'll do the same for his wife." Sound reasoning that. Billy had worshiped Maggie (who had held on with steely reserve until after her son's bout with Louis), and throughout their marriage, he treated Mary Louise the same way.

Did Conn ever get another crack at Joe Louis? I'm glad you asked. To quote from Frank Deford's masterpiece, "The Boxer and the Blonde," June 17, 1985, in *Sports Illustrated*: "After Pearl Harbor, Conn fought three more times. Nobody knew it then, but he was done. Everything ended when he hit Louis that last big left. The best he beat was Tony Zale, but even the fans in the Garden booed his effort, and he only out-pointed the middleweight. It didn't matter though, because all anyone cared about was a rematch with Louis– even if both fighters were going into the service."

The rematch was in the works for that summer of '42, when Fate stepped in and nixed the whole deal. In the middle of May, Pfc. Billy Conn got a pass to come home for his firstborn's christening. Pittsburgh's Art Rooney, the child's godfather, thought it might be the perfect time to heal the rift between Billy and his father-in-law, Greenfield Jimmy Smith. Rooney entreated Billy to come on over to Mary Louise's parents' home for the party, that Jimmy was ready to "smoke the peace pipe."

There was no peace pipe. Rather, there was a war dance, with Smith goading his son-in-law into a confrontation. Sitting atop the stove in the kitchen, his legs dangling, Billy took the verbal spurs for as long as he could, finally leaping off his perch to have a go at his father-in-law with his best– a left hook.

The problem was that the shorter Jimmy ducked, and Billy caught him square on his hard head, injuring himself worse than ever he had in the ring. Conn knew straightaway he had broken his hand. He was so angry over blowing his chances for a rematch with Louis, to make matters worse, he put his good hand through a window on the way out the door to the emergency room. The next day the *The New York Times* said Billy looked "as if he had tangled with a half-dozen alley cats."

What was particularly disturbing to Billy was that ole Jimmy didn't have a mark to show for the brouhaha. Years later, when Louis ran into the Kid, he asked, laughter dancing in his dark eyes, "Hey, Billy, is your father-in-law still beating the s— out of you?"

That June, Secretary of War Henry Stimson announced that Joe Louis would *not* be making anymore public appearances, and the champ began a round of morale-boosting tours.

The brawl at the christening had cost the Pittsburgh Kid any real chance of victory over Joe Louis.

Joe and Billy both fulfilled their patriotic duty during the war; both being patriotic men. Billy, however, disliked army life. No small wonder. Being told what to do did not sit well with him. It never had. Other than Maggie, Johnny Ray, and Mary Louise, few people ever got away with that in civilian life. "You got a million bosses in the Army," Billy liked to say.

Shortly after D-Day, Conn received word that his unit was leaving for Europe. One incident that took place aboard the transport ship en route to England merits retelling. With dozens of enlisted men at attention on deck before him, a hulking platoon sergeant, new to Conn's outfit, bellowed out in a thick Southern accent a typical military challenge: "If anybody here thinks he knows how t' fight good 'nough t' lick me, step outta line right now!" The entire unit remained in formation, though every pair of eyes shifted to Billy.

The brawny sergeant repeated the challenge, his booming voice rising to a double-dare level. "Anybody he-ah thinks he can lick me, step outta line!" Again, the platoon remained in formation, but this time a number of heads turned in Billy's direction.

Now, you might think that Conn was an Irishman always bent on confrontation, but in all honesty, his habit was to try and avoid conflict. Reluctantly, he took a step forward, waiting at attention. Swooping down on the bold-as-brass private, the big sergeant barked, "So– you think you kin take me, huh? Is that what you think, Soldier!"

In a respectful but firm voice, the private responded to the query with succinct honesty, "Yes, Sergeant."

"What's yore name, Private?"

"Billy Conn, Sergeant."

The non-com looked startled for a moment, almost as if Billy's famous left hook had stung him, then he slapped an arm round Billy's broad shoulder. "That goes f'r everyone 'cept you. C'mon, I want you t' meet the admiral."

"Well, Sergeant ... I'd just like to have some eggs."

A smile played at the corners of the sergeant's mouth. "Don't worry; you'll git all the eggs you kin eat ... with grits, though you already got plenty-a that, boyo!"

During Conn's stint in the Army, there was another near-fisticuffs, this time with a cantankerous mess sergeant who didn't like to give seconds and who, like the NCO on the transport, didn't know who he was messing with ... excuse the pun. Words were exchanged after he refused to refill Billy's plate. A close-at-hand lieutenant deftly stepped between the two strapping men, saying, "I think we can arrange for you two to box, if you'd like that."

"Fine," roared the burly sergeant. "I'll *kill* him!"

The lieutenant nearly choked. "I think you ought to be introduced first, Sergeant. I'd like you to meet Billy Conn."

The loud-mouthed sergeant's face blanched, and a long moment of awkward silence followed, with the fellow sheepishly extending his big paw to shake Billy's proffered hand. "Seconds for everybody!" he yelled.

During a USO tour, Conn was placed in another unit, and his became an all-boxing expedition. Late into the tour, Billy and his group were, en cavalcade, rolling along a lonely road in Italy when an American fighter jet crash-landed nearby. The men watched as the plane burst into flames, leaving the unconscious pilot trapped inside. Conn and a few of the others rushed to the wreckage, fought through the blaze, and pulled the pilot to safety.

Within the span of six months, Billy had traveled over 50,000 miles, from England, to France, to Italy, Sicily, Corsica, and back again to France. He boxed about four nights a week, though his wartime boxing was nothing compared to Johnny's rigorous training.

When he was offered a promotion, he turned it down. He liked being "one of the guys." And besides, he wasn't in the Army for the long haul. "Boxing's *my* game," he told them.

World War II dragged on, and with those years went some of Billy's boxing skills. Those in the fight game say the legs go first. In Conn's case it might have been true- for a time.

Billy was with Bob Hope at Nuremberg on V-E Day. At long last peace arrived, and the lights came back on in the world. The Pittsburgh Kid's homecoming revealed that he was no longer down-for-the-count with his father-in-law. Greenfield Jimmy Smith had mellowed toward him; but Sweet William was happy, most of all, to be reunited with Mary Louise and his boys.

After settling in with his family, the first thing on Billy's mind- and fight fans everywhere- was a rematch between the now twenty-eight-year-old Conn and the thirty-two-year-old Louis. The long-awaited match was scheduled for 19 June 1946. It was before this fight that Joe Louis coined the famous phrase (referring to Billy's speed) "He can run, but he can't hide."

Billy told the press he wanted to make one thing perfectly clear, that all the talk was just hype for the upcoming show. He was telling the truth. He and Louis had become fast friends, and they would remain so. "Joe's a nice guy. ... I just want that title of his; that's all. He's had it a long time now, and I'd like to have it ... ."

When the big day rolled around, Mary Louise (as was her custom) remained at home with the boys, at their house in Squirrel Hill. She said she'd listen to the fight on the radio. "I'm not particularly worked up about it," she told a reporter. Good thing, as it turned out.

For the first time, ringside seats sold for a hundred bucks, and a $2 million gate was realized. There is no point in relating this fight to you, round for round, because it was unbelievably bad. Someone once said that "... sometimes the best way to deliver a punch is to take a step back, but step back too far, and you ain't fightin' at all!"

Billy "bicycled" all over the ring, which confused Louis who thought it was a trick, and neither fighter mixed it up. Baffled, from start to finish, by Conn's performance, the champ finally went in for the kill, ending the boring affair in the eighth.

This time, it was Johnny Ray who cried. He knew it was over for Billy. Billy knew it too, calling his second performance with Louis a real "stinkeroo."

Pittsburgh was stunned. At the Conn home, Billy's little sister, the tough, defiant now-sixteen-year-old Peggy cried out and wept bitterly.

After reading everything I could lay hands on about Billy Conn, in addition to speaking at length several times with Conn's first son Tim, I am convinced Billy was drugged before his rematch with Joe Louis.

"My father was fully prepared to meet Louis, physically and mentally," Tim told me. "He had trained hard and readied himself for that decisive bout. More than one sportswriter penned that they had never seen a 'better conditioned or a more confident challenger in camp' than Dad before his rematch with Joe Louis.

"The day before the fight, Dad disappeared for several hours with 'friends,' who would have had sufficient opportunity to put something in his food when he dined with them. Over the years, several witnesses remembered his strange behavior during his weigh-in, behavior that was translated as 'jitters' back then.

"My grandfather Greenfield Jimmy Smith was with my father in the locker room before the Louis rematch, and he saw immediately that Dad was in no condition to fight. He demanded that the fight be postponed but to no avail.

"The man who came into the ring that night was not Billy Conn. *That* man was a mere shadow of Billy Conn. Looking as though he were in a daze, a stupor, with deep, dark circles rimming his eyes, that faint imitation of my father looked as though he hadn't slept for days. His performance was a nightmare, and, as it is with many bad dreams, he remembered virtually nothing about the fight afterward.

"And another thing: Johnny [Ray] was drunk the entire time Dad was in training. He was in a drunken stupor through the whole fight, so he was absolutely no help to my father as a trainer. Johnny had a drinking problem, sure, but his condition surrounding the events of the Louis rematch was unusual, to say the least. Was someone keeping him in that state? I suppose we'll never know.

"Bear in mind that there was a lot of money riding on that long-awaited rematch, the first fight with such a huge gate. Betting was heavy, very heavy. That my father was drugged is the *only* thing that makes sense."

Tim Conn was never alone in his belief that Billy lost that fight, not from "ring rust," but because he was drugged by a conspiracy that was hoping to get an edge in the massive betting. One example I will cite is a November 7, 1948 article written by Harry Keck, Sports Editor for the Pittsburgh *Sun-Telegraph*, the "*Sun-Telly*" as it was called around the Burgh.

Under the header "Is This What Happened to Billy Conn?" the famed sportswriter, while discussing how horses in important races can be drugged to win or lose, speculated: "Maybe, now that he's doing a comeback, we'll find out one of these days just what happened to Billy Conn before his second fight with Joe Louis. You never saw a more conditioned or more confident challenger in a training camp than Billy or a more unimpressive-looking heavyweight champion than Louis. [And this was widely reported by the press, making Billy the favorite.] But the day of the fight Conn suddenly went limp. He doesn't remember going to the weigh-in, has only a vague recollection of the fight [a situation that remained till the day Billy died]. He was walking like a man in a dream. There have been many rumors that he was drugged by persons interested in the betting angle. As bad as he was, it took a fumbling Louis eight rounds to catch up with him.

"I wonder if Dan Parker, the New York columnist, had Billy in mind when he wrote the other day, '... Why not saliva tests for fighters in main bouts? It would be quite practicable, and the result could be determined quickly. ... More than one fighter has claimed he was doped after a fight in which he was beaten, and it wasn't always just a cheap excuse. I know a manager who says a gambler offered him $200,000 to slip a pill to a heavyweight champion in a fight some years ago on which a large amount of money was bet. ... Why wouldn't it be in order for the examining physician to make a test before and after important matches to see if anyone had tampered with the fighters? One or two Phenobarbital-pills will make a chump out of any champ.'"

Referee Eddie Joseph told Pat Robinson of the *International News Service*, "I knew there was something wrong when I saw those circles under Conn's eyes."

Billy Conn had wanted that crown more than he had wanted anything in his life, except for Mary Louise. I've read, heard, and discussed how he wanted it so badly he could taste it. Something happened to him in the hours leading up to his rematch with Joe Louis, something dark and sinister. To this day, mystery shrouds that fight, a tangled web that likely will forever remain in the shadows.

Boxing is not like other sports. A professional sports figure can be good in a lot of sports to scrape by with a good career. But to survive, boxers have to be *very* good. If not, they'll end up badly injured- or dead.

Don't misconstrue what I'm saying here. Billy Conn was very good. Remember, approximately a third of his seventy-five fights had been against world champions, and he had beaten them all- save for Louis. Time after time, when the experts had said that Billy wasn't ready, that he was in over his head, he had proven them wrong. At age nineteen and twenty, he had beaten all of the best middleweights in their prime. At twenty-one, he had won the world light-heavyweight championship. Conn had dominated the division so thoroughly, he had to fight heavyweights to find a challenge. Barely 170 pounds, he had beaten the heavyweight contenders with ease.

And in that memorable first match with Louis, he had taken the fight to the Brown Bomber, plausibly the greatest heavyweight champ of all time. For twelve thrilling rounds, Billy had proven the boxing connoisseurs wrong again, taking the bigger man's punches and even staggering him in the previous round. Remember too that Billy had tipped the scales at just a tad over 169 that morning to Joe's 200, yet it was Louis who was hurting and trailing behind for most of that fight.

Allow me the fancy footwork I need to skip ahead in time and let you know that Billy Conn garnered several awards and accolades over the years, such as: Light-Heavyweight Champion of the World (1939); the Edward J. Neil Memorial Award for Fighter of the Year (1939); the first-ever Dapper Dan Award (1939, for the sports figure who did the most to publicize Pittsburgh that year); *The Ring* magazine's Fighter of the Year Award (1940); the 1945 Dapper Dan Award; and induction, in 1965, into *The Ring* magazine's Hall of Fame.

In 1978, the Boxing Writers Association named Conn, via a nationwide poll, the Best Light-Heavyweight of All Time.

In 1988, Billy received the honor of Grand Marshal in Chicago's famous St. Patrick's Day parade. The subsequent year of 1989 marked Billy's induction into the initial class of the International Boxing Hall of Fame in Canastota, New York.

In 1998 (after Billy had passed away), the city of Pittsburgh honored the Pittsburgh Kid by christening the corner of Fifth Avenue and Craig Street, in the Oakland district, near where the Duquesne Gardens once stood, "Billy Conn Boulevard." Billy won eleven of twelve fights there, defeating six world champions.

In the year 2000, the *Associated Press* listed Billy among the Top Ten Fighters of the Twentieth Century. And in 2004, the Western Pennsylvania Sports Hall of Fame opened its doors in downtown Pittsburgh. There, an entire room is devoted to the area's boxing history, with the spotlight on Billy Conn's glittering legacy. A Light-Heavyweight Championship belt is on display, courtesy the Conn family, and a videotape of highlights from the first Louis-Conn match runs continuously.

Oh, yes, Billy Conn was *very* good at what he did. To quote biographer Kennedy: "Conn was as skilled a boxer as anyone who ever laced on gloves. He had great speed of hand and foot, and ring smarts. He had phenomenal physical stamina, and (after reaching physical maturity at age twenty) an almost inhuman ability to take a punch."

Yet today, there are those boxing enthusiasts who contend that there never was a better fighter than Billy Conn, a better stylist anyway. Speak the words "Sweet William," and their minds flash back to that unforgettable June night in 1941.

Later, much later in time, Conn jokingly put this question to Louis: "Hey, Joe, why didn't you let me have that title for six months?"

Joe, who hadn't been as quick on his feet as Billy, but who was always quick with a good quip, had laughed in his good-natured way, answering, "Billy, I let you have it for twelve rounds, and you couldn't keep it, so why would I let you have it for six months?"

Boxing fans, that championship bout between Louis and Conn back in '41 was as good a fight as ever there was. And the thing was it had been Billy's one-and-only unhindered chance at the glittering heavyweight crown. When he walked out of the Polo Grounds that night, he left his boxing career behind him. With some things in life, you only get one chance.

After hanging up the gloves for good, Billy gave up physical exercise, took to smoking, which he had never done before, and developed a taste for Scotch. As a fighter, he had rarely indulged in alcohol. During the 1950s, he invested some of his money in oil wells in Texas and Oklahoma, lent his good name to a car dealership, and purchased a few race horses. With the money he made from boxing and his smart business deals, he and his family were comfortable.

Billy shunned public appearances, even avoiding many of his children's activities. He was no longer comfortable in the limelight, and he visibly gritted his teeth when anyone came up to him, patted him on the back and called him "Champ."

He had his small coterie of close friends, and a few select clubs and bars he frequented, but in his post-career days, he was no longer comfortable, as I said, with the public. Sundays, he and Mary Louise attended the earliest Mass, the one with the fewest people.

In the basement of their Squirrel Hill home, he taught his boys to box, at the same time lecturing them on the dangers of the sport.

Occasionally, Billy refereed a boxing match; and for a while, he dabbled in teaching amateurs the sport. Though he had been a stylist- some would even say a genius- in the ring, he was an *impatient* teacher. "He expected everyone to be perfect, like him," the late veteran trainer Frank "Spacky" Delio said of Conn's training endeavors.

In 1963, Billy moved his family to Las Vegas where he accepted a lucrative job offer in which he would be in charge of public relations at the famous Stardust Hotel. His sons worked as busboys at the hotel, meeting all the stellar acts who performed there.

Though it was, in a sense, a glamorous life, the whole family missed Pittsburgh. Billy and Mary Louise became increasingly uneasy with the Vegas lifestyle, particularly were they worried about the effects of the place on their kids. Their old friend Bob Hope agreed with them, telling Mary Lou: "You get your nice family out of here."

After nearly three years in the Nevada desert, the Conns returned to Pittsburgh, to their home in Squirrel Hill. They had not sold the house, only rented it, so the move was coordinated rather quickly- and the Pittsburgh Kid came home *for good*.

In July 1972, the Irish government invited Billy Conn to the land of his ancestors to help promote the fight in which Muhammad Ali defended his title against Alvin "Blue" Lewis in Dublin. As always, when Billy was away from home, he missed it and was glad to return to the Burgh.

In the 1980s, the saga of the true Pittsburgh Kid was revitalized with a media rebirth. In the January 1981 issue of *The Ring*, the magazine reported that a poll of boxing historians voted the first Louis-Conn match as the Greatest Fight of All Time, beating out the Frazier-Ali and the Tunney-Dempsey battles.

Then, in 1985, sportswriter Frank Deford penned his wistfully nostalgic article for *Sports Illustrated*, "The Boxer and the Blonde," that interlaced Billy and Mary Louise's romance with Conn's quest for the heavyweight title. The memorable piece- recounting one of boxing's greatest stories- is still one of the most popular articles in that sport magazine's history.

Early one spring morning in 1990, after attending a novena service for their daughter who had been diagnosed with breast cancer, Billy and Mary Louise stopped at a convenience store en route home. Mary Lou went to the back of the store for coffee. Billy purchased a newspaper, opened it and began reading as he stood near the check-out counter, waiting for his wife.

Within a few moments, a young hood entered the store, and pointing (from under his sweatshirt) what he said was a gun at the proprietor, demanded the money from the cash register. The punk paid little attention to the elderly fellow near the counter, holding a newspaper. From the rear of the store, Mary Louise could see the whole scenario, and a troubling thought leaped into her mind, "Someone is going to get killed, either Billy or that kid." She knew her husband well- knew he would not be able to stand by and do nothing.

When the thug grabbed the store owner, Billy ordered in a stentorian voice, "Leave him alone!" As the thief turned from the proprietor to the "old man," the famous Conn left hook slammed into his face, sending him crashing through the cookie display. Billy then reached for the crook with something of his former self, the expression on his face telling. Literally taken aback, the punk flung the newspaper rack at the energized ex-boxer and fled the store as if the Devil himself were after him, not pausing to pick up anything but his feet, in the fray leaving behind his wallet that easily led police to apprehend him soon afterward.

"I hit him with my best punch," Billy told reporters. "I interrupted him. He won't be robbing any stores for a couple of days."

On the fiftieth anniversary of the first Louis-Conn fight, June 18, 1991, newspapers and magazines all over the country carried articles about the "Greatest Fight of All Time." ESPN sent boxing commentator and former Lightweight Champion Sean O'Grady to Billy's home to interview him. Billy Conn's era had long since passed into history, but the Pittsburgh Kid had not been forgotten.

Round about 1992, Billy began suffering from a condition known as "pugilistic dementia," words that always spark a question in this author's mind: "Why isn't head gear mandatory in professional boxing?"

Billy had maintained "damage control" during the years he had fought due to his superb defensive skills, but he had engaged in seventy-five fights all told, mostly against top contenders. He had gone thousands of rounds of hard sparring. Likely, he had kept his faculties for so long because he had enough sense to retire at the relatively young age of thirty-one.

For Billy, Death came quietly, on silent cat paws, as the saying goes, and he went in his sleep on May 29, 1993. He was seventy-five.

Newspapers nationwide carried the headline that one of boxing's greatest legends had passed away. Billy's widow informed the Pittsburgh media. "The champ is gone," she pronounced softly.

Mary Louise's words took the City of Champions reeling back once more to that sultry June night in 1941, to the bell at the close of Round Twelve when Billy was "dancing" on top of the world and cuffing the heavyweight champion's ears. Within those remaining six minutes, long-past and never to return- Billy's dream just might have been.

John Greenleaf Whittier was not a boxer. He was a poet, but the stark truth of his words has defined many a fighter, and none more than Pittsburgh's sweet Billy Conn--

"Of all the sad words of tongue or pen, the saddest are these- it might have been."

Yet Billy's story is not wholly sad. He rose from poverty to find fame, fortune, his one true love, and a caring family, and his was a long and healthy life for a prizefighter.

In Mary Louise's Pittsburgh apartment is an entire room devoted to her late husband, a sort of Billy Conn shrine, where pictures of the couple with celebrities paper the walls.

The largest photograph is the most compelling, that of Billy and Mary Louise holding hands and dashing with silent peals of laughter out of the rolling surf at the Jersey shore, the ocean foaming at their feet. It's 1941. They are young, so beautiful- and so much in love. To echo Paul Kennedy, "It is how they should be remembered."

As the true Pittsburgh Kid, Billy Conn was the symbol of a tough city, and an even tougher era. Should his story fade with the passage of time, his phenomenal record will stand firm.

Paul Haggis, the *Million Dollar Baby* screenwriter, said, "If there's magic in boxing, it's the magic of fighting battles beyond endurance, beyond cracked ribs, ruptured kidneys, and detached retinas. It's the magic of risking everything for a dream that nobody sees but you."

Billy Conn had that dream- and for a time, he was part of that magic, created by his sheer guts, his famous left hook, dazzling footwork, lightning speed, his incomparable style- and the magic that Johnny Ray had spun for him from his own shattered dreams.

Like magic, the Billy Conn legend embraces allure and mystery, a glittering facet in the diamond-hard realities that make up the intricate world of boxing.

Among the litany of the sport's ace pugilists- Billy Conn stands tall as one of the greatest.

"They Came to America, Echoes from Our Past"

"When we came in, towards Ellis Island, the ship slowed, and oh, I felt better ... I was happy. When we saw Miss Liberty, I can't tell you the feeling we had. ... We started to sing ... America!"
–Hungarian immigrant, Ellis Island, 1922

"Give me your tired, your poor, your huddled masses yearning to breathe free, the wretched refuse of your teeming shore. Send these, the homeless, tempest-tost to me, I lift my lamp beside the golden door!"
– From Emma Lazarus' famous poem, "The New Colossus," graven on a plaque within the pedestal of the Statue of Liberty, "Liberty Lighting the World," 1883

Ancestors of nearly one half of all the people living in the United States today came to America through the great immigration portal of Ellis Island. They *were* tired. They *were* poor, and yes, they *were* yearning to breathe free!

In several segments of the previous four volumes of my *County Chronicles* Pennsylvania history series, I have proffered to my readers cherished memories garnered through interviews from fellow Pennsylvanians. In the premier volume, trolley memories took us on a magic-carpet ride into the past. In the third volume, we relived World War II via the home front and battlefront memories of those who lived it. The fourth volume took us back to the 1950s, the last age of innocence in America.

In this volume, I want to share with my readers "... Echoes from our Past," memories of our ancestors who came to America with a shared dream, that of making a better life for themselves and their children.

It was not easy for immigrants at the turn of the last century. After sailing across what very likely was a turbulent ocean for as many as thirty-odd days, huddled below deck in cramped and fetid steerage quarters, you can bet they were yearning to breathe free!

Between 1820 and 1920, some thirty million European immigrants arrived in the United States. Most came through the port of New York, and after 1892, most were funneled through Ellis Island.

In the early years, due to "The Troubles" at home, most of the immigrants came from Ireland, though many came from Germany as well. During the Famine period in Ireland (1845-1852), an estimated half-million Irish were evicted from their cottages. Unscrupulous landlords basically used two methods to remove their penniless tenants. The first involved a legal judgment for back rent against the male head of the family. The second method was simply for the landlord to ship the unwanted tenants overseas. This was cheaper than sending them to the workhouse. With phony promises, British landlords packed the tenants off in overcrowded, poorly built and often unseaworthy sailing vessels that History aptly christened with the sinister name "coffin ships."

In the years when Ellis Island was the busiest, southern and eastern European immigrants predominated. In 1906, when activity at Ellis Island was at its height, 1,100,735 immigrants poured into America. Though they encountered some restrictions, they were generally welcomed until 1921 when quotas on immigration commenced. By 1927, only 335,000 immigrants, typically from northern and western Europe, were permitted into the country, and that figure was never exceeded in subsequent years.

For immigrants coming to America in steerage, the trip across the wide expanse of ocean was nothing short of dreadful. Shipping-line advertisements promised a "sea voyage on a fine ship, including a plentiful supply of cooked provisions." However, the truth of the situation was this: The cooked provisions were scarcely edible- soggy rye bread and a barrel of herring for the Slavs, Swedes, Germans, and Jews traveling on the northern routes; sardines and soggy wheat bread for Italians, Greeks, and Armenians who came by way of the Mediterranean. The wise packed wicker baskets of food to take with them.

Steerage quarters below deck were horribly crowded. So great was the crush of humanity, tempers often flared, in a fiery explosion of languages. Blankets suspended on ropes separated the men from the women and children. Without portholes, these low-ceilinged rooms had no ventilation and carelessly maintained toilets. The stench was appalling.

In stormy weather, the steerage hatchway doors were locked and roped securely shut to make certain no one seeking the deck got swept overboard. This practice cut the immigrants off from fresh air and water, since the only drinking water was on deck. Thus, foul weather delivered both nagging seasickness and agonizing thirst. Many of the poor immigrants were seasick and unable to get to the overflowing toilets or onto the deck to vomit overboard. In the reeking atmosphere, in a diversity of languages, prayers rose to their God to let them die.

Inside the steerage cabins were bunks, two or three tiers high, topped with thin mattresses thoroughly populated by lice. Women with babies or toddlers had to sleep with their arms locked round their children who might easily roll out of bed whilst the ship rolled with the ocean's tireless waves.

With the crying babies, the moaning and groaning of the sick, the tempest tossing of the ship, and the noisy engines pounding and banging beneath them, it would have been virtually impossible for steerage passengers to even rest, let alone sleep.

After a long, arduous journey, the waters calmed as the ship steamed into New York Harbor. At this point, most of the newcomers changed into the best clothes they had with them. Or more likely, they put their finest clothing on over top what they already were wearing, resulting in less to carry.

Eager to catch sight of their new home, a flux of immigrants hastened to get on deck. Many of them had heard stories of the Statue of Liberty, though most were not certain of what she was. Nevertheless, as the great Lady appeared before them, they all felt exhilarated, filled with the thrill of Freedom, Opportunity, and Hope!

Many began to sing in their native languages. Most uttered prayers of thanksgiving. Some even saluted the Lady, with men taking their hats off to her. Others were so overwhelmed with this symbol of their dreams that they simply stood and gazed at her majestic form, her hand held high, lighting their way, as tears streamed down their upturned faces.

From the harbor, the ship carrying the immigrants sailed up the Hudson to a pier where first and second-class passengers debarked, their passage through immigration normally quick and courteous. Whilst these passengers were being cleared, those in third-class/steerage were kept waiting ... and waiting.

When steerage passengers finally did disembark, they were prodded and hurried along like so many cattle, to the ferry that would carry them to Ellis Island. Waiting was no picnic, for it often meant standing in the rain, snow and icy winds, or in the heat of a blinding, broiling sun. And all that waiting provided the newcomers with plenty of time to worry about making it through immigration.

As each boatload of immigrants started across the bay for Ellis Island (originally a sandbar), the huddled masses could see the large Romanesque Reception Center with its distinctive four towers, the red and white brick building low in the water, a number of other ferries and barges secured alongside in the ferry basin.

Once on Ellis Island, the immigrants lined up in front of the doors of the main processing building. Before setting sail from their native lands, the ships' crew had prepared lists of all their passengers, including steerage, detailing information about each. By use of these manifest lists or simply "manifests," immigrants waiting to enter the immigration center were divided into groups of thirty, tagged and labeled.

Inside was an imposing stairway that led to the processing area. Immigrants could leave heavy baggage on the crowded floor downstairs (if they dared) before heading upstairs to the Registry Room.

A great many prayers were uttered here. If we could somehow reverse time, we would hear, the length of that historic stairway, a litany of pleas in Gaelic, German, Italian, Slovak, Hungarian, Polish, Romanian, Romany (the language of the Gypsies), Yiddish (spoken by Jews of central and eastern Europe), etc., to watch over luggage, to blind officials to flaws, and enlighten them to virtues.

At the top of the steps was a group of uniformed officers. Little did the immigrants realize that among this cluster of men was at least one doctor who intently watched for signs of weakness as the immigrants climbed the stairs, signs that would require a more thorough medical examination.

Up top was the Great Hall, a vast room- 200 feet long and 100 feet wide, with a fifty-six-foot-high ceiling- thronged with people, where the motley crew moved slowly but steadily through aisles rimmed by iron rails. Here again was a long wait as those immigrants ahead were examined by the physicians. Babies were carried but children who had reached the age of two had to walk- to prove they could.

Doctors examined scalps for lice or other health issues. They thumped chests and inspected skin and fingernails, for bluish nails might indicate heart problems.

The Immigration Service employees wore dark uniforms that frightened many of the immigrants, who took them for army officers. To so many Europeans, an army officer spelled *danger*.

The segment of the physical exam the immigrants feared the most was the eye exam. Here, the medical examiners used an instrument to turn the eyelids upward, checking for trachoma or other diseases that could result in blindness. If trachoma were found, the immigrant was chalked with the letter "E" that meant almost certain rejection.

I don't know if it was true or not, but the scuttlebutt in my family was that the examiners used button hooks to turn the eyelids upward. The hooks I refer to were used to fasten the high-button shoes of the era.

A century ago, in the shadow of the Statue of Liberty, the Ellis Island Hospital emerged and quickly grew into a massive facility, soon sprawling over two islands. If an immigrant failed the medical exam, he or she was detained at the Ellis Island Hospital, where the doctors, nurses, and aids dealt with every kind of disorder that plagued the world at that time.

Immigrants make their slow but steady way through the Great Hall's aisles at Ellis Island's main building circa 1907.

According to the WQED documentary, *Forgotten Ellis Island*, approximately 3,500 immigrants died at Ellis Island Hospital; however, bear in mind that few vaccines had been developed during that long-ago era. About 350 babies were born there, and these instant citizens were ofttimes named for the doctors and nurses who delivered them.

The medical inspection was, as touched on above, directed mostly at the third-class/steerage passengers rather than first and second-class. For those poor souls in steerage, the medical exam stood between them and the United States of America.

As many as 6,000 immigrants per day were herded past the Ellis Island doctors, who had about thirty seconds to judge if each new arrival was healthy or not.

One in five got a chalk-mark indicating that something was wrong, that this particular individual had a suspected condition. This meant separation from the rest of their family, detainment at the Ellis Island Hospital, and possible deportation. It meant tears as well. Ellis Island was, to immigrants with their shimmering dream of America, the Isle of Hope, but it was also the Isle of Tears.

Be that as it may, less than 1% were sent back for contagious diseases, in any given year, and 2% for other reasons.

The Ellis Island Hospital was the place where America's ideals were tested. Let it be said here that many of the sick immigrants were not only treated at E.I. Hospital but *cured*. The techniques, technology, and the care at the E.I. Hospital were the best anywhere. That stands to reason since the staff there had to deal with such a variety of medical conditions. Their experience rendered them the best health givers anywhere at that time.

In the entire E.I. experience, it was the policy that immigrants be treated humanely. No rough language or rough treatment was tolerated. Nurses, especially, at the E.I. Hospital, are remembered as being kind as well as efficient.

Fear was the immigrants' worst affliction, for most had never experienced, for example, an X-Ray. Some had never had a bath in which their entire body was submerged. Patients at the hospital would get downright nasty if the nurses tried to take away their clothing. The E.I. Hospital staff soon discovered why. Before leaving their homelands, immigrants often sewed money or other valuables into the hems and seams of their clothing.

For children detained at the hospital, it must have been especially frightening, not knowing if they would ever see their parents again. It was difficult for the staff to make some of these quarantined youngsters understand. Languages varied greatly, and so many of the immigrant children spoke nary a word of English.

After only three short decades, at the end of the era of America's heaviest immigration at the turn of the last century, the Ellis Island Hospital fell into decay and ruin in the erosive salt air of New York Harbor.

Today, Ellis Island is part of the National Park Service. After thirty years of abandonment, the main building has been completely restored. It opened as a museum in 1990.

In spite of it all, most immigrants did make it through the feared medical ordeal, and they were herded onward.

The subsequent trial was the feared *tête-à-tête* with the Primary Inspector, the man who would finally grant- or withhold- permission to go ashore. At this point, names were checked against those on the manifest lists. Sometimes names were anglicized. However, I want to state for the record that, though Americans stubbornly hold to the belief that immigrants' names were anglicized at Ellis Island, such changes more frequently occurred on the opposite side of the Atlantic, at immigrant processing centers located at European ports of debarkation.

The Primary Inspector asked each immigrant a total of twenty-nine questions; for instance, if he or she could read or write, his or her age, marital status, etc. I suppose the most important question asked was "Have you work waiting for you in the United States?"

I was surprised to discover in my research that the correct answer was "No." The importation of contract labor was illegal though quite common. Male immigrants were always tempted to answer in the affirmative. Relatives already in America had assured them that jobs would be available to them. Many had been promised employment, and most men were eager to make it crystal clear they would be self-supporting and would not end up as public charges. However, those who answered "Yes" were detained until it became clear that they were not illegally imported by a labor contractor.

Once the immigrants made it through the Primary Inspector, they were guided to a sign that read "Money Exchange," where they could change their foreign currency to American money.

Armed with their papers stamped by the officer at the Primary Inspector's desk, and their small life's savings converted to American currency, they were now ready to enter the United States of America. After passing through that final gate- America's Threshold of Liberty- they were more than ready to begin living their long-nurtured dream. *For most immigrants, the Golden Door did open.*

In this Chronicle, I will share memories harvested through interviews with fellow Pennsylvanians, of stories passed down in families from their ancestors who came to America. To get things started, I will begin with my family.

My father's family came from Ireland, my mother's from the Naples-Bay area of southern Italy. Salerno, the name of the Italian province, was an early Jewish community in Italy. My mother's family goes back to Andalusia in southern Spain. Some were Catholic, others Jewish. Yet today, there is a large faction of Spanish Jews in the Naples-Bay area of Italy.

Andalusia was also a district rich with Celtic lore. Family stories prompted me to research this, and I discovered that region of Spain even had its own unique bagpipes, so the family tales held truth.

My mother's people were doll makers in Spain and in Italy. What is notable is that none of us knew this until quite recently, but Mother used to design her own dolls. She is gone now, and I treasure those handmade *objets d'art*.

Another example of what I call "genetic remembering" is this: My mother's father, my maternal grandfather, used to play guitar and mandolin, gypsy and flamenco music, quite well actually, though he never took a music lesson in his life. Mother and I loved Spanish music, and I studied flamenco dance for several years.

Flamenco is a word replete with a swirl of colorful images and emotions. It is most associated with the region of Andalusia, connected to the gypsies in Spain who settled that area in the fifteenth century. It was the gypsies who first used flamenco as a form of entertainment, expression and art. Toward the end of the 1800s, the guitar became the musical instrument of flamenco. Like a fine wine, flamenco has matured and evolved into the art form it is today.

I cannot express in words, though I fancy myself a writer, the deep-rooted feelings that flamenco evokes within me. I have loved it passionately from the first moment my mother introduced this time-honored music and dance to me when I was but a small child. I am proud that it is part of my heritage.

My maternal grandfather's name was Mariano Bello. He had served in the cavalry in Italy before coming to America, and I suppose it is from him that I inherited my great love for horses. Grandpa loved horses, and as I was growing up, he shared his cavalry remembrances with me. His handsome sepia-tone image in cavalry uniform hangs on a wall here at Tara in my home-office.

Author's maternal grandfather Mariano Bello in his cavalry uniform, Italy, circa 1905

He arrived in America on the *Indiana*, a ship built in 1905 that flew the Italian flag and traveled the Italy-New York route. His point of departure was Naples, not too distant from his family home in Capaccio, in the province of Salerno. He was nineteen when he came to his adopted country, passing through Ellis Island on July 7, 1906.

Grandpa Bello settled in Connellsville, Pennsylvania, where he worked on the railroad. He counted himself lucky to have a job, but he hated his boss. The man was from a section of Italy where a long-time vendetta existed for those from the area where my grandfather hailed. Though Grandpa was a small, slender man, his boss, who was much younger and brawnier, made certain to give him the heaviest work, out in the foulest weather, and he humiliated my grandfather every chance he could, even accentuating his harsh words with a well-timed shove whenever he had a mind to do it. That would have been especially difficult to take, for my grandfather was a proud man who, all his life, walked erect with a quiet charm and an innate dignity.

I can recall my grandmother (whose heritage was the same as her husband's) telling us the story of how hard Grandpa labored. They had four girls, my mother and my three aunts. Once when the girls wanted something that the family could not afford, Grandmother bundled them all up and dragged them in the early-morning chill down to the railroad where Grandpa was employed. "There," she pointed to him working like a slave in the freezing cold, "see how hard your father has to work for the little he makes. Now, maybe you'll understand why we are so careful with our money."

Though a good and decent man, Grandpa exhibited a fiery Latin temper. One day, he decided he had had enough of his boss' abuse, and he cached his cavalry pistol in his lunch pail. Thank God my grandmother had forgotten to add something when she packed his repast that day. When she reopened the pail and discovered the weapon, she screamed (a rarity, for I never heard that saintly woman raise her voice), "Bell!" (For their entire life together, Grandmother addressed her husband as "Mr. Bell," or "Bell," the anglicized version

Author's maternal grandparents, Mary Camille Bello and Mariano Bello, on their wedding day, 1910

of his surname.) "Why are you taking your gun to work!"

"If that boss calls me names again today, I am going to kill him," he answered flatly. What was chilling, Grandma said, is that he stated it simply, without emotion, but his manner and his expression validated his words.

Needless to say, my grandmother confiscated the weapon, reasoned with my grandfather, and later hid the pistol. Never was it seen again for many years.

It was not easy for immigrants who came to this country. There were no streets of gold, no welcome committees. They each had to hack out a place for themselves with the sweat of their brows and the labor of their hands. I once said in one of my *Chronicles* that though the powerful moguls such as Andrew Carnegie and Henry Clay Frick made this country the leading industrial nation in the world- they did it on the backs of the immigrants who labored for them.

Though my maternal grandfather was proud of his heritage and often used the language of the old country with Grandmother and his neighborhood cronies, he was even prouder of the fact that he had become an American. His sentiment about that was: "Whenever anyone asks you what nationality you are. Hold your chin up, look that person right in the eyes, and answer him proudly, 'I am an American.' "

To the immigrants who came to this country during the great influx prior to WWI, becoming Americanized was their foremost goal- that and educating their children. The credo of my grandparents and my parents was "Get an education! That is something no one can ever take away from you." I might add that most of those early immigrants, though they rightly retained their ethnic pride, learned to speak and write English.

Approximately one and a half million Irish came to America during the 1840s and 1850s alone, their search for work blending perfectly with the *heyday* of the coal mines and coke ovens (1870-1929) in my hometown of Connellsville, making it a boomtown. Today many of the descendants of those Irish immigrants still reside in this area, because of the roots their coal mining, coke-making ancestors sowed. I am proud to be one of them.

This was an era when many Irish left Erin, hurriedly, in the dark of night. A member of the "Young Irelanders," my great-grandfather, Francis Xavier McDonough (O'Hanlon), was active in that early movement for Irish freedom. Too active, for his actions, whilst he was employed at the Dublin Post office, were noticed; thus, at eighteen, he fled with his first cousin Father John O'Hanlon's identity and the priest's swift Catholic blessing in his ear, never again to return to the tortured land he so loved.

He had come to America hastily, as many a better and worse Irishman before and since, with the clothes he had on his back, a couple of shillings above his passage money in his brogan, and a hefty price on his head. But 'twas a good head he carried on his brawny shoulders, and in his adopted country, he fared well.

Like many in his position, he continued his work for "Home Rule." Every payday, among his fellow coal miners at Broad Ford (Broadford), the Connellsville area, he took up a collection to be sent to the "Old Sod."

Already a member of the *Ancient Order of Hibernians*, a Catholic society born out of defiance centuries earlier in Ireland, he devoted much time to building the organization in Fayette County, serving as its financial secretary for a number of years. At the time of his death, my great-grandfather, at the age of ninety-four, was thought to be the oldest member of the Hibernians in the world.

Like his ancestors, my father was staunch about his religion and his politics, but despite his hair-trigger temper and the intensity of his stances, never did he belittle or berate anyone else's. As fiercely loyal as he was about his beliefs, he was equally adamant that others had a right to theirs. "This," he always told us with vehemence, "is what America stands for, what Americans have always fought for, what our ancestors came to America to enjoy!" My brother and I were never permitted to speak ill of anyone in regard to race, religion, or even politics within the perimeters of our home.

Over the years, at the place where my father was employed, he was asked on occasion to join a certain organization. He did not feel that it was right for him to have to do so in order to make foreman. Consequently, it took him longer to attain that position, but he would never compromise his belief that he should be judged on the merit of his work and not on whether he was a member of that particular organization that included all the bosses.

Times have changed, and those things are no longer tolerated in today's workplace. Dad made a great foreman, and when he passed away, so many who had worked under him related to me how fair he was, how good to work with.

Let's move on now to another family's memories and others of those who- came to America.

~ ~ ~

"My maternal grandfather's name was Donald (*né* Donato) Papa. However, I never remember anyone calling him 'Donato.' Everyone always called him 'Donald' or 'Don.' He was born October 5, 1897, in the Province of Benevento, near Naples, Italy. "Grandpap," as I always called him, came to America in 1913, at the age of sixteen.

"The story of how he came to America goes like this: In Italy, Grandpap had an older, married step-sister with whom he was very close. She and her husband had four children, but she loved and treated my grandfather as one of her own brood.

"Her husband left for America alone, so he could prepare a home for his family at Bridgeport, Connecticut, where he settled. After four years, he sent for his wife and children. When Grandpap heard that his step-sister and her children were leaving for America, he cried. He loved them all so much, and he knew how much he would miss them. Seeing how distressed he was, his step-sister offered to take my grandfather with her to America.

"Grandpap's step-father, Michael Bartoli, was not in favor of this. He wanted his step-son to stay in Italy to work. Grandpap's mother, Marguerite, understood her son's feelings, and she wanted more in life for him. She knew America was the 'Land of Opportunity.' She knew too Europe was on the brink of war, and that Grandpap would have to fight. In those troubled times, she feared for his life in Italy.

"Marguerite's older son, Mike (Grandpap's brother), was already in America. He had come in 1905, settling in Uniontown, Fayette County, Pennsylvania, and was doing quite well. It took some fancy talking, but in time, Grandpap's step-sister and his mother succeeded in persuading his step-father to let him make the crossing. Besides, his step-sister said, she had four children of her own- what was one more! She promised Grandpap's mother that she would watch over him with maternal love and supervision.

"In November of 1913, my grandfather, age sixteen, left Castelfranio, Italy, his place of residence. His journey to America would begin- and it would be the last time he would see his mother. Many people today don't realize that immigrants who left for America rarely ever saw again their homelands or the family members they left behind.

"The steamer Grandpap sailed on was the *Verona*, a ship destined to be sunk by a German submarine in 1918, during the Great War/WWI. The *Verona*'s port of departure was Naples. My grandfather's port of entry to the United States was Ellis Island in New York Harbor. The date was December 1, 1913.

"To digress a bit, I traveled with my husband and daughter, in the late 1990s, to visit the renovated, newly opened Ellis Island. From there, we took a ferryboat tour around Liberty Island and the Statue of Liberty. I remember thinking, as we slowly sailed by the majestic 'Lady Liberty,' 'This is what Grandpap saw on that frigid December day in 1913, as he entered the gates of America and a whole new world- a whole new life.'

"If your readers visit Ellis Island, they will see walls covered with names near the main building. Donald (Donato) Papa's name is etched in stone among those thousands of others who so bravely left their homelands, their families, the cultures, traditions and languages familiar to them, to enter the United States of America through that great portal to freedom and opportunity.

"To return to my grandfather's journey: That evening, after all the processing and test-taking, Grandpap boarded a train in New York City, bound for Bridgeport, Connecticut, and his first job in his new country.

"For several months, he labored at the Bridgeport Brass Company, a factory that manufactured springs. That was his day-job. In the evenings, he worked in a barbershop owned by his step-sister's brother-in-law Tony. Grandpap was an apprentice barber, which meant that he received no pay. However, he was learning the trade with hands-on training.

"After six months, he quit his job at the factory. For the next two years, during the daytime hours, he did odd jobs around the town, with his evenings still at the barbershop.

"In 1915, he visited his brother Mike, who, as mentioned earlier, lived in Uniontown, Pennsylvania. Mike was overjoyed to be reunited with his younger brother, and he begged Grandpap to move to Uniontown, so they could always be near one another. My grandfather agreed, though the arrangement did not set well with his step-sister. She reminded Grandpap that she was the one who brought him to America, and that she had given her word to his mother that she would watch over him in his adopted country.

"Grandpap did not want to be separated from either his older brother or his step-sister and her children; it was a difficult decision to make, for he loved them all. He finally told his brother that he would remain in Uniontown with him if he could secure him a job at the enamel plant where Mike was a foreman.

"Mike, however, was reluctant to see his younger brother labor in that place, and he told him firmly to learn a trade. What, he asked my grandfather, was he interested in? Grandpap readily replied that he was already familiar with the barber trade, but he voiced a concern that since he would have to start in a Uniontown shop as an apprentice, he would not make enough to pay Mike room and board. Mike answered without hesitation, 'You learn the trade, and I'll keep you.' And so he did.

"In January 1915, Grandpap went to work as an apprentice for Mike's barber. For the first five months, he earned a scanty fifty cents a week. However, after fifteen months, his salary was increased to union scale. Twelve dollars a week! It was a fortune. In those long-past days, a haircut was twenty-five cents, and a shave fifteen cents.

"On July 1, 1925, Donald Papa and Julia Pierro (my maternal grandmother) married before a judge at the Fayette County Courthouse in Uniontown, Pennsylvania. Grandma was nineteen, Grandpap twenty-eight.

"Their first home was an apartment on Uniontown's East Main Street. One of the many stories Grandma used to relate was that of her lost engagement ring. Here is the story: One morning, my grandmother got up and began to dress for the day. All of a sudden, she realized her engagement ring was not on the dresser where she always set it at bedtime. She remembered putting it there the night before, and becoming ever-more frantic, she called for my grandfather. They searched everywhere but could not find the cherished token of their vows. Grandma was terribly upset, but Grandpap had to leave for work at the barbershop, so he sadly left her alone with her tears.

"That evening, when he returned home, he went up to their bedroom to change his clothes. In doing so, he heard a 'Ping!' as something dropped out of his pants and hit the wooden floor. There was the ring! Evidently, it had been swept off the dresser, either the night before or very early that morning when he dressed for the shop, and somehow landed in the cuff of his workpants. Imagine that! Grandpap had walked to the barbershop, worked all day, then walked home that evening and up the flight of steps to their apartment with Grandma's engagement ring in the cuff of his pants!

"When the Stock Market crashed in 1929, it took a toll on everyone, including my grandparents. In 1930, Grandpap was forced to cut the number of chairs and his staff in half and move his business to a smaller/less expensive location. He and a sole barber employee moved from his South Gallatin Avenue location to a new site on North Gallatin Avenue that was conveniently only two and a half blocks from his home.

"Here is another family story Grandpap used to tell involving the 'Black Hand,' aka the 'Cosa Nostra' or the 'Mafia.' One morning when my grandfather arrived at his barbershop, he discovered he had been robbed. This was during the Great Depression, and times were hard, so there was more crime. The thief or thieves not only took cash, they made off with some of my grandpap's necessary barber tools– razors, scissors and such.

"There was at that time a patron who came to the shop, who was suspected of being involved in the 'Black Hand.' Of course, the man never spoke of his reputed underworld connections, but there were whispered rumors about him and said connections around the town. Grandpap told us that irrespective of the gossip, the man always spoke and acted as a gentleman.

"On a side note, my grandfather had many different customers, from all walks of life and from all socio-economic levels. He treated each of them with the same courteous respect. If a patron wanted to talk, that was fine with Grandpap, and he conversed with him. If a patron was silent, that was fine too.

"Getting back to my prior story: During the suspected 'Black Hand's' next visit to the barbershop, Grandpap mentioned, in passing, that he had been robbed and that some of the needed tools of his trade had also been taken. A day or so afterward, as Grandpap approached the shop, he espied a package wrapped in plain brown paper at the foot of the barbershop door. The opened package revealed his stolen razors and scissors! I can't recall from that old family tale if the stolen money was among the tools or not. I do know this, however, the next time that customer came to the shop, he casually inquired if my grandfather ever got his tools returned to him. Grandpap answered 'Yes,' and nothing more was ever said. Though he could never prove it, my grandfather always believed that gentleman had a hand in the recovery of his stolen items.

"During the next fifty-six years, a familiar sight around 'the avenue' was Don Papa walking to and from his barbershop Mondays, Tuesdays, Thursdays, Fridays and Saturdays. In the early years, his work-days extended into evenings. After all, he had a family to take care of. Wednesdays and Sundays were

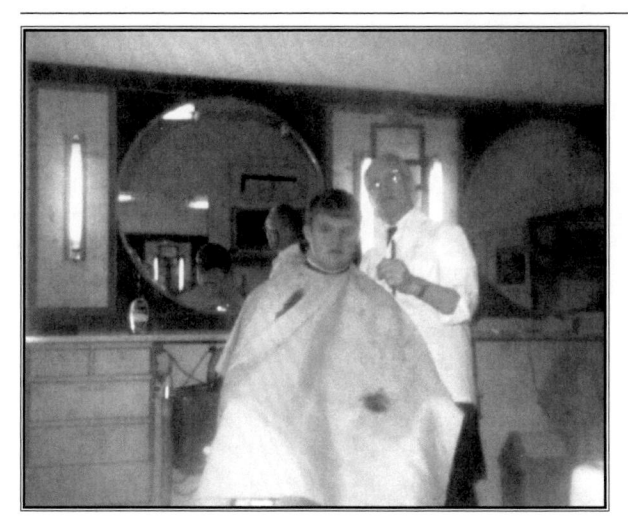

Don Papa cutting his grandson William R. Ziska Junior's hair, 1977

off-days, usually to get chores done around the house.

"Over the years, there must have been thousands of people who sat in Grandpap's barber chairs during the total seventy-two years he barbered– and my grandfather was a friend to them all.

"Our family lived on Uniontown's Askren Street, one street over from Coffey. I can remember seeing Grandpap, between 5:00 and 5:30 p.m., taking long, slow strides up Coffey Street, a neatly folded newspaper tucked under one arm. Sometimes he would be clutching, in his other hand, a white paper bag, filled with delicious hard rolls from Young's Bakery.

"A hot dinner, lovingly prepared by Grandma, awaited him. Always quiet as a church mouse, Grandpap's habit was to enter his home through the basement door, climb the stairs (that he pronounced 'stays') from the basement to the kitchen, then ever so gently open the door leading into that room fragrant with the rich smells of Grandma's supper. If they were dining at our house, he quietly entered the back door. Either way, this always seemed to startle Grandma, and I can still hear her exclaiming, 'Oh, Donald, you scared me to death!'

"And he, with a smile and a look of love in his eyes, would touch or tweak her cheek and answer, 'Oh, Julie. My Julie.'

"The way Grandpap entered a room was indicative of his nature, at all times soft-spoken and gentle. Donald Papa was the kind of man who did not receive public recognition for his good deeds (and these were countless), did not make the history books; but he left a lasting impression of goodness, decency, and honesty upon each of those with whom he came in contact.

"Grandpap was well-known in the community where he lived all those years. At the Gallatin Bank he was able to secure small loans on his good name and sterling character.

"Lucille Conn Everly, a bank teller, became a co-worker of mine at the bank. Grandpap did a lot of banking with Lucille over the years. When I was hired in 1972 and introduced to her, I told her I was familiar with her name because my grandfather, Donald Papa, had spoken of her many times. When she heard who my grandfather was, she smiled. 'Donald Papa is a true gentleman!' she pronounced. Everyone who knew him said as much, for it was true.

"Between his work, his lodge meetings, his dart-ball league, and household duties, Grandpap was a busy man. I cannot recall him ever being idle. Nevertheless, he always found time to visit a sick friend or a patron in the hospital. Each and every time one of his customers died, he paid his respects at the funeral home. We would often joke that Grandpap was forever going to the funeral home, and he

Don and Julia Papa, Christmas 1979
Papa photos courtesy Nancy Anderson, Uniontown, PA

would reply, 'I have to go. He was my good customer, my good friend.' We wondered how one man could have so many good customers and good friends ... *but he did.*

"Because Grandpap knew in his heart that he would not have much time remaining with his beloved Julie- my grandmother had cancer- he decided to retire, and in the summer of 1986, he sold his barbershop. When he reluctantly closed the doors that final day, it was the end of seventy-two years of barbering. He had loved his work and the time spent with his customers.

"My grandfather was such a wise man. His wisdom came from life-experience and with age, and his education from his customers. He loved to talk with his customers, and, as I said, they came from all walks of life, laborers, doctors, lawyers, accountants; Grandpap got them all. He knew how to talk to each of them, what to ask, and what not to ask. Grandpap was a great listener too, and that's why I say he was educated by his interesting array of customers.

"When any of us had troubles, he always had a story ready to tell us, to ease our pain or our worries. These were old tales carried with him to America from Italy. He had many words of wisdom; some were his own, gained from living; others, the famous words of one of his many heroes.

"On the subject of money, he told us from the day he started his first job, he always put money in his savings. He said any fool could make money, but it took a wise man to know how to handle money. Mostly, though, he always told us to 'love one another and live a good, clean, Christian life.'

"Grandpap always kept a neatly clipped and folded article from a trade magazine tucked away in his wallet. It was an article about a barber who retired after sixty-nine years. His self-imposed goal was to top that fellow- and he did. I think he would have continued to barber until he was a hundred, if Grandma had not taken ill. To him, spending precious time with his Julie was ever so much more important. My grandmother's passing meant a dramatic change in Grandpap's life ... a *dramatic* change.

"In the early morning of December 23, 1987, my grandfather suffered a stroke while visiting with my aunt in Pittsburgh. He passed quietly away and with dignity on the morning of December 27, 1987. He is greatly missed.

"I'd like to share with you the following newspaper article that appeared on the editorial page in the Uniontown *Herald-Standard* two days after Grandpap passed over. It was written by his one-time neighbor and longtime friend, newspaper reporter and local historian Walter 'Buzz' Storey: 'Donald Papa, One of America's Heroes' topped the article as the header.

" 'Donald Papa died Sunday at the age of ninety. He had been a barber in Uniontown for seventy-two years, an incredible record of longevity, persistence, dedication and attention to duty. When he finally left his shop on North Gallatin Avenue last year, it was the passing of an institution. Quiet, soft-spoken, devoted to his family, a friend to thousands over the years, he epitomized the kind of good citizens- unsung heroes, if you will- who make America great.'

"My dear grandfather was laid to rest, on December 30, 1987, beside his Julie, in the main mausoleum at Sylvan Heights Cemetery, Uniontown, Pennsylvania. Gone now to their heavenly home, Grandpap and Grandma will live forever in the hearts and minds of their children and grandchildren. Their rich legacy of honesty and decency will enduringly be cherished within the bosom of our family. I pray we honor them by continuing their traditions.

"When I visit their resting place, my thoughts are these: My grandparents were proud people who loved God, their family, their Italian heritage, and their adopted country. An era is gone with their passing but not forgotten, for a new era begins, and the cycle of life continues."

Nancy Anderson, Uniontown, PA

Author's Notes: Popular barber Don Papa was, indeed, a Fayette County institution. He cut hair from the quarter-a-haircut era through the "flat-top" and the hippie-long-hair epoch into the modern age of men's hair styling- that's five generations of Uniontown area's families.

Mr. Papa remembered when barbershops administered massages, shampoos, and singes, and the more elite and/or discriminating had their own shaving cups on the barbershop shelf, engraved with their names in gold lettering.

After World War II, the barbershop business started to pick up when the "flat-top" made its entrance into the realm of men's fashion. It was good for business because it required extra attention. Customers came for a haircut every two weeks.

Mr. Papa's specialty, however, was what he referred to as the "gentlemen's haircut" that involved a lot of scissor work to style the hair and shape it attractively round the head. It took skill and patience, things for which Don Papa was known.

Barbering was a pleasure to that special man, and he took keen satisfaction in seeing, on nearly a daily basis, old and new friends. To echo the late Buzz Story, "[Donald Papa] epitomized the kind of good citizens- unsung heroes, if you will- who make America great."

Nancy Anderson is the treasured reader who planted the idea of this Chronicle in my mind. I hope you enjoyed her cherished memories of her grandfather.

Clara Demarco, whose family story follows, is a remarkable woman, whom I have come to know and love over the years. I admire her fortitude, her strong sense of family, duty, and responsibility, traits inherited from her immigrant ancestors.

Kathy Sawyer, Eleanor Shutsy Michalowski, Janet Gabelt, Ralph Mazer, Tony Zuback, and Carol Zuback Alexander are also readers, who, with warmth and sweetness of soul, were willing to share their interesting family stories with me for this book.

Bob Cole, Drenda Gostkowski, and Barbara M. Neill are fellow writers with whom I have shared kindred sentiments and for whom I have the deepest respect. Barbara and I once taught in the same school district. I have always admired her positive outlook as well as her extraordinary zest for life!

Marcia Mountain and I were classmates. How much she seems to have inherited from her ancestor Susan Kern! For one thing, Susan, as you will read, was known round about for her sewing skills. During our high school years, Marcia would often take up pattern and material on Saturday afternoon to sew a new dress for church on Sunday morning.

Francis Mongell is a nurse manager in my hometown hospital. In addition, he is president of the local school board. In fact, he has been a public servant in my home area for many years. It is not uncommon for him to go several weeks without a day off. He takes both his jobs seriously and to heart, and he gives to both 110%. It is not easy to make the assessments he sometimes is forced to make, but he is not afraid to make a decision and to stick by it. On top of all that, Francis is a loving husband and a beloved figure in his neighborhood. I remember calling him one evening only to learn that he was next door, giving an IV to the neighbor's cat that was suffering from kidney problems.

These people did not come by their admirable qualities by accident, though each of them did pick them off a tree- their family trees. From their ancestors, they inherited their love of country, their deep-rooted sense of responsibility and duty, and their strong work ethics.

You won't find the names of their pioneer and immigrant ancestors in typical history books, but, dear readers, you will most certainly find them in mine. *A cross section of the people who get overlooked and lost to history are the people I am presenting to you in this Chronicle- just everyday folks who had their own poignant stories to tell.*

These unsung heroes were not perfect. Like the heroes you will find in conventional histories, these unacclaimed, obscure heroes possessed weaknesses and faults along with their strengths, because they were not demigods; they were human. And like their conventional history counterparts, they shared common denominators of courage and perseverance.

Though most of these family stories are about immigrants who passed through the portals of Ellis Island, a few are family tales of pioneers. Pioneers and immigrants alike carried with them from the old countries their traditions, their foods, their music, and their tried-and-true home remedies. These facets of their homelands helped sustain them as they adjusted to their new country.

The word "pioneer" always evokes images of hard work. Americans pushing westward labored hard to conquer forests, mountains, prairies, and rivers. They battled Indians, sicknesses, and the elements to own the land they worked. I have related throughout the preceding volumes of my *County Chronicles* stories of heroic pioneer women struggling to sustain family and home by working long hours under the most trying conditions.

Work. That word is totally unavoidable when discussing these early Americans.

The Native Americans too worked hard, to hold on to their lands and the old ways, and later to assimilate into the American fabric of life.

After the Civil War, America became a land of immigrants. And ponder this, readers, these were the most daring and energetic members of the nations from which they emigrated.

They did not come here thinking they would be idle. Jobs- work- the chance for a better life for themselves and their children is what drew them in such great numbers. Even those who fled the old countries to escape religious or social oppression came to seek work in America's industrial revolution. Immigrants infused the American ideology with the virtue and efficacy of hard work. Like the pioneers, immigrants to America endured many hardships. Pay was minimal; working conditions were poor and often dangerous, and health and death benefits were non-existent.

This bright tapestry of ethnic peoples created the great melting pot that is America, the very first of which was our own noble commonwealth of Pennsylvania. These courageous trailblazers are the true "stuff of legends"- the "stuff of America." These were the people who molded this country and made it strong! They and their descendents are the reason America endures!

And those hardworking, stalwart, courageous pioneers and immigrants are the people we should try and emulate today!

Now, let us continue with more of their remarkable stories.

~ ~ ~

"My father, Carl Izzo, came from Naples to this country through Canada. I do not know why he didn't come through the port of New York like so many others of his era, but he didn't. Perhaps the shipping line was British, and it docked in Canada. Perhaps that line offered a better price for passage to America; I don't know. I do know that he was just a boy, only ten or eleven years of age, when he immigrated here over a century ago. On his journey, he was accompanied by his stepfather.

"After disembarking from their ship, they traveled a short distance by train, debarking at a small Canadian town, the name of which I have long forgotten. At the railroad station, my father's life, unbeknownst to him at the time, was about to change even more drastically than it already had. His stepfather told him to wait there at the railroad station, that he had some business to attend to, after which he would return to pick him up.

"My father waited there all day, and still his stepfather did not return for him. He was dog-tired, hungry, and thirsty, without so much as a cent in his pocket. He was also frightened. Can you imagine how he must have felt, a youngster alone in a strange country with no money, and only knowing a word or two, if that, of the language? I think all he had in his possession was one small bag of clothing, smaller than what we'd call today an overnight bag.

"Finally, the man at the railroad station came over to him and said, 'It's late, I don't think anyone is coming for you.' My father, trying desperately not to cry, answered in Italian, broken English, and with gestures, attempting to make himself understood to the railroad agent that someone *was* coming to pick him up.

"He sank back down and waited longer, for what, I am sure, must have seemed like an eternity; and again, the ticket agent came over to him. By this time, the poor boy had fallen sound asleep on one of the hard wooden benches in the railroad station waiting room.

"The kind man gently shook my father awake and offered to take him home with him for the night. It was a lucky break, for my dad ended up residing with that railroad fellow and his family and working on the railroad as a water boy. That sympathetic stranger was my father's welcome to the New World and a whole new life.

"I know you're wondering if my father ever saw his stepfather again. *He did not.* The incident remains to this day a family mystery. The man was never seen or heard from again.

"As I was coming of age, I remember that my father always said he came to America to find a better place, with better opportunities than they had in the old country. People did not come here because they had it so good where they came from. They did not. I know my father always placed a great deal of importance on education. That was the *key*, he said, to having a better life. He always said that he was, from that first frightening experience in the railroad station, *determined* to learn English, to learn to speak it properly and to read and write it well. He did too.

"My father worked in many places before he finally settled in Fayette County, Pennsylvania. I remember him saying that he labored in Michigan, and then in New York before he came to southwestern Pennsylvania. As a child, I asked him once, 'Papa, how did you ever end up in Dunbar [Pennsylvania]?' His answer was that it was a prosperous town, a boomtown before the dawn of the twentieth century.

"Located in the heart of industrial Pennsylvania, it surely was. In the early days, there were several industries here, iron ore, coal and coke, and wire glass, to name a few. The promise of employment for better pay drew him, and he stayed ... so Dunbar became our family's permanent home.

"After working hard and saving every penny he could, my father, in his twenties, began thinking about taking a wife. At the time, my mother's brother was working with him, and the two had bonded in friendship. Back in the old country of Italy, they each had a sister whom they wanted to introduce to the other. Soon, letters were exchanged, and the pen-pals became sweethearts, with the promise of marriage.

"My father journeyed back to the Naples Bay area to marry my mother, Mary Moliterno. They wed in Italy and made the trip together to America, not in steerage, as my father had first come here, but second-class. This was right around 1900, and yes, they did enter through the great portal of Ellis Island; but since they had come second-class, their entry was accomplished with relative ease.

"For my mother, this was a dream-come-true, and her first sight of Lady Liberty in New York Harbor was an unforgettable thrill. The Statue with its raised arm lighting the way was symbolic of America, and on the ship's crowded deck, she shed tears of real joy.

"When my parents first set up housekeeping in Dunbar, where my father worked, they had an apartment in the Soldano Building. Outside one of the windows, across the way, my mother could see a vacant lot. During her daily household duties, she would often pause to look at the empty tract of land in reverie. She told me how she dreamed of buying that piece of ground one day and building a house on it. Within a few years after they married, she and my father did just that.

"No sooner, however, did they realize their dream of owning their own land, their own house, when who should show up at their door, bag and baggage from Italy, but my father's mother! She moved in and stayed till she died at the age of ninety-four. And my parents had a big family! I had nine brothers and sisters. I am the youngest and the sole surviving sibling.

"After my paternal grandmother had a stroke, she became bedridden, and there were those who told my mother she should put her mother-in-law in a home. But mama would not do it. 'No,' she said, 'she helped me raise my children, and now she needs me. I will return the care she gave us.'

"My mother spoon-fed my grandmother those last three or four years of her life, and when she died, my mother knew she had done the best she could for her. Of course, we all pitched in. That was the way it was then; families helped one another. Along with the traditions, customs, and wisdom from the old countries came a deep-rooted sense of responsibility. We took care of our own.

"One final thing I want to say concerns education. My family, that is my brothers and sisters, were mostly self-educated. My eldest sibling did go to college. He became an electrical engineer. My parents wanted each of us to go for higher learning, but the Great Depression put the damper on that dream. We each, though, worked hard in life; each became self-taught. When it came to *life experience*, we were all graduates *cum laude*.

"I have always led a good life, one sated with hard work and more than my share of responsibility, the deep meaning and significance for which I inherited from my parents, and passed down through three generations to my great-grandchildren. I have had my share, perhaps more than my share, of sadness, but I have laughed a lot too. I have lived nearly a century, and every night when I say my prayers, I thank God for all my blessings."

– Clara DeMarco, Dunbar, PA

~ ~ ~

"The coal mines of northern England employed large numbers of miners during the seventeenth and eighteenth centuries. Among them were generations of my ancestors, the family Cole.

"By 1880 the patriarch of the family was one Richard Watson Cole. Twice widowed, he lived at Cambois Colliery just north of Newcastle Upon Tyne, close by the remnants of Hadrian's Wall.

"Richard Watson had five sons; all but the youngest worked in the mines. He had two daughters, one of whom had already married a miner. The future showed no promise of fulfilling his mother's fervent wish that her descendants be free of digging deep in the earth for coal.

"Whether it was the promise of higher wages or a desire to fulfill the wish to escape the grueling labor in the coal mines, we will never know, but the Cole family began their steady exodus from England to America.

"Richard Watson's oldest son Nicholas, with his wife and two children, embarked from Liverpool, and arrived in New York City on May 3, 1880. The second son, John, and his wife arrived on the *SS Illinois* at the port of Philadelphia on May 23, 1881. Richard Watson Cole, patriarch of the family, and his youngest son arrived in New York Harbor aboard the *Anchoria* on November 16, 1881. A fourth son, Fenwick Barnfather Cole, departed Liverpool on the *SS Ohio* and arrived in Philadelphia on December 23, 1881. Another son, James, and the youngest daughter, Mary Ann, arrived about the same time. The last daughter, Isabella, and her husband, Richard Watson Postgate, left England in 1882 or 1883. Only one son of Richard Watson remained in England by 1884.

"The emigrant Cole family traveled to western Pennsylvania where they entered the coal mines in supervisory positions. They all became naturalized citizens of the United States of America with the words of the Naturalization Papers, stating, for each of them, that '... *he would support the CONSTITUTION OF THE UNITED STATES, and that he did absolutely and entirely renounce and adjure all allegiance and fidelity to every foreign Prince, Potentate, State or Sovereignty whatever, and particularly to the Queen of England ... .*'

"Life in the New World did not immediately provide escape from the dangerous work beneath the earth, in the dark, dank pits of the coal mines. Eldest son Nicholas worked in a number of mines before becoming a foreman of No. 2 Furnace in Dunbar, Pennsylvania. He died unexpectedly in the bathtub of a heart attack after a hard Saturday morning shift at the furnace. Second son John eventually settled at Boswell in Somerset County, Pennsylvania. He held the position of Assistant Superintendent of the Boswell Mine when he was killed in a devastating explosion. The third son, James, worked in the coal mines at California, Pennsylvania. The fourth son, Fenwick Barnfather, worked in the mines near Dunbar before moving to Vesta No. 4 Mine at California, Pennsylvania. Daughter Isabella's husband worked in the coal mines too, primarily in Pennsylvania's Fayette County. The family departure from the coal mines, however, would begin with daughter Mary Ann and son Richard William.

"Only one grandson of Richard Watson Cole ever worked in a coal mine. With his generation, the Cole family entered the fields of education, music, journalism, and banking. Richard Watson Cole's mother, I am certain, was unquestionably pleased.

"Today the descendants of Richard Watson Cole inhabit the far reaches of the United States where they engage in any number of careers. Someday perhaps there will be a book to remind them of the struggles of their ancestors– the people who set them free of the back-breaking, choking, and death-defying life in the grim cavernous pits of the coal mines."

– Robert E. Cole, author/historian, Hilton, NY, formerly of Fayette County, PA

~ ~ ~

"My great-grandfather, Giovanni Volpe, came to America with his little family in 1899. He was thirty-three years old, his wife Angelina was twenty-eight, and their two children, Vincenzo and Giuseppe were seven and four respectively. They would welcome six more children after their arrival in America.

"Giovanni and Angelina with their two children made the long, treacherous journey to the United States via the ship *Ems,* a Scottish-built ocean vessel that held 1,250 passengers. Of that number, one thousand were third-class or steerage passengers. I have no doubt that my ancestors were four of the poor 'huddled masses' in the bowels of their vessel.

"The ship manifest from the *Ems* lists Giovanni and family as passengers on a voyage that landed at the Port of New York on May 4, 1899. They were processed through Ellis Island. My great-grandfather declared that he paid for the tickets himself, and his monetary worth upon disembarking at America's great gateway to freedom was a grand total of $19.00!

"His journey had begun in the village of Torchiara, which is located in the Southern Italian province of Salerno along the Amalfi

Vincenzo Volpe and wife Rose Marie on their wedding day, 1916

coast. Somehow, that journey ended in New Salem, Fayette County, Pennsylvania.

"Although Great-Grandfather spoke with a thick Italian accent, he did not encourage his children to speak Italian. When I questioned my father about this, he said the family sentiment was 'You are American, you will speak English.'

"All of Giovanni's children Americanized their names as further evidence of the allegiance the family felt for their new country. My grandfather, Vincenzo Gennaro, became 'James Vincent Volpe.'

"In his later years, Great-Grandfather Giovanni, who became known as 'John,' worked as the maintenance man at the New Salem Christian Church, where he occasionally attended the services, always seated in the rear pew.

"After his death, the church held a memorial service in his honor. My mother attended the service and recalls the pastor stating, 'We will sorely miss the little man in the last pew.' In addition, some of the hymnals at the Christian Church bore a dedication to John Volpe.

"My father was born February 14, 1926, to his Italian immigrant parents and christened James Vincent Volpe, Jr. Daddy was short in stature but huge in presence. He impacted my life in ways that are still being revealed to me. I saw him in so many different lights throughout our years together: He was a Roman God in my childhood. His rule and power were absolute. In my teens he was Superman, able to build or repair anything and taking on three jobs to provide for us.

"When I was in my twenties, my father became 'human.' I never saw him weep until the death of his father, and that experience will stay with me forever. He came to me where I was working and told me the news. He was standing there with his heart breaking right in front of me. I gathered him into my arms as I had never done before and held him as tightly as I could. Yes, he was my father, but that day he was also a lost, very sad, little boy.

"As I approached my thirties, and he neared the end of his life, I became acquainted with his inner-self. It was through my father's dying that I learned of his living. We spent countless hours together in the kitchen, in the car, and in the radiation unit of Pittsburgh's Mercy Hospital.

"His years underground in the dusty coal mines of southwestern Pennsylvania were claiming their due. Regardless of illness- or perhaps in spite of it- his life was filled with a deep appreciation for laughter. When he chose, mirth would literally spill out of him, and he laughed with his whole being, his whole essence.

"He derived great satisfaction in telling me some of the worst jokes I think I have ever heard. When I would tell him so, he would throw his head back and laugh till he cried, the tears rolling down his cheeks. That was his gift, you see, the great gift of laughter. He could always raise our spirits ... make each of us feel better. It was- *magical.*

"He taught me to love Steeler football, how to play a first-rate game of poker, and how to cook, all the while telling me the stories of a life that would become inextricably bound up with my own."

– Kathy Sawyer, Taylors, South Carolina, formerly of Fayette County, PA

~ ~ ~

"My Baba (grandmother), Katarzyna Mech, came from Poland to Pittsburgh with her brother's wife. She obtained employment at the Pittsburgh Athletic Association in Oakland as a cleaning lady. There, she met my Judak (grandfather), Waclaw Gostkowski, who was head of the cleaning staff. He had arrived in the Pittsburgh area before Baba. They married at Saint Stanislaus Polish Church in the Strip District, subsequently residing in that general area of the 'Strip' for many years. Their first three children, Valeria Stella, Henrik, and Anna, were baptized in that church.

"Then Judak obtained factory employment in the small riverfront town of Groveton, Pennsylvania, near McKees Rocks. I think it rather romantic that, during this period, my grandparents lived in a cosy houseboat on the Ohio River, and it was there that my father Walter was born. He was baptized at SS Cyril & Methodius Church in McKees Rocks.

"Soon after, Judak went to work at a Harmarville coal mine. Then, they lived in company housing even after Judak contracted miner's asthma.

"To keep body and soul together, Baba, like so many other immigrant women, began taking in boarders. However, once Judak was no longer able to work, money became scarce.

"This was during the era of Prohibition; thus, Baba's boarders encouraged her to become a bootlegger so they would not have to go elsewhere for their drink. A relative of hers also encouraged her, soon afterward teaching her how to make whiskey.

"In no time at all, my baba was in business, making lots of money while sending the kids round about to make deliveries. However, when the mining company found out she was bootlegging, the family was ordered to vacate- immediately.

"The Gostkowski's then moved to Verona, where they occupied a rented house until they built their own home on Penn Street. It was here that the bootlegging really took off. All the children made deliveries to Baba's ever-increasing list of thirsty customers.

"My aunts tell how they would hide the bottles under their aprons while they rode the local trolleys to the delivery destinations. They constantly worried about getting caught with 'the goods.'

"My father recalls that, as a young boy, he delivered to the folks in Harmarville. This was before the Hulton Bridge was built. Near

Katarzyna Mech Gostkowski, in her late twenties, circa 1921
Photo courtesy Drenda Gostkowski

where the bridge stands today, a Mr. Hulton owned a ferry. My father Walter would catch the ferry from Verona to Harmarville, and then hop the trolley that ran along that side of the river to his customers.

"Although the family made whiskey, Judak had a lifelong passion for making wine. One year, his wild-cherry wine went sour; so, 'waste not, want not,' they ran it through the still and made excellent wild-cherry brandy. My father remembers yet how crazy people were for that wild-cherry brandy. For that, they got double the money!

"Bootleggers paid off the local police, and my family was no exception. In truth, many of the 'boys in blue' drank in the Gostkowski kitchen ... but once in a while, there was a raid.

"For many years I heard the 'tsk tsks' of the family as they told how my 'cad of a grandfather' ran out the back door, leaving poor Baba to go to jail. That was until I spoke to Baba's oldest child, my Aunt Stella. I was 'tsk tsking' myself when she said, 'Oh no, you got it all wrong.' The story she told was wonderful.

"Baba did get hauled before an official; however, if it had been Judak whom the police had carted off, he surely would have had to do real jail time in addition to having to pay a hefty fine. Baba, being a woman, and a wily one at that, did not have to spend time in jail or pay a fine. When she went before the judge, she cried big Polish tears about how she was just a poor, pitiful woman trying to raise her four children. She sobbed prettily that she had no other way of making enough money to do that. Of course the judge fell for the tears and her story and let her go with a mere slap on the wrist.

"During one of the raids, the police found the still. It was hidden in the crawl space above the attic. The Gostkowski family always felt it was someone they knew well who tipped off the police. The police smashed the still, and as Prohibition had just been repealed, Baba never replaced it with another.

"Judak, however, continued to make wine. My mother claims he made the best wine she ever tasted. I personally remember him cultivating grapes and bringing jugs of his wine to our house for us.

"The irony of all this is that none of the Gostkowski family ever touched a drop, except for one uncle and my father when they came of age, and they were only light drinkers at best."

— Drenda Gostkowski, Cabot, PA

~ ~ ~

"My paternal ancestors did not enter this land through the portal of Ellis Island, since they made their passage long before it was designated the first Federal immigration station.

"There follows the text of the *Certificate of Character* presented by Covenanter Church to James Lyons when he left Ireland in 1763: 'These are to certify that the bearers hereof, James Lyons and his wife Martha "alias" Dobbins, lived within the bounds of this congregation for many years immediately preceding the date hereof and always behaved themselves soberly, honestly and religiously, and now, at their leaving this, are free of all public scandal, and any grounds of reproach, and as they are about to go to North America, may be received into any Christian Society where providence may order their lot. Given under my hand at Monyrsask in the County of Down, Ireland, May 6, 1763, S. McKean, Depending Minister.'

"Within this *Certificate of Character,* the word 'alias' could be translated *née,* meaning 'born,' for Dobbins was Martha's maiden name.

"At the remove of nearly 250 years, the tone of moral authority in the abovementioned document sounds almost comical. But, in the context of the era in which it was written, it would have been perceived as a solemn stamp of approval for James and Martha Lyons. Considering the enormity and uncertainty of their undertaking, it was no doubt comforting for the couple to possess this letter of entrée with its positive affirmation of merit as they embarked on an unknown destiny.

"One could also conclude that this couple had great confidence in their convictions and in themselves, for such a fateful crossing required unwavering courage. Mortals who had once lived by the words 'For King and Country' found on the Lyons coat-of-arms, James and Martha would no longer serve a sovereign nation. Their allegiance would be pledged to a home in the new world that proffered the promise of hope and freedom.

"The Alexander Lyons branch of the James Lyons family from which I am descended has but three remaining male members– Donald Curtis Lyons (my father), Jon Edward Lyons (my brother), and his son Zachary David Lyons (my nephew). At this moment in time young Zach is the 'last man standing,' and, as yet, knows very little of his Lyons ancestors and their storied past.

"Perhaps, one day Zach will learn, as I did, of his early forbears by reading the family history his grandfather compiled. He will discover the men of Scotch-Irish Presbyterian stock who made their way– at a time of eternal vigilance– from the southeastern sector of Penn's Woods to the newly formed Indiana County on the precarious westerly frontier.

"My kinsmen were feisty pioneer farmers who acquired land, cultivated and harvested crops, married, reared (and often buried) children, battled disease, fought in the Revolutionary War and the War of 1812 and died– unsung heroes. These original settlers cleared the way for one family's American journey, literally and figuratively. Others soon followed in their sure footsteps.

"Ensuing generations had their share of trials and tribulations, shining hours and glory days in turn. Lyons men continued to serve their country in war and in peacetime. Newton, son of William and Eliza DeVinney Lyons, died while serving the Union during the Civil War at Vicksburg. Over the work-filled decades, sickness and plague continued to ravage households. Before the advent of the miracle drugs, Dudley C. Lyons and his wife Anna Margaret Rhea Lyons lost three small children- Newton, Morris and Laura- to the scarlet fever epidemic of 1891. It was never easy, but sturdy stock persevered.

"Eventually migrating to neighboring Westmoreland County, some family members continued as landowners and farmers; others found work in the factories of the now-booming industrial nation and later in the companies of the technology-driven land; several established their own business enterprises. The risks taken were many, the obstacles ably overcome, and the accomplishments hard-earned. An oft-repeated family stance during my lifetime has been: *The first ninety-nine years are the hardest.*

"For now, the lives of James and Zachary Lyons embody the brackets of an ancestral saga- the former's contributing text long-ended; the latter's newly-begun. My fervent wish for my nephew and in due course his issue, male and/or female, is an abiding *belief in self* and the positive reinforcement of that belief no matter 'where providence may order their lot.'

"Author Jack Gibb once said, 'Self-confidence is the result of a successfully survived risk.' My ancestors and, certainly, those of each *County Chronicles V* vignette contributor and reader are proof positive of that!"

- Barbara M. (Lyons) Neill, Latrobe, PA

~ ~ ~

"After a long voyage in steerage across the Atlantic, my maternal grandmother, Gertrude Emma Gramm, arrived, circa 1920, at Ellis Island from her native Germany. During the lengthy screening process, as she waited with other steerage passengers on a bench, one of the kind officials handed her an orange. Never having seen one before, she had no idea how to eat it. Famished, she gratefully bit into the thick, bitter rind, completely unaware that the sweet, edible portion of the strange fruit was hidden just beneath the surface.

"After enduring two more bites, she found it too difficult- *impossible*- to continue eating. Grandma agonized over throwing away a precious piece of food, for she knew well the value of food- through hunger. Finally, she did discard the acrid orb, but lo! She carried the guilt for many years to come.

"Gertrude came to America under the sponsorship of her oldest sister's employers, a wealthy family in Chicago. There, she worked as a maid and a cook for a few years till she met and married a handsome American soldier, my grandfather.

"For years, I could not imagine how she managed it, but my dear grandmother learned to speak English- and speak it well- by reading the local newspapers. It just goes to prove, as 'Miss Daisy' advocated in that now-classic film, that if you learn your alphabet and learn how to sound out the letters, you can teach yourself to read. It proves too that where there is a will, there is a way. And that persevering immigrant resolve became- the American way."

- Marla K. Mechling, Butler, PA

~ ~ ~

"My grandparents, Alex and Anna Honjosky, came from Austria-Hungry in the late 1890s. The Henry Clay Frick Coal Company had sent recruiters to Austria to recruit workers for the coal mine in the Leisenring #1 coal patch.

"For those of your readers who do not know what a 'patch' is, allow me to explain. A patch was a community of coal miners' houses that looked exactly alike and were built by the coal company. These (usually double-family) dwellings were not built for aesthetics, to be sure, but they must have been built to last because most of them are still standing and are still being lived in.

"I don't think the officials at Ellis Island approved of recruiting workers from overseas, but it was done all the time. The recruited workers were schooled by the recruiter how to respond to certain answers when they went through Ellis Island. The fact is that America was hungry for laborers- muscle- and so many in the old countries were eager to come to America and provide that muscle, so it all evened out.

"My grandfather was recruited, as I said, by the H.C. Frick Company, and in time, he was sent by that coal company back to his homeland as a recruiter himself. Actually, he made several trips as a recruiter and to visit his mother in the old country.

"I should tell you that Granpap had been educated in a monastery in Europe by his uncle, and he spoke seven different languages. That was quite unusual for someone of his station in life. My family has always been a believer in education.

"Grandpap also did a tour of duty in the cavalry for Emperor Franz Josef before he came to America. *It was the law.* Whatever the emperor said, you did- no questions asked!

"Before Grandpap embarked on his first recruiting assignment, he convinced Henry Clay Frick, the coal and coke mogul, to build a church for his workers. My grandfather felt strongly that would make recruiting more successful. His efforts led to the construction of Saint Stephens Church (Byzantine rite) in Leisenring #1. H.C. Frick donated the land and paid for the construction of the church building, and for as long as the coal company existed in Leisenring, Frick donated the coal for the church and the rectory, the priest's house.

"Some folks said that Frick was a hard man, cold and greedy. Others said he paid a better wage and was fairer than other coal magnates. I guess it all depended on who you were talking to. By the way, the patch at Leisenring #1 was the *heart* of the famous Connellsville Coking Basin.

"To quote from the premier volume of your *County Chronicles*: 'The Connellsville Coking Basin was a long, narrow land of extremes, ugly by day, smoky and cruelly dirty, with banks of beehive coke ovens, tipples, railroad sidings, and fields and meadows gnawed to the rock-bone with strip-coal operations. Old-timers still vividly recall what a losing battle, during "King Coal's" sway, the women had with the ubiquitous dirt.

" 'Windows and curtains had to be washed constantly; contents in bureaus had to be covered with protective cloths; silver and brass, that tarnished nearly overnight, required continuous polishing; while each spring demanded demonic housecleaning of walls, rugs, upholstery, cabinets, closets, drawers, and, of course, windows and curtains. Author Muriel Earley Sheppard in her book, *Cloud by Day*, stated: "Even the daisies in the fields had dirty faces." Yet, this area was luridly beautiful by night, when, burning through the haze, the glare of those endless rows of ovens painted the sky with *magic*!'

"Eventually, after working hard and saving every cent he could, my grandfather returned to his homeland to marry my grandmother, with whom he had corresponded on a regular basis. When they came, together, to the States, they traveled in steerage, and the dreadful journey took days, thirty days, to be exact. The poor third-class/steerage passengers sat on long benches in the bowels of the ship during the daytime. Nights, they slept on those hard benches.

"Patch housing, as I told you, was provided by the coal company for which the coal miners labored. This meant that if a miner lost his job, he lost his home too. The coal company had an ironclad control over its workers in this manner.

"The early company houses that my immigrant grandparents lived in had no running water or indoor plumbing. There was an outhouse out back for each dwelling, and each kitchen sink had a hand-pump. Laundry was done all by hand, in a large tub with a washboard and strong lye soap. Clothes could also be laundered by boiling them in a large copper kettle. This was necessary due to the black coal dust that embedded itself deep into the miners' clothing- as well as in their skin and their lungs!

"I was in high school, in the mid-1930s, before my grandparents' company house had electricity. I can still recall the kerosene lamps they used before they got electricity. Those lamps, about twelve inches in height, with their glass chimneys, were placed within holders/brackets on the walls. My sister and I used to clean those sooty glass chimneys, and if we broke one, it came out of our allowance. We got a nickel a week spending money. The glass lamps cost fifteen cents a piece.

"During most of his working years, my grandfather hacked out coal in the 'pits'/mines on his knees. When he dug coal, he wore heavy leather coverings on his knees to protect them, but nothing spared the miner of chronic aches and pains. That came with the territory!

"The miners were paid twenty-five cents a wagon for dug-coal. Sometimes their pay was reduced if the hump of coal on the wagon was 'not high enough' to suit the pit bosses.

"Once, my grandfather suffered a serious head injury during a cave-in, and when the others who survived it carried him home, they laid Grandpap on the kitchen floor. The summoned doctor sat on my grandfather's chest to stitch up the gaping wound. No hospital.

No antiseptic. No nothing! The doctor did not even bother to clean the coal dust out of the wound! Thus, for the remainder of his life, Grandpap had a large black blotch on his forehead.

"Every member of the family pitched in and worked in the old days. I say 'the old days' at age ninety now. Those strong work ethics were a carry-over from the old country. Everyone worked, even the children. We kids walked to the coal dump, picked up as much coal as each of us could carry and lugged it home. This provided heat for the company house, and fuel for cooking.

"My mother was twelve when she began working, by then she was ready for the job market. She worked as a maid for a Jewish family in Connellsville. Hers was a live-in job, but once a week she took the streetcar back to Leisenring for a visit; so homesick was she for the family.

"I should tell you that every patch house had a garden behind it, and many folks had a cow. This helped supplement the food purchased at the company store. The backyards of the patch also contained an outdoor bake-oven. I don't mean to say that there was an oven in everyone's backyard. There was not. Several families shared an oven that was central to a number of families. I seem to remember the thing being shaped like a brick igloo. You could bake half-a-dozen loaves of bread in it at a time. A long-handled, wooden paddle was used to slide the dough in and take the bread out when it finished baking.

"Miners and their families had to shop at the company store or risk losing their jobs ... and their homes. Things were dear in those stores, but you dared not shop anywhere else, because if the company officials found out, those who made purchases elsewhere were promptly fired. The coal company took back every cent they paid out in wages, in the rent they collected for the company houses and in the monies spent by their workers in the company stores.

"After my grandparents were settled in from Europe in their company house, a young couple moved into the patch not far from them. They had a newborn baby when the big flu pandemic during World War I claimed both the parents, leaving the child an orphan. Since the couple had no relatives in this country, my grandparents took that baby and raised him as their own.

"Patch neighbors always helped one another in times of crisis. If someone was sick or there was a death, the neighbors all pitched in, preparing the meals, doing the laundry, cleaning, or whatever. That too was a carry-over from the old country. It was the way it had been done in the village where my grandparents came from. And they, like other immigrants, brought their traditions to America with them, along with their strong work ethics and their strong faith in God. Though they were eager to become American citizens, they held fast to their ethnicity.

"Having grown up under the iron rule of Emperor Franz Josef, Grandpap was so proud when he finally had the opportunity to vote. Come Election Day, he would ask round about, 'Did you vote today?' Heaven help those who said 'No,' for they were in for a long, ardent lecture. He drilled in his children, in each of us, the importance of voting and living a clean life as a good American citizen.

"I remember the story passed down in our family about Grandma. En route to America with my grandfather, a passenger in steerage gave birth to a baby. The babe died and was wrapped in a cloth and buried at sea. Combined with the whole sickening steerage experience, that made a lasting impression on my grandmother. Years later, when the family wanted to give her a trip back to the old country, she flatly refused. Everyone assured her that she would have a private cabin and all the comforts, but she would not go. On the other hand, my grandfather made about seven trips back to the homeland.

Anna and Alex Honjosky, circa 1930
Photo courtesy Eleanor S. Michalowski, Bay Village, OH

"I was born in that patch house in Leisenring #1. During my ninety years on this earth, I have seen a lot of history. Hard work has never been a stranger to me. But neither has laughter, nor love of family, God and country. I came from good, stalwart stock, 'thoroughbreds' all of us ... able to run on a dry or wet track.

"For example, my sister, Florence Shutsy-Reynolds, was a WASP (Women Airforce Service Pilots), the first women to fly military aircraft during World War II, and one of only a handful of women to do so. Many of those missions took sheer guts. As you wrote in 'Wings of Athena' in *CC II*, the 'WASP did more than carry military personnel and matériel, they carried the future, because they opened a door for women in both commercial and military aviation.'

"At the time they served, the WASP weren't considered actual military, though they did fly for our country during World War II. However, in 1977, a bill signed by President Jimmy Carter finally awarded these women their well-earned veteran status. Recently, a bill has passed the Senate to award the Congressional Gold Medal to the WASP. My sister told me it took all of fifty-two seconds for the bill to pass. It has gone through the House, the Financial Committee, and to the President's desk. President Barack Obama signed the bill into law on July 1, 2009. So now, it is a sure thing. The WASP will receive the Congressional Gold Medal. I told Florence the medal ceremony will warrant a trip to Washington for our whole clan! From the moment my grandfather landed here, ours has been an ultra-patriotic family.

"Another example of the 'stuff of our ancestors' is the fact that my daughter Janet Barvincak is a police officer, a special breed who works, in addition to her regular patrol, as a hostage negotiator and counselor to rape victims. Once, when Janet and I accompanied my sister to a Wasp reunion, one of the Wasp appraised my daughter with words I shall never forget. She said, 'Janet has the ability to silently project that she is an authority ... very professional, with understanding and compassion for others.' My daughter has a pile of letters in her police file to prove it! I am so proud of her!

"My brother Irvin J. Shutsy earned a PhD. He was a professor at California University of Pennsylvania, and my younger brother, Aloysius J. Shutsy, a Ship's Master, earned his captain papers in the Merchant Marines.

"My grandparents came to America before the turn of the last century. They labored hard to make a permanent place for themselves and their offspring in this Land of Opportunity. They learned to read, write, and speak proper English, becoming good, productive citizens of their adopted country, and they lived honest, decent lives. They instilled in each of us the value of an education, and we each took their advice to heart.

"My Honjosky grandparents left their mark, and though they are not in typical history books, they were, as you say, 'unsung heroes.' Most importantly, they left behind a rich legacy for our family to carry on- one of which I am rightfully proud."

- Eleanor Shutsy Michalowski, Bay Village, Ohio, formerly of Leisenring #1, PA

~ ~ ~

"The family stories most familiar to me are those from my mother's side, the Kern family. They came to America much earlier than the influx of immigrants who came through Ellis Island. When you asked me for a story passed down in our family, I thought of the Kerns, because I know more about them, thanks to the impressively researched, well-documented *Kern Family History* compiled by Tilden H. Kern and printed in April 1956. Among our family members, this paperbound booklet is a cherished item.

"The Kerns hailed from Württemberg (formerly Wirtemberg), in southwest Germany. They set sail for America in the year 1752. A son William may have been born on the ship during the difficult month-long journey. I have also read that he was born near Easton, Pennsylvania, and there seems to be more evidence that he was born *after* the family settled in their adopted country.

"Upon their arrival, the family Kern established themselves along the Schuylkill River in eastern Pennsylvania. That much is for certain. William came of age and eventually married a woman named Catherine Hoover.

"He served in the Continental Army with George Washington, distinguishing himself in the Battle of Brandywine on September 11, 1777, thereupon ascending to the rank of lieutenant.

"At the end of the Revolutionary War, in 1782, William and wife Catherine crossed the Allegheny Mountains, making a new home for themselves in the Indian Creek Valley of Springfield Township in what is now Fayette County, Pennsylvania.

"The tract of land they chose, unbeknownst to them, had already been claimed by someone else through Tomahawk Right. That means this fellow (whose name I do not know) had blazed the trees bounding the tract with a tomahawk, claiming that land for himself. William traded a good rifle for the tract, which was approximately six hundred acres.

"William Kern lived peacefully with his neighbors and was known in the district as a staunchly moral man. He and Catherine were Lutherans, and they traveled by horse and buggy to services at the old Back Creek Lutheran Church in neighboring Saltlick Township.

"William lived ninety-two years, a rarity in those short-lived days on the rough Pennsylvania frontier. My mother's family history indicates that he passed away in 1844.

"William's wife, Catherine Hoover Kern, was a strong woman, emotionally and physically. Like other pioneer goodwives, she had to endure many hardships during her life on the western Pennsylvania frontier. A story survives that one day, in the spring or summer– I don't know which, though I do know it was in the warm season– a noteworthy incident occurred after Catherine had taken the horses out to pasture and was returning from the field.

"Hearing a chilling animal noise close behind her, she turned to see a large bear coming toward her ... coming fast at a good clip. I have always thought that, while executing her chore with the horses, she had somehow gotten between a mother bear and her young, for the angry bear seemed determined to harm her.

"At any rate, when the bear was right on her heels, she wheeled around and whacked it as hard as she could across the back with the bridle she was carrying. She either injured it or stunned it enough that it did not continue following her, as she dashed the short distance to the cabin, slamming and bolting the door before arming herself in case the bear came to the log dwelling in pursuit. It did not; and ever after, with the telling of this victory, Catherine always exhibited a quiet look of satisfaction.

"This stalwart lady gave birth to fifteen children, seven of whom died in infancy due

Joshua and Susan Kern about the era of the American Civil War
Photo courtesy Marcia Ghost Mountan, Connellsville, PA

to sickness, and more than one to a smallpox epidemic. Those who lived were: Solomon, Abraham, William II, Jacob, Jonathan, Joshua, Rosanna, and Mariah. I always thought the names so pretty.

"Of those Kern ancestors, I'd like to relate a little about William and Catherine Kern's sixth child, Joshua, and his wife Susan Marietta Kern. They were my great-great-great-grandparents. I find them the most interesting because of Susan. Susan's family had come from Maryland to settle in Fayette County, Pennsylvania.

"After Joshua and Susan married, they moved, over a number of years, to different sites across Springfield Township. Susan gave birth to seven children, and due to a life of hard work and childbearing, she was not an especially robust woman. She suffered from neuralgia (pain along the course of one or more nerves) and rheumatism (arthritis); however, she was not a complaining woman, and few knew of her ailments.

"Joshua too was afflicted with inflammatory rheumatism, and likely that was why his last farm was not so large. He could not do as much physical labor as he had done before the affliction. He was a quiet, peaceful man who loved the woods, hunting and fishing. He had a reputation of being a good hunter, both for deer and bear. Within the *Kern Family History*, I read that Joshua loved to spin a yarn; loved to swap hunting and fishing stories with a friend before a cheery evening fire in the warmth and comfort of his own hearth. Then, he was no longer quiet but a most fluent raconteur!

"The vicinity of Fayette County between the Indian Creek Reservoir and White Bridge became the site of Susan and her family's permanent cabin. The humble dwelling was one and a half storeys high, four rooms, with glass in the windows. The kitchen boasted a three-cornered cupboard and a large open hearth.

"Here, Susan cooked in iron kettles suspended over the fire. She did her baking in a Dutch oven, including pies, cornpone, cakes, gingerbread, biscuits, and bread. Bread-baking required patience, because she could only bake one loaf at a time, allotting an hour per loaf. Since women in her day were never idle, I am sure she kept busy while each loaf baked.

"Except for the table-and-chairs sector of the kitchen, the remainder of the cabin served as sleeping areas for the family. Susan had at least two trundle beds that were stored under the regular beds days and pulled out nights for sleeping. The cabin's upper level was also for sleeping purposes.

"Joshua and Susan had two out-buildings on their property- a barn, and a springhouse. They always kept at least one horse and a cow.

"Susan is remembered in our family tales as a courageous woman. A favorite story that survives is how she discovered two copperhead snakes sunning themselves on the large stone that was the exterior foundation of her fireplace. Her children were playing all about, and the men were away working for the day. With the safety of her youngsters foremost in her heart and mind, Susan dashed inside for her iron teakettle. Returning, she poured the boiling water over the snakes, scalding them to death.

"Life on the frontier meant sacrifice and heartache. Joshua and Susan's eldest daughter Polly was fatally stricken with typhoid fever, passing away at the age of twenty. Not long afterward, their son John left the area to take a drove of cattle east. John virtually disappeared, and it was seven long years before the family finally heard from him.

"He had written several times to tell his parents and surviving siblings that he had decided to remain 'out East,' but none of his letters had reached his former home. It was only through an accident of fate that the family learned of his whereabouts and his life since his 'disappearance.'

"It happened like this: Another man from the Kern home area started eastward with a drove of cattle. When he paused in his journey at Fayetteville, Franklin County, in south-central Pennsylvania, he heard John Kern's name mentioned in the tavern where he had stopped to take refreshment. After making inquiries, he discovered that John had married, had a son, and was living nearby. Soon afterward, John came home to visit his folks for a time before returning to Fayetteville.

"John was killed in the Civil War, as was Susan's son James, who was of an age to serve. Susan's daughter Sarah's husband also served. Sadly, none of them returned home after that long and bloody struggle.

"Susan Kern is referred to as a 'prize' in the *Kern Family History*. Throughout her life, Susan was known across the countryside for her unselfish deeds of kindness to family, friends and neighbors alike. Regardless of how tired she was, if she received news that someone was ill, she would go to them, either on foot or horseback, with her familiar black lace cap on her head.

"Susan was also known for her sewing. She not only made clothing for herself, she made clothing, especially men's clothing, that she sold for needed income. For a man's overcoat, she usually received two dollars.

"The thing I found amusing was that Susan smoked a pipe. Supposedly, it provided relief when she was suffering from one of her 'smothering spells.'

"Susan's grandchildren used to watch at the road for their Grandma Kern. Frequently she would come riding up on her horse, perched atop a lady's sidesaddle, the black lace cap covering her dove-grey hair. She'd pass the day sewing for the household and/or playing with the children. Summer evenings would always find her sitting cross-legged in the yard, contently smoking her pipe, with the grandchildren crawling over her and drinking in the wonders that only Grandma Kern could supply!

"My mother's family, the Kerns, I told you, hailed from Württemberg, Germany. Years ago, someone claimed that the Ghosts, my father's family, also came from Württemberg, so who knows? Maybe there was a previous connection, in Europe, between my father's ancestors and my mother's. Stranger things have happened!"

– Marcia Ghost Mountan,
Connellsville, PA

~ ~ ~

"My husband Paul's family, the Gabelt family, has its roots in Germany. Their reason for coming to America was to work for the Overholt Distillery. We believe they were recruited by the Overholt family who owned the whiskey distillery. The period in history in which the Gabelts arrived in America was approximately the late 1890s.

"The whole family worked at the distillery, which was a stone's throw from their homes in Owensdale, a community located on the old Everson Road, between Connellsville and Everson [Pennsylvania]. My in-laws derived a good living from their employment, and I remember hearing them say that the labor force at Overholt's was like one big family. As I said, they all worked there, the aunts too.

"The Burke family was also employed at the distillery, and they were related to the Gabelts by marriage. Irish and German marriages are common around here. So, in essence, the Overholt Company *was* 'one big family.' In fact, it was a big, *happy* working family. In olden times, families were all hard-working, and since the Overholts treated all their employees like family, it was, *all in all*, a good place to work.

"A few words about Old Overholt rye from your *County Chronicles Volume II*: 'This large, commercial distillery, established in 1853, was located in the Connellsville area at Broadford (also Broad Ford), eight miles distant from Overholt Village. Overholt's "Old Farm" pure 100-proof rye whiskey was produced at the distillery on the Village's farm, whilst Monongahela Rye (called thus despite the fact that the distillery was located on the Youghiogheny River and not the Mon) was produced at the commercial distillery at Broadford, the label becoming, in tribute to Abraham Overholt after his death, "Old Overholt." This rye became legendary and flourished at that site for over a century, despite two major fires in 1884 and 1905.

" 'Old Overholt is one of the oldest, continuous distilled products in America. After a roller coaster ride through the long tunnel of time, including Prohibition, the brand, with its original recipe, has wound up in Kentucky at Jim Beam, and is still available today. I have talked to several old-timers, however, who swear that Old Overholt was better when it was made here at Broadford, in the Connellsville area of our state.'

"In closing, my husband's paternal grandparents spoke very little English upon arrival, if any. They soon learned it, however, and they made certain their children learned English. And that's a point I wish to make. In the past, people from the old countries came here to *assimilate* into our culture; they did not come to change it."

– Janet Gabelt, Connellsville, PA

~ ~ ~

"My father's people, the Mongell family, came from Nusco, from the province of Avellino, in south-central Italy. My mother's side came from Ireland, just north of Dublin, County Meath, in the province of Leinster. Their family name is Haggerty.

"My Irish ancestors came to America first, followed a decade or so later by my Italian ancestors. Intermarriage between Irish and Italian was common here in this area, for both groups had a large representation, and both were, for the most part, the same religion, Catholic.

"I never met my great-grandparents, but I knew both sets of my grandparents. I don't really have a family story to proffer, but I do have family memories to share with your readers.

"From family discussions over the years, I can tell you that relatives on both sides of my family appreciated the opportunities that America provided them. They valued the jobs they held, and each of them worked hard at those jobs. On both sides of the family, they were all well-thought-of, well-liked, and that was evident by the numbers in attendance at weddings, wakes, and funerals.

"Another thing I remember from family talks is that everyone had the utmost respect for the law ... for rules in general. And the mothers, Irish and Italian, were the rule-enforcers. Every time one of us kids stepped outside to go anywhere, our grandmothers and/or our mothers would reiterate the rules, of what to do- and not do.

"Both sides of my family are large, close-knit kinfolks. Always, I was taught by my Italian as well as my Irish relatives to take care of family, to protect family. For each of us, a family member's tragedy is the whole clan's tragedy until the problem is soothed or corrected. We have always come together in times of sickness and death, in family crisis of all sorts, to pitch in and help one another. I can remember the family elders saying that was the way it was done in the old countries- and it was a good way.

"My grandparents and my parents embraced the Golden Rule, and drilled that thinking into each of us. As I said, *respect* was at the top of the list in our family, respect for God and country, respect for the law, and respect for others.

"My immigrant grandparents put in long days at hard labor; so did my parents, and so did each of us kids. Growing up, we all had chores, responsibilities. We were taught the value of a dollar early on, and we learned the feeling of satisfaction after a job well-done.

"Education, we were taught, was the *key* to relief from back-breaking work, and we were encouraged to excel in school and to pursue higher education. When immigrants came to this country, they came with an express, shared goal to make a better life for themselves, and especially for their children.

"When I look at the Connellsville immigrant families where I grew up on Limestone Hill, and on West Side Hill where my cousins lived, almost every single one of them produced children who went through college or some training beyond high school. Think of that! Those poor immigrants who came through Ellis Island at the turn of the last century with only pennies in their pockets, carrying one or two small bags containing everything they owned in the world, so many of them not speaking a word of English- and a generation or two later, they have children and grandchildren who are nurses and doctors, lawyers, teachers, and entrepreneurs. That says something for those 'huddled masses yearning to breathe free!'

"It speaks volumes about the immigrants themselves, of their perseverance and fortitude, and it speaks volumes about America. Never would they have been able to achieve so much in the old countries. There, they would never have been able to break free of the strict European caste system.

"Everything I have ever set out to do in life is the result of my family's teachings. I can hear to this day, echoed deep within my being, the voices of my grandparents and my parents telling me that whatever I chose to undertake, to do it to the best of my ability. 'Your work is a reflection of who you are,' they used to say- and I have never forgotten it."

- Francis Mongell, Connellsville, PA

~ ~ ~

"My family came to America from Poland in the 1920s. I say Poland, for the area where my ancestors hailed is part of Poland today. My mother, Mary Garson- that is the Americanized version of both her first name and her maiden name- was the youngest in her family. Others of the family had already emigrated to America, and those older siblings wanted to bring their baby sister over too. They waited until she was old enough to survive the hardships of the long sea voyage, all the while saving their money to pay her passage here.

"By the time Mother was approximately five or six years old, the family in America had gotten up enough money to pay an immigrant agency to escort her to America. There existed in those days, during the great influx of immigrants to the United States, immigration welfare societies, such as the Italian Welfare League, the Polish Society, and the Yiddish-speaking Hebrew Immigrant Aid Society. Such organizations were necessary because immigrants were readily recognizable, easy targets for unscrupulous people lurking on board ship and on the docks to rob them or perpetrate worse crimes, much worse.

"It is very likely that my family either contacted the Hebrew Immigrant Aid Society or the Polish Society to hire an escort to bring my mother over to join her brothers and sisters in America. Thus, after her family here paid the fee, my mother set sail for the New World with an escort from one of those organizations.

"However, she journeyed only as far as Liverpool, England. At that point, for whatever reason, she was abandoned by her adult escort from the agency. Mind, these agencies carried good reputations, but like any organization, they were only as good as their current agents. The reason the agent abandoned my mother is still a mystery.

"Perhaps there is no mystery at all, and it was simply greed. Possibly the agent had already been paid the fee, and in consequence, decided to dump the child in a remote area devoid of witnesses in order to abscond with the money. Whatever the reason, my mother, who was only a small child- and one who did not speak a word of English- was taken to a lonely, marshy spot near the seaport of Liverpool and left completely to herself.

"Can you imagine how frightening this must have been for the poor child! Alone, with no family anywhere in the whole country- a strange country- in which no one spoke her language! However, Providence was watching over her.

"After three or four terrifying days in the wetlands, alone and crying, near starving and literally chilled to the bone, a compassionate man, passing by, heard my mother sobbing and fetched her home to his house near Liverpool. There, his kindly wife bathed her in heated water, washed her clothes, fed her, and administered to her, desperately trying to get the poor child to stop shaking, so cold and frightened was she.

"Thank God my mother's identification papers were still on her person when the sympathetic stranger came upon her. The agency's name and the names of my mother's relatives in America were also on those papers. Therefore, the good samaritans were able to contact that Immigration Aid Society, explain to them, as much as they could ascertain, what had happened; and not long afterward, with a new and responsible escort, my mother was able to complete her journey to America, where she was met at Ellis Island by a relative. At long last, after an arduous journey and what became a haunting experience, my mother entered the gates of America, at New York Harbor, more than ready to begin her life in her new country.

"As a result of those three or four days in the damp and the chill of the English wetlands, Mother became asthmatic, though, with time and care, she did outgrow the condition. My mother never forgot her ordeal and was always thankful to be warm, fed, and in the bosom of her family."

- Ralph Mazer, Connellsville, PA

~ ~ ~

"My grandfather, Metro Zuback, was an immigrant to this country from Austria-Hungary. He came over first, found work, and then sent for Grandma Anna and their two children. They all entered the United States through Ellis Island, settling in the coal mining community of Van Meter, on Jacobs Creek, Westmoreland County, Pennsylvania, where Grandpap labored in the Darr Mine with many other Hungarian immigrants.

"The Pittsburgh Coal Company owned the Darr Mine, and the truth of the matter is they valued their mules and horses more than they ever did their workers. There was always another man, fresh off a boat, ready to step into an injured or killed worker's place in the mines. Horses and mules cost the company money!

"Conditions then would never be tolerated today, and there was no such thing as workers' compensation.

"Faced with the realities and harsh life in the pits, immigrants helped one another in times of crisis. They also formed fraternal organizations or 'lodges,' and after December 1907, those who did not already belong to such organizations, readily joined them.

"December of 1907 is literally known as the worst month in coal mining, recorded in the annals of history as the 'Bloody Month' as well as the 'Dreaded Month.' Whichever label you place on it, it was, by far, the darkest month in mining history.

"On December 19, 1907, something at once miraculous and horrific occurred at the Darr Mine. A tremendous explosion took place that claimed the lives of 239 souls, men and boys. Boys often went down into the pits to help their papas dig coal; some of them were only eight, nine, and ten years old.

"In those days, child labor was common in the dark, dusty depths of the coal mines. Some of the water boys were as young as five or six! That's partly why the actual death count after the Darr Mine disaster was not feasible.

"The Darr explosion, due to methane gas and coal dust, shook the entire Youghiogheny Valley. With the speed of a galloping horse, the highly flammable coal dust propagated through the mine caverns, causing continuous violent explosions, rendering the Darr Mine a huge and immediate tomb.

"Like I said, the entire Yough Valley shook and trembled with continuous ear-shattering blasts- **Boom! Boom! Boom! Boom! Boom!**- heard many, many miles away.

"Widows had to identify their husbands and sons by the bits and pieces of the bodies found afterward, by a fragment of a shirt on a torso or an arm, or from a chunk of pants on a leg.

"What is also sad is that some of the survivors of the December 1, 1907, mining explosion at Naomi in neighboring Fayette County, in which thirty-four miners had been killed, found work at the Darr Mine, hoping for a better life there. The Naomi and the Darr mines were only about ten miles apart.

"My grandfather and several of the other Hungarians were not working the historic day of December 19, 1907, due to the observance of the Feast of Saint Nicholas. Though his pay would have been docked (and believe me, my grandparents, like all those poor miners, needed every cent earned and then some), he did not go to work on Saint Nicholas Day. The coal bosses, who normally had complete control of their labor forces, *knew* they could not force the Hungarian miners to work on the Feast of Saint Nicolas.

"In fact, my grandmother had *forbidden* Grandpap to go to work in the Darr Mine that fatal day so that he could attend Mass at the Greek Catholic/Byzantine church in honor of the patron saint of the old country.

"I am so glad she did forbid Grandpap to go into the pits that deadly day, for my father (John Zuback) was not born until 1911, and if Grandpap would have died in 1907, neither my father nor any of us children would ever have been born!

"My father worked for a time as a coal miner, then he got a job on the B&O Railroad as an engineer, at which time we moved to Connellsville, Pennsylvania.

"But the Darr Mine story of December 19, 1907, is but *one* piece of the Saint Nicholas miracle of that dreadful month. The rest of the account goes like this: Earlier that same month, on December 6, 362 miners were killed in a huge explosion in the mines in Monongah, West Virginia, about fifty miles southwest of the Darr Mine. There was no church of the Greek Catholic rite in that area, so the Hungarian miners and their families attended Mass at the local Roman Catholic church. Roman Catholics observe a different calendar, and thus, the date for the Feast of Saint Nicholas is different on that calendar- it is December 6.

Sadly, the rescue team after the Darr Mine disaster served only as a recovery team. The man on the extreme left is Metro Zuback, who was in church at the time of the explosion.

Photo from the author's personal collection

The Hungarians attending Mass that day for the observance of Saint Nicolas were all saved from the Monongah mine disaster.

"In our family yet today, you can bet Saint Nicolas is our favorite saint!"
- Tony Zuback, Venetia, PA and Carol Zuback Alexander, Sterling, Virginia, formerly of Connellsville, PA

~ ~ ~

People have migrated to the New World through every historical shock, and in great waves of longing and desperation. Beneath the majestic statue of "Liberty Lighting the World," the images of our stalwart ancestors pass into shadow- like memories of so many dreams.

Reminiscent of the brave pioneers before them, immigrant newcomers courageously came to America, and like the early settlers, they too have become echoes from our nation's boisterous past.

The passing years, however, have faded their spectrum of voices and withered their patchwork of noble images. Time, someone once said, is a relentless peddler who deals in dust. That is why it is important to keep family stories *alive*. Treasure yours, and pass them down to your children- lest they are lost to the ages.

"Pennsylvania Wilds"

"In every walk with nature one receives far more than he seeks."
- John Muir

"When you watch wildlife without causing a reaction, you are seeing what is truly wild."
- Mark Duda

"No where in this country, from sea to sea, does nature comfort us with such assurance of plenty, such rich and tranquil beauty as in those unsung, unpainted hills of Pennsylvania."
- Rebecca Harding Davis

"Those who contemplate the beauty of the earth find reserves of strength that will endure as long as life lasts."
"Those who dwell ... among the beauties and mysteries of the earth are never alone or weary of life."
- Rachel Carson

"The human spirit craves- desperately needs- places where nature has not been disturbed or rearranged by the hand of man."
- Ceane O'Hanlon-Lincoln

Pennsylvania is a beautiful state teeming with outdoor thrills- charming towns and villages rich in history, incredible rustic scenery in our mountains and in our deep and endless woodlands.

Our bright tapestry of ethnic people makes visitors feel at home in this unsurpassed beauty. Here, you can click your heels together thrice and repeat that time-honored phrase, "There's no place like home," and mean it! Or you can wish upon a star, where, away from city lights, the stars appear brighter in the night-sky over one of our splendid state parks.

Whether you are a camping, hiking, biking, fishing, hunting, nature or wildlife enthusiast, Pennsylvania has something for you. From trout fishing to whitewater rafting to taking in the sights along our gorgeous rails-to-trails hike-and-bike nature paths, Pennsylvania offers wilderness buffs of all kinds riveting scenery with a myriad of wildlife.

There is nothing more healing or relaxing than the quiet and solitude of a walk in the woods. The state parks, mountain trails, gorges, and serene country roads of our Pennsylvania wilds provide every type of hiking adventure about which you could possibly dream. And remember to walk softly and silently, for you just might encounter deer, a bobcat, a fox, a river otter, a bear, or elk, not to mention a wide variety of our feathered friends.

Our 375 species of songbirds are forever staging a melodic show for your enjoyment! Pennsylvania is also home to owls, falcons, hawks, eagles, and ospreys (thanks in large part to Pennsylvania-born Rachel Carson; see "The Salient Spring of Rachel Carson," this volume).

Pennsylvania Histories

I like to include Native American totems with each animal discussion. If you enjoy this Native symbolism as much as I do, then make certain to read "Camelot" in the premier volume of my *County Chronicles* Pennsylvania history series.

It is my hope this Chronicle will prompt you to lace up your hiking boots, grab your camera, your protein bars, and your water, as Rachel Carson advocated, "... to contemplate the exceeding beauty of this earth." When you can do this, "... you will find calmness and courage for your life."

The turning wheel of the seasons is a constant delight in Pennsylvania. Spring is an experiment in green, lush and fragrant, the rolling hills carpeted in shimmering emerald velvet. Our state flower, the mountain laurel, blooms in late May, and its pink and white blossoms are evident well into June.

Pennsylvania summers are abundantly splashed with colorful wildflowers and a myriad of flora. Then, the flickering sunlight through the thick, black-green canopy of trees is almost mystical throughout the forest "cathedrals" of Penn's Woods.

Autumn, though, is my favorite time of year, when the light is golden, and the sky is low and a glorious, unbroken blue. How I love the trees- the forests- cloaked in their bright autumn splendor! The Pennsylvania fall season is *dramatic*- except for the frequent evergreens that stand tall and straight like disapproving dowagers who shake their heads and purse their lips over the wild, untamed beauty of the oaks, maples, birch, ash, elm, walnut and others who dare to show their true colors. But the contrast is gorgeous. "Poems are made by fools like me, but only God can make a tree!" So saith Joyce Kilmer.

Fall comes bearing a chill in the air that is electrifying, and on wooded paths, the fallen leaves, when stepped upon, crackle too,

Cucumber Run, Ohio Pyle State Park, Fayette County, PA
Photo taken autumn 2007 by professional nature photographer Glenn E. Mucy

sending up a delightful, nutty scent that is transporting to autumns past, to the warm hearth of reminiscence and longing.

Indian summer is special. This unchartered season is like a fickle woman, a flame-haired woman of deep passions, who comes and goes on a whim in garments of jewel-tones that match her mettle- energetic colors of red, orange, purple, and rust. One never really knows how long she'll stay, or, in fact, if the capricious lady will come at all, but when she does, her warmth- laughing and vibrant- keeps winter at bay.

She leaves when Jack Frost blows in with his backbone of ice, leafless trees, sunless skies,

County Chronicles

Serene, snow-dusted Cedar Creek Park on the Youghiogheny River, Westmoreland County, PA
Photo taken winter 2009 by Glenn E. Mucy

and frozen ground. Comes the snow then, and oh, how enchanting the first snowfall of a Pennsylvania winter, when the fields, hills and vales, the mountains and forests are glittering white with it– a virtual fairyland! Aren't those first silent flakes– each a lacy work of art and no two alike– truly magical?

I cannot understand anyone wanting to live in a warm climate all year long. The seasons, to me, balance nature ... and man. I believe mankind yearns for the cycles and rhythms of nature. We still have so much to learn, and to gain, from nature, from the seasons, the trees, the rivers, the mountains, from the animals. I believe that the further man removes himself from nature, the more unbalanced he becomes, the more easily stressed and dis-eased he is. Nature heals, and it provides wisdom, creativity, and stability.

Forests have always been important to the inhabitants of Penn's Woods. Due to Pennsylvania's geographical location, its varied terrain supports approximately 108 species of native and other trees brought from Europe and Asia. For instance, the Chinese chestnut was introduced here because it is resistant to the blight that nearly wiped out the American chestnut that was formerly the most common and arguably most valuable tree in Pennsylvania for both its wood and its nuts.

Pennsylvania is home to a variety of stately oak trees, maples, birch, hickory, walnut, willow, ash, elm, redbud, dogwood, pine, hemlock, spruce, a spectrum of apple and other fruit-bearing trees. That, of course, is but a sampling of our fine foliage.

I recommend that my readers go online and research historic/famous/witness trees, for we host many within the perimeters of our commonwealth. For example, Valley Forge is home to several champion trees and a few really historic ones. The Pawling Sycamore is located in the flatlands area of the Valley Forge National Park. It is a magnificent tree that is estimated to be between 260 and 285 years old. Its widest spread is 147 feet.

Gettysburg is home to several trees that witnessed and survived the great battle, including a copse of oaks that beheld the infamous "Pickett's Charge." In the Gettysburg National Cemetery, defying time and the elements, stands a grand old honey locust near the spot where, on a somber November day in 1863, President Abraham Lincoln stood to deliver his Gettysburg Address.

Cook Forest in northwestern Pennsylvania- see "The Forest Primeval," in *County Chronicles IV*- is home to awe-inspiring old-growth segments of forest. Many of its heaven-reaching trees exceed three feet in diameter. Referred to by many as "William Penn Trees," these lofty giants are often 300 years old, dating to the era of and even before William Penn, thus the name. Within the Forest Cathedral old-growth segment, soaring over 180 feet in height, is Cook Forest's famous Longfellow Pine, the tallest tree in the northeastern United States.

One of the few remaining Olympic gift oaks from the historic 1936 Olympic Games in Berlin (awarded to the gold medallists) resides in my hometown of Connellsville, the John Y. Woodruff Olympic Oak.

Oh, if those venerable old witness trees could talk, tell their tales! I have sought out each of them, and perhaps, in a sense, they *have* spoken to me.

Trees are living entities just as we are. They ooze energies, along with a powerful aura and a spiritual essence. Trees are one of our greatest natural gifts.

I have always had a penchant for trees, and, for me, it is heart wrenching to see a tree felled. I remember years ago when I was exhausted with life and quite unsure of my own direction. I was taking a long tramp on a rutted back road near my residence when I came upon a scarred old oak. It quickly became a favorite tree of mine, marking the spot where, after brief repose during my evening walks, I would turn round and start back home. One night, absorbed in self-pity, as I was looking up at the starry sky through the lacy tangle of its lofty branches, I began to wonder how such a giant tree could survive lightning, wind and the power of years of summer storms. I knew and noted that it bore evidence of carvings and even car crashes, yet it had endured.

Suddenly my own life raced through my mind. I thought that if this ancient oak could survive after being hacked, burned, and vandalized, surely then I could pick myself up and reach skyward. I felt as if that tree had spoken to me, comforted me in my confusion and melancholy, and renewed my crippled spirit. It was then that I began to write.

When I relocated from Westmoreland back home to Fayette County, I missed that valiant oak "whom" I still consider an old friend.

Trees provide a renewable source of lumber, paper, nuts, and chemicals. And never forget that they are essential as living filters, removing pollution from the air we breathe and the water we drink. In addition, trees provide homes and food for wildlife, and they offer beauty to our own homes with comforting shade from the glare of summer heat and the chill of winter winds.

With wise management, our Pennsylvania woodlands will continue to produce these benefits to future generations as they have to Native Americans, frontier farmers, and Pennsylvanians in the past.

Yet true to its name, *Pennsylvania* is about sixty percent forested with approximately seventeen million acres of woodlands. And today, we still derive much of our economy and many comforts from the bionetwork of Penn's Woods. Medicines, foods, and lumber, a cleaner environment, tourism and recreation are all provided by our fantastic forests.

In regard to the diverse Pennsylvania flora and fauna, "been there, done that" does not apply. Each nature walk or exploration is fresh, and that is the best thing about nature study.

In an interview with professional nature photographer Glenn E. Mucy, the artist related to me: "While I've always had an appreciation for nature, I think my interest in photography came about as a result of my fascination for birds of prey, accompanied with a desire to capture the sense of freedom I felt the first time I watched a red-tailed hawk soaring gracefully across the Pennsylvania sky.

"My passion for nature photography was sealed once I realized how each animal is perfectly designed for its specific niche in life. I am constantly in awe of the absolute beauty of everything God has created."

I invite you now to come with us, via text and images, most notably the photographs of nature photographer Glenn E. Mucy, for a wonderful trip into the vast and unforgettable- Pennsylvania wilds!

~ ~ ~

Let's begin with the black bear, *Ursus americanus*, that ranges through much of wooded North America. These bears exhibit life patterns, pelt coloration, as well as size and weight according to the region in which they live.

Most Pennsylvania bears are glossy black, though a few are brown. Powerfully built animals, black bears average anywhere from 140 to

400 pounds. Males, sometimes called "boars," tend to be considerably larger and heavier than females, "sows." The largest Pennsylvania bear on record (2005 bear season) was one from my home county of Fayette. He was 733 pounds and estimated to be about fifteen years old.

Bears walk in a flat-footed manner, with a sort of waddle. Though their walk may appear lumbering and even clumsy, don't be fooled into thinking they cannot move fast when they want to. Their top speed is around thirty miles per hour! Bears are extremely agile for their size, sometimes standing erect on their hind feet to see and smell better. They are excellent climbers and good swimmers.

They have an acute sense of smell– their strongest sense– though their eyesight is not that keen, nor their hearing. As for their verbal capacity, bears occasionally growl or emit a "woof." When injured, they will sob and bawl, much like humans. Mother bears communicate to their cubs with grunts, low huffs, and mumbles.

Though bears are essentially nocturnal, they sometimes move about and feed during daylight hours. Alert and usually wary of humans, bears tend to avoid open areas, keeping to the woodlands. While most of these creatures will shun humankind, a female with cubs is a special consideration. If a human has the misfortune to inadvertently come between a mother bear and her young, the sow could attack if she feels her cubs in danger.

The more accustomed bears become to humans (in a park for instance), the less likely they are to run away– and the greater their potential danger.

Since their sense of smell is their forte, bears locate their food primarily by scent. Opportunists, with a largely vegetarian diet, they grab what they can, where they can, including berries, acorns and beechnuts, succulent leaves of hardwood trees, insects, honey, plant roots, amphibians, reptiles, small mammals, fish, carrion and yes, even garbage. Bears drink water frequently, and in hot weather, they love to wallow in cooling streams.

Early June to mid-July is bear-mating season. They are polygamous, and the males take no part in rearing the young.

Autumn is the season for bears to fatten themselves for winter hibernation. I have read

Adult black bear. Taken in natural habitat at Fayette County's Woodland Zoo, 2008, by Glenn E. Mucy. Courtesy the photographer and Jill and Sonny Herring, Woodland Zoo, Farmington, PA

and heard that the more fat they have on them, the deeper and longer they sleep. But that is not 100% true.

Their winter den can be a hollow tree or log, a crevice in a rock ledge, a cave, even a drainage culvert. Normally, females select more sheltered hibernation sites than males. Some bears choose to line their dens with bark, grasses or leaves for more warmth and protection, and most of these more diligent homemakers are females.

Denning bears in winter become dormant, lapsing in and out of deep sleep- from which, be advised, they can be roused. In fact, they may emerge from their dens on warm, late-winter days to forage for food.

Males den alone, as do pregnant females, who give birth in the den, usually in January. Litter size ranges from one to five cubs, three being the most common in our Penn's Woods. Newborns are exceptionally tiny compared to the size they will become as adults. Covered with fine, dark hair, they are about eight to nine inches in length and weigh from ten to sixteen ounces, with ears and eyes tightly closed. Cubs den with their sleeping mother the first winter, instinctively nursing on their own.

In the den, after about six weeks, the cubs open their eyes. They are walking about within the subsequent two weeks. After three months, the youngsters leave the den, and they are weaned by seven months. Young bears put on weight *rapidly*, normally weighing between sixty and 100 pounds by their first autumn. Bear cubs are exceptionally playful. Wrestling with their littermates is a favorite pastime. As touched on earlier, Mother Bear is ultra-protective, sending her cubs straight up a tall tree if danger threatens.

Most females are ready to breed when they reach the age of two and a half. A female raises but one litter every other year.

In the Pennsylvania wilds, a bear might live to twenty-five years, though those bears over fifteen would only make up about one percent of the total Pennsylvania bear population.

It is important to play it smart- and by the rules- when it comes to bears. Do not feed wild animals! Food placed outside for wildlife, such as corn for squirrels, may attract bears. Even bird feeders can become "bear magnets."

A curious black bear approaches bird feeders at my publisher's home in Butler County, PA
Photo courtesy Al and Marla Mechling, Chicora, PA

You can safely feed the birds, however. Audubon Pennsylvania offers tips on how. If a bear shows up in your yard, contact the nearest Game Commission immediately- and keep a safe distance. When camping, keep all foods tightly covered. To avoid food smells near your tent, cook several meters downwind from your campsite. If you've acquired food smells on your person, wash up and change your clothing. Always seek out, study, and obey the safety rules in bear country and other locales where wildlife abounds.

The bear has played a prominent role in Native American cultures. Because of its power and fearlessness, Bear has always been a highly desired ally, spirit guide and teacher. The Natives believe that the power of the Great Spirit lives through this very special animal-brother, and it was because of this that a constellation was named for it- *Ursus Major*, meaning "The Great Bear."

The gifts that Bear offers are strength, introspection and great and wondrous knowledge. Bear can sometimes be too quick to anger and too sure of his own power. However, keep in mind that while Bear has little to fear, he can forget caution- an important trait to have. If Bear is *your* totem, then be careful not to toss caution to the wind. Being unaware of your limits in certain areas can be disastrous.

I want to clarify something. Compliant with Native American values, "animal medicine" translates as an individual's perspective on life, the way an individual looks at life, the way in which he acts and reacts to life. Animal spirits/guides, according to the Natives, provide humankind with guidance. There is a difference between the two.

Throughout life, each of us has one animal medicine totem (who we really are) and several animal guide totems that can change during the course of a life, remaining for only a limited time, depending on the direction each life is headed and the obstacles on the horizon of each person's lifepath.

Adolescent Native American males seeking spiritual power learn through a vision the identity of animal spirit guides; in fact, this is called a "vision quest."

Animal totems are important for each individual to come to know him/herself. They help us to return to our earthly roots, reconnect with nature, and remind us that we are all interconnected within the Great Circle of Life.

If you do not know your animal medicine or your animal guides (most Natives believe there are nine animal guides per person at any given time), then ask yourself these questions: What animal do I feel the most drawn toward? For which do I have the most interest, the most kinship? That is likely your animal medicine. Thus, research everything you can about that animal, for it will help you to come to know yourself better, your strengths, your weaknesses.

Animal guides can show up in your life everywhere you look, or in dreams. Remember that animals are both teachers and messengers. When you dream of an animal, look up everything you can about that creature, so you can understand its message in your life.

I possess Cougar Medicine. It is who I am. Like the cougar, I am oftentimes solitary – I value my privacy– and I am quite sure of my purpose in life. I have always admired the cougar's great courage, mystery, magic, and leadership qualities. My animal guides are wolf, bobcat, cat, eagle, bear, bat, horse, snake, owl, and boar. Some of those totems have remained with me for years, others come and go. If you feel drawn toward Cougar, be sure

Adult female cougar, Woodland Zoo, Fayette County, PA
Photo taken in 2008 by Glenn E. Mucy
Courtesy the photographer and Jill and Sonny Herring, Woodland Zoo, Farmington, PA

and read "Ghostwalkers" in *CC III*, where I have discussed this very special animal-brother at great length.

One does not have to possess Native American blood to respect, love, and learn from animals. We must share this planet with all different races of humankind and a great variety of animals. *When*, I ask, are we going to learn to do this! Must we constantly rob the poor animals of freedom and dignity? Must we constantly *destroy*? So many of our animal-brothers are already extinct. So many more are threatened with being crowded out forever. Rachel Carson taught, "The more clearly we can focus our attention on the wonders and realities of the universe about us, the less taste we shall have for destruction."

In conclusion, this segment, if ever Bear shows up in your life, in the woods, in a dream, or in some other way, give consideration to your current mind-set; i.e., take a long, reflective look inward to examine your own thoughts and feelings and how you act and interact with others. Use discernment in all you do and discriminate with care. Bear teaches us how to make choices from a position of power.

Bears, to the Native Americans, represent great strength and healing. They also symbolize dreams, because bears hibernate/sleep the winter through when their metabolism significantly slows down.

Those who possess Bear Medicine are said to have the bear's great strength. Bear Medicine people prefer to stand on their own two feet (as the bear can do). These people are dreamers, but they have the strength to realize their dreams.

~ ~ ~

Pennsylvania is home to the red and the grey/gray fox, small, agile carnivores belonging to the same family as the dog, coyote, and wolf. These are highly intelligent predators with extremely sharp senses of sight, smell, and hearing. Did you know that a fox can hear a mouse squeal at about 150 feet? Amazing, isn't it!

The more common red fox, *Vulpes vulpes*, is between twenty-two to twenty-five inches in length, with an additional fourteen to sixteen-inch tail, and weighs between eight to twelve pounds. I must state for the record that, due to their lush fur, foxes always look heavier than they actually are.

The red fox has full, thick reddish-orange fur that is slightly darker along the back. The red's ears, legs and feet are black, providing beautiful contrast.

The grey/gray fox sports a somewhat coarser coat with buff-colored underfur. Grey foxes can be slightly larger. Both colors have long, bushy, well-insulated tails that they like to curl over themselves for warmth in the cold season.

Foxes are swift runners, and they can swim if they have to. The greys can climb trees, the only member of the canine family with this ability! Both reds and greys are, in essence, nocturnal.

When it comes to feeding, foxes are *the* supreme opportunists. Their variety-packed menu includes mice, rats, rabbits, woodchucks, opossums, porcupines, domestic cats, chickens, insects, squirrels, game birds, songbirds, bird eggs, and fruits. These little opportunists will also feed on road and winter-killed animals. Both the red and the greys have basically the same diet, and both cache away uneaten food (to which they will return) by burying it in loosely dug earth.

The males are sometimes referred to as "dogs," the females as "vixens."

Have you ever heard a fox barking at night in late winter? They do this to announce their presence to the opposite sex. Mating usually takes place in February. Red foxes have a gestation period of about fifty-one days, the greys approximately sixty-three days. Litters can be large, ranging from four to ten pups that are born in the den.

Red foxes are prone to take over a groundhog's/woodchuck's burrow, though they can also den in hollow logs. Greys too will den beneath ground as well as crevices in rocky ledges. For both species, underground dens will usually have several entrances/exits.

Mothers nurse their pups in the den for approximately one month. When the growing pups emerge, both parents keep them supplied with solid food for two or three months, until they are completely weaned. By mid-July or August, the young foxes leave the den, at which time they may forage with their parents for another few weeks until the family disbands. Foxes are sexually mature at ten months and may breed during their first winter.

Proof of the resiliency of foxes was their ability to weather decades upon decades of persecution through bounties across Pennsylvania and elsewhere. Foxes are often blamed for decreasing game populations; however, most of the time, the number of game birds and animals taken by foxes and other predators is insignificant compared to other natural causes.

Young red fox with squirrel. Note that proud expression!
Photo taken in Westmoreland County, PA, 2008, by Glenn E. Mucy

I am happy to report that more and more people are accepting predators as valuable members of our natural world. *Every creature has a purpose in the workings and the balance of nature!*

According to an article that appeared in the Sunday, November 2, 2008, "Focus" section of the *Tribune-Review*, "The dramatic migration of wildlife into the city of Pittsburgh tells a tale of successful conservation and animal adaptation. ... Pittsburgh is geographically unique– built [around] steep hills and ravines that could not be developed, providing wildlife corridors, swaths of undeveloped land that allow animals freedom of movement. ... Such corridors have been proposed for decades by biologists. Who would have known Pittsburgh would have become testimony to such thinking!" There's virtually no hunting in the city ... few predators ... . "So, Pittsburghers, keep your eyes open. Eagles, ravens, otters, coyotes, and bobcats, even when glimpsed for a moment, can provide an exciting experience." I personally have seen deer feeding on wooded, steep Mount Washington from the window of the incline I was riding.

To the Native Americans, Fox speaks of the need to develop the art of camouflage, invisibility and shape shifting. Fox is agile, skilled, and rather unpredictable, not to mention sly, clever and cunning, giving rise to the expression "sly as a fox."

When Fox is pursued by hounds, he will dash across the tops of walls, cross water diagonally, double back on his own trail, run in circles, and do anything and everything to break the continuity of his scent. He possesses great ability to outwit both predators and prey. As the Native Americans have always known, Fox is a great teacher to the ranger, scout, or woodsman.

Those with Fox Medicine are clever and witty, but they must remember to keep their crafty nature balanced, or it will backfire.

The appearance of Fox in your life, in the woods or in a dream, could translate that your actions might well be too obvious, and the lesson you need to learn is discretion.

Fox is one of the most uniquely skilled and ingenious animals of nature. Because it is a creature of the night, it is often imbued with supernatural powers. Foxes are usually seen at dawn and dusk. Those are "between times" when the magical world and the world in which we live intersect. The ancient Celts as well as the Native Americans thought of Fox as a magical/mystical creature. Because he ventures out "between times" and lives "betwixt and between" woodlands and open lands, the Celts believed Fox to be a guide into the faerie realm.

Actually, Fox has a long history of magic, cunning and cleverness associated with him. He can move in and out of situations restoring order or causing confusion, even mayhem, depending on the situation. If Fox is your totem, he is a powerful ally and medicine to have, but be certain to use his skills for the good of all.

~ ~ ~

Spotting a bobcat in the Pennsylvania wilds is a tremendous thrill! Tawny, tireless, and truly beautiful, bobcats are an elusive predator.

Efficient and wary, *Lynx rufus* possess sharp senses of sight, smell, and hearing in addition to sharp, cutting teeth and sharp, retractable, hooked claws. Thus, they come well-equipped to the hunt.

Despite its small size, the bobcat is a fierce fighter. Mature cats, approximately two feet tall, average thirty-odd inches in length, including the stubby tail that provides this feline with its name. Weight varies anywhere from fifteen or twenty pounds (the Pennsylvania average) to as heavy as thirty-five or more pounds, though in some areas of the country they can weigh up to fifty pounds.

Pennsylvania bobcats are usually light brown, i.e. tawny to reddish-brown. I have discovered through my research that they are more grey than red in the winter, I am certain, for camouflage. Like the cougar, they are born with spots that fade as they grow, though the bobcat, to maturity, retains its tabby coloration.

The captivating bobcat face has broken black lines which radiate onto attractive, broad cheek ruffs. The short tail is distinguished by two or three black bars and a black tip; the underside is buff, cream, or white. As with most species, the males are usually larger than the females. This cat likes forest as well as rocky, grassy, or scrub lands.

Though these cats are considered nocturnal, they sometimes venture out in the daytime. Their diet is varied, consisting largely of small animals, mice, rats, shrews, chipmunks, rabbits, squirrels, and birds, especially ground

Adult male bobcat
Photo taken in 2008 by Glenn E. Mucy
Courtesy the photographer and Jill and Sonny Herring, Woodland Zoo, Farmington, PA

birds. These predators too are opportunists, and will take whatever they find, including mink, muskrat, skunk, frogs, fish, certain insects, and even foxes. Bobcats have been known to bring down deer, usually weak or crippled deer, but they have little or no effect on Pennsylvania's deer herd.

Like the lynx, the bobcat has a great liking for hare and rabbit. Their keen sight and hearing as well as the soft pads on their feet aid them in the hunt. They habitually hide in brush, waiting to leap out at a rabbit or squirrel. Using their claws and sinking their sharp teeth into the neck of the prey, cougar-fashion, is Bobcat's quick-kill technique.

Male bobcats, however, will hunt larger game, such as deer in the winter months, as I said, bringing down a weak or sickly one. They have been known to take fawns too, but the number is negligible.

Bobcats can only eat about three pounds of meat at a meal; therefore, larger prey is dragged off and cached away, hidden under leaves and such, then revisited and eaten till the meat starts to rot. Bobcats will feed on winter-starved or road-killed deer as well, as long as the meat is still fresh.

Basically nocturnal (as are most of their prey), bobcats like to hunt when rabbits are at their peak of activity, dawn and dusk. During the cold winter months, these diurnal creatures are more active during daylight (again corresponding with their prey).

Bobcats can run up to thirty miles per hour. An interesting point is that they place their back feet in the same spots where their front feet stepped. In this manner of walking, they snap fewer twigs, making less noise.

Bobcat tracks are easily distinguished with a rounded shape and four toes. The track is generally twice the size of a domestic cat's print, loosely resembling that of a dog, but more rounded, with *no* claws evident. Like most cats, the bobcat's claws are kept sheathed and thus sharp. Like most cats, they are shy, and as it is with the cougar, they keep their distance from humans.

Smaller than their lynx and cougar cousins, bobcats are less secretive than the mountain lion, but more aggressive than the lynx. Like the cougar, the bobcat is an excellent climber, and this cat, too, will often lie in wait in trees to pounce on prey.

Although the bobcat generally breeds between February and June (depending on geography), they have been known to breed year round. They can have large litters, one to six (though two to four is average), born after a gestation period of approximately sixty days.

Bobcats like to den- under logs on the forest floor or even in the root mass of a fallen tree. Mother cats bring live mice back to the den, so that the babies can practice hunting. Offspring are independent of their mothers (usually in autumn) after ten to twelve months. In the wild, bobcats live about a dozen years. Under proper conditions in captivity, they can reach their mid-twenties. Predators of the bobcat include cougars, coyotes, wolves- and man.

Native Americans believe that people with Bobcat Medicine are often solitary like their totem animal. Bobcat teaches how to be alone without being lonely. Bobcat people often become the keeper of secrets. Bobcat's lesson here is never to break the silence and a friend's confidences.

Bobcats hold magic and power, and those who carry their medicine should learn to be silent about the magic and the power they hold, for speaking of it dissipates the power. Learning to know when to speak, when to listen, and what to share with others is essential for bobcat people. These folks, like their totem, are usually night people, who can be both psychometric, having the ability to sense objects in total darkness, or clairaudient, having the ability to hear something not quite present to the ear. Bobcat people should learn to trust their senses and what is often called "gut feeling."

~ ~ ~

Recognized as our state animal since 1959, the graceful white-tailed deer can be found from the most remote forests throughout the Commonwealth to our most developed cities.

Because so many Pennsylvanians are affected by deer, differences of opinions regarding them are common- and sometimes even heated. Pennsylvania's deer program is guided by biological and social goals. Hunters, homeowners, farmers, municipal officials, foresters, and others have all contributed to the Pennsylvania Game Commission's focus on our state animal.

Widespread throughout Pennsylvania's woodlands and brush, as well as over a good portion of the United States and southern Canada, this deer is not as heavily built as

White-tailed deer. This beautiful buck has an eight-point rack. Photo taken during the 2008 rutting season by Glenn E. Mucy in Westmoreland County, PA

the western mule deer. Whitetail females weigh from ninety pounds to a bit over 200. A buck's weight will range from 130 to 300 pounds. Most Pennsylvania bucks average around 200 pounds.

A glimpse of this deer's "white flag" tail disappearing into the tangle of a Pennsylvania forest is a thrill to those of us who enjoy hiking. The whitetail deer is reddish-brown most of the year, with a coat that turns greyish-brown to almost blue-grey during the winter. This, of course, is for camouflage purposes.

Deer eat twigs, fungi, grasses, crabapples, apples, nuts, clover and acorns, to name the most common elements of their diet. Their keen sense of hearing, sight, and especially smell enable them to flee humans or animal predators, usually without being seen. Their white-flag tails flip up instantly when they sense danger as they vanish into the thick cover of Pennsylvania's ubiquitous woods.

These animals are excellent swimmers, and that is why you will find them on lake and river islands. They can run up to thirty-five mph, leap obstacles eight feet high or more, and cover a distance of approximately thirty feet in one awesome bound.

They are not a vocal animal, though I have read that they can make several different sounds, the most common being the snort they emit when their keen sense of smell detects danger.

Young males get their first set of antlers when they are yearlings. A buck begins growing a new rack each year in the early spring. The developing antlers are "in velvet"; that is to say, the antlers are covered with a thick, velvety skin rich with blood vessels and nerves. The rack begins to harden; and by late August or September, bucks will remove the velvet from the antlers by rubbing them against trees. Males are now ready to compete for doe with a set of hard, polished antlers.

Rutting season can begin as early as mid-October and run through mid-January, so that the females can drop their young in the warm seasons of spring and summer. Once the rutting season is over, bucks shed their antlers.

Doe always go with the winner after a fight. And I have heard from hunters that bucks engaged in such a contest over doe can lock antlers with one another, causing fatal problems for both rutting males. Bucks "in rut" have even been known to attack humans.

Bucks chase doe for several days before mating actually begins. A buck will mate with a doe several times, keeping other deer at bay. Then he moves on to other doe, mating with as many as possible before the rutting period ends. Bucks do not assist doe with their young in any way.

Deer are graceful to watch running across an open meadow or field, or when they leap from a virtual standstill to clear a high barrier.

Pennsylvania drivers should pay special attention when traversing areas marked "Deer Crossing," especially from October through January when these animals are the most active. Deer can be active round-the-clock, though less during daylight hours. Nocturnal, they like to sleep in thickets on soft pine needles during the day. Whitetail seem more on the move at dawn and dusk.

The Native American symbolism of the deer carries the attributes of grace, peace, love, beauty, swiftness, spirituality, fertility, and watchfulness. The ancient Celts too looked upon the deer as graceful, linking it to the arts, specifically poetry and music. The Celts also believed that deer were associated with the faerie realm, in that faeries would troop behind a stag as he swiftly cut a path through a thick, nearly impenetrable forest.

Both Celts and Native Americans considered the deer to be savvy when it came to locating the best herbs. People of both cultures would follow deer to prime herb patches, many of which proved to be highly beneficial in their medicinal purposes.

In art symbolism, the image of a slain deer with herbs in its mouth is symbolic of unrequited love, lost love, or love sickness.

~ ~ ~

Owls are interesting birds of prey, holding sway over the night where hawks hunt by day. Superb, specialized hunters, owls find, catch and kill prey quickly and efficiently.

Eight species of owls either live in Pennsylvania or visit our commonwealth winters. Barn, screech, great horned, barred, and long-eared owls are permanent residents. The fabulous snowy owl is occasionally spotted here in the winter, especially in Pennsylvania's northern counties. Other species come and go.

The owl's plumage is dense and soft, making these birds appear heavier than they actually are. Their drab-hued feathers are excellent camouflage, blending this adept hunter into a variety of backgrounds. Both sexes are marked and colored essentially alike, though with owls, unlike many birds and animals, the females are usually larger. The feathers on owl legs provide both insulation and protection.

Owls have extraordinary vision and hearing. Extremely large retinas make their vision up to 100 times more effective than human eyes! Owls also possess binocular vision meaning that each eye views the same scene from a slightly different angle, therefore improving depth perception. Owl eyes are fixed into the skull. To look to the side, an owl moves its head. Some species can turn their heads almost the entire way round.

Another thing an owl has going for it is its wings. Lightweight wings with a large wing surface render noiseless flight. An owl descends to its prey in a silent, purposeful glide, gripping and killing its quarry with its lethal talons.

What I found amazing during my research is this: An owl's stomach absorbs all the nutritious parts of the animal it eats, forming indigestible matter– such as hair, feathers, bones and claws– into little round pellets that are regurgitated a few hours later.

As with most predators, owls are often blamed for killing more game and poultry than they actually do. Respect that owls are beneficial birds that feed on many pests. And remember that all owls are protected by the Game Law and Federal regulations.

Most owls call out to announce individual territory and to the opposite sex during mating season. We will discuss their sounds a bit later.

Owls don't build nests. Rather, they take possession of abandoned crow or hawk nests, or they will make good use of holes in trees. In fact, a hollow tree is prime owl real estate. Some owls add or refresh the lining in the nests they take over.

This was an interesting discovery for me: Owls are early nesters, some laying eggs in late winter. Thus, by the time the fledglings leave the nest, baby rabbits and the offspring of other prey abound– easy pickings for the inexperienced young owls.

Female owls lay anywhere from three to five round, white eggs, and incubation is her responsibility, while the male hunts and brings her food. Once the eggs are hatched, both parents feed the young.

For lack of space, I shan't discuss each owl species in Pennsylvania; rather, I have selected a trio of personal favorites.

The great horned owl is sometimes referred to as the "tiger of the air." It is our most powerful owl, and the fiercest, weighing up to three and a half pounds; though, as I said, it looks a lot heavier. It is about twenty-three inches tall with an incredible wingspan of nearly five feet. Its most prominent feature is its ear tufts, the so-called "horns," that can reach up to two inches in length. This majestic bird is known for its deep, resonant call, three to eight (usually four or five) booming hoots: *hoohoohoo- hoooo.*

It is believed that great horns mate for life. They fiercely defend nests with young, even attacking humans who get too close. These birds prefer solitude. You won't find them in densely populated regions of the state. They favor heavily forested land in remote wilderness areas. They are not solely Pennsylvania birds. Great horned owls are found over much of North America.

The screech owl is the only small Pennsylvania owl with ear tufts. It is about ten inches tall, weighing approximately six or seven ounces, with a twenty-two inch wingspan. There are two colors, a rust shade and a grey, but the grey is far more common within the perimeters of our Penn's Woods. This owl's call is a "quavering whistle," i.e., a long, protracted, mournful wail: *huhuhuhuhuhu.*

Screech owls prefer hollow trees, often moving into abandoned woodpecker dwellings. The females lay their eggs in March, and incubation takes twenty-six days. After breaking through their shells, the young remain in the nests for about a month before taking on the woodsy world. Large insects, like grasshoppers, beetles and moths, mice, shrews, flying squirrels, small birds, and frogs, are the basics of the screech owl's varied diet.

The barred owl is a large bird of the deep woods. Its head is rounded, and it sports no horns. What is rather unique about this

Adult barred owl
Photo taken in 2008, Washington County, PA, by Glenn E. Mucy
This owl was an injured bird that was rehabilitated and released into the wilds by the good folks at Wildlife Works, Inc., Youngwood, PA. Check them out online; they are always looking for volunteers. In addition to their rescue program, Wildlife Works, Inc. educates people about Pennsylvania wildlife.

creature is its eye color. Except for the barn owl, it is the only other Pennsylvania owl with brown eyes. The remainder of our owls have yellow eyes. This bird ranges over the eastern United States, its distribution coinciding with that of the red-shouldered hawk.

Though, like other owls, it looks heavier, the barred owl usually weighs up to two pounds, with an impressive forty-four-inch wingspan and a body length that can reach up to twenty inches. Its plumage is a drab grey-brown with white spots on its back. The white underside is barred with a buff or brown hue, with barring on the chest as well as the belly.

The barred is the most vocal of all the PA owls. Its hoots are more insistent than even those of the great horned owl, though not as deep or resonate. The barred owl's call usually consists of eight strongly accented hoots, in two segments, each with four calls: *hoohoo-hoohoo ... hoo-hoo-hoo-hooooaw.*

A humorous side note to the barred's call is that Pennsylvania folks have been known to describe it as "Who cooks for you? Who cooks for you allllll?" The barred owl's habit is to call early in the evening, at dawn, and occasionally on dark, cloudy days.

This species of owl almost always nests in hollow trees, laying two to four eggs that hatch in twenty-eight to thirty-three days. Pairs have been known to display strong attachment to the same nesting area, returning year after year.

Unfortunately, the secretive/mysterious habits of the owl, its quiet flight, and various calls, from whistles, screeches and hoots, have made it an object of fear and superstition. I remember hearing, from childhood, that the hoot of an owl was a message of death. Creator made no evil creatures; they each have a purpose, and we are always discovering new ones.

The Native Americans believe that Owl often visits those who are teachers, therapists and counselors. Owls are wise, you see. A visit from wise old Grandmother Owl may indicate a need to peer into the gloom and face existing fears. It could also mean that, within your life, a great mystery is about to unfold, one that will soon be revealed to

Adult male osprey with fish. Note the female in the nest.
Photo captured in Westmoreland County in 2007 by Glenn E. Mucy

you. During waking hours or in dreams, Grandmother Owl comes to those who need to let go of some portion of their lives that is no longer needed or useful. As an animal spirit guide, Owl teaches us to see and hear past shadows, beyond fears and darkness, to the illuminated flip side- to happiness and knowledge, i.e. *enlightenment*.

~ ~ ~

According to the PA Game Commission, Pennsylvania's nesting osprey population has been on the rise in recent years. Back in 1986, we had but one known nesting pair of ospreys. As of 2004, about seventy pairs of ospreys were documented in seventeen PA counties.

Ospreys are large, striking, fish-eating birds of prey often sighted around water. They can exceed two feet in length and sport wingspans of nearly six feet. Dark brown on top, white underneath with faint brown streaking on their breasts, ospreys have prominent dark eye stripes and black patches at the crooks of wings. Some folks call them "fish hawks," and that, I suppose, is their common name.

Ospreys prefer lakes, rivers, ponds and marshes bordered by trees. They nest in large trees, but may be found nesting on telephone poles, chimneys, and manmade platforms built for their use. They require open water with adequate fishing opportunities.

I saw my first osprey in 2009 at Annapolis, and learned that the world's largest nesting population of ospreys, approximately 2,000 pairs, is in the Chesapeake Bay area each spring. Osprey pairs typically return to Pennsylvania in late March to early April to nest.

Osprey populations were decimated through the effects of insecticides like DDT. Use of that killing agent unleashed a slow but steady stranglehold on ospreys, eagles, and other birds of prey. By eating contaminated prey, the birds ingested the insecticide, causing them to lay eggs with extremely thin shells. So fragile were the shells that they broke when the mother bird sat on the eggs to incubate them. Unable to reproduce, ospreys all but disappeared from Pennsylvania. Eagles suffered the same effects from DDT. For more information on this subject, please read the Rachel Carson segment of this volume.

~ ~ ~

Thanks to Pennsylvania's Rachel Carson and others like her, our nesting bald eagle population is also on the rise. In 1980, there were only three nesting pairs reported in the Commonwealth. In 2005, there were, at least, ninety-six reported pairs within the borders of Pennsylvania; again, as per the PA Game Commission.

Bald eagles are among the largest birds of prey. They can weigh ten to fourteen pounds and have up to seven-and-a-half-foot wingspans. Bald eagles can be readily identified by their white heads and tails; however, they do not attain this characteristic plumage until they reach the age of five; thus, they can be confused with golden eagles until they acquire the above-mentioned white head and tail.

Eagles nest in large trees near water where they can fish. Bald eagles don't begin nesting until the age of four or five, then producing, normally, one to three young per year. Adults will continue using the same nest for years, seasonally adding to that nest to strengthen and pad it.

This is the majestic bird that is the symbol of our nation, yet it was on its way to extinction from the deadly effects of DDT. Thanks to recovery efforts, these noble symbols of America may once again be found throughout our state at any time of the year.

For Native Americans, the keywords for the eagle are freedom, strength, courage, spirituality, and rising above. Eagle teaches us to see the highest truth or highest viewpoint. Eagle's energy is pure. It is spiritual energy in its highest form. Eagle teaches us, when we find the courage to do so, that we have the ability to reach great heights.

People with Eagle Medicine need time alone. If Eagle makes an appearance in your life, when you are awake or in a dream, he is reminding you that you need some solitary time before you will be able to take flight.

Eagle People, because of your great beauty and grace, there are those who (lacking good self-esteem) may see you as a threat. However, do not let others prevent you from flying like an eagle. With your great vision (for eagles have remarkable vision), you are likely seen by the more enlightened as a mentor. Whether you actively seek that position or not, there are many who look up to you- for you have great wisdom to share.

County Chronicles

What a sense of freedom is the majesty of an eagle in flight!
This is likely a sub-adult due to the white mottling under the wings and the black markings on the tail.
Photo taken in late-winter 2009, in Bedford County, PA, by Glenn E. Mucy
These images and others by professional nature photographer Glenn E. Mucy are available by calling 724-379-8370.

If you do not have Eagle Medicine and would like to harness it, then read as much as you can about these majestic birds to learn from Eagle, the great teacher. Learn to meditate, and spend as much time as you can in nature, reconnecting to the spiritual. Meditate on a high hill with beautiful rustic scenery surrounding you.

There, conjure your highest vision for yourself, ask to attain it– and *believe* that you can bring it to fruition.

Remember that in Native American culture, the eagle, as the bear, represents the Great Spirit. From the dawn of time, Eagle has been a symbol of Divinity in many cultures.

People with Eagle Medicine know instinctively that freedom is our birthright.

"This is Pittsburgh!"

"As I got down before the canoe, I spent some time in viewing the rivers, and the land in the fork, which I think extremely well situated for a fort, as it has absolute command of the [three] rivers ... . The land at the Point is 20 or 25 feet above the common surface of the water; and a considerable bottom of flat, well-timbered land all around it, very convenient for building ... ."
- George Washington, from his Journal in regard to the Point at Pittsburgh, autumn 1753

"[Pittsburgh is] Hell with the lid taken off."
- James Parton, 1868

"Steel, coal and coke may have built Pittsburgh, but this city has come a long way from its smoky, gritty past. Today, Pittsburgh is a fantastic cultural center, for the arts and the performing arts; a superior medical center, and a vibrant corporate hub. Pittsburgh today is a gorgeous city. And no where in the entire world can you view a more beautiful- a more dramatic- city at night."
- Ceane O'Hanlon-Lincoln

Pittsburgh's strategic location and wealth of natural resources, combined with a steady flow of labor to the area, practically guaranteed, from its beginnings, its commercial and industrial success. One of this city's finest natural resources has always been its people- a magical medley of ethnic peoples from the four corners of the globe.

Pittsburghers say that America was not born in Philadelphia, Pennsylvania's queen city, but in Pittsburgh, the Commonwealth's princess city. Nearly every Pittsburgher is a "historian"; never argue with a Pittsburgher about the history of his/her beloved city! In a way, they have a valid Point ... forgive the pun.

The Point, at Pittsburgh, was prime real estate in the 1750s, when western Pennsylvania became the focus of the entire western world. It is the spot where the Monongahela and the Allegheny rivers meet to form the Ohio, fittingly christened by the Native Americans and the French explorers *la Belle Rivière*, the "Beautiful River."

The world's two superpowers during this period were France and England. The great rivals gingerly descended the path to war when, in May 1754, the first shots between them rang out in a remote corner of my home county of Fayette in what became known as the "Jumonville Affair." There, the young British officer in charge would get his first taste of war. His name was George Washington.

Not long afterward, the two superpowers clashed again, in July of that year, at Great Meadows, where the French retaliated against Washington at his hastily built Fort Necessity, resulting in the one and only time the future Father of our Country surrendered an army in the field to an enemy.

Deciding that the Point must be taken, the King of England sent over 1,500 regular troops the following year (1755) to accomplish what the British believed would be a relatively easy task. In charge of this force was Major General Edward Braddock.

Though a brave and seasoned officer, Braddock was not skilled in fighting Indians, and ignoring the wise counsel of both Benjamin Franklin and George Washington not to underestimate the Native element, about two-thirds of his flying column was defeated in what became known as the Battle of the Monongahela. Amid the bloodcurdling war whoops and scalphulloes of the Indians, the slaughter was terrible- over 900 British falling in less than four hours, like so many leaves in a sudden and devastating storm. Braddock himself was mortally wounded.

It was not until three years later, on 25 November 1758, that another army- made up of 6,000 British and Colonial soldiers led by General John Forbes- reclaimed the Point for the British Empire. Once Forbes secured the fort, he commissioned a temporary fortress be built to replace the one the French had left in ashes after they had abandoned the site, fleeing down river.

The subsequent permanent fort, just east of the ruins of the French Fort Duquesne, Forbes named in honor of William Pitt, the British prime minister who had led the successful war against France. The area surrounding the Point was christened "Pittsbourgh (pronounced *Pittsboro* with a Scottish trilled "r" that quiets at the end of the word, thus the emergence of the "h" at the end of Pittsburgh). Almost immediately, the name evolved into "Pittsburgh."

Fort Pitt became one of the largest British strongholds in North America and one of the few British forts to withstand a Native American siege during Pontiac's War that was, in essence, the Indians' war for independence. During the siege that lasted from May to August 1763, hundreds of settlers took refuge inside the sturdy walls of Fort Pitt. It was only when Colonel Henry Bouquet led combined Highlander and American ranger troops to victory, that August at Bushy Run (midway between Fort Ligonier and Fort Pitt), that the long siege on Fort Pitt was lifted. The victory at Bushy Run was the first time White warriors had clashed in the forest with Red and won.

Though short-lived, Pontiac's War was nothing to scoff at. The damage wreaked by the Indians was considerable. United in their efforts, they had killed or captured 2,000-plus settlers. Many captives would not be reunited with their families for years, though several would be returned the next year. Others would never again live with Whites.

The French and Indian War and its aftermath, Pontiac's War and Dunmore's War, unleashed Colonial passions that provoked America's War for Independence. The frontier outpost of Fort Pitt and the eventual settlement of Pittsburgh soon became a hub of the new American nation, rendering the frontier town the "Gateway to the West."

In the succeeding decades, this focal city grew into one of America's significant centers of industry, innovation and invention. Here, the making of steel turned Pittsburgh into the "heartbeat of America."

In the not-too-distant town of Connellsville, in Fayette County, coke production (a by-product of bituminous/soft coal) that began in the 1840s provided a vital ingredient to the making of steel. In fact, the Pittsburgh mills grew insatiably hungry for Connellsville coke!

By the way, readers, the word "coke" is derived from COal caKE, since that is essentially what coke is- soft coal baked, at a high temperature, into a sort of cake.

Prior to the Civil War, steel was one industry among many in Pittsburgh, but the great conflict brought a major change to this city- and steel became the indisputable king.

The first method of making steel inexpensively and in large quantities was the Bessemer process that gave birth to the modern steel industry. Rapidly, this drew a flood of immigrants- German, Irish, Welsh, Scottish, Italian, Polish, Slovak, Croatian, and Hungarian- who began weaving the Steel City's rich tapestry of ethnic cultures and traditions. These immigrants came armed with hope and a fierce resolve for a better life, strong backs, and a great willingness to work- *and work they did.*

The "men of steel" who went into the hell that was the hot-end of the steel works, stepped into a virtual war zone on a daily basis for the pennies a day they made to keep body and soul together. Mind, there were no safety conditions in those long-past days, no workmen's compensation, no insurance, no minimum wage. Their pay was low and their hours long, but for wives and for the want of something better for their children, they braved the fierce ovens with the glare of extreme heat and the horrible stench of gases, whilst everywhere- *everywhere*- was the Devil's own shower with its deafening hiss and omnipresent danger of escaping steam!

In the mills' early days, puddlers, for example, had their jobs down to a science, or perhaps I should say *an art*. These skilled craftsmen had once overseen the difficult mixing and heating of the ore, watchfully keeping their keen, knowing gazes fixed upon the molten metal for subtle signs of what to add and when to finish.

In the hot, yellow glare from the furnaces, they had pushed the heated iron around, stirred it, and literally spat in it, judging it by its color and the hue of the flames that shot out of the oven to announce when the "cooking" was done.

But with the advent of the great bulbous brute called "Bessemer," things changed. The Bessemer converters, in the late 1880s, eliminated the skills of the puddlers, along with the *hold* the iron craftsmen once had on production. No longer did mill owners need the master craftsmen who had run the former iron works. Now, they needed muscle. And the influx of immigrants provided that muscle!

When Big Bess began to rumble and belch, and from her gaping mouth, high overhead, her huge scarlet-flame tongue licked at the smoky Pittsburgh sky, the usual cacophony of noises was drowned in one fearful, ear-shattering triumphant **R-O-A-R**, as a rush of cold shot liquid fire into her great belly. When the blower signaled that the blow was ready, and that biting blast of air, with ferocious temperature contrast, struck the workers' sweating bodies, the men visibly shuddered, and it was no small wonder pneumonia was the greatest death trap of all the mills' hazards.

Now commenced a battle more astonishing than man had ever before witnessed. The flame, steady and frightfully red, began to change color, a descending spectrum of bright flashes- a spectacular "fireworks" display- reflecting and reverberating from the warring elements, oxygen in a life-and-death struggle with carbon.

Inside the grand beast, steel was being born. And from the great thundering mouth, the solid fire transformed from scarlet to indigo, to orange, to yellow, the roaring subsiding to powerful throbs and heartfelt echoes- *the heartbeat of Pittsburgh, the heartbeat of America*- the vivid flames changing ultimately to the blinding dazzle of a most brilliant white.

Then, when the enormous, egg-shaped Bess began slowly to tilt, via her tall trunnions, like a gigantic cannon in the war of the industrial titans, *this* was the most incredible of the sights and sounds of steel, the cascade of liquid death- *breathtaking*- with a coral flare too vibrant to describe. From it, and around it, poured light and heat, intense beyond human endurance; and as the liquid fire flowed into the enormous pot below it, *a magical veil of blazing, hissing sparks shot up and sprayed the entire scene- like a gigantic dragon's fiery breath!*

Fresh off the boat, immigrants didn't need to speak English to use a shovel or tote a heavy load of pipes. *Tchekai*, the Slavic word for "Watch out!" often reverberated through the hot-end of Pittsburgh-area steel mills when a crane was taking a huge ladle of hot metal overhead- And oh, a ladle of liquid steel was a lovely terror!- or when a torrent of red-hot cinder was shooting out of a gaping furnace door. After a while, even English-speaking workers began to shout the strident warning. *Tchekai* was a word that cried out to the ears of Slavic workers in their sleep.

Regardless of ethnic origin, every one of the immigrant workers was forged in this miracle of birth- with each definable aspect of the heat and hammering that changed iron into steel- *the best steel in the world*. The miracle *belonged* to these men of steel. They knew it, and they held fast to it!

Some of the nation's bloodiest labor conflicts took place in the Pittsburgh area. In 1892, Pinkerton detectives hired by Henry Clay Frick and strikers at the Carnegie Steel Works clashed in a horrific battle (involving most of the town) at Homestead. For the whole thrilling account, please read "Homestead!" in *CC II*.

Here is an excerpt from that Chronicle: "At midnight on 5 July, tugboats pushed two covered barges, carrying roughly three hundred Pinkertons armed with Winchester rifles, down the Monongahela River. But union guards stationed along the waterfront spotted them at the Smithfield Bridge. A Pittsburgh journalist penned that at about 3:00 a.m., *à la* Paul Revere, '... a horseman riding at breakneck speed dashed into the streets of Homestead, sounding the alarm as he sped along. "They're coming! They're coming!"'"

County Chronicles

"The mill had forged a brotherhood in the community; and ten thousand strikers, their families and sympathizers flung off sleep and, armed with guns, pipes, bricks, shovels, rocks, and even brooms and umbrellas, poured down to the riverbank where the silent mill stood. Homestead- where once the roar of a thousand lions forged steel from iron. *Now there awaited lions of a different sort.*"

Yes, readers, after the Civil War, Pittsburgh with its steel industry rightfully claimed its place as the "Heartbeat of America." Some might say the "Hearth of America." The Pittsburgh steel industry played a major role in defeating our enemies in all of America's struggles from the Civil War hence. Pittsburgh steel outfitted the Allied Forces, and at the height of World War II, this mighty city and its environs produced about thirty percent of the nation's steel.

However, everything comes at a price. To quote *Forging Ahead, Pittsburgh at 250*, "[The city] bore the scars of the Industrial Age." In addition to its soubriquet the "Heartbeat of America," Pittsburgh was labeled "Hell with the lid off" and the "Smoky City." And each label was well-earned, well-deserved.

Pittsburgh in future years would experience a renaissance battle for cleaner air, thanks to people like Mayor David L. Lawrence and others. We'll discuss some of Pittsburgh's visionaries a bit later.

During the post-WWII years, big steel continued in Pittsburgh, to quote again from *Forging Ahead*, "... filling demands for cars, washing machines, and building materials."

Then, in the mid-1980s, "Pittsburgh's backbone of steel turned to rust" when cheaper steel imports came into the country as Pittsburgh mills struggled with higher production costs. By 1986, the once-massive Homestead Works shut down forever. The great roaring lion had been put to sleep.

I can vividly recall, over the long years, seeing the Pittsburgh nighttime sky- a fiery drama- when the mills were in blast, gone now but not forgotten. I remember how I felt when so many of the steel works closed their doors back in the 1980s. I thought, "What will happen to Pittsburgh?" But it did not take me long to realize that Pittsburgh, a shot-and-a-beer kind of town, was a *tough* city. Before long, it picked itself up, dusted itself off, and forged ahead, just as it had always done in the past.

The nighttime magic of Pittsburgh's Golden Triangle from the West End Overlook
Photo by John Craig

Today, the 251-year-old (at this writing) Pittsburgh is a beautiful city, clean, the air breathable, the skies no longer smoky. On the historic site of the former Homestead Works is the **Waterfront**, providing, with magnificent Victorian ambience, 260 acres of upscale shopping, entertainment and fine dining.

Reflecting its bright tapestry of ethnic peoples, Pittsburgh is resolute and resilient- *a survivor*. The city continues to adapt to meet the demands of its residents and the nation, even the world. The modern, revitalized Pittsburgh is an impressive cultural center- for the arts and the performing arts. Our commonwealth's princess city is also a superb medical center as well as a vibrant corporate hub. And no city, no where, is as dazzling as Pittsburgh at night! From Mount Washington, from the deck of one of the famous Pittsburgh riverboats, from Station Square, nighttime Pittsburgh aglow with its jewel-like lights is incomparable.

Pittsburgh and the surrounding region are home to architectural masterpieces designed by such noted architects as Henry Hobson Richardson, including, on Grant Street, the Allegheny County Courthouse and former jail with its arching stone bridge, the **Bridge of Sighs**, one of the few remaining such structures in the nation.

Let's talk for a moment about Pittsburgh's ubiquitous bridges. Known as the "City of Bridges," Pittsburgh, with three rivers converging at the Point, can boast approximately 320 bridges. Three of those bridges are charmingly called the **"Three Sisters,"** and these are: the Roberto Clemente Bridge that crosses the Allegheny between downtown and the North Side; the Rachel Carson Bridge, formerly the Ninth Street Bridge; and the Andy Warhol Bridge, formerly the Seventh Street Bridge.

Pittsburgh has its noteworthy tunnels too. To name a few: The Armstrong Tunnel opened in 1927, the Squirrel Hill Tunnel in 1953; the Liberty Tubes began use in 1924, and the Fort Pitt Tunnel opened in 1960.

The twin Liberty Tubes are listed among America's oldest automotive tunnels, com-

The Monongahela Incline about a century ago. Note the spelling of Pittsburgh on this vintage photo/postcard. The most misspelled city in America, Pittsburgh dropped the "h" in 1890, only to restore it again in 1911. It should be noted that most Pittsburghers had refused to drop the "h."

pleted about three years earlier than the famous Holland Tunnel in New York. Did you know that about 200,000 vehicles motor in and out of the Fort Pitt Tunnel, on the city's South Side, and the Squirrel Hill Tunnel, to the east, every day?

Now let's talk inclines. Called "funiculars" almost everywhere else, Pittsburgh's inclines are super-charged with history. Only two remain today, the **Duquesne and the Monongahela inclines** that carry passengers up and down the steep, scenic slopes of Mount Washington. Years ago, they carried workers from their various neighborhoods to the mills.

Oh, there were footpaths, but it was difficult going to reach those ultra-steep hilltops. In Pittsburgh's smoky past, inclines not only carried workers but, believe it or not, horses and light freight too!

The Monongahela Incline, that began operation in 1870, travels about six miles per hour up and down Mount Washington on one of the steepest funicular rides in the entire country (about 369 feet). The Duquesne Incline, that began operating a few years later in 1877, travels up and down Mount Washington from Carson Street to the aptly named Grandview Avenue.

Known internationally for its historically precise reconstruction, the Duquesne Incline, together with its observation deck, can claim one of the most impressive panoramic views of the Golden Triangle- especially spectacular is it at night.

In fact, in 2003 the *USA Weekend Magazine* ranked this the "Number-Two" most beautiful view in America, second only to the Red Rock Country of Sedona, Arizona. With all due respect to the magazine and the great state of Arizona, I have seen both and would rank Pittsburgh's nighttime Golden Triangle first, but of course, I am biased.

Pittsburgh's glittering night skyline is not the only highlight of this Chronicle, however. This city has been the home of some pretty impressive human luminaries, such as **Andrew Carnegie,** who, at thirteen, left his native Scotland in search of wealth in America, beginning his life here as a bobbin boy in a cotton factory, where he earned about a dollar a week.

To say that Carnegie had a successful life would be a gross understatement. By thirty, his business interests included iron works, steamers, railroads, and oil wells. But it was his ensuing involvement and virtual control of steel production that chiseled his name in the annals of history.

Carnegie opened his largest steel plant, the Edgar Thomson Works- named for the president of the Pennsylvania Railroad- at Braddock in 1875.

In 1901, the "Little Scott" sold the empire he had forged in the steel furnaces of Pittsburgh for $400 million, making him literally the richest man in the world. A champion for education, Carnegie donated more than $350 million for the construction of libraries, as well as for other educational and cultural institutions.

While Andrew Carnegie was the "Steel King," **Henry Clay Frick** was the "Coke King." Even when he became the undisputed person in charge of the coke industry, Frick never slacked work. He frequently collapsed at the front door of his Pittsburgh/Point Breeze home, **Clayton House**, exhausted from his exertions.

Frick was meticulous and exacting in everything he did, from his elegant attire to the smallest detail of his busy daily schedule. To be sure, he ran a "tight ship." H.C. Frick was at once a notorious union-busting, "get-out-of-my-way" industrialist and a refined gentleman and connoisseur of the arts. He was hard-nosed, ofttimes ruthless and uncompromising in his business dealings; but when it came to family, he was a loving husband, father and grandfather.

From his mother's side of the family, Frick borrowed money in the amount of $75,000. He later borrowed $20,000 from Mellon Bank in Pittsburgh, which he had no trouble securing. Always neat and careful about his appearance from early on, H.C.'s innate elegance- his quiet dignity- was a principal facet of his power. Immediately then, he began building beehive coke ovens to turn out coke, the valuable by-product of bituminous coal for the production of Pittsburgh steel.

By 1870, the steel-mill operators in Pittsburgh had discovered that the Connellsville coke was the best in the world for manufacturing steel; and the subsequent year, the assiduous young man, who had been born with the Midas touch, organized the H.C. Frick Coke Company. A couple of years hence, the financial panic of 1873 allowed the cool-headed Frick to acquire the properties of his rivals. *He gained over eighty percent of the Connellsville coke.* This incredible coup would knock open the door to his partnership with steel tycoon Andrew Carnegie.

By 1879, Frick controlled about 35,000 acres of coal and thousands upon thousands of beehive coke ovens. At the age of thirty, Frick was a millionaire residing in his Pittsburgh mansion, Clayton House, with his new bride, the beautiful Adelaide Howard Childs, whom he had met at a Pittsburgh reception with Andrew Mellon in June of 1881.

As enamored as Frick was with Adelaide, nevertheless, during his honeymoon, the "Coke King" seized the opportunity, at a chance meeting with Carnegie, to discuss business and partnership with the "Steel King."

The alliance made perfect sense, for Carnegie's Pittsburgh mills were, to reiterate, insatiably hungry for coke to make steel.

Before long, Frick became the director of several companies, and in 1901 he took an active part in the negotiations that resulted in the formation of the United States Steel Corporation.

From 1889 to 1900, the workaholic coke mogul was elevated to Chairman of the Board at the powerful Carnegie firm, and it was during that period when his actions at the Homestead Strike of 1892 led to his attempted assassination by anarchist Alexander Berkman. Berkman, who had no real connection with the strike, fired three bullets into Frick's neck and stabbed him several times.

A carpenter working in the area subdued Berkman and was about to bash his head in with a hammer, when Frick shouted, "No! Don't hit him! Leave him to the law... but raise his head, and let me see his face."

Frick finished his day's business with this message to Carnegie who was in Scotland: "Don't come home. We'll fight this strike out, even if it kills me!"

As it turned out, the Homestead Strike did not kill Frick, but the violence did claim the lives of several others. Frick hired Pinkerton guards who shot and killed ten striking steelworkers in the Homestead streets. To be fair, there was violence on both sides. At the time of the Homestead troubles, as mentioned above, Frick's partner, Andrew Carnegie, was conveniently at his castle in Scotland, leaving the dirty work to Frick. Carnegie's desire to suppress unions was just as intense as Frick's, if not more so, but in the years following, Carnegie always tried to disassociate himself from the Homestead Strike that, by the way, set labor back for over four decades.

Of course Carnegie *knew* what the tough-minded Frick would do to put down that strike. Nevertheless, the episode tore a deep rift between Carnegie and Frick that never healed.

Along about 1900 Frick left Carnegie Steel, and the partnership broke up, though Frick continued his business interests in New York. Years later, an absolving Carnegie sent a message down Fifth Avenue to his estranged colleague to meet and tidy up the past; but Frick was having none of it. "Tell Mr. Carnegie," he retorted in terse summation, "I'll meet him in hell, where we are both going!" Never again did the Scotsman offer the olive branch to his former partner.

Henry Clay Frick died in 1919, the same year Andrew Carnegie left this world, and the same year, ironically, that Frick-would-be-assassin Alexander Berkman was released from prison and deported back to his native Russia, quipping to reporters, as he strode up the gangplank of his ship, that he was glad Frick left the country before he did. For more true stories and events connected to Carnegie and Frick, see *County Chronicles I* and *II* of my PA history series.

Another Pittsburgh luminary who passed from this earth that year was **Henry J. Heinz**, a food processor who first gained fame from his horseradish. Determined to prove his product's quality over the competition, he marketed his horseradish in clear glass bottles.

H.J. Heinz provided variety to America's diet, and that prompted his company's famous slogan– "57 varieties." And let us not neglect to cite that little green pickle pin that tops the list of promotional gimmicks of all time.

Heinz was an innovator when it came to food processing, marketing, and food safety, utilizing the latest developments in steam-pressure cooking, vacuum canning, and railroad refrigeration cars. He moved his company from Sharpsburg (a suburb of Pittsburgh), where he had established it in 1869, to Pittsburgh's North Side in 1882, the same year he patented his soon-to-be-famous ketchup in its distinctive glass bottle.

When Henry passed away in 1919, the H.J. Heinz Company included twenty-five food-processing plants and about 200 smaller works that ranged from container and bottling factories to farms and H.J. Heinz offices around the globe.

Andrew Mellon's name conjures banking and finance. The Pittsburgh-born financial wizard developed his banking expertise from the time he was a teen when he joined his father's banking firm. Like other magnates of his era, Andrew Mellon was a workaholic. He helped to organize the Union Trust Company as well as the Union Savings Bank of Pittsburgh. With the passing of years, Mellon expanded his vistas and his fortune. In addition to banking, his interests included steel, oil, construction, and shipbuilding.

In 1933, **Richard King Mellon** took over as president of Mellon Bank. In the ensuing thirty-odd years, with R.K. at the helm, the bank underwent rapid growth that helped to establish Pittsburgh as a major financial and corporate center.

A veteran of both World Wars, after WW II, Mellon undertook the task to bring Pittsburgh into the modern age. His mission included new downtown buildings and a center for medicine, incorporating research and education. Lauded by *Time*, the magazine christened his efforts "Mellon's Miracle."

In 1947, the far-seeing man created the Richard King Mellon Foundation, today one of the nation's largest independent endowments. The RKMF largely bestows grants in the southwestern corner of our commonwealth, focusing on economic development, land preservation, and watershed restoration and protection.

Though **George Westinghouse, Jr.** was not a Pittsburgh native, he made our princess city his adopted hometown in 1868. Here, he formed the Westinghouse Electric Company. The hard-working, prolific inventor had already built generators that harnessed the incredible power of Niagara Falls; and with his electric company and his use of alternating current, he rendered electricity practical for lighting, transportation, and machine operation.

From the age of fifteen with his first patent, a rotary engine, Westinghouse's fertile mind was constantly generating new and better ideas. A myriad of historians would agree that George Westinghouse's influence on industry in America- especially on the nation's railroads- is considerable, perhaps even unparalleled. His nearly 400 patents include the automatic railroad air brake, electrical transformers, and air shock absorbers for automobiles.

The financial panic of 1907 was hard on Westinghouse, and after losing control of his companies, he passed away in 1914.

David L. Lawrence was Pittsburgh's only four-term mayor, serving in that office from 1946 to 1959. His name shall ever be associated with the city of his birth.

During the Great Depression, Lawrence was named (1934) Chairman of the Democratic Party for the state of Pennsylvania, and it was he who put into place the Democratic machine that is still operating today. His efforts broke the firm hold the Republicans had on Pittsburgh for decades prior to the Great Depression.

Lawrence nearly always advocated compromise. He liked to jest that he had learned to do so as a boy, because he and his brothers were forbidden to resort to fisticuffs. The fact that he was a staunch Democrat did not dissuade him from building a good working relationship with Republican Richard King Mellon.

Though the pair had little in common, they piloted and propelled **Renaissance I** forward for the betterment of their hometown. Renaissance I, readers, was one of the very first urban renewal plans in America, as well as the first earnest endeavor to reduce and control the city's industry-related pollution problem.

In 2003, the David L. Lawrence Convention Center opened in Pittsburgh along the Allegheny River, the largest building to meet rigorous requirements created by the United States Green Building Council for GOLD Leadership in Energy and Environmental design, thus spurring additional "green" Pittsburgh construction.

A second Renaissance was undertaken by Democrat Mayor **Richard S. Caliguiri**, who took the helm of the city of Pittsburgh in 1977. Caliguiri was the leader who helped Pittsburgh evolve bigger and better than ever after the requiem bell had tolled the end of the steel industry. His **Renaissance II** project included construction of a subway system and skyscrapers- One PPG Place, One Oxford Center, and One Mellon Center. In addition, he fostered development of Station Square and the Pittsburgh Technology Center. Bridges were repaired, potholes patched, and streets, parks, and neighborhoods cleaned up.

When Caliguiri sadly passed away at the age of fifty-six (an untimely death from the fatal build-up of proteins in the organs), this man who cared little for politics, and even less for fame, went down in history as one of Pittsburgh's most popular mayors.

City Council President **Sophie Masloff** stepped into Caliguiri's shoes upon his death. You can read about this unique Pittsburgh mayor in "The Right Stuff ..." this volume.

Moving on in our discussion, polio, a once relentless disease, is now virtually eradicated thanks to a University of Pittsburgh scientist, **Dr. Jonas Salk**, who developed the first effective polio vaccine.

Hundreds of local schoolchildren- known as "Polio Pioneers"- tested Salk's vaccine that contained a dead polio virus rather than the live virus (preventing the injections from infecting patients). Announced to the public on April 12, 1955, Salk's polio vaccine was welcomed, lauded and cheered as a great success, cementing the University of Pittsburgh's reputation for medical research and innovation.

Over the years, Pittsburgh has also earned its rightful reputation as a nucleus for organ transplants and as a burn-treatment center.

In addition to the **polio vaccine**, Pittsburgh has provided the nation with other firsts. The **first World's Series**– Boston Pilgrims vs. Pittsburg(h) Pirates– was held in 1903 in Pittsburg(h) with the final score Boston 5, Pittsburg(h) 3.

Built in 1909, Pittsburgh's **Forbes Field** was the nation's first major-league baseball concrete-and-steel stadium.

The **world's first gas station** was built by Gulf Refining Company in Pittsburgh at the corner of Baum Boulevard and St. Clair Street in 1913. I wonder what the price of gas was then?

Pittsburgh is also the proud home of the **first commercial radio station, KDKA,** which began broadcasting in 1920. There are other firsts discussed elsewhere in my *CC* series.

Also in the early 1920s, **bingo** was Pittsburgh-born. After creating the game and subsequently taking it to carnivals nationwide in 1924, Pittsburgher Hugh J. Ward penned an official book of bingo rules in 1933.

Now let's talk culture. Did you know that few areas of our nation can compare with western Pennsylvania for its number of world-renowned native sons and daughters in the arts? To name a few of these shining stars, let's begin with one of the great pioneers of modern dance, **Martha Graham**.

Graham, who was born in 1894 in Allegheny City, now the North Side, was influenced by the dances/movements performed by Native Americans during their religious ceremonies. I suppose we could say that Martha Graham's influence on dance could be compared to Stravinsky's influence on music, Pablo Picasso's on art, or Frank Lloyd Wright's influence on architecture.

In essence, what Graham did was to invent a whole new language of dance that unleashed, through expressive movements, passion, rage, ecstasy– the whole circuitous route of human emotions.

For over seventy years, Martha Graham danced and choreographed exciting performances, the first dancer ever to perform at the White House, the first ever to travel abroad as a cultural ambassador– the first dancer ever to receive the highest civilian award– the Presidential Medal of Freedom.

Gene Kelly is another Pittsburgh dance legend. No other male dancer I can think of could combine masculinity and grace quite like Kelly. A graduate of Peabody High School, he earned a degree in economics at the University of Pittsburgh, graduating in 1933. After he appeared on Broadway in a couple of shows, he was offered a movie contract, and the future star was on his toe-tapping way!

Known for his athletic, energetic dance routines, Irish good looks and charm, and his likable characters on the Silver Screen, Kelly is best remembered for his performances in such classics as *Singin' in the Rain* and *An American in Paris*. The recipient of several esteemed awards, Gene Kelly dominated musical film from the mid-1940s to the late 1950s, almost single-handedly rendering ballet commercially acceptable to movie audiences everywhere.

Frank Gorshin, Michael Keaton, Shirley Jones, Jimmy Stewart, and **Sharon Stone** are other big-name actors who hailed from the Pittsburgh area. I wrote about Indiana, Pennsylvania's admirable– *heroic*– Jimmy Stewart in *County Chronicles II*, and Smithton, *Pennsylvania's – America's– Sweetheart* Shirley Jones in *CC III*.

In the late 1970s, I was blessed to have dined a few times with **Fred Rogers** at the Latrobe County Club. He and I shared a close mutual friend, and that's how those memorable evenings came about. Fred was born in Latrobe in 1928. I remember him as sweet-natured, kind and gracious, much as he appears on his nationally syndicated, four-time Emmy-winning show *Mr. Rogers' Neighborhood* (1968-2001).

In addition to his television career, Rogers was an ordained Presbyterian minister. Though he wasn't really interested in preaching, he did God's work in so many other ways, entertaining and teaching thousands of children and ushering them into the "Neighborhood of Make-Believe." The beloved figure passed away at the age of seventy-four in 2003. His legacy and his TV show, however, live on.

An iconic movie producer of the Golden Age of Hollywood, **David O. Selznick** was born in Pittsburgh in 1902. He is best known for producing the epic classic (1939) *Gone With the Wind,* debatably the best motion picture ever made, copping seven Oscars, additional special awards, and the highest amount of money at the box office of any film ever (adjusted for inflation). Selznick made history by winning the Best-Picture Oscar two years in a row for *GWTW* (1939) and *Rebecca* (1940).

Here's a Selznick tidbit I think you'll like, readers: His real name was simply David Selznick. He had no middle name. The "O" stands for nothing. In his own words: "I had an uncle whom I greatly disliked, who was also named David Selznick, so in order to avoid the growing confusion between the two of us, I decided to take a middle initial and went through the alphabet to find one that seemed to me to give the best pronunciation, and decided on 'O.'"

Pittsburgh has produced so many outstanding people in the various arts that we should not neglect to mention a couple of its fine painters. **Mary Cassatt**, about whom I wrote in *County Chronicles II*, was born in 1844, in Allegheny City (now Pittsburgh's North Side).

Cassatt enjoyed a privileged childhood within the affluence of her family. Her parents instilled zeal in their children for education, especially in the arts. Mary's father, an investment banker, constantly sought advancement, moving the family to a variety of Pennsylvania locales throughout her youth. The family eventually relocated to Philadelphia, and it was after their move east that the Cassatts began to immerse themselves in the increasingly sophisticated cultural arenas of Philadelphia, London, Paris, Heidelberg and Berlin, creating for them- *la bonne vie*.

About a month before her sixteenth birthday, Cassatt enrolled at Philadelphia's eminent Pennsylvania Academy of Fine Arts. The school gave her a good foundation for her artful quests. After the American Civil War ended, Cassatt studied art in Paris.

A movement of new artists, who deviated from the norms of the art world, was emerging onto the Paris scene, such men as the self-confident Claude Monet, the son of a grocer, who was in love with the sun, the sea and the wind; Pierre-Auguste Renoir, the son of a tailor, whose art was consumed with a love of life and happy, bright-eyed people; and then there was the imperious Edgar Degas, whose fascination for the ballet dancers destined him for immortality.

It was while strolling past a Paris gallery one sunny April afternoon in 1874, when Cassatt first espied, in the window, a bold pastel by Edgar Degas. His ballet dancers threw her imagination into a whole new gear, and in that pivotal moment, within the quick movement of a danseuse's whirling pirouette, she arrived in the exciting realm of the Great French Impressionists. She drew in her breath. The effect the Degas had on her was *dizzying*.

Mary Cassatt became the only American to ever exhibit with the great French Impressionists. In addition to her well-earned fame as a painter, Cassatt was always a strong advocate of women's rights. She believed women could be homemakers and professionals, one or the other, or any combination therein; the choice, she advocated, was theirs.

Pennsylvania's Mary Cassatt, one of the greatest artists America can claim, was more than anything an artist of surprises- sometimes small, often subtle, but always profound. She left behind a glorious legacy of art and with it, the story of her life, proving that a woman could be, in her own words, not "something"- but *somebody*.

Another innovative Pittsburgh artist was **Andy Warhol**. Born in 1928, Warhol graduated from Carnegie Mellon University, majoring in pictorial design. He eventually surfaced as a leader in the visual art movement known as "pop art."

After a successful career as a commercial illustrator, Warhol gained international acclaim as a painter, avant-garde filmmaker, author, and public figure known for his membership in coteries of bohemians; Hollywood celebrities; wealthy, eccentric aristocrats; and distinguished intellectuals.

It was Warhol who coined the phrase "fifteen minutes of fame," stating, "In the future, everyone will be world-famous for fifteen minutes."

As a child, Warhol was sickly, suffering from Saint Vitus' dance that may have been a complication of scarlet fever. He became somewhat of a hypochondriac, developing a fear of hospitals and doctors. Repeatedly bedridden as a child, an outcast to his schoolmates, Andy bonded strongly with his mother. From his bed, he took up drawing and surrounded himself with pictures of film stars. Warhol said later that this lonely period turned out to be significant in the development of his personality and artistic skills and preferences.

Warhol's work redefined modern art when he turned everyday commercial products, like a Campbell's soup can, into pop icons. His most famous work embraces a series of celebrity silk-screen prints featuring Marilyn Monroe, Elvis Presley, and countless self-portraits.

Warhol loved music, and he designed fifty record covers, his first in 1949, and his last the year he died in 1987. Perhaps his most famous were the bright-yellow-banana Velvet Underground cover and the 1971 Rolling Stones album "Sticky Fingers" for which he used an actual zipper on the record sleeve. Notably, Warhol created album covers for Artie Shaw, Count Basie, Aretha Franklin, Diana Ross, Blondie, and for a special recording of Tchaikovsky's *Swan Lake*.

Visitors to Pittsburgh can view more than 4,000 works by Warhol in the **Andy Warhol Museum** that opened its doors on the city's North Side in 1994. Those works include drawings, paintings, prints, photographs, sculptures, and films.

Yet another Pittsburgh-area artist is **Robert Griffing** whose biographical sketch I included in *County Chronicles II*. Griffing's paintings are windows to the past. Each of his images draws us into history, where before, there had been only words to take us there.

"Griff," as he is known to family and friends, engages in meticulous research before and during the creation of each new painting. A stickler for authenticity, there is never any guesswork. The clothing, uniforms, weapons and accoutrements illustrated in his art are all authentic to the period. So, too, are the backdrops. This devotion to the truth is rooted in Griff's lifelong love of history.

Robert Griffing was born on June 9, 1940. A native of Linesville, Crawford County, Pennsylvania, he grew up in an area rich in natural beauty and Native American legend and lore.

Membership in the Boy Scouts intensified Griffing's keen interest in Native American culture, and for a time, he entertained the idea of becoming an archaeologist. But Destiny intervened in the guise of his high school art teacher, who urged him to pursue a career in art, so telling were the young man's drawings.

A graduate of the Art Institute of Pittsburgh, Robert Griffing enjoyed a lucrative thirty-year career in advertising, where he was recognized as a superior logo designer and art director.

By the early 1980s, Griff felt the strong magnetic pull of the easel with his desire to paint Native Americans and Native American scenes. He began doing just that in his spare time, until he retired from advertising in 1992, after which he dedicated his energies toward his first love, the eighteenth-century Eastern Frontier and the Eastern Woodland Indians. His devotion to his craft has reaped well-deserved awards. In 1999, he received the prestigious John Forbes Medal for his notable contribution to the study and promotion of Pennsylvania frontier history. The artist has said that was one of the proudest moments of his life.

I first met Griff in the spring of 2004, when I was invited to his Pittsburgh-area studio to meet with him and his agents, Cathy and Gerry Seymour, the result of their perusal of my work where color plates of the artist's paintings would appear in *County Chronicles*.

In April 2005, I was invited to the special unveiling of Robert Griffing's *The Wounding of General Braddock (Battle of the Monongahela, July 1755)*, at Fort Pitt, in commemoration of the 250th anniversary of Braddock's Defeat. When the drape was drawn from the masterpiece, the hushed audience breathed a sound of appreciation and wonder. "This is not a painting," I exclaimed to my husband, "this is alive... it pulses with life and emotion... with *history*!"

One of the things of which I am most proud is that I have met Robert Griffing, spoken with him, learned from him and his work. I am pleased and grateful, too, that select color plates of his paintings appear, courtesy of the artist and Paramount Press, in this volume, as well as other volumes of my *County Chronicles* Pennsylvania history series.

One of the most respected artists in his genre today, Robert Griffing is destined, through his media of expression, for immortality.

Now, let us discuss a few of Pittsburgh's outstanding museums– the **Carnegie Museum of Art** and the **Carnegie Museum of Natural History** (both on Forbes Avenue in Oakland); the **Senator John Heinz History Center** (on Smallman Street in the Strip District); the **Frick Art Museum** (at the **Frick Art and Historical Center** at Point Breeze); the unique **Mattress Factory** (on the North Side), the first of its kind in the country; the awe-inspiring **Carnegie Science Center** (North Side); the learning-is-fun **Children's Museum of Pittsburgh** (also on the North

Side); the **Fort Pitt Block House** (at the Point; Point State Park).

The **Carnegie Museum of Natural History** began in Pittsburgh in 1895. After its team of paleontologists discovered the skeleton of a huge dinosaur, nicknamed "Dippy," in Sheep Creek, Montana, in 1899, the "creature's" massive size meant the Carnegie Museum of Natural History had to move to a larger home. The current, very impressive, building opened in 1907.

Today, this museum's majestic, marble corridors lead thousands of visitors a year to galleries where they can discover thrilling African wildlife, or where they can time-travel to ancient Egypt, and to exciting Native American cultures. One of the best of its kind in the entire country, Carnegie houses an extraordinary collection of over twenty-two million objects and specimens with about 50,000 displayed at any one time.

I have loved this museum since childhood, and as a former teacher, I sponsored and chaperoned field trips there annually. Yet, I can honestly state that each visit is a fresh learning experience; each is memorable.

The **Senator John Heinz History Center** is- and I state this proudly- the largest history museum within the commonwealth of Pennsylvania. The Center opened its doors in 1996. The building has seven floors. In 2000, it became an affiliate of the Smithsonian Institution, and in 2004, the Center added a Western Pennsylvania Sports Museum. This pride of Pittsburgh is named for Senator John Heinz who perished in a plane crash in 1991.

The History Center is one of my favorite Pittsburgh museums. There are permanent exhibits, of course, but visit the Center on-line to learn what *special* exhibits are being displayed at any given time. Each one is more exciting than the last! Three of my personal favorites in the past were "George Washington, the Man behind the Legend"; the "French and Indian War Exhibition"; and the "First Ladies Exhibit."

Constructed in 1764, the **Fort Pitt Block House** was, at different times in Pittsburgh's layered history, a military structure, a trading post, and even a private residence. It opened its doors to the public as a museum in 1895, rendering it the oldest continually operating museum in Pittsburgh. A Pittsburgh must-see, admission is free. Artifacts on display include musket balls, shards of pottery, and other items unearthed during archaeological excavations.

The Pittsburgh area has bred several famous singers and musicians, among them **Stephen Foster, Perry Como,** and **Bobby Vinton. Henry Mancini** grew up in the Pittsburgh suburb of Aliquippa.

In the perpetual shadow of the Cathedral of Learning, at 4301 Forbes Avenue, Oakland, stands a limestone building aglow with jewel-like stained-glass windows. Most people don't even know it's there. It is the **Stephen Collins Foster Memorial.**

Dedicated in 1937, this awe-inspiring Pittsburgh museum houses books, sketches, instruments, and personal items used by and connected to Stephen Foster. Open 9 a.m. to 4 p.m. weekdays, admission is free to the public. Guided tours, for which there is a small fee, must be scheduled in advance by telephoning 412-624-4100.

A somewhat enigmatic figure with an unwavering singular devotion to song craft, Foster became impatient and upset when people interrupted him at his work. Though he dedicated his life to music, and he wrote songs that eventually the whole world would sing, his efforts did not yield him the windfall such a songwriter would reap today. According to Deane L. Root, curator at the Stephen Foster Memorial, Foster's fortunes would have been healthier if he had chosen to be a performer as well as a composer. Though he was a competent singer with a light baritone voice, the songwriter was shy about performing in front of an audience. Foster left it to others to spread the word of his work across the country via his sheet music.

Oh! Susanna premiered in 1847 at a Pittsburgh ice-cream shop. It was soon picked up by the era's popular minstrel troupes, and by the autumn of that year, singers were belting it out from the glitzy stages of New York City. By late 1848, gold miners out West were crooning *Oh! Susanna,* having altered the lyrics from "Alabama" and "banjo" to "California" with a "wash pan on my knee." By the subsequent spring, natives of south-central America were singing or humming the catchy tune to travelers passing through the Isthmus of Panama!

In 1860, just prior to the Civil War, Foster relocated with his family to New York City. However, a year later, his wife and daughter Marion moved back to Pittsburgh. Remaining in NYC, Foster kept writing his songs, spending the rest of his life in lodging houses and hotels to be near the theater district. Sadly, he died in January 1864 at Bellevue Hospital three days after he collapsed from fever and cracked his skull on a washbasin. He was only thirty-seven years old. His wallet (that can be viewed at the Stephen Foster Memorial) contained thirty-five cents in Civil War scrip, three pennies, and a cryptic note with the words "Dear friends and gentle hearts."

Born on the Fourth of July in 1826, Stephen Foster was America's first superstar. His haunting, toe-tapping songs- the bedrock of American music- that favored melody over harmonics, live on in the bright fabric of culture and tradition we call "Americana": *Oh! Susanna*, *My Old Kentucky Home*, *Old Folks at Home/Suwannee River*, *Camptown Races*, *I Dream of Jeannie/Jeannie with the Light Brown Hair*, *Nelly Bly*, and *Beautiful Dreamer*, to mention a few.

Though Foster's songs predated the movies and television, both the Silver Screen and TV have lovingly embraced his music. In *Gone With the Wind*, for instance, Foster's music was incorporated into the soundtrack to establish the time period. In the final episode of *M*A*S*H*, one of the doctor-regulars directs a Korean band playing *Old Folks at Home*, tendering a distinct American artifact.

In July 2009, the Lawrenceville Historical Society held its fourth annual **Stephen Foster Music and Heritage Festival- Doo Dah Days**. This event includes a variety of bands playing, of course, Foster's enduring- and endearing- music, horse-and-buggy rides, children's activities, and Civil War reenactors. The Festival usually runs from noon to 5 p.m. Admission is free.

Pittsburgh has it all: The **Pittsburgh Opera**, founded in 1939, was housed initially at Carnegie Music Hall; after 1945, in the **Syria Mosque** in Oakland; and since 1971, in **Heinz Hall**. The **Pittsburgh Symphony** and the **Pittsburgh Ballet Theater** also perform at Heinz Hall.

Pittsburgh proffers great theater. Historically speaking, Pittsburgh was home to theater since the city's beginnings in the 1700s; and by the Civil War era, there were at least a dozen theaters operating along Penn and Liberty avenues. The dawn of the twentieth century ushered in professional theater companies that have endured to the present day. The influential **Pittsburgh Playhouse** opened its doors in 1933, and **Pittsburgh Civic Light Opera** began right after WWII, in 1946. The **Pittsburgh Public Theater** staged its first performance in 1975. City Players that became the **City Theatre Company** also had its beginnings in the 1970s.

Pittsburgh has turned out some prominent pen folk as well, chief among them author/historian, lecturer, narrator and teacher extraordinaire **David McCullough**, who was born in Pittsburgh on July 7, 1933, and was educated there and at Yale. When I chose to include him in "The Right Stuff" segment of my *CC II*, I knew this prolific, popular author had received several awards for his work, but when I began garnering the research for that Chronicle, I was amazed at how many. The very readable writer has received not one but two Pulitzers for his *Truman* (1993) and *John Adams* (2002), two National Book Awards (1978 and 1982), and twice has he been the recipient of the coveted Francis Parkman Prize (1978 and 1993).

McCullough has accumulated accolades from everyone, everywhere, including a mile-long list of academia. As if that were not enough to illustrate the depth and significance of his work, the impact it has had- is ever having- teaching American history in its storytelling way to readers around the planet, here is one other indication of this author's greatness: He has *no* books out-of-print.

In many ways, David McCullough is the *ideal* historian, because he brings meticulously researched, first-rate scholarship, to a wide audience, not just to die-hard history buffs- but to everyone. McCullough's shorthand response to that is: "I try to write the kind of book that *I* would like to read. If I can make it clear and interesting and compelling to me, then I hope maybe it will be for the reader."

Like his *Truman*, David McCullough is the "Captain with the Mighty Heart," for, in addition to his outstanding histories, that is precisely what he gives to each of his readers and to his country- *heart*.

The "City of Champions," Pittsburgh is the quintessential sports town, with, to illustrate my point, six Super Bowl wins. This segment of this Chronicle could roll on forever!

Pittsburgh athletes have created some of the greatest moments in sports history. Who could ever forget the 1960 World Series, plausibly the most thrilling Series ever played!

I dedicated an entire Chronicle to it in *CC IV* entitled "... Sometimes Even a Religion." When, at the bottom of the ninth, **Bill**

Mazeroski smashed that historic long drive (that sent daggers through the hearts of Yankee fans everywhere) over Forbes' vine-covered left center field wall and into Schenley Park- over the rainbow and into the luminous realm of sports history- we Pirate fans were over the moon!

The Pittsburgh Pirates copped the 1960 World Series by a final score of 10-9. Fans at the ballpark, those throughout the Pittsburgh area and beyond, even students on the roof of the University of Pittsburgh's Cathedral of Learning in Oakland, with their birds'-eye-view of Forbes Field, burst into screams of joy as "Maz" sprinted round the bases like a kid let out of school for a long-awaited vacation. As he skipped over second, he yanked off his ball cap, waving it gleefully. With his cap in hand, he whirled his arm like a propeller and bounded onward for home, where he was nearly overwhelmed by a "reception committee" of teammates and errant fans who congratulated him with unbridled gusto!

"We had 'em allllllllllll the way!" The improbable Pittsburgh Pirates, who were outpitched, outhit and outscored had pulled off a miracle and a World Series victory to boot! It was the most *dramatic* climax to a World Series we had ever seen- a *classic* moment; yes, even a *magic* moment- *and the home run of the century.*

In fact, nearly half a century later, in 2008, Bill Mazeroski's walk-off homer in the 1960 World Series was voted by fans (despite five of the Steelers' Super Bowl championships) as the best moment in Pittsburgh sports history.

What brilliant luminaries are the Pittsburgh sports figures! In addition to matchless Maz, the City of Champions can claim such men as **Honus Wagner**, considered by some to be baseball's greatest player; **Harold "Pie" Traynor**, one of the best third basemen in baseball history; the incomparable **Roberto Clemente**; the great Pirate manager **Danny Murtaugh**; **Franco Harris**, whose "Immaculate Reception" in 1972 made NFL history; **Joe Greene**, anchor of the famed "Steel Curtain" defense; **Terry Bradshaw**, leader of the super-seventies Steeler offense; **Jack Lambert**, whose speed and intensity personified Steeler defense; **Lynn Swann**, one of the best drafts in NFL history; **Chuck Noll**, the coach who led the Steelers to glory; Hall of Fame tight end **Mike Ditka**; Hall of Famer and Heisman Trophy winner **Tony Dorsett**; Pitts' legendary football coach **Johnny Majors**; Hall of Fame left fielder **Stan Musial**; and Duquesne's legendary basketball coach **John "Red" Manning**.

Then there's Pittsburgh's **Johnny Unitas** and those legendary football stars who helped give rise to the saying that "Western Pennsylvania is the cradle of quarterbacks," to quote sportswriter Paul Zimmerman, "soft coal and quarterbacks, such as Connellsville's **Johnny Lujack** [one of the greatest players in the history of Notre Dame football, who won a Heisman in 1947], **Namath** from Beaver Falls, **Marino** from Pittsburgh, **Montana** from Monongahela, **Blanda** from Youngwood, **Clements** and **Fusina** from McKees Rocks, **Galiffa** from Donora, and **Hanratty** from Butler."

And we haven't finished naming sports luminaries yet! Let's not forget powerful Steeler running back, **Jerome "The Bus" Bettis**; superstar Penguins **Mario Lemieux** and **Sidney Crosby**; western Pennsylvania's most famous golfer **Arnold Palmer**; the original "Pittsburgh Kid," **Billy Conn**, arguably the greatest light-heavyweight of all time; and the list goes on ... and on.

We've even had our share of Olympians from the Pittsburgh and southwestern Pennsylvania area: Gold-medal runner (from my hometown of Connellsville) **Johnny Woodruff**; bronze-medal long jumper **Herb Douglas**; gold-medal hurdler **Roger Kingdom**; silver-medal sprinter **Lauryn Williams**; gold-medal basketball player **Swin Cash**; gold-medal wrestler **Kurt Angle**; and gold and bronze medal basketball player **Suzie McConnell-Serio**.

Within *County Chronicles*, I have penned revealing segments about several of these sports luminaries, such as Johnny Woodruff and Johnny Lujack, Herb Douglas, Bill Mazeroski, Roberto Clemente, Danny Murtaugh, and Billy Conn, to name a few.

The oldest professional franchise in Pittsburgh, the **Pirate Ball Club** can trace its roots to the 1876 Pittsburgh Alleghenies who played in the minor league International Association in 1877.

The Pirates were National League champs in 1901, '02, and '03, but did not win a World Series crown until 1909. They did not claim a Series again until 1925, and then it would be another thirty-five years, till 1960, when the Bucs upset the "invincible" New York Yankees for the Series crown that historic baseball season. During the 1970s, the Pirates were a dominant force, winning the World Series against Baltimore in 1971 and again in 1979.

Considered one of the classic ballparks in Major League history, **Forbes Field**, located in the section of Pittsburgh called Oakland, was home to the Pittsburgh Pirates for over six decades. Built in 1909, Forbes was, as mentioned previously, the nation's first major-league baseball concrete-and-steel stadium.

Forbes Field was named in honor of General John Forbes, the British general of Scottish extraction and previously mentioned hero of the French and Indian War. The Pirates played their first game at Forbes Field against the Chicago Cubs on June 30, 1909. It was the beginning of an era.

That extraordinary Pittsburgh ballpark helped usher in a new wave of ballparks with modern elements the likes of which the nation had never before seen. Forbes became one of the first stadiums to have luxury suites that were located on the third tier of the grandstand. It was also the first ballpark to have ramps to lead patrons to their seats and elevators to carry them to the third level.

Forbes Field had one of the grandest exteriors of any ballpark ever built; and for those of my readers who remember, I know you will heartily agree with that statement.

Until its closing, Forbes changed little. The Pirates played their final game there on June 28, 1970. When it ended, fans swarmed onto the dear, old field, grabbing anything they could carry off for souvenirs.

Today, the site of Forbes Field is part of the campus of the University of Pittsburgh, the location of its library and dorms. However, with a plaque stating the date of the last game at Forbes, home plate remains on display, under Plexiglas, in the building next to the library. "Home" had to be moved a bit from its original spot. If it had not been, it would, at present, be situated in a women's restroom.

In addition, a portion of the Forbes Field wall still stands. There is a plaque marking the spot where Pirate Bill Mazeroski's home-run ball cleared the left center field wall to beat the Yankees in the 9th inning of Game Seven of the 1960 World Series. Under it, a second plaque conveys a bit of Forbes Field history. Across the street is another portion of the wall, as well as the flagpole. That brick wall still has the markers showing its distance from home plate- 457 feet.

The University of Pittsburgh does a terrific job preserving these significant pieces of sports history. Be certain to visit there, the next time you're in Pittsburgh. Then stand and relive those electrifying moments of the 1960 Series' final game, when Maz knocked that deciding ball out of Forbes Field to the elation of approximately 37,000 fans in and about the ballpark, to the joy of hundreds of thousands listening on transistor and car radios, and those lucky enough to be watching on black-and-white television sets- to the excitement of Pittsburgh Pirate fans everywhere.

Three Rivers Stadium on the North Side began hosting both the Pirates and the Steelers in 1970, witnessing two Pirate World Series and four Steeler Super Bowls.

The new home to the Pirates, **PNC Park** on the North Side, with its spectacular views of the Allegheny River and the Pittsburgh skyline, opened in 2001.

In 2001, **Heinz Field** opened its portals on nearly the same spot where once stood Three Rivers Stadium. Heinz is the home field of the Steelers and Pitt Panthers football teams.

The Pittsburgh **Steelers** *are, at this 2009 writing, the only professional football team ever to have won six Super Bowls. To be sure, they have become a model franchise.* Successful seasons were not part of early Steeler history, however. From 1933 to 1970, they claimed only seven winning seasons. The situation changed when a young assistant named Chuck Noll came aboard as head coach in 1969. Noll led his team to four Super Bowl wins in six seasons- in 1974, 1975, 1978, and 1979. And there just might have been a fifth ring within that glorious stretch of years had it not been for injuries late in the 1976 season.

And who could ever forget the legendary Pittsburgh sportscasters! **Bob Prince** was one of the most distinct voices in sports broadcast history. Best known for his memorable stint, from 1948 to 1975, as the voice of the Pittsburgh Pirates, he earned, during those nearly three decades, the nickname "The Gunner" due to his colorful, barking comments.

With his gravel voice, unabashed style, clever player nicknames and catch phrases, known as "Gunnerisms," Prince became a cultural icon in the Pittsburgh area. In 1966, he devised a good-luck charm he christened the "Green Weenie," a plastic rattle fashioned in the shape of a huge green hotdog that Pirate fans used to jinx opponents. "Never underestimate the power of the Green Weenie," Prince announced reassuringly to Pittsburgh fans everywhere.

Bob Prince died on June 10, 1985, of the cancer that had plagued him for the past several years. To read more about this Pittsburgh legend, see "...Sometimes Even a Religion" in *CC IV*.

Another legendary sportscaster was **Myron Cope**. A Pittsburgh symbol of hope and joyfulness, he retired from the Steelers' broadcast booth, where he had spent thirty-five years, in 2005. If Prince had his "Gunnerisms," Cope had his "Copeisms," like "Okel dokel," which meant, of course, "Okie dokie."

One of the last great sports characters, Cope– "Double Yoi!"– was a "character," colorful, to be sure, and one-of-a-kind. A myriad of national broadcasters and sportswriters attempted, over the years, to describe Cope's distinctive voice, as well as his wit and wisdom, but none captured the magic (despite the screechy expletives) that was Mr. Cope's alone.

Born Myron Kopelman in Pittsburgh in 1929, he lived most of his life in his hometown, save for the brief period in 1951 when, after graduating from Pitt, he took his first job with the *Erie Times*. It was there that his editor changed his byline to "Cope."

Myron Cope was the originator of the "Terrible Towel," a gimmick that has long since become the symbol of Steelers passion, and the thing with which he is most associated, perhaps even more than his great writing. The "Terrible Towel" is now a trademark that benefits the Allegheny School, an institution for the mentally and physically disabled, where his son was enrolled in 1999. In addition to his sports career, Myron Cope's charity work is also legendary.

According to KDKA, Cope did not come up with the expression "Immaculate Reception"; a caller did, but Myron bestowed that name upon Harris' catch on the eleven o'clock news the night of the game. At first, Dan Rooney hadn't really liked the term, thinking it sacrilegious, but he eventually came round to accepting it.

When Myron Cope passed away in 2008, he was seventy-nine, the only sports commentator in the national Radio Hall of Fame.

Pittsburgh's **Penguins** have successfully surmounted the professional hockey summit (at this writing) thrice, winning Stanley Cups in 1991 and 1992, coming mighty close, just two games short, in 2008, and most recently, defeating their 2008 nemesis, the Detroit Red Wings, in a right-to-the-line exhilarating triumph in 2009. When the youngest captain to take the Pens to a Stanley Cup, Sidney Crosby, hoisted the prize, injured knee and all, it was the perfect ending to a thrilling season. "It's a dream come true!" exclaimed "Sid the Kid." You bet it was! The Pens had just rendered Pittsburgh the only city in America to have both Super Bowl and Stanley Cup victories within the same year.

All this sports talk has made me hungry, so how about a sandwich? Pennsylvania's queen city can rightfully boast of its famous Philly steak sandwich; however, for a true taste of Pittsburgh, we must proffer **Primanti Brothers' famous sandwich.**

There are currently fourteen Primanti Brothers Restaurants in the Pittsburgh area, with the original, since 1933, still operating in Pittsburgh's celebrated Strip District. Primanti Brothers Restaurants started out as a wooden lunch stand in the Strip, serving hearty, pit-stop sandwiches to Depression-era truckers who rolled in to load and unload their wares at the railroad docks across the way.

What makes Primanti Brothers unique is their famous sandwich, called a "sammich" in the language of the Burgh. The nearly six-inch high marvel begins with thick Italian bread. Then comes the main filling of your choice, meat(s), cheeses, or eggs and sardines, whatever you choose from their menu. Since the Great Depression, the huge creation is always topped with tomato, coleslaw, and the Brothers' special fries. Even if you are eating in, the sandwich is served wrapped in waxed paper, and *voilà*, a meal-in-hand– and a Pittsburgh tradition! Or should I say, "It's a Burgh thing!"

The Strip District, the "Strip" as it has always been called, is a one-half-square-mile neighborhood of Pittsburgh, northeast of downtown. The north border is the Allegheny River. To the south is the extension of Grant's Hill. The east and west boundaries are 11th and 33rd streets.

From its beginnings, the Strip's location and access to transportation made it ideal for industrial development. As early as the 1820s and '30s, it was home to iron mills, foundries, and glass factories. In the late nineteenth century, the produce merchants began to relocate to that district, to be nearer to the Pennsylvania Railroad Station, and the Strip became the hub of the wholesale produce business in Pittsburgh.

Then, in the 1920s, grocery stores set up along the Strip. The post-WWII years saw

Jones and Laughlin Steel Mills, stretching along the Monongahela River at Pittsburgh, sometime prior to WWII. The great J&L Works turned the Pittsburgh night sky into a fiery drama!

trucks gradually replace the railroads. In the 1950s, there were about seventy wholesale produce dealers in the district, and by the 1970s, that number had sharply increased.

Today, the Strip is known for its retail produce, as well as its colorful mosaic of ethnic food stores, restaurants, and coffee shops.

Another Pittsburgh tradition is **Kennywood Amusement Park**. Since 1898, people have come to Kennywood to make memories. Whether it was a first kiss at the top of the Ferris wheel or in the tunnel of love, a special school or company picnic, or an unforgettable day spent with someone who has since passed over, Kennywood has always been known as a southwestern Pennsylvania "Memory Maker."

And speaking of memories, Pittsburgh stages a three-day, Fourth-of-July, fun-packed, action-packed **Three-Rivers Regatta** on the city's North Shore, the first of which took place over thirty years ago. Approximately 400,000 visitors attend annually, rendering this the region's largest community event and largest inland Regatta in the nation. Pittsburgh's Regatta includes water sports- or perhaps I should say *extreme* water sports!- children's activities, concerts, and a dramatic fireworks display.

For the past fifty years, Pittsburgh has hosted, in early June, the **Three Rivers Arts Festival** that includes a vast artists' market, as well as family-friendly visual arts and events, such as live outdoor concerts.

Another family-friendly place to visit is the **Pittsburgh Zoo/PPG Aquarium** that dates back to 1898, when it first opened its doors as the Highland Park Zoological Gardens. Today, the seventy-seven-acre Pittsburgh Zoo/PPG Aquarium is home to over 400 species, including twenty-two threatened and endangered species. My favorite segments of the zoo are the big-cat areas, where visitors can get nose-to-nose with lions lapping a cool drink. The beautiful tigers and leopards too are in their natural habitats. At Water's Edge, visitors are transported to the world of polar bears and sea otters with up-close viewing of these fascinating creatures. Here, in a forty-foot tunnel, visitors will be wowed by the huge sharks. In fact, you can't get any closer- not even in the wilds!

There are so many facets of Pittsburgh, so many things that make Pennsylvania's princess city unique. First and foremost, Pittsburgh is a city of neighborhoods, a city teeming with ethnic restaurants, festivals and events.

There are ninety-one neighborhoods in Pittsburgh, and each possesses a unique character created by the ethnic groups who settled them.

Bloomfield, settled in the early 1800s by Germans, evolved after WW I as an Italian neighborhood. Today, it is still known as Pittsburgh's "Little Italy."

Hazelwood began in the late 1700s as a German neighborhood. A century later, with the opening of Jones and Laughlin's Steel Mill, the promise of work attracted Irish, then Hungarian, Polish, Croatian, and Slovakian immigrants.

Prior to 1851, **Mount Washington/ Duquesne Heights** was known as "Coal Hill," where the immigrant mill workers were of German and Italian extraction.

Before the turn of the last century, the **Hill District** was home to many Jewish immigrants as well as newcomers from Syria, Poland, and Russia. Circa 1890, an influx of African-Americans arrived from the South. Today, "The Hill," as it is called, is still predominately Black.

The Jews relocated to **Squirrel Hill**, and yet today, this area is Pittsburgh's Jewish community.

In the late 1800s, Polish immigrants began populating **Polish Hill**, and it has remained a Polish neighborhood to present day.

The **South Side** began as a German community, then with immigration, took on Irish, and later eastern Europeans.

The **North Side**, once a separate entity known as Allegheny City, was home, early on, to English and Scottish, as well as German immigrants. Then came the Irish, followed later by the eastern Europeans, and in more recent times, African-Americans. Today, all these colorful threads are evident in the North Side's never-ending story.

Composer Stephen Foster's Pittsburgh neighborhood of **Lawrenceville** was home to German, Irish, and Polish immigrants who came to the Pittsburgh area to labor in the mills. Descendants of these ethnic groups are still there, along with others who came later.

Troy Hill is an old German neighborhood that includes Irish.

The Irish were the first group to come to America in large numbers, and **Pittsburgh's Irish**, who make up nearly a quarter of the population of Allegheny County, spread out everywhere rather than settling in pockets. Such a strong Irish influence has resulted in many Irish organizations throughout the region. Each year in September, the city hosts the ever-growing **Irish Festival**. Created in 1991, its express purpose is to contribute to the rich cultural awareness of Irish history and traditions that exist in the vicinity of Pittsburgh.

For over a half-century, the **Pittsburgh Folk Festival**, held annually at the beginning of May, has been on a mission to "preserve unity in diversity" by highlighting Pittsburgh's cultural mosaic. Why travel the world over when you can visit Pittsburgh? At the Irish Festival and the Folk Festival, you will sample a variety of old-world dishes, enjoy the cultural exhibits, as well as the crafts, music and dance of Pittsburgh's colorful ethnic peoples.

Pittsburgh has its **mysteries** too. One about which I wrote in *CC II* is the still-puzzling scandal that rocked the Smoky City in 1902, involving Kate Soffel, wife of the warden of the Allegheny County Prison. Kate assisted the notorious Biddle Boys in their daring escape from the hangmen's noose only to meet a barrage of bullets in a bloody shootout on 31 January, near Prospect, PA, a few miles west of Butler.

Another intriguing Pittsburgh story has its focus on the plane that mysteriously disappeared into the Mon on another frigid January 31st over half a century later.

About 4:10 in the afternoon of 31 January 1956, an Air Force B-25 crash-dived into the Monongahela River, a few miles east of the city- *and vanished.*

The weather that winter day was typical for Pittsburgh, about twenty-seven degrees with a ten-knot wind out of the northwest creating a ten-degree wind chill. River conditions were also typical for mid-winter; about a ten-knot current with the water about thirty-five degrees.

Out of the plane's crew of six, four men survived. The aircraft sank into the depths of the icy water, and to the best of public knowledge, has never been found.

Over half a century later, the incident is still a mystery. If you love reading about unsolved mysteries as much as I do, then I recommend *The Incident that Could Have Killed Pittsburgh*, by Robert H. Johns and edited by Robert E. Cole. It will get you thinking.

Pittsburgh has always been a special place for me. I have so many glittering memories and preferred sites there, it would be impossible to choose one favorite spot. Here are but

The then-and-now magic of Pittsburgh captured, from the West End Overlook, through the lacy boughs of a stately old tree
Nighttime Pittsburgh photos by professional photographer John Craig/Craig Photography
These and other prints available by contacting Craig Photography: www.craig-photography.com, craigphotography@mac.com, 724-355-9079.

a few: strolling through Heinz History Center, the Carnegie Museum of Natural History, any one of Pittsburgh's fine art galleries, or the colorful Three Rivers Arts Festival when I know I have the whole day to enjoy and learn from all the interesting exhibits; taking in a play, the ballet, or the symphony and having dinner in one of the fabulous restaurants atop Mount Washington with the Point, below, awash with lights and its glorious fountain; spending a Saturday morning (the best time to shop the Strip) at the diverse Strip District, with a stop for lunch at one of the unique ethnic cafés; taking a cruise on one of the riverboats from the fabulous Gateway Clipper Fleet; having dinner at Station Square at a table overlooking the river shimmering with the city's night-lights; riding one of the historic inclines anytime but especially at night when the Golden Triangle really shines; standing before the Bessemer converter "Big Bess" at Station Square and pondering Pittsburgh's vibrant steel past; taking the carriage ride (whence my husband proposed to me) at Station Square; touring Clayton, the opulent Henry Clay Frick mansion (the sole remaining great manse along what was once called Pittsburgh's "Millionaires' Row"), wandering the grounds with occasional repose on the benches beneath the magnificent trees, breaking for an inimitable lunch at their charming tearoom, then leisurely pondering the fabulous Frick art collection and, in their car and carriage museum, the horse-drawn and horseless carriages that transported the Frick family during the Gilded Age; attending one of Pittsburgh's fabulous festivals with no thought to dieting; eating a huge Primanti Brothers "sammich" with no care of calories or cholesterol; touring the Nationality Rooms in the romantically gothic Cathedral of Learning in Pittsburgh's Oakland neighborhood; Christmas shopping at the charming Waterfront, then collapsing at that fabulous burger place across from the shops on the river; returning home from the airport after a trip and exiting the Fort Pitt Tunnels to catch yet another breathtaking view of nighttime Pittsburgh!

In 1989, in the *New Yorker* magazine, the late Brendan Gill claimed, "If Pittsburgh were situated somewhere in the heart of Europe, tourists would eagerly journey hundreds of miles out of their way to visit it. Its setting is spectacular, between high bluffs where the Monongahela River and the Allegheny River meet the Ohio."

The wondrous woven magic that is Pittsburgh holds a *special* charm for me- it's a history-lover's paradise. Several times in the past, as I stood at the lookout on Mount Washington, I imagined the Point as it was in Colonial times with its high bluffs thick with woods, a birch bark canoe, with its dusky, painted passengers, gliding silently across the tranquil water.

In a place as deeply rooted in history as Pittsburgh, one cannot help but live both in the past and the present. And as I said, one would be hard-pressed to select just one or two favorite things to see or do in this city that continues to reinvent itself, in this city of so many soubriquets, so much nostalgia, color and culture. Here, you can find something special going on almost any weekend; and no matter when you visit, you'll love Pittsburgh's hospitable character. Twice rated "America's Most Livable City" (1985 and 2007), not withholding the British magazine *The Economist*'s jolly good number-one rating in 2009, Pittsburgh *is* a big small town- a city with a surplus of good, including small-town friendliness!

The whole Pittsburgh area makes me feel like clicking my heels together thrice and uttering that time-honored phrase, "There's no place like home!"

This is my tribute to Pennsylvania's princess city- one of America's most tenacious, unique and unusual urban settings. And though this is not nearly all I could include here, so proudly do I conclude-

This is Pittsburgh!

"THE RIGHT STUFF: SOPHIE MASLOFF"

"Her great sense of humor, her integrity, and her straightforward manner are the keys to Sophie Masloff's abiding likeability and charm."
- Ceane O'Hanlon-Lincoln

In the first four volumes of my *County Chronicles*, I lauded several Pennsylvania natives whom I greatly admire. The title of those Chronicles is "The Right Stuff," and I have included a "Right Stuff" segment in each volume of my *County Chronicles* Pennsylvania history series.

What exactly do we mean by the "Right Stuff"? I defined the phrase as the essential or requisite qualities, such as self-confidence, courage, stability, dependability, organizational skills, and specific knowledge appropriate for application in a given field or situation.

I have researched the lives of many Pennsylvania as well as national heroes— George Washington, Captain Molly Cochran Corbin, Rachel Carson, Abraham Lincoln, and George C. Marshall, to name a few. I discovered that these exceptional people had common denominators. They all had a strong belief and faith in God; and by extension, faith and belief in themselves and their own capabilities. However, each was a humble person.

Abraham Lincoln once said, "I have been driven many times upon my knees by the overwhelming conviction that I had nowhere else to go."

And certainly Right Stuff people possess courage. Lincoln retorted in the face of relentless adversity, "I say 'try.' If we never try, we may never succeed."

My grandmother used to say that is all anyone can do. At the end of my life, I do not want to lament via Rebecca McCann's rhyme: "It's not the things I failed to do/That make me wipe this eye/It's the things I should and could have done/And simply failed to try."

This reminds me of a story Harry Truman liked to tell of a tombstone he happened upon in an old graveyard in Arizona: "Here lies Jack Williams. He done his damnedest." Not a bad epitaph to work toward!

It was the longstanding conviction of America's thirty-third President that if you did your best in life, did your "damnedest" always, then whatever happened, you would at least know it was not for lack of trying.

Truman was also a great believer in the role played by luck, by the forces quite beyond effort or determination. His greatest biographer, Pennsylvania-born author/historian David McCullough, wrote of this heroic President: "[Truman] stood for common sense, common decency. He spoke the common tongue. As much as any President since Lincoln, he brought to the highest office the language and values of the common American people." And there was nothing passive about Harry Truman. He was the Commander-in-Chief in law– and in fact.

Right Stuff candidates do the best they can, one day at a time, to be the best they can be. These valiant companions have polished skills and accumulated knowledge, yes. Stability and dependability, most certainly. Yet, something else led to the greatness of each of these matchless individuals– something *extra*. And that, I soon perceived, was *persistence*. When actress Hattie McDaniel won the Oscar for Best Supporting Actress for her brilliant portrayal of "Mammy" in *Gone With the Wind* (1939), she said, "I did my best, and God did the rest." Ms. McDaniel was the first African-American to win an Oscar.

Another discovery I made was that Time does not alter these essential, requisite qualities. The same basic qualities were necessary for greatness in George Washington's era as they were in George Marshall's.

A good friend of mine says that luck occurs when preparation and persistence meet opportunity. Shakespeare said of great men, "Some are born great; some achieve greatness, and some have greatness thrust upon them." Philosopher Eric Hoffer once said, "A great man's greatest good luck is to die at the right time."

Personally, I believe being in the right place at the right time has something to do with it. And by "it," I mean luck, or destiny, the *magic* that helps to spiral individuals to eminence.

I believe in God. I believe in Destiny. I believe in that magic we call "luck." However, I think "luck" can be spelled two other ways, both of them four-letter words: w-o-r-k and g-u-t-s. In a word- *persistence*. Successful people make their own luck.

And be assured, as this Chronicle will clearly illustrate, Right Stuff people have a driving sense of *duty*.

In each "Right Stuff" Chronicle of my Pennsylvania history series, the peerless men *and women* are drawn from a variety of life's callings. How proud we should be of these shining stars!

In this volume of my *County Chronicles*, I am proffering the story of a very special lady. The daughter of Jewish Romanian immigrants, her name is Sophie Masloff, and she was Pittsburgh's first- and, to date, only- woman mayor. She was also the first and, to date, only Jewish mayor of this city.

Born Sophie Friedman on December 23, 1917, on Roberts Street in Pittsburgh's Hill District, the then-enclave of Jewish immigrants, Sophie was the youngest of four children. Her father Louis was an insurance salesman, who died when Sophie was but two years old, leaving her mother Jennie with the four children to rear on her own. One can only imagine how difficult this was for Jennie, who did not speak English, and who could not read or write.

Around the corner from the tenement where the Masloffs lived was a tobacco factory. Sophie's determined mother went there seeking work after her husband passed away. "She rolled stogies," Sophie remembered in an article that appeared on her ninetieth birthday (Sunday, December 23, 2007) in the Pittsburgh *Tribune-Review*. "[With the money she earned,] she'd buy two bananas. We'd each get a half. We were very, very poor, and in some ways, it was a horrible life for a child, but I came through it, and just think of the great honor I had! What an *incredible* honor it was for me to be elected mayor of Pittsburgh. My mother, if she were alive, would never have believed what happened to me."

I must interject something here. Someone once said that parents do not rear heroes. They rear sons and daughters. But if they treat them like sons and daughters, there is a darn good chance they will turn out heroes.

Sophie spoke only Yiddish until she began attending school in her Lower Hill District neighborhood. The school was Miller Elementary. It is still there, and Sophie makes a practice of visiting it.

In 1935, she graduated from Fifth Avenue High School. (This was a former school that served the Lower Hill District.) Her classmates forecast that she would make someone a fine secretary.

Actually, her first job out of high school was bookkeeper for a butter and egg company in the Strip District. At the age of eighteen, Masloff began her long career working as a civil servant. She worked as a secretary, as her high school chums had predicted, in several county government jobs.

In 1938, she began a thirty-eight-year stint as clerk in the Allegheny County Court of Common Pleas. Sophie was elected in 1976 to Pittsburgh City Council, eventually heading that board as its president.

When Pittsburgh's Mayor Richard Caliguiri (See "This is Pittsburgh," this volume.) died in office on May 6, 1988, the city dictated that the city council president was next in line to assume the office and the duties of mayor.

To quote KDKA-TV at that time: "The tragic death of Pittsburgh Mayor Dick Caliguiri ... left a huge void in the city. Luckily, we have someone who is capable of keeping the office running smoothly, without rancor, and free from political brawls- Mayor Sophie Masloff."

Seventy and a grandmother of two at the time she took office to become the fifty-fifth mayor of Pittsburgh, Sophie was characterized by her petite stature, her red hair, her raspy voice and, we might also say, her fluency in speaking "Pittsburghese," that unique dialect of Pittsburgh that includes such phrases as "How's about a sammich and a cupa coffee?" And: "We're sposda go dahntahn for ... ."

There has never been anything pretentious about our Sophie. Her "little Jewish grandmother" image rendered her a *beloved* figure in Pittsburgh, well-liked even by those who did not always agree with her administration.

Masloff served out Caliguiri's term– a tough act to follow– and, triumphing over five men in the Democratic primary for mayor, was reelected in November of 1989. That spoke volumes about the job she was doing.

"I was told I'd never win," Sophie related to me in an interview, reminding me of something famed aviatrix Amelia Earhart once said: "A woman must do the same job better than a man to get as much credit for it."

Here's a humorous Sophie story I ferreted out while researching for this Chronicle: In 1992 when Bill Clinton was campaigning for President, he telephoned the Pittsburgh mayor's office to introduce himself. Masloff, thinking a prankster was on the line, responded, "Yeah, and this is the Queen of Sheba," ringing off with a titter and a toss of her curly red head.

Clinton too had a chuckle over the incident, and he became one of her favorite Presidents. After Sophie's sextuple heart bypass operation in 1999, he penned her a hand-written note from the White House, wishing her well.

Masloff's all-time favorite President, however, was Harry Truman. Once when the President's daughter Margaret, who had aspirations for a singing career, booked the Syria Mosque for a 1947 performance, only a few tickets sold. The then-mayor David L. Lawrence galvanized into action by putting the newly formed Democratic machine to work selling tickets. Lawrence was counting heavily on Masloff, one of his veteran party loyalists, who worked for the county. He called her into his office, telling her that Pittsburgh could not embarrass the President of the United States. He did not have to explain further. Masloff hastened to city and county employees, to department heads, and straightaway got all the tickets sold.

In January 1988 when Sophie became president of the city council, it was the culmination of a lifetime of dedication and work within the Democratic Party and in local government. In fact, during the Great Depression, Masloff had worked alongside Lawrence to create the party machine that wrestled control of city government from the Republican Party, establishing Pittsburgh as the Democratic stronghold it is today.

"Mayor Lawrence was a dear friend," Sophie told me during our talks. "I had a profound admiration for him."

Certainly, she seemed to have followed in Lawrence's footsteps when, years later, she was at the helm of the city of her birth. Both mayors used humor when attempting to settle heated matters. Both put their constituents first. Both put financial matters at the top of their list of priorities. And both were scrupulously honest with an abundance of integrity.

To quote Masloff's former chief-of-staff, attorney Joseph S. Mistick, "Sophie Masloff came from an era when great politicians engendered unfailing personal loyalty."

Did you know that Sophie was the first public figure to suggest that Pittsburgh's baseball and football teams each have their own stadiums? Though her idea was not well-received at the time she pitched it, it was implemented several years later, and I am certain that there are many Pittsburgh-area sports fans who wish that PNC Park and Heinz Field had become realities much sooner.

In honor of Masloff's ninetieth birthday in December 2007, the city of Pittsburgh renamed a section of Federal Street near PNC Park after her. There is no more appropriate spot for *Sophie Masloff Way*, since her visionary "Clemente Field" was a dream (for which she had received heavy criticism) that foreshadowed PNC Park.

Embraced warmly as a Pittsburgh icon by dignitaries and passersby alike, Sophie appeared, on the day of the street-sign unveiling, a bit shy about the whole affair. "I am embarrassed by all of this, but I am so happy to be here today ... happy to be anywhere as a matter of fact! I really do appreciate this honor, though I really don't deserve it. I did what I was supposed to do. ... This is a great compliment, of course ... it's wonderful for me to be remembered by the city I love."

After the requiem bell tolled for the steel industry in Pittsburgh, Sophie Masloff's administration was faced with urban flight, a shrinking industrial sector, and crumbling infrastructure. Was this seventy-year-old grandmother up to the huge task ahead of her? Time, our greatest historian, has proven she most certainly was.

With fiscal responsibilities her top priority, Masloff stepped up to the plate- and hers was a full plate!- and privatized numerous costly city assets, such as the Pittsburgh Zoo and PPG Aquarium, the National Aviary, Phipps Conservatory, and the Schenley Park Golf Course, thereby lifting a great financial weight off the citizenry of Pittsburgh.

One humorous aspect to the above is this: Behind the scenes, when rhetoric became heated over the idea of privatizing the National Aviary, Mayor Masloff quipped to a staffer, "Why don't we just open the window and let them fly out!"

Like her hero Harry Truman, Sophie has always been a what-you-see-is-what-you-get kind of person. Allow me to share with you two more examples of Sophie's keen wit.

She would often begin her speeches with, "As Henry the Eighth said to each of his wives, 'Don't worry; I won't keep you long.'"

Masloff, like all politicians, had her speech writers, but no prepared communication could compare to her own straight-to-the-core words, to her own insight, or her infectious sense of humor.

Sophie Masloff during her stint as Pittsburgh's first- and, to date, only- woman mayor
Photo courtesy Sophie Masloff

Once when she was posing for a photo with an official from Yugoslavia, she remarked, "You know, I have never been to Czechoslovakia."

With a start, the official answered, "Madam Mayor, I am from Yugoslavia." Without missing a beat, Sophie pulled herself up to her full five feet, stating with dignity and her warm smile, "I know that, but the truth is I have never been to Czechoslovakia." The whole room erupted in laughter- something that Sophie's magic brought about time and again- laughter, by the bye, that included the Yugoslav representative and Sophie herself. Here was a politician who was not only honest but who could laugh at herself- a treasure to be sure.

In addition to the above fiscal accomplishments, Masloff, due to her no-nonsense attitude and strong sense of honor and integrity, created a five-member ethics board to listen to complaints from people against city officials and employees.

In 1991, she had guts enough (shades of her hero Truman) to force, via a Commonwealth Court judge, striking Port Authority employees to return to work after a twenty-six-day walk-out.

One of the things she is most proud of during her time in office was the Crawford-Roberts Housing Development. "I was instrumental in getting the funding we needed for that project. I literally twisted arms," she stated. "It was rough going because the Lower Hill District was so blighted. I mean it was such a distressed area that it made things tough, but I persevered, and we did it."

The development began opposite the Mellon Arena where there was a deplorable slum. The project then expanded to include a good portion of the Lower Hill District. "Today," Sophie concluded, "it is a significantly improved area."

Though she had met her obligations with determination (one of her salient strengths) and skill, Sophie declined to run for a second full term. Retiring in 1994 to her Squirrel Hill home, she was succeeded in 1993 by Democrat Mayor Tom Murphy.

However, since leaving the mayor's office, Sophie has been far from idle. A Democratic committeewoman, Masloff attended (excluding 2008) every Democratic Convention since 1956, and she had been a delegate for each convention since 1960. This loyalty and devotion is rooted in her teen years. From the age of seventeen, when Sophie first saw the then-first-lady Eleanor Roosevelt dedicate the Bedford Dwellings Housing Project in Pittsburgh, she was inspired to become a political activist.

Upon both her daughter's and her doctor's advice, Sophie did not attend the 2008 Democratic Convention. In an interview with WPXI Pittsburgh TV, she responded to their query about everyone's concern that she would not be attending the Democratic Convention: "I'm flattered that so many people are interested in me, but I am also feeling very sad because I am not going. The Convention has always been a delight for me, not only for the Convention business but [because of] the people I meet. I've met news people from all over the world. I've met all the candidates. But I know this is in my best interest."

Masloff, who, at that moment in time, endorsed Hillary Clinton, would have been the oldest delegate attending the 2008 Democratic Convention. "I am really very sad," she said in wrapping the above TV interview, "because I feel physically able to go, but maybe I am not as tough as I thought I was."

Sophie's husband Jack, a security guard, passed away in 1992 while Sophie was still Pittsburgh's mayor. They had been married for over fifty years. Sophie and Jack had one child, Linda. Linda is married to Nicholas Busia, and they have two grown children, Michael and Jennifer. The family is close-knit. Theirs is a loving family with old-fashioned values, many passed down, I feel certain, through Sophie.

As I said, the former mayor keeps busy. She has even done a few Pittsburgh pierogi commercials. On the phone with her during our interviews, I felt as though I had known her all my life. Again, it was Sophie's magic at work, putting others at ease, and it has not faded one bit.

In the course of our discussions, I was surprised to learn that Sophie had relatives in my hometown of Connellsville. "Yes," she told me. "I feel connected to Connellsville. My sister lived there for years, and I still have relatives there, nieces and nephews. Griglak is their surname. I will always have a soft spot in my heart for Connellsville; we used to go there a lot."

Sophie Masloff's warmth, her natural, unpretentious manner is chicken-soup for the soul, as that old saying goes. When I asked her if she still had her nearly two-decade-old Cadillac, she responded, "Yes, I'm the typical old lady who only drives her car to church. I suppose still owning my car gives me a feeling of security, though I no longer drive at night, or in foul weather, or in high-traffic areas. Now it's only short hops in the neighborhood, but I love that car, and I hate to get rid of it … in a way, it's like an old friend."

"I think," she told me with her wonderful laugh, "My claim to fame might be that I've outlived a lot of people. When a paper like the *New York Times* calls me to get my take on something that happened a long time ago, they always begin with the words, 'There aren't many of you left.' I often think about how lucky I've been.

"Here I am, the daughter of immigrants, with little education- though I have a vast knowledge of people and life-experience. Think about it; I've been all over the world, representing the great city of Pittsburgh. Above all, I've been fortunate to have met so many wonderful- truly wonderful- people."

As soon as I asked Sophie to relate to me her feelings about Pittsburgh and its people, I was rewarded with this: "Of course, I *love* Pittsburgh … and its very special people. There are no people like Pittsburgh people! I couldn't live anywhere else. Pittsburgh is home, and it always will be.

"And Pittsburgh has so much potential! It is my ardent wish that those who follow will always take advantage of that powerful Pittsburgh potential!"

When I asked what she was most proud of during her stint as Pittsburgh's mayor, Sophie responded that there were, in fact, many things that gave her satisfaction, several things that she had persevered to accomplish. "I was, in addition, a day-to-day housekeeper for the city. I insisted that Pittsburgh be swept at regular intervals and kept clean and attractive."

Like all "Right Stuff" people, Sophie Masloff is not a braggart. There is no bravado, no boasting of any kind when she speaks of her time at the helm of Pennsylvania's princess city. In fact, I found, during our conversations, that Sophie is almost shy about all the things she accomplished for her hometown. She is the kind of person who did what she did in a quiet way, though the things she did were done most effectively. And if I had not known she would be ninety-two at the end of this year (2009), I would never have guessed it. Her energy, her quick wit, her clear thinking and ability to express herself are all there, sharp as ever.

While we were talking, and I likened her to a female Harry Truman, she commented with her usual zest: "I told you he was my favorite President, so it is an *honor* to be compared to him. I met him once in 1947, not long after he took over as President. It was when he was here in Pittsburgh, and I never forgot it. President Truman was very human, very down-to-earth, and completely unpretentious. That's what I really liked about Harry Truman, that straight-talking way he had. To know him was to love him."

My final question was how Sophie wanted to be remembered by the city she so loves. "I would like to be remembered as the 'First Woman Mayor of Pittsburgh Who Got Things Done Without Any Hoopla'!"

I have no doubt that she will.

"Historic Connellsville ... Hometown Memories"
What a Wonderful World ...

"There was a time in America when our society was not as welcoming to minorities as we are today. A time in America when the value of a man could be discounted or diminished solely because of the color of his skin, rather than the purpose and intent of his mind, his character, and his heart ... ."
- Captain Tony Barnes, USN

On October 30, 2007, Connellsville's Olympic hero, John Y. Woodruff, passed quietly away at the venerable age of ninety-two. A memorial service, on November 18, was held in his hometown at the Connellsville stadium, under the golden majesty of his Olympic Oak Tree.

While I was preparing John's eulogy with all of his accomplishments and accolades, I was disquieted by the one thread left untied around the gift that was his exceptional life.

After John's powerful nine-foot stride had carried him across the finish line in Berlin, Germany, for the 800-meter gold medal at the historic 1936 Olympic Games, he returned the subsequent fall to the University of Pittsburgh, where, on scholarship, he was the core of the Pitt track team. There came then a time when Pitt was to compete against Navy, but Annapolis refused to run against Pitt if John Woodruff, a Negro, was among their team members. John was left behind.

The autumn before John passed away, in October 2006, his alma mater, the University of Pittsburgh, invited him and his family to a sports event at the campus for a formal, public apology in regard to the incident. But Navy had never made such a gesture.

I decided to make the present-day Superintendent at the United States Naval Academy cognizant of John Woodruff's story; and thus began my quest. I was determined to tie up that one loose end of John's remarkable life.

After about a year of ardent letters, emails, and countless telephone calls to Annapolis, Navy agreed to make a formal apology to John Woodruff, posthumously, through his family.

The time and place were perfect. America had just elected and sworn in its first African-American President, Barack Obama, and Navy had just dedicated its fabulous new sports arena/field house to the first African-American, Wesley A. Brown, to have graduated from the Naval Academy. In addition, it was almost February, "Black History Month." So, finally, nearly seventy years after the hurtful incident had occurred, the date for the apology was set for Saturday, January 24, 2009, and off we went to the United States Naval Academy at Annapolis- John's widow Rose, John's son John Junior, my husband Phillip, and yours truly.

Let me begin by saying that Navy could not have been more gracious to us. We were all invited for the entire weekend, and what a memorable weekend it turned out to be!

Upon arrival, we were put up over the Officer's Club, in the VIP quarters. The suites there are beautiful and ultra-comfortable.

I was given a keepsake coffee-table book about the United States Naval Academy, signed

USNA Superintendent VADM Jeffrey L. Fowler presenting Rose Woodruff with Navy-etched crystal vase
Photos courtesy the USNA

by the distinguished Vice Admiral Jeffrey L. Fowler, the Academy's 60th Superintendent. VADM Fowler presented to Rose, courtesy the USNA, a beautiful crystal vase etched with the proud Navy insignia.

Friday, after an enjoyable lunch in the USNA mess hall (the world's largest cafeteria) among all the midshipmen, we were given a private walking tour of the campus. That evening, following a pleasant drive through the charming town of Annapolis, we were treated to dinner at the Yacht Club overlooking the moonlit Chesapeake Bay, the water aglitter with twinkling harbor lights. The delicious meal with our Navy escorts was replete with fellowship that created an indelible memory for all of us.

What's more, our Navy guide served us the breakfast of our choice in our rooms Saturday morning. Then we all headed over to the new Wesley A. Brown Field House for the ceremony that was followed by a Navy track meet.

The speaker who delivered the formal apology was Captain Tony Barnes, USN. Here is a bit of what he said that significant day: "As you know, there was a time in America when our society was not as welcoming to minorities as we are today. A time in America when the value of a man could be discounted or diminished solely because of the color of his skin, rather than the purpose and intent of his mind, his character, and his heart."

Captain Barnes then went on to honor John Woodruff by telling his incredible story, the tale of a man born a champion, on July 5, 1915, one of twelve children to Silas and Sarah Woodruff of South Connellsville, Pennsylvania, and the grandson of former Virginia slaves. He told of John's great passion for running, of how he emerged as an exceptional athlete at Connellsville High School, owning school, county, district, and state records.

Captain Barnes related how several Connellsville businessmen saw to it that John secured a scholarship to the University of Pittsburgh, and how Johnny set off with twenty-five cents in his pocket, in the sheriff's car, for that institution of higher learning and a whole new world.

The captain recounted to those listening that historic day at Annapolis how hard John worked at school, earning his meals by keeping the campus grounds and the stadium tidy, and that his room was not at the dorm, but at the "colored" YMCA where Johnny had to fight the bedbugs for sleeping space.

As the audience listened in rapture, Captain Barnes continued, telling them that, as a Pitt sophomore, John Woodruff made the United States Olympic Team, and in the summer of 1936, won, with a storied daring move, a gold medal for his country in the 800-meter race, the first time in twenty-four years the United States had won that honor.

For those who may not know, when Johnny found himself boxed in during his history-making race, he accomplished what one sportswriter called the "most daring move on a track." Not taking a chance of jostling another runner and being disqualified, he came to a dead stop, waited till everyone passed him, and moved two lanes wide to the outside, running a longer race than all the others but winning the gold nonetheless.

Captain Barnes told the assembly that the US track team, more than anyone in those historic Games in Berlin, roundly disproved Adolf Hitler's cruel theory of a "Master Race."

Toward the end of his segment about John Woodruff's life, Barnes stated: "There came a time, after John returned to university, when Pitt was to run against Navy. John Woodruff was not permitted to compete here. That was truly a tragedy for which we condole with you.

"However, we are proud to say that despite this tragic circumstance, John Woodruff believed in himself and his country, and remained committed to uphold and protect its borders. Mr. Woodruff went on to serve with distinction in the Army during World War II and later in Korea, where he was decorated for valor.

USNA midshipmen shaking hands with Rose Woodruff. What memories we garnered at Annapolis!

"Today, we are happy to have with us the widow of John Woodruff, Mrs. Rose Woodruff, and John Woodruff, Jr., the son of John Woodruff, Sr. We are humbled and honored that they have graciously agreed to join us here this afternoon.

"Mrs. Woodruff, John, we would like you to know that all of us here at the United States Naval Academy apologize, and are truly sorry for what Mr. Woodruff faced in the past.

"This is not a time to cast blame, although certainly many deserve blame. Now is the time to look at our bright future. Our new President reminds us that this is a time to act and act in a manner that will produce change.

"Today, we honor our brother John Woodruff for his unwavering commitment to military service, his country, his community, and his remarkable and legendary achievements.

"Under the leadership of our Superintendent, Vice Admiral Fowler, and our entire leadership team, including our athletic director, we are making great strides. I am pleased to tell you that our current class, the Class of 2012, is the most diverse in the history of the Naval Academy. We have indeed come a long way, and together we will blaze a trail into the future."

Readers, in the past years, I came to know John and Rose Woodruff well, and I can honestly tell you that John never harbored bitterness over the Navy incident or other racial slights. He told me stories, plenty of stories, for instance, of how, when the team bus stopped to eat somewhere, he could not go into many of the public restaurants to eat with them, but was forced to take his meals on the bus.

John lived such an exemplary life; I so wanted that apology for him. What incited me to action was that John mentioned to Rose before he died that he had received an apology from everyone but the Naval Academy. He wasn't complaining. He was merely stating a fact. I only wished he had lived to receive the apology in person. Rose and I both know he would have accepted it graciously, with a simple but heartfelt "Thank you."

But I can tell you this, readers, Johnny *was* there that memorable day. He was with us in spirit. Here is the reason I say that: After the ceremony, I told Rose I had a keen feeling that John was looking down on the event that Saturday afternoon at Navy. "We will get a sign," I told her.

I must back up in time for just a moment here, to October 30, 2007, to the day John died. As soon as I had learned that John had passed away, I telephoned Rose in Arizona (where the couple made their home for the past several years). As we were talking, I asked her about the Louis Armstrong tune *Wonderful World.* "It keeps playing in my head, Rose. Did John happen to like that song?"

"Like it!" she exclaimed. "It was his all-time favorite." And so, I requested the musicans play it at his memorial service. Little did I know at the time, that song- John- would speak to me again. "We will get a sign," I had told Rose. *And we did.*

As my husband and I were returning home from Annapolis, just as we came down our street, where near our house a marker announces "Welcome to Connellsville," *Wonderful World,* with Sachmo's gravelly voice singing the haunting words, issued clearly from our car radio. Coincidence? I don't think so.

The next day, Rose Woodruff telephoned me. "I must tell you something, Ceane. You are not going to believe this, but as soon as I got home, as is now my habit, I switched on the television, because then it is not so lonely in here for me, and what do you know? Over the waves came *Wonderful World!*"

Rose and I both knew that Johnny had seen and heard that USNA apology. Indeed, he had- *and he was pleased.*

John Woodruff's quiet but powerful struggle for racial equality paralleled that of Wesley A. Brown, who, as mentioned above, was the first African-American to graduate (1949) from the USNA. I will leave you with Mr. Brown's valiant words, for they so aptly echo his own life as well as the life and times of our hometown hero Johnny Woodruff.

"Go where there is no path and blaze a trail."

~ ~ ~

Connellsville's Heisman Hero Returns Home ...

"This new facility helps bring [Connellsville High School] into the twenty-first century."

- Jeff Immel, Connellsville Football Coach, July 17, 2009

The 1947 Heisman Trophy winner Johnny Lujack (at this writing, 84) returned to his hometown of Connellsville on Friday, July 17, 2009, for a weekend packed with honors.

The initial event took place at Connellsville's Falcon Stadium on Friday afternoon with the dedication of the Johnny Lujack Training Facility. Lujack had donated $50,000 toward the construction of the state-of-the-art facility, stating, to quote from a July 18 article in the *Daily Courier:* "When I was young, people worried that they'd get muscle-bound and wouldn't be able to operate if they lifted weights. Now, all that has changed. Connellsville didn't have an adequate weight room, and they needed it ... ."

Saturday, July 18, Mr. Lujack was part of the inaugural class inducted into the Fayette County Sports Hall of Fame. Another member of that class is, of course, Connellsville's Olympic hero, Johnny Woodruff.

Known as the "Connellsville Kid," Lujack was a member of the champion 1941-42 Connellsville Coker football team. He took over as quarterback for Notre Dame as a sophomore in 1943, catapulting the Irish to three national titles and establishing a reputation for himself as one of the great T-formation signal-callers in college football history. In his initial start in 1943, he threw for two scores, ran for another, and intercepted to secure a 26-0 victory over Army.

He spent nearly three years in the Navy during WW II, but returned in time to earn consensus All-American his junior and senior years, in 1946 and 1947, when the Fighting Irish did not lose a single game.

No slouch as a runner- he also played halfback as a sophomore- Lujack punted, as well, and probably made his greatest individual play on defense. As a junior, he finished third in the Heisman voting behind Army's Glenn Davis. As a senior, he earned his Heisman plus the Associated Press' "Athlete of the Year" award, landing him on the cover of *Life* magazine.

Lujack played for the Chicago Bears for four years, leading the team in scoring each year, tying a record with eight interceptions as a rookie, throwing a record 468 yards in one game in 1949- a new NFL record at the time- and playing in the NFL Pro Bowl his last two seasons.

An Irish backfield coach for two years following his retirement in 1952, Lujack then ran an automobile dealership in Davenport, Iowa, until he retired in 1988. In 1960, he was the youngest man ever to be inducted into the National Football Hall of Fame.

"But nothing compares with being honored in your hometown," Lujack told me.

Johnny Lujack is one of the few athletes to have earned letters in four sports at Notre Dame in a single year. In addition to his stellar football performance, he was a starting guard on the basketball team, played baseball, and ran track.

I met up with Mr. Lujack in the lobby of his hotel on the Saturday morning of his 2009-homecoming weekend. In the past decade, while immersed in my *County Chronicles*, I had spoken to him on the phone numerous times. When I met him in person, I was not disappointed. Though our visit was brief, I was duly impressed with our Heisman hero. To succinctly echo what famed Pittsburgh sports writer Jim O'Brien said in my "Right Stuff" segment of *CC I*: "Johnny Lujack is a class act." Needless to say, it was a thrill to finally shake his hand.

The name "Johnny Lujack" will forever be linked to Connellsville and Fayette County, Pennsylvania. Upon graduation, the Connellsville Kid was heralded as the "Greatest Athlete in Notre Dame History," the most publicized college football player since Red Grange. As Jim O'Brien likes to say, " 'Johnny Lujack' is one of those names you just want to say aloud, over and yet again."

Johnny has some words he likes to reiterate too: "Always give a hundred percent ... then give another ten." *That standard and his loyalty to his hometown- he has always held near to his heart.*

~ ~ ~

An Honor and a Privilege ...

"... Jimmy is truly a good man who never forgot where he came from."
- J. William Lincoln, PA Senator (Ret.)

James E. Shaner had not always dreamed of becoming a Pennsylvania State Representative. The thought of running for public office never even entered his mind until sometime after he graduated from college. To honor this deserving public servant, let us back up to his school days, for that was when he began to develop his strong work ethics.

Jim, as he is known to family and friends, took his first job when he was in junior high school. The job was delivering newspapers in his community near Dunbar, Fayette County, Pennsylvania. To say that Jim Shaner was always a hard worker is rather an understatement.

Around the same time he took on his longtime paper-delivery route, Jim worked hard digging out a basement for his parents. This huge undertaking took preference over his beloved sports, and the young Shaner learned early on to set priorities in life. Also during his school years, it was his responsibility to help his grandfather harvest and haul coal from the coal dump back home for the family's winter heat. Life wasn't easy.

Summers, Jim labored on a nearby farm for two dollars a day. It was hot, heavy work for the pennies he earned, but that job, along with the others, taught him invaluable lessons about earning and saving money- and life in general.

In addition to his significant work responsibilities, Jim convinced the local "patch" baseball team to sign him on (at a younger age than was the norm) as a player.

For those readers who might not know, a "patch" is the term used in western Pennsylvania for a coal community. These coal towns were made up of houses (virtually all alike except for the coal boss' house) constructed by the coal company for their workers. In this manner, the coal companies kept their workers under their firm control. If a miner lost his job, he also lost his house. To keep up morale, and to keep the ofttimes "rowdy" miners out of trouble, the coal companies sponsored patch baseball teams.

All his life, Jim Shaner has loved sports. During his high school years, he walked miles to get to team practices. After the games, the bus dropped him off on Route 51, which meant that he had to walk home several miles in the dark in all kinds of weather.

Keep in mind that in those days, very few students had access to an automobile, and those families lucky enough to own a car, had but one.

Upon graduation from Uniontown High School in 1955, Jim worked at Anchor Hocking, a local glass plant located in South Connellsville. After a short time, he decided that was not the career for him, and he made up his mind to go to college with the money he had saved.

There were no grants in those days; thus, Jim worked long and hard to finish school and pay for his tuition. He finally secured a student loan. His college years at Fairmont State College (of West Virginia, now Fairmont University) were crammed with work, and he was often so tired he could hardly hold up his head to study, falling to sleep the instant his head hit the pillow at night.

During the regular school year, he attended classes, met his college work load, and to satisfy college expenses, labored at two jobs simultaneously. Summers, he took more classes, working full time to meet the rising costs of a college education.

How he managed to play college football and baseball and still keep up his grades, in addition to working two jobs to pay for his tuition and expenses is beyond me! But those are the facts, and what I am telling you is true.

It was at Fairmont where he met his wife, the beautiful Mabel Jeanette Gum. For Jim, it was love at first sight. With that first look, he turned to the fellow sitting next to him at the Student Union, remarking with conviction, "That is the girl I am going to marry."

Jim and Mabel were wed on June 25, 1960. "We will soon be married nearly half a century, and I can honestly state that it's been a wonderful union!" Mr. Shaner related to me during our interview.

Since Fairmont is an out-of-state school, the tuition, for Shaner, was higher. Though it was rough going, in his heart, he knew he could do it, and he did, graduating in 1961 from Fairmont State College with a Bachelor's Degree in Secondary Education.

The Shaners had one child, a daughter, Shawn Ivann, at this writing, a teacher in the Uniontown School District, who is married to Robert Pfrogner (of *Bob the Builder* fame) of Monessen, Pennsylvania.

After college graduation, Jim Shaner worked full time teaching and coaching in Ohio before securing a teaching/coaching position in his home area of Fayette County, Pennsylvania. Now, as before, he found himself with multiple duties and commitments. At the same time he was teaching and coaching, he began traveling to West Virginia University to take classes toward his Master's Degree. Soon, the extra expense for tuition meant taking on yet another job.

It was at this point in his life when he started his painting business. Teaching and coaching, taking classes toward a Master's, and doing interior and exterior house painting was exhausting; but again, he knew he could handle it. One whole summer, he was forced to abandon his studies to work full time on a pipeline. Finally, in 1966, Shaner was able to complete his requirements for his well-earned Master's Degree.

Due to the years of hard work, when he finally did seek Pennsylvania State office in 1994, he was successful in getting the votes he needed to push him over the top for election. People who knew Jim Shaner admired his strong work ethics. They knew he would serve them with the same intensity and dedication, with the same honesty and integrity that he had always exhibited in his family life and business affairs. From 1995, his first year in office, until he retired as a Pennsylvania State Representative in 2007, Jim Shaner did just that, working as hard for his constituents as he had in every other endeavor he had tackled in his life.

Jim Shaner still attends church services regularly, a practice that goes back to his early childhood when his mother instilled in her family the importance of cultivating a deep faith.

Mr. Shaner has taught history, physical education, and drivers' education in the Pennsylvania school system. He has coached football, owned and managed his own painting business, as well as his own restaurant, and he has served his Pennsylvania constituents of the 52nd District faithfully, honestly, and to the best of his ability as a State Representative, retiring after twelve years from public office.

It should be noted that during his stint in the PA House, Shaner always answered his phones, returned his calls, and followed up on the day-to-day problems in his district. He fought hard for grant monies, and because of his perseverance, many of the much-needed community projects in his district were realized. Another thing he did was to make it a practice to recognize the many accomplishments of the people who made up his district. I can personally vouch for this.

Not long after I received the Athena Award for career excellence, awarded by the Chamber in my hometown of Connellsville, I opened my mail one day to find a Special Recognition Award from the Pennsylvania House of Representatives- the result of State Representative James E. Shaner keeping abreast of events that involved his constituents.

My *County Chronicles* (that had begun life as an upbeat history column in my hometown newspaper *The Daily Courier*) had gained attention locally, and had been well-received. Mr. Shaner recognized the importance of rewarding hard work. *After all, who would know more about the subject?*

When I asked him about his years serving in the PA House as a State Representative, he responded, "It was an honor to serve the people of the 52nd District. They saw fit to give me that job, and never asked much in return. I tried to the best of my ability to serve them. All in all, it was a great privilege."

While writing this segment of "Historic Connellsville..." I asked several people about Jim Shaner. All were positive and admiring in their responses, including my brother-in-law, State Senator J. William Lincoln, (Ret.), who

PA Rep. James E. Shaner at microphone, speaking to his constituents, and PA Sen. Richard A. Kasunic (fore/left) at the South Connellsville Rod and Gun Club in 2001

served Pennsylvania first as District Justice, then in the House (1973-1978) as a State Representative, and subsequently as a State Senator from 1978 to 1994. Lincoln was Majority Whip in the Senate from 1985 to 1992, then Senate Leader in 1993 and 1994, as well as the Commonwealth's Chairperson of the Democratic Party from 1991 to 1994.

Lincoln and Shaner both hail from the Dunbar area, so if anyone knows Jim Shaner well, it's Bill Lincoln. "Jimmy has always been exactly the kind of person we'd want to represent us," he pronounced with feeling, "because he is a truly *good* man who never forgot where he came from."

I have known Jim and his charming wife Mabel for several years, and I personally want to comment on the reliability and the warm, kind spirit of each of them, for no finer people can be found anywhere.

It is both an honor and privilege *for me* too- to call the Shaners "friends."

~ ~ ~

Two Firsts of Connellsville ...

Two "Firsts" of Connellsville are Suzi Pilla-Fetsko and her mother, Cookie Pilla. In 1986, Suzi was crowned the first-ever "Miss Connellsville." One of the prizes for the first Miss Connellsville was an exciting trip to the nation's capital in Washington, DC. A runner-up for "Miss Pennsylvania," Suzi was named "Miss Photogenic" in the 1989 Miss Pennsylvania USA Pageant.

More than thirty local women were nominated for the city's first-ever Athena Award in 1988. That historic year, Isabella "Cookie" Ambrosini-Pilla won the city's coveted Athena statuette for outstanding community service and her exceptional record in selling over a million dollars of real estate in 1986 and over 1.6 million dollars of real estate in 1987. Cookie led production at Century 21. According to the firm's Athena nomination, "She was not content with simply providing a service to the public. She provides that service in a personal, caring, professional way, always giving over 100 percent."

In addition to her real estate career, Cookie was the longtime bookkeeper for the family businesses. Over the years, her community participation has included monthly delivery of Meals on Wheels to the area's shut-ins, assistance with the Heart Telethon, volunteer work for local political campaigns, active membership in St. Rita's RC Church of Connellsville, where she has participated in their annual street fairs, bake sales, and various functions, as well as membership in the city's chamber of commerce. At the time Cookie won her Athena, the Greater Connellsville Chamber of Commerce was known as the North Fayette Chamber of Commerce. When her two children, Shawn and Suzi, were in school, at the Verna Montessori School and at Geibel High School, Cookie was faithfully active in their school affairs, serving in numerous positions on related boards and committees.

Today, both her children have demonstrated this inherited strong work ethic, perseverance and integrity, proving themselves capable and successful entrepreneurs.

A 1987 graduate of Geibel Catholic High School of Connellsville, Uniontown's Finesse Modeling School, and the Uniontown Beauty Academy, Suzi Pilla-Fetsko went on to establish her own beauty business, Excursions, in Connellsville. Her brother Shawn Pilla is the president and owner of the successful Carryall Products, Inc.

Cookie Pilla is a dear and loyal friend, and I consider her one of my cherished muses.

~ ~ ~

Local Rails, Tales and Trails ...

In harmony with the wistful Helen Alt painting– "The old RR Station, Dunbar, PA"– on the cover of this volume, I am happy to report that the Dunbar Historical Society is successfully pairing nostalgic train rides with attractive historical tours.

The Fayette Central Railroad that operates in Uniontown, Dunbar, and Fairchance provides a half-hour layover at the Dunbar Historical Society. To quote the group's secretary Donna Myers, "Since Dunbar was a major player in Pittsburgh's steel industry in providing coke, we want people to have the opportunity to explore our town's industrial heritage with exhibits and memorabilia.

"The FCRR, in cooperation with the DHS, offers a pleasant [rail] trip with narration of the history of our region," Myers told me and the *Tribune-Review* in August of 2008. "The most popular train forays are during Hallowe'en when the FCRR stages thrilling haunted rides and pumpkin-trips for the children." Adults with a hankering for Hallowe'en adventure will equally enjoy this ride, and I can personally vouch for that!

According to local short-line operators, train rides catering to children are among the most popular. And, of course, nostalgic appeal attracts riders of all ages to our region's scenic railroads. Tickets may be purchased at the train. So–

All aboard! Let's make tracks!

In May 2008, Dunbar's Sheepskin Trail officially opened for biking and hiking. The 2.1-mile trace connects to the Youghiogheny River Trail at Wheeler Bottom near Connellsville and enters Dunbar Borough next to the Dunbar Historical Society. A comfort station on Railroad Street and Trail parking are conveniently located within the same block.

Sated with history, this segment of the Sheepskin Trail is the first leg of the thirty-two-mile-long trail that will extend through the heart of Fayette County to Point Marion. As per the Dunbar Historical Society's web site (www.dunbarhistoricalsociety.com), the Trail will connect to the West Virginia Rail-Trail system at the state line, which will connect to the American Discovery Trail, an impressive 6,300-mile-long hike-and-bike-system that stretches from coast to coast, from Delaware to California!

Using the Sheepskin Trail affords tourists and locals the wonderful opportunity of visiting the Dunbar Historical Society's education center and to see the building of a bona fide beehive coke oven.

At this writing, the Dunbar Historical Society is in the final stages of building an authentic- in every way- beehive coke oven. I am so proud of this energetic group for taking on the coke-oven project! I laud their efforts in preserving this significant era of Pennsylvania's layered history.

As Time marches on and the glowing era of the beehive coke ovens fades, it is ever more important to educate people, especially young people, about the area's rich coal and coke heritage. To quote again the DHS' web site, "Today's generation has little knowledge of the struggle that took place in this region by the men and women who tried to eke out a living in the dirt and smoke of the coke-oven era."

I remember the ovens in full blast when the sky at Leisenring #1, for instance, mirrored that of the Pittsburgh sky- a fiery drama, breathtaking in its vibrant beauty. But, for those born after the coke era dimmed and faded, it would be virtually impossible to imagine both the grime and haze by day and the blazing spectacles by night.

The youth of today will not have to try to conjure these historic images. Instead, they will be able to see and touch a real beehive coke oven. The DHS was fortunate to locate and purchase, along with other necessary materials, old-stock coke-oven bricks that had been safely stored and cached away in the vicinity of Shamrock, PA, inside some old coke ovens that had guarded their secret for decades. While Dunbar is surrounded by coke-oven sites, as stated by their web site, used materials are not feasible for constructing a coke oven, since ovens once fired take on a glass-like appearance, and the old material easily crumbles.

With the generous gift of cut-stone from the old Bryson house, by owners Karen Ross and her husband, the late Louis Ross, together with wrought-iron fencing from the Dunbar Reservoir, donated by the North Fayette County Municipal Authority, the society is in possession of everything it needs to construct a beehive coke oven to proper size and scale, based on plans used by none other than Henry Clay Frick, the "Coke King" himself.

Another interesting fact is that the society is planning to make use of corrugated wire glass panels for the roof that will shield the coke oven. This wire glass has been in DHS' possession for many years, and was manufactured in Dunbar at the Pennsylvania Wire Glass Company. A sample of this unique glass can be seen at the DHS.

The coke-oven dream was born in 2006, and from its early stages, the society has been fortunate to have Albert "Cutty" Caruso, former coke-oven builder, as their experienced consultant.

During the spring of 2009, the footer was completed, then it was simply a matter of time, some additional funding, and volunteer support. In late summer 2009, the DHS finally began seeing their dream nearing completion when the project advanced to full-swing under the guidance of mason Barry Pritchard of Scottdale, PA.

"He has been a blessing," Donna Myers told the *Tribune-Review* in an article published, Sunday, August 23, 2009, in that paper's Fay-West section. "[Mr. Pritchard's] help with our coke-oven project is more than we could have imagined."

"I saw an article [about the society's coke-oven dream] in the *Tribune-Review*," Pritchard related in the above article, "and I ... drove by the site. I thought that I'd like to see what I could do to help." A mason for more than thirty years, Pritchard recently moved back to the Fay-West area of southwestern Pennsylvania, discovered the project, heartedly believed in it and decided to volunteer his services. "Though," stated the *Tribune*, "Pritchard never constructed a beehive oven before, his knowledge and years of experience made the transition an easy task."

After contacting the society and discussing the project with them, it was decided that he was the man for the job, and Pritchard put his nose to the proverbial grindstone. He began with research, including driving around and studying old coke ovens in the area.

When the actual work got under way, Pritchard and the volunteers made slight modifications since the original plans are from the early 1900s and the materials are dated from the 1940s and 1950s, but the DHS avows that the changes are "minute."

The authentic Frick beehive oven will be a magnificent part of a large tourism draw for Dunbar, a wonderful educational opportunity for students and visitors alike. The DHS, with additional funding, hopes to build a pavilion with education signage to create a place where recreational as well as educational programs will be staged. This energetic, dedicated group- true stewards of our area's rich

County Chronicles

heritage- welcomes your support. Contact information is on their web site.

A drawing of a cross-section of a coke oven; a ten-foot panorama illustrating the fifty-mile long, narrow strip of land (from Latrobe to Fairchance and the West Virginia line, a rich vein of coal, seven to nine feet in thickness, unsurpassed anywhere in the world for steel production), that was the famed Connellsville coking area; genuine coke; and sample coke-

Sheepskin Trail & Dunbar Historical Society Dunbar, Pennsylvania

The beginning of the Sheepskin Trail 2.1 miles from Dunbar, Pennsylvania

The old-stock coke-oven bricks inside the coke oven where they were cached away for decades in the vicinity of Shamrock, PA

A tranquil view of the Youghiogheny River from the Fayette Central RR

Cutty Caruso and Barry Pritchard, stone masons discussing wall corner

The Sheepskin Trail, Dunbar Creek for trout fishing, Coke Oven Park, the FCRR tourist train, and the DHS Education Center are all within the same block, town center, Dunbar.

oven bricks are all on display at the DHS. Go and have a "look-see"!

Just a reminder, readers: The coke workers used to refer to the baked coal as a "coal cake," for that is what the burned coal resembled. Thus, COal caKE was shortened to "coke."

The coal and coke era is a rich legacy, and one that deserves preservation for posterity's sake. What could be more exciting in this region known in the annals of American history as the "Coke Capital of the World"!

The "Rivers of Steel" in Pittsburgh have termed the Connellsville coking region, the "Mountains of Fire." And, to quote Pam Seighman, curator of the Coal and Coke Heritage Center, at Penn State Fayette, "Without the 'Mountains of Fire,' there would have been no 'Rivers of Steel'!"

Readers can read more about historic Dunbar in "Old Irishtown Reminiscences," "A Moment of Remembrance," and "Small Town Tapestry" in the premier volume of my *County Chronicles*, as well as in "The Right Stuff ... the Knights of Irishtown" in *CC IV*.

~ ~ ~

Electricity is installed to the oven for night illumination
Dunbar photos courtesy the Dunbar Historical Society Archives

Circus, Circus!

Here is an interesting tidbit I discovered in the *Daily Courier* archives: In 1893, the same year as the "great circus train wreck" included in the opening Chronicle of this volume, Connellsville experienced its own circus woes. In those days, circuses entered the towns on their tour route with a big parade and all the fanfare they could muster. Unhappily, Barnum and Bailey's heavy circus wagons and elephants proved too heavy for the new pavement on Pittsburgh Street. They broke

Circus parade entering (possibly) nearby Mount Pleasant circa 1900. Note their brick-paved street.

Lions! Vintage circus photos courtesy Nancy Sova Hrabak

through the bricks in several places. According to a Friday, October 13, 1893 article in the *Courier*, the ruined pavement did not speak well for the contractor. Contractor J. W. Hallam, however, repaved the street. Thus, it was reported in the paper's Saturday, October 27th edition that the job was complete, and Connellsville could boast of having "the longest [brick-] paved street in the entire county." In accordance with the *Courier*'s poll taken in regard to the paving job, though most of the citizenry believed the contractor was not at fault, they were pleased that he "made good" and repaved the street.

~ ~ ~

The Connellsville Cultural Trust ... "The buck stops here!"

"We must take care of our historic places and be ambassadors for them."
 - Author/historian David McCullough

Michael Edwards and his partner Daniel Cocks moved to Connellsville in 2001 to open the Newmyer House Bed & Breakfast. The Newmyer House is one of the most historic houses in Connellsville. Before I discuss these two enterprising young men further, let's review the history of their house.

Located on South Pittsburgh Street in Connellsville, the Newmyer House is a stately 1890s Victorian mansion in the Queen Anne style. This was a style that was fashionable in both England and America from the 1870s to the turn of the last century, the spacious porch one of its striking features.

The turreted brick Newmyer, rich with the gingerbread trim and stained glass so popular in the late Victorian/Edwardian era, was the former home (circa 1873 to 1913) of P. S. Newmyer, a prominent Connellsville attorney.

Speaking of stained glass, Dan Cocks, who is self-taught in this art, has added to the stained glass in the Newmyer manse. He obtains his glass locally from Connellsville's Youghiogheny Glass. One of the stained-glass windows that he added to the Newmyer mansion depicts a Japanese scene. The war in Japan at the turn of the last century had forced many wealthy Japanese families to sell valuable family heirlooms, and so Japanese art became popular.

My favorite of Dan's stained-glass creations (that I admired at their Gallery MD) was *The Girl with the Pearl Earring*, shades of the famous seventeenth-century baroque painter Vermeer's oil that has often been called the "Dutch Mona Lisa." At this writing, Dan is working on a stained-glass window depicting an iron furnace surrounded by irises and birch trees for the Gibson House, the oldest house in Connellsville proper and the home of the Connellsville Historical Society.

While we're on the subject, let's scan the history of stained glass, for so much of it brightens the former Connellsville coking basin.

There is a *mystery* to glass. It is a form of matter with gas, liquid, and solid properties, though a super-cooled liquid rather than a true solid. Stained glass captures light and seems to glow from within.

As I have often pointed out, Connellsville's heyday was circa 1870 through the 1920s, and during most of this era, stained glass for private residences was very much in vogue.

The origins of the first stained glass are lost to history. However, the technique probably took root in jewelry-making, cloisonné, and mosaics.

Stained-glass windows emerged during the Middle Ages, likely around the 1100s with the Rose Window of Paris' Notre Dame a model for French Gothic cathedrals. It was at this time that depictions of Biblical scenes were used in the stained-glass windows of French, German, and English cathedrals.

In the mid-1800s, England saw a revival in most everything Gothic. During this period, stained glass became a fashionable addition to residences and public buildings, in addition to churches. Though painted glass had been in vogue since the Renaissance, several amateur art historians and scientists rediscovered the medieval glass techniques. Pieces of glass were tested and their color secrets unlocked.

John LaFarge and Louis Comfort Tiffany were two American painters who began experimenting with glass. Contemporaries, but working independently, they soon became competitors. LaFarge developed and copyrighted opalescent glass in 1879. Tiffany popularized it, and his name became synonymous with opalescent glass and the American glass movement.

The numerous stained-glass windows, several signed, of the Victorian and Edwardian homes in the Connellsville area are iridescent treasures reminiscent of an era when Connellsville was the "Coke Capital of the World," when millionaires and near-millionaires were fairly common, and income tax was an obligation of the future. This was an epoch- the modality of elegance and opulence- unparalleled in the *beaux arts*, architecture, fashion and jewelry- *unparalleled in America*.

The coal and coke barons built their "castles" to attest to their success, and they furnished and decorated them with the best their "black gold" money could buy. I am so grateful that people like Michael Edwards and Dan Cocks have seen fit to restore and preserve so much of Connellsville's rich legacy. And I am thrilled that stained glass, nearly a lost art, has made, in recent years, a strong comeback.

Based on tours of the Newmyer mansion and research into its history, I know the house has twenty-eight rooms, including a charming trilogy of parlors on the main floor.

The manse's original owner, Porter Strickler Newmyer, was an enterprising businessman as well as a successful attorney, who entered the study of law at the Fayette County seat and was admitted to the bar in March 1871. In May of that spring, Newmyer began his law practice in Connellsville, where he also chose to reside.

In addition to a lucrative law career, attorney Newmyer engaged in real estate and other significant endeavors. For instance, he was one of the organizers of the *Keystone Courier* that later became *The Courier*, then *The Daily Courier*, and to date, the *Daily Courier*.

In April 1873, Newmyer married Mary A. Davidson, and the couple settled on Apple Street before building their Queen Anne mansion in 1893. Then, the "Talk of the Town," a popular segment of the *Courier*, reported that P. S. Newmyer was building "a handsome and costly home on Pittsburgh Street."

In addition to his private residence, the community-minded attorney had the first public theater, the Newmyer Opera House, constructed on the corner of Pittsburgh and Peach streets.

There, during our smoky town's boom era, a great variety of theatrical entertainment, from drama to comedy and "everything in between," came from New York City and the world to the theater-going folks of Connellsville. The three-storied brick structure, the "finest and most imposing" in this city, was erected in 1881 at a cost of $25,000.

Connellsville's coal and coke era paralleled perfectly with "*La Belle Époque*," the "Beautiful Age," also known as the "Gilded Age," the peak of luxury living, when the city's *beau monde* indulged themselves, taking in the Newmyer Opera House's exciting theatrical performances.

Michael Edwards discussing Connellsville Cultural Trust plans for historic Connellsville

Now, let's talk some more about the two laudable men, Michael Edwards and Dan Cocks, who have preserved significant Connellsville landmarks.

Michael and Dan opened their Newmyer home to Bed and Breakfast guests for several years, purchasing and restoring a second old Connellsville mansion and opening a second B&B, as well as Gallery MD, an art gallery where local artists could display and sell their work. The reason they christened the artsy endeavor "Gallery MD" was because the building was the site of Connellsville's first hospital, not to mention that the letters represented their first names. This was the third historic building that the pair had restored and saved.

In 2005, Pennsylvania's Governor Ed Rendell visited Gallery MD during an open house given in his honor.

The subsequent year, Edwards and Cocks bought and improved a fourth Connellsville building, the former Immaculate Conception convent. They then opened that building to various local groups for special events.

Michael and Dan have hosted every one of my *County Chronicles* book debuts, the first at the Newmyer House, the second at Gallery MD, the third at the Convent, and the fourth again at the Gallery. Each was a sumptuously staged soirée, with the most delectable foods and delightful music, decorations and ambience. In addition, we were blessed to have the nation's ace bagpiper, the founder and director of Pittsburgh's Balmoral School of Piping and Drumming, George Balderose, at these affairs, rendering each book debut truly memorable.

In 2006, the year of Connellsville's bicentennial, Edwards and Cocks formed the 501(c) 3 nonprofit Connellsville Cultural Trust with its mission of valuing and preserving the historical and cultural assets of the city and celebrating the arts.

The Heritage Trail was the Trust's first project. Successfully completed in 2008, it constitutes eleven signs that take visitors on a pleasant two-mile walk through historic Connellsville. In this way, newcomers, guests of the city, and visitors can learn the basic history of our town.

Further Connellsville Trust plans include the restoration of our historic Armory and the renovation of the auditorium of the former Connellsville High School to the Edwin S. Porter Theatre, a community theater and performing arts center.

For those who may not know, here is a bit about the historic Connellsville Armory and the importance of preserving its rich legacy.

Long before the Declaration of Independence, Americans were fighting for freedom. These men were not professional soldiers. They were farmers, blacksmiths, and merchants- ordinary citizens.

To protect their homes during times of common danger, the steadfast colonists formed militia units. Those in Massachusetts became famous as the *Minutemen*- citizen-soldiers who could be called upon at short notice to defend their colony. This spirit has been a fundamental part of our American heritage for well over three and a half centuries. In fact, the National Guard is the oldest component of the United States Armed Forces.

Connellsville can claim its own celebrated Guardsmen unit from the Spanish-American War- Company D of the 10th Regiment, mustered May 5, 1892.

In July of that year, the regiment, with others, was sent to Homestead to put a peaceful end to the labor war there. Connellsville's Company D had not yet received their uniforms, and thus, in mufti, was somewhat scornfully addressed by the strikers as the "Tenth Regiment Pinkertons." Though they remained at Homestead over a month, Company D restored order without fray or bloodshed.

From left to right: Dan Cocks, Michael Edwards, Connellsville Mayor Judy D. Reed and husband Dex Reed at CC IV book debut "Bringing History Alive" at Gallery MD in 2008. Those attending came as historical figures from my County Chronicles PA history series. Can you guess who these attendees represent?

The 10th Regiment, including Company D, left for the Philippine Islands on May 18, 1898, entering Manila Bay on 17 July. By the end of the month, the men saw action for the first time, standing their ground like seasoned veterans and displaying great courage. The Tenth fought in several hard-hitting engagements, including the valiant charge on Manila, later battling with Filipino insurgents at La Loma Church in February 1899.

The regiment saw its severest action *after* its term of service had expired. The conscientious volunteers served for more than two months after the peace treaty with Spain was ratified in April 1899, and their term of enlistment had expired. If these Guardsmen had been mustered out, the small force of regulars left behind would have been rendered helpless and most likely destroyed, due to the outbreak of the insurrection.

Upon the President's recommendation, the Tenth- known now as the "Fighting Tenth"- received a special Medal of Honor for its noble service above and beyond the call of duty.

The regiment sailed for home July 1, 1899, arriving in San Francisco, where they were mustered out on August 22, after a service of fifteen months and an unforgettable journey to and from the jaws of death.

A special train carried them to Pittsburgh, where they were received at Schenley Park (where Pennsylvania erected a monument to them in 1904) with great fanfare in a ceremony that included President McKinley.

When Company D returned home to Connellsville the following day, August 29, the citizens of our hometown greeted them at the railroad station with a roaring, flag-waving welcome. Bunting and flags were everywhere. The air resonated with patriotic music, the streets with cheering people. After the lively parade and the speeches concluded, an elegant banquet honored the brave lads at the sumptuous Newmyer Opera House.

Guardsmen were reorganized into the 28th Division in 1917, arriving in France on May 18, 1918. These soldiers participated in six major campaigns during World War I, the unit's fierce combat abilities earning it the title "Iron Division" from General "Black Jack" Pershing himself, Commander of the American Expeditionary Force.

The oldest division in the armed forces of the United States, the 28th's coat of arms graces the entrance and great halls of Connellsville's historic Armory.

The insignia's red and yellow colors represent its artillery; the chevron signifies support and attack; the fleur-de-lis represents the unit's combat service in France during World War I; and the castle is a keen reminder of the assault at Normandy that in 1944 opened France- the Continent- to invasion and consequent liberation.

Thus is a capsule history of the valiant Division of our old Connellsville Armory- an Armory that was built by the State of Pennsylvania in 1907-08, and is the second oldest armory within our commonwealth.

With its parapet roof and Romanesque doors and windows, the Connellsville Armory is an impressive, fortress-like red brick building on Washington Avenue. The old Connellsville Armory was placed on the National Register of Historic Places on November 14, 1991, by the United States Department of the Interior. The historic brass plaque was placed on an exterior corner of the building in June 1993 by Thomas W. Scott, Sr. and Thomas W. Scott, Jr.

World War I veteran Thomas W. Scott labored with Max C. Floto and other WWI veterans of our Fayette County for several decades to secure a day of recognition for America's combat veterans, finally realizing their dream when Veterans' Day became a *national* holiday honoring America's warriors.

At this writing, Connellsville's new armory is located in Connellsville Township, but Michael Edwards, Dan Cocks, and the Connellsville Cultural Trust are determined that the old "Keystone Guardian" on Washington Avenue will not be forgotten or neglected, for it served and protected the people of Pennsylvania and the nation for over a century, and it is now up to the citizens of Connellsville to protect it.

There are several ideas under discussion about how this grand old building can continue to serve. Whichever plan materializes, I pray Connellsville will be as vigilant a protector of the "Keystone Guardian" as the old armory has been over the long years for its citizenry. To borrow a phrase from the Guardsmen handbook: "The answer is found in the unspoken appreciation of the entire town"; and that town, a place where patriotism has always run high- the home of Max C. Floto, our nation's recognized and official "Father of Veterans' Day"- is historic Connellsville.

If you do not know why Michael Edwards and the Connellsville Cultural Trust harbor a dream of converting the old Connellsville High School (the Community Center on the corner of Prospect and Fairview) to the Edwin S. Porter Theatre, allow me to review the story of Connellsville's movie legend Edwin S. Porter.

He was christened "Edward" by his parents, but as a youngster, his friends called the pudgy boy "Betty." By the time he joined the Navy in 1893, he had traded the "Edward" for the more impressive "Edwin Stanton," after Abraham Lincoln's Secretary of War.

The fourth of seven children, born April 21, 1870, in Connellsville to Thomas and Mary Clark Porter, Edwin S. Porter became America's first major filmmaker.

During the 1880s, while working as an usher and ticket taker at Connellsville's Newmyer Opera House, the young man was exposed to the theater's wide range of amusement. He quickly became enraptured with entertainment.

Despite the above, for some unknown reason, he chose to become a tailor; however, economic realities thwarted his success in this unlikely career, and the small tailor shop closed its doors on June 15, 1893.

Just ten days earlier, Porter had displayed his romantic nature by eloping with Caroline Ridinger of nearby Somerset. Once the adventuresome groom declared bankruptcy, the pair relocated to Philadelphia, and there, Edwin joined the Navy.

Upon completion of his three-year hitch in the service, Porter secured a job in 1897 as a projectionist in New York, that City of cities that would become, for many years, the heart of the entertainment world. Subsequent to a circuitous outset, Edwin Porter was finally following the yellow brick road to his destiny.

At the Eden Musée, a New York City amusement center, Porter was hired to show scenes from the Spanish-American War, the first war ever filmed. Soon, he began manufacturing motion picture equipment.

By 1900, Thomas Edison's film company was in a bit of trouble due to its lack of photographic skills. Business was falling off. The genius needed some fresh, new ideas, thus he hired Edwin Porter, not solely as a mechanic, as some have reported, but also as a producer/director for the short films produced for Edison's Kinetoscope.

The invention of the motion picture was a *windfall* to Porter. He had always loved to tinker, and what could be better than to work with his longtime idol, Thomas Edison! The age had dawned to tell a story with film, and Connellsville's Edwin Porter would do more than anyone to coin the phrase, "Lights, camera, action!"

If you were to view one of his films today, you might think it primitive, but Porter was one of the earliest directors to use a panning camera. Essentially, he moved the camera to follow actors or objects, creating a panoramic effect. He was also the first to use dream sequences, close-ups, fades (fade-ins and outs), chase scenes, and special effects, such as split-screens and double-exposures.

The man had an intuitive *feel* for what a motion picture ought to be, and it was only a matter of time until his films began to improve. As cameraman, Porter was responsible for *all* the film elements, not only cinematography, but also developing the negative and editing, which, at first, was little more than trimming. He even selected subject matter and worked on story development, demonstrating a definite flair for comedies.

Porter did some pretty good editing in his 1901-02 productions, but it was 1903, his banner year with Edison, when he made *The Life of an American Fireman* that enthusiastically captured public attention. This breakthrough film had a real plot, plenty of action and suspense, and even a close-up of a hand pulling a fire alarm. What drama!

Nonetheless, it would be his next endeavor that put the name "Edwin S. Porter" in lights.

Back in August of 1900, Butch Cassidy and his "Wild Bunch" had robbed the Number Three Train on the Union Pacific tracks near Table Rock, Wyoming. The gang stopped the train and forced the conductor to uncouple the passenger cars. They then blew up the mailcar's safe, and in a cloud of dust and a thunder of hooves, the daring bandits absconded with $5,000. The romantic, inventive Porter had read about the robbery, the elusive Wild Bunch, and their super-posse pursuers in the newspapers. The event haunted him, and he decided to make a film of it.

A twelve-minute action film, *The Great Train Robbery* utilizes camera movements and continuity editing to advance the story. "The film's commercial success," Charles Musser recounts in his *Before the Nickelodeon*, "was unprecedented and so remarkable that contemporary critics still tend to account for the picture's historical significance largely in terms of its commercial success and its impact on future fictional narratives."

The film is still considered a *classic*, bestowing on Connellsville's Edwin S. Porter fame, recognition, and immortality, along with the following lofty titles: the "First Major Filmmaker," the "Father of American Story Film," the "Father of Film Editing," and the "Father of the Western Movie."

Every shot in *The Great Train Robbery* contained action, from the first scene when the telegraph operator is assaulted, to the final shootout after the posse catches up with Butch's gang. The most exciting scene is the one in which one of the bandits, played by Charlie Barnes, fires a pistol- *point blank*- at the audience.

Porter had positioned his villainous-looking actor in front of a solid-black background, after which he placed a thick piece of glass over the camera lens to protect it from flying wadding and powder burns. At the conclusion of the film, the audience was/is *riveted* to the sinister gunman's dark penetrating gaze- to the menacing barrel of his cocked six-shooter!

That scene never failed to send front-row viewers diving for cover! Needless to say, audiences were thrilled. They had never experienced anything like this. *The Great Train Robbery* played to packed houses everywhere it opened.

Stop and think, readers. Connellsville's Edwin S. Porter- our little "Bettie"- had just given birth to an American film genre known affectionately as- the great American Western! *Train Robbery* was also a crime tale, and thus it had an influence on future police dramas as well.

When Edwin S. Porter died on April 30, 1941, shortly after his seventy-first birthday, sadly, the world hardly noticed his passing.

The question begging is this: Will Porter's birthplace let this legendary figure pass from history? Not if Michael Edwards, Dan Cocks, and the Connellsville Trust can prevent that from happening!

For more information about the Connellsville Cultural Trust, please visit www.connellsvilleculturaltrust.org.

The fortitude and resolve Michael and Dan have exhibited are evident in the awards they have received by the Connellsville Area Chamber of Commerce. Their efforts were recognized in 2003 with the Beautification Award and in a 2007 award for their establishment of the Connellsville Cultural Trust. In addition, the Pennsylvania Legislature has also presented them with Special Recognition for their undying service to the historic Connellsville community.

In July of 2008, Edwards was hired as the Executive Director of the Connellsville Redevelopment Authority. Edwards serves on the board of the Greater Connellsville Chamber of Commerce, and Cocks on the Planning Commission.

Prior to coming to Connellsville, Dan Cocks served in the US Air Force as an MP from 1981-2001 when he retired from military service. One of his duties included accompanying President Bill Clinton on Air Force One.

Michael Edwards owned and operated his own catering business in the metro DC area for twelve years. A 1987 graduate of Philadelphia's St. Charles Seminary, Edwards holds a bachelor's degree in philosophy.

Michael Edwards and Dan Cocks possess what I like to call in my books "The Right Stuff." They continually persevere, ofttimes in the face of great adversity, to preserve the historical and cultural assets of our city, and to celebrate the arts.

As a person who writes history and reveres it, I *urge* the citizenry of historic Connellsville to aid them in any way we can to achieve their- *our*- goals for a better and more beautiful community.

The great author/historian David McCullough concluded a talk, in October 2005, at Fayette County's Fort Necessity with this sagacious advice: "We must take care of our historic places and be ambassadors for them."

Readers, *we* are the stewards of our heritage, of our historic buildings and our historic sites, and we had better embrace a Harry-Truman attitude about our rich legacy, for-

"The buck stops here!"

~ ~ ~

"Duty, Honor, Country" ...

"I've known Bill Colvin since we were in high school together ... and that's longer than I care to mention. Since then, my opinion of

him has never waned– Bill is a man of honor and supreme integrity."
– Ceane O'Hanlon-Lincoln

Connellsville native son, William D. Colvin, is a graduate of the Kiski School in Saltsburg, Pennsylvania. An alumnus of the College of Wooster, Ohio, with a joint Bachelor's in theatre and United States history, he also holds a Master of Art's degree in International Affairs from Salve Regina University in Newport, Rhode Island. In addition, Colvin is a graduate of the United States Army War College, the Command and General Staff College, among an impressively long list of military training completed, including the Infantry Officer Candidate School at Fort Benning, Georgia.

In 2000, Colvin was inducted into the Infantry Officer Candidate School Hall of Fame.

Among his impressive decorations are the Legion of Merit, Defense Meritorious Service Medal, the Meritorious Service Medal with two oak leaf clusters, the Joint Service Commendation Medal, the Army Commendation Medal with oak leaf cluster, the Army Achievement Medal with three oak leaf clusters, the Army Reserve Medal with silver hour glass, Army Overseas Service Ribbon, Army Service Ribbon, Army Reserve Components Overseas Training Ribbon, Joint Meritorious Unit Award, Pennsylvania Distinguished Service Medal, Pennsylvania Meritorious Service Medal, Pennsylvania Governor's Unit Citation, Pennsylvania Service Ribbon with four stars, Pennsylvania Twenty Year Medal with star, the Maj. General T. R. White Medal, the General T. J. Stewart Medal, and the National Guard Master Recruiter Badge.

Brigadier General, Pennsylvania, (retired) William D. Colvin was a traditional Army National Guard officer who began his career with the 1-110th Infantry Battalion. During his military career, he commanded at every level from platoon through battalion.

This patriotic, duty-bound man spent twenty-one years training officer candidates and junior officers at the Pennsylvania National Guard Military Academy. He served the last seven years as Chief of Tactics. Among a myriad of leadership positions, General Colvin served as Program Manager for the transition of an infantry battalion to an armor battalion for which he wrote the Program of Instruction that was adopted by the Armor Training Center at Fort Knox, Kentucky.

As the commander of the Division Rear Operations Center and Chief-of-Staff Rear for the 28th Infantry Division, General Colvin developed the Standard Operating Procedures for Rear Area Operations, and later tasked to organize and serve as the first commander of the 128th Forward Support Battalion.

During his long stint with the Guard, General Colvin served in *countless* staff positions both stateside and overseas to include: Deputy Assistant to the Chairman of the Joint Chiefs for National Guard and Reserve Matters and the European Command's Joint Contact Team Program Team Chief in Vilnius, Lithuania, as an advisor to the Minister of Defense, as well as a member of the United States Ambassador's Country Team.

In October 2001, after thirty-one years of service, then-Colonel William D. Colvin retired from the Guard and was promoted to Brigadier General on the Pennsylvania Army National Guard Retired List.

Brigadier General Colvin (PA) (Ret.) currently serves as the Pennsylvania State Co-coordinator of the United States Military Academy Admissions Field Force.

Bill recently retired from teaching theatre and English at Connellsville Area Senior High School. In addition to classroom instruction, he annually produced and directed the senior class play, was the technical director for the annual Broadway musical, and sponsored the local chapter of the International Thespian Society and the Camera Club.

Not surprisingly, Colvin was selected for inclusion in *Who's Who Among American Teachers* for the years 1996, 1997, 1998, and 2005. He retired from teaching in 2007 with over thirty-five years of dedicated service.

Talk about a heavy schedule! Bill is also a member of the International Brotherhood of Magicians, as well as a member of the Order of Merlin, an elite group of those magicians who have dedicated over twenty-five years of uninterrupted service to the International Brotherhood.

As if that were not enough in his civilian capacity, Bill has served as a member of his local parish council and finance committee, as a hockey coach and charter member of the board of directors of the Fay-West Hockey Association, as a member of Geibel Catholic High School's development board, and as technology coordinator for Conn-Area Catholic School.

He must have been a great teacher. I say that because, while engaged in the endless hours of proofing my books, I have telephoned him often with military, history, punctuation or grammar questions. He is always patient, and his explanations are clear and easy to understand. Over the years, I have learned a lot from Bill. No matter how busy he is, he always returns my calls. What's that old saying? "If you want to get something done and done right, ask a busy person to do it." And this man is busier than the proverbial beaver!

Presently, he is hard-at-work on his third career. Since retiring from teaching and the PA Army National Guard, Bill Colvin is working for Defense Solutions, serving as the Director of Information Management and Security, as well as Program Manager for Combat Vehicles.

Established in 2001 and based out of Exton, Pennsylvania, with branch and satellite offices on three continents, Defense Solutions' goal is to deliver the best equipment, technology, and training to our service members with minimum risk to their lives and well-being.

Bill's two sons, Sergeant William Justin Colvin and Second Lieutenant Alan Shuda Colvin, are following gallantly in their father's (as well as their ancestors') soldierly footsteps.

When I asked Bill for a photograph of him with his sons in uniform, he said, "It is appropriate that my wife Judy be in the picture too, because the bottom line is that spouses and mothers also serve. Without them, the soldier can not be successful."

Brigadier General William D. Colvin (PA) (Ret.) is married to the former Judith Reed of Connellsville. Judy and Bill have four fine children, Dr. Bridget L. Colvin, PhD, Megan E. Colvin, Pennsylvania State Police Tpr. Wm. Justin Colvin, and 2nd Lieutenant Alan S. Colvin, United States Army.

Since the Colvin family motto seems to mirror that of West Point- "Duty, Honor, Country"- I think it best if I let BG Colvin tell you about his sons.

"From the time they could walk, all of my children, on occasion, accompanied me to the armory on an administrative night. Justin and Alan in particular liked to run their remote-controlled cars all over the big drill floor where there was no furniture to get in the way.

"When I left the infantry to become a 'tanker,' I needed to learn fire commands. I practiced them with Justin. At the armory in Johnstown, there was a tank gunner simulator called a VIGS that Justin learned to use. One memory that perpetuates, not only with me, but also with other members of my unit is the night that the Battalion Master Gunner 'took on' Justin on the VIGS. This encounter proved to be a source of embarrassment to our Master Gunner for many years, since Justin thoroughly trounced him in the competition. Justin was five years old.

"From the time he was old enough to have college as a goal, Justin repeatedly said that he was going to join the Guard, 'so you don't have to pay for my college, Dad.'

"When I was stationed in Lithuania, I received an email from Judy, informing me that she was faxing a paper for me to sign for Justin. It was a bit annoying. Why couldn't *she* sign his sports consent form? Within minutes, his enlistment papers arrived by way of the fax machine. I needed to sign the parental consent for him to enlist at age seventeen. I missed swearing him in over the phone by six hours.

"The summer following his junior year in high school, Justin attended Basic Combat Training, and after graduation Advanced Individual Training to become an Infantryman. He had joined the same company and battalion that I had joined in 1970.

"During his sophomore year at Juniata College, Justin learned that the 28th Division Headquarters was to deploy to Bosnia. He asked me if I could get him a slot to go. I did; and at the end of his college sophomore year, he deployed to Eagle Base in Bosnia for a year, including his training. When he returned to school to continue his education, his friends were a year ahead of him.

"At the end of his college junior year, he was notified that his unit was mobilized for deployment to Iraq; and after six months of training, he deployed for a one-year tour in 2005, right in the middle of the Sunni Triangle. His brigade combat team, 2BCT 28th Division, was attached to the First Marine Division in Ramadi, and Justin's battalion, 1-110th Infantry, was located apart from the brigade in Habbyaniyah. His job: Assistant Operations Sergeant.

"That's what it was on paper. I found out later that what he really did, much of the time when he wasn't posting maps, was to serve as a Rifle Squad Team Leader with one of the Rifle Platoons that patrolled the area.

"Subsequently, in an email that made its round-about way- from its starting point with his battalion commander, to the commander's son at West Point, there to Justin's brother

Alan at the Point- to me, I saw in the attached picture Justin being pinned with the Combat Infantryman Badge- the *definitive* award for an infantryman who has seen combat. I only know a few sketchy facts given to me by his brother, but I am proud to say that Justin *earned* this coveted award. He is, and always will be, my hero.

"Following his tour in Iraq, Justin returned home, completed his college studies with a degree in Criminal Justice, became engaged to a lovely girl, and graduated from the Pennsylvania State Police Academy. He is currently assigned to the Lancaster barracks, and he and his wife Michele have a beautiful baby girl, Evelyn Jane Colvin.

"My younger son Alan was in sixth grade when he decided that he wanted to attend the United States Military Academy at West Point to become an Army officer. He set this as his goal, and from that period in his life, everything he did was in preparation for that objective, from self-motivated physical conditioning, earning his Eagle Scout award, to maintaining a solid academic average.

From left to right: Sgt. William Justin Colvin, Brig. Gen. William Colvin, 2Lt. Alan Shuda Colvin, and Judy Colvin
Photo courtesy William D. Colvin

"He was so serious about his chosen career that, during his junior year in high school, he joined the Army National Guard, the unit his brother Justin was in, again the same unit I had joined at the beginning of my military career. This time, I had the honor of conducting the swearing-in ceremony.

"The summer of his junior year, Alan attended Basic Combat Training at Fort Benning, Georgia, and opened his candidate file with West Point. He was so certain about what he wanted to do, that he only applied to two schools, West Point and the Citadel, his 'backup school.'

"Though Alan's sights were clearly set on West Point, he was invited to interview for a Presidential scholarship at the Citadel. A month before the interview, he interrupted me in the middle of a student's singing audition (for the annual school musical). He proceeded to tell me that he 'was *not* going to the Citadel interview,' whereupon, I answered him quietly that we could not afford the Citadel without the scholarship. He responded flatly that he was not going, 'because,' he said, 'it is a waste of time.'

"By this point, while the young lady on stage was still singing her heart out, I was vibrating about four feet off the floor. I told him this was neither the time nor the place to discuss the matter. A grin tugged at the corners of Alan's mouth, prompting me to ask if he knew something I did not.

"That familiar mischievous grin of his spread rapidly across his face as he informed me, 'Congressman Murtha called me today in school. I got into West Point.'

"The yell I let out reverberated throughout the auditorium. He had me hook, line, and sinker. *And I could not have been prouder.*

"Alan's was an early admission, but that did not stop his mission of attainment. He continued to improve his academic average, and upon graduation from Geibel Catholic High School, was awarded the Arlene Severin English prize for excellence. He left for West Point in late June.

"I am proud to say that Alan made the Superintendent's List (Dean's List) each of his eight semesters at the Point, while preparing for and participating in the Sandhurst Competition, a tough International Military Skills

Competition. His senior year, he became his company's team squad leader, recruiting and training his own squad for the competition. His hard work and academic excellence paid off.

"A Military History major, he graduated in May 2008 in the top twenty percent of his class, qualifying for both his choice of assignment and branch. He chose the Infantry and Fort Campbell, Kentucky. Judy and I pinned Alan with the same Second Lieutenant bars my parents had pinned on me in 1971. It was, needless to say, a moment packed with emotion- and one that is forever etched in our minds and hearts.

"Alan is now Airborne qualified, and when he arrives at the 101st Airborne Division (Air Assault), he will be Ranger Qualified as well. With his choice of branch, he could have chosen a myriad of easy assignments. He did not. He chose to be an Infantry Officer.

"Alan's class is the fourth class made up of patriotic cadets who sought out West Point *after* the attack on the Twin Towers in New York City, knowing that in four short years, they would be headed to war in defense of their country.

"My sons represent the fourth generation of military service in my immediate family. Our military service dates back to the Revolutionary War. Their paternal great-grandfather, William M. Colvin, served in the Great War as a sergeant in the 840th Aero Squadron in France; their paternal grandfather, William F. Colvin, M.D., served in the Medical Corps during World War II and after, as a captain in Korea; and their maternal grandfather, Blaine C. Reed, served as a sergeant in the Big Red One during World War II. Service to their country flows through their veins with the blood of their ancestors.

"In April 2005, the Commandant of West Point referred to the young men and women of today as the 'Second Greatest Generation.' I couldn't agree more. Those young men and women who go into harm's way to keep America safe, and in particular *my* sons, are my greatest heroes."

This author will succinctly conclude this segment with the trilogy of words that are the United States Military Academy at West Point's guiding principle: "Duty, Honor, Country." And, readers- *that says it all.*

About the Author

Ceane O'Hanlon-Lincoln is a native of Connellsville, Fayette County, Pennsylvania, though she resided in neighboring Westmoreland County's Ligonier Valley for eighteen years, where she taught high school French until 1985. Already engaged in commercial writing, she immediately began pursuing a career in writing history, as well as historical fiction. "History has always been my first love," the dynamic author has stated. "I'll read a history book the way many read a novel."

In 1987, O'Hanlon-Lincoln won honors at Robert Redford's Sundance Institute, when two of her screenplays made the "top twenty-five," chosen from thousands of nationwide entries. In 1994, she optioned one of those scripts to Kevin Costner; the other screenplay, *A Toast to Destiny*, she adapted, with a fellow teacher, to a compelling mystery novel of the same title.

Ceane has also had a poem published in *Great Poems of Our Time*. Winner of the Editor's Choice Award, "The Man Who Holds the Reins" appears in *County Chronicles II* and in the fore of her anthology, *Autumn Song*, a medley of stories threaded by their destiny themes and autumnal settings. William Colvin, a Fayette County theatre and English teacher said of her *Autumn Song*: "The tales rank with those of Rod Serling and the great O. Henry. O'Hanlon-Lincoln is a *master* storyteller."

Robert Matzen, writer/producer of Paladin Films said of *Autumn Song*: "I like the flow of the words, almost like song lyrics ... very *evocative*."

From February 2000 to March 2002, Ceane authored, in her hometown newspaper, *The Daily Courier*, her own bimonthly column, "County Chronicles," in which she focused on local history. A vivid assortment of places, people and events that affected and shaped Pennsylvania, *County Chronicles*- the series- is the result of the numerous requests for a compilation and continuation of her exciting Chronicles.

Author Ceane O'Hanlon-Lincoln with her Athena
Photo courtesy the author's husband Phillip R. Lincoln

In February 2004, O'Hanlon-Lincoln won the prestigious Athena, an award presented to professional "women of spirit" on local, national and international levels. The marble, bronze and crystal Athena sculpture symbolizes career excellence, community leadership, and the light that emanates from the recipient.

In the tradition of a great Irish *seanchaí* (storyteller), Ceane has been called by many a "state-of-the-heart writer." Soon after the debut of the premier volume, the talented author won for her *County Chronicles* a Citation/Special Recognition Award from the Pennsylvania House of Representatives, followed by a Special Recognition Award from the Senate of Pennsylvania.

Ceane shares "Tara," her restored, century-old Victorian home, with her husband Phillip and their champion Bombay cats, Black Jade and Black Jack O'Lantern. Her hobbies include travel, nature walks, theatre, film, antiques, and reading "... everything I can on Pennsylvania, American, and Celtic history, legend and lore."

~ ~ ~

What Readers Have To Say...

"Ceane, this is Shirley Jones calling. Your book is just wonderful! I've never read such an extensive ... comprehensive account about myself. It's just incredible, really incredible! I really am very grateful ... very appreciative to be in your Pennsylvania history series. In fact, I think it's great what you're doing for Pennsylvania ... ."
— Shirley Jones, celebrated actress/singer, from an October 2007 telephone message to the author, in regard to "Pennsylvania's Sweetheart- the Inimitable, Indomitable Shirley Jones," *County Chronicles III*

"Your Chronicle about Shirley [Jones] in *County Chronicles III* is splendid. It is by far one of the best accounts I've seen, and as her best friend for over sixty years, I've seen many. The whole book is great ... ."
— Charlotte Morrison-Lynn, NY

"Dear Ms. O'Hanlon-Lincoln: *County Chronicles* is a beautiful book that demonstrates the love and loyalty you have for your very special home area. ... I am sharing your fine book with members of my staff. ... I appreciate your passion for honoring ... the history of our great commonwealth."
— Pennsylvania Governor Edward G. Rendell

"A true state-of-the-heart storyteller, Ceane O'Hanlon-Lincoln is an *exceptionally* gifted writer with a talent for bringing history alive like no other author I have ever read. In each of O'Hanlon-Lincoln's books, I am *there*. I have smelled the coal smoke drifting on the Pennsylvania winter air. I have smelled the smoke of battles fought and heard the roar of guns. I have *experienced* history; and thus, understand it better. And I have come to know the *human* side of many of our historic figures."
— Judy D. Reed, retired teacher and Mayor of Connellsville, PA

"Ceane O'Hanlon-Lincoln truly presents a colorful and vivid interpretation of historical events."
— Mike Bell, retired history teacher, Dunbar, PA

"Ceane O'Hanlon-Lincoln is Pennsylvania's Margaret Mitchell!"
- Jim Stefano, Dunbar, PA

"Ceane O'Hanlon-Lincoln's *County Chronicles* is the perfect bedside/fireside reader. The more I read, the more I want to read. I *know* what kind of painstaking research goes into work like this. In *Autumn Song* and in each volume of *County Chronicles*, O'Hanlon-Lincoln's style is fascinating, from beginning to end. *She is a master storyteller.*"
— William Colvin, retired theatre and English teacher, Connellsville, PA

"What an interesting and well-researched chronicle!" (Regarding "George Washington's Secret Weapon," the Pennsylvania Rifle, in *County Chronicles*' premier volume)
— Stephen Molstad, author of *The Patriot*, the novelization, Los Angeles, CA

"Ceane O'Hanlon-Lincoln, I applaud you for your initiative and vision in bringing area history to new audiences! Keep up the good work!"
— Robert Matzen, Paladin Productions, Pittsburgh, PA

"Ms. O'Hanlon-Lincoln: Your chronicles on Washington and Lee are excellent! 'Honor Answering Honor' in *County Chronicles*' premier volume is a fantastic piece- interesting, warm, memorable, moving ... congratulations on excellence!"
— President Thomas Burish of Washington and Lee University, Lexington, VA

"Ms. O'Hanlon-Lincoln: I found your chronicle on George C. Marshall, 'Soldier of Peace,' most interesting, well-written and accurate. We are happy to include it, along with its wonderful photos, in our permanent files in the Marshall Research Library."
— Joanne Hartog, Director of Research Library/Archives, Marshall Foundation, Lexington, VA

"Ms. O'Hanlon-Lincoln: The *County Chronicles* Pennsylvania history series is a welcome addition to the Pennsylvania Senate Library. The rich history you provide will help anyone researching Pennsylvania.
The first four volumes have been well received and offer our patrons a glimpse into the history and fabric of Pennsylvania. I perused the books as they arrived in the Library and was astonished at the wealth of details and the fascinating stories they told. You provide an in-depth window into what makes this commonwealth remarkable. Each PA county provides a unique history, and you have captured the essence with each splendidly."
— Pennsylvania Senate Library

"*County Chronicles* is a wonderful collection of stories that fill a void in ... Pennsylvania history, a region with as colorful and varied a past as any in the USA. Each volume is stocked to the brim with stories worth telling over and over again. Many of the Chronicles touch historical events and lives that go far beyond [Pennsylvania] ... this series deserves a place on any bookshelf that is concerned with American history."
— George Baldrose, Director, the Balmoral School of Piping, Pittsburgh, PA

"Ceane O'Hanlon-Lincoln, you deserve a gold star for *County Chronicles Volume IV!* I am an avid reader, and I've always enjoyed history, but ... never have I enjoyed it as much as I do *your* presentations. You bring events and people to life with your beautiful, unique, expressive way of writing. You are truly a gifted author.
"I am a devoted fan of yours, most likely one of your oldest readers. Thank you for your excellence, and I urge you to continue with your well-researched, honest reports of history, not only for those of us in the present, but for the benefit of those who will come after us. I am looking forward to your next volume!"
— Tena Pitzer, Sun City, FL

"Ms. O'Hanlon-Lincoln: I have just finished reading your Chronicle on General 'Mad' Anthony Wayne, from 'Haunted Pennsylvania' of *CC III,* to my classes. The students responded well to the reading. Our textbook devotes only two pages to Wayne. So it was nice to have your Chronicle on him as a complimentary piece. The students were interested in the content, especially since this particular Chronicle delivers both the historical and the supernatural elements of Wayne's impressive story. I asked students to provide me with feedback, even going so far as to ask them to compare your Chronicle with their textbook. I received numerous comments. The students were impressed with the detail and the more personal portrayal of Wayne that your Chronicle delivers as opposed to the cut-and-dry information the textbook supplies. Last but not least, the students liked the quotations at the beginning of this Chronicle, which help to highlight the colorful character that was 'Mad' Anthony Wayne."
— Joshua Scully, history teacher, Uniontown, PA

"Ms. O'Hanlon-Lincoln, every volume of your *County Chronicles* is so vivid! Each makes the reader feel as though he is right there witnessing history being made! I especially like your Chronicles on the Eastern Woodland Indians, as well as those on the Civil War. I have the whole *CC* set, and am looking forward to the next volume!"
— Donald Brown, South Connellsville, PA

"The rich history of Pennsylvania is vividly brought to life by Ceane O'Hanlon-Lincoln in her *County Chronicles* PA history series. This author combines meticulous research with expert storytelling to transport her readers back in time.
"One can relive the bloodbath of Picket's Charge, experience the danger and fortitude of the Pennsylvania frontiersmen, or witness the fascinating tale of Kate Soffel and the Biddle Boys. It's all there– over 300 years of fascinating people and events that have created our Pennsylvania. *County Chronicles* is a must-read for anyone who loves history. I highly recommend it."
— Tim Conn, Pittsburgh, PA

"Author Ceane O'Hanlon-Lincoln certainly has a way with words! I started reading the premier *County Chronicles* as soon as I received it, and I wasn't able to put it down much until I completed it. I think the *County Chronicles* series should be used in the schools across Pennsylvania ... ."
— John Lujack, 1947 Heisman Trophy winner

"I minored in history in college, and I want to say that *County Chronicles* is well-written,

well-researched ... a very *fine* work. I personally congratulate Ceane O'Hanlon-Lincoln on a job well done."
— John Y. Woodruff, Gold Medalist,
1936 Olympic Games

"The historical facts come alive with the author's account of vivid details. This series is a *must* for anyone interested in the development of Pennsylvania— of America! It is obvious that Ceane O'Hanlon-Lincoln puts her heart and soul into her beloved Chronicles. Read, learn, and most of all— *enjoy*!"
— Frank C. Gyimesi, M.D., Lost Creek, WV

"I am thrilled with *County Chronicles*— the beautiful color images brighten the pages! I am most pleased to include it in the Law Library of our Fayette County Courthouse. Ceane O'Hanlon-Lincoln has done an excellent job!"
— Elida Micklo, Law Librarian, Fayette County Courthouse, Uniontown, PA

"*County Chronicles* reads like whip cream; it is so smooth! It is my contention that this Pennsylvania history series should be a supplement for the local history courses taught across our commonwealth."
— Gloria Rock, Connellsville, PA

"I love how all Ceane O'Hanlon-Lincoln's books read. I can feel the cold, the exhaustion, the hunger of George Washington's army. I see, smell and feel the acrid smoke of battles lost and won."
— Janet Hiltabidel, Connellsville, PA

"Ceane O'Hanlon-Lincoln: Your books are the Ruby Slippers of OZ– they make us all realize 'There is no place like home!' I never tire of your stories; they bring the best of Pennsylvania and its people alive in such a warm and homey way."
— Kathy Sawyer, Taylors, SC

"Ms. O'Hanlon-Lincoln: Your books make me proud to be a Pennsylvanian!"
— Barb Hallenbaugh, Connellsville, PA

"I really love how Ceane O'Hanlon-Lincoln writes and the little personal insights she adds on the various subjects. I can tell she enjoys her work– *it shows*. It's hard to put her books down!"
— Jen DeOre Gordon, Chicago, IL

"Ceane O'Hanlon-Lincoln: I just love, *love* your books! You know why? I love a book I can pick up and put down easily; the short stories fit comfortably into my lifestyle."
— Joy Connor, Murfreesboro, TN

"Ms. O'Hanlon-Lincoln: I just finished reading *County Chronicles Volume II*. I told my husband how much I enjoy your books. The funny thing is I was totally uninterested in history in school ... but after each of your Chronicles, I want to hop in the car and visit the place I've just read about. I never realized how much history we have in Pennsylvania! You are my favorite author. Please keep writing, and I'll keep reading. I love your *County Chronicles*!"
— Nancy Anderson, Uniontown, PA

Selected Bibliography

In addition to a myriad of interviews with rangers at historical sites, curators of museums, tour guides, other authors, reenactors, history teachers and professors, as well as with the many fascinating and knowledgeable individuals connected to the people and the subjects of the Chronicles in this volume, including (among numerous others) Susie O'Brien and Paula Zitzler (summer 2008), author and paranormal expert Patty A. Wilson (autumn 2008-spring 2009), Gettysburg's Tillie Pierce House proprietors Leslie and Keith Grandstaff (autumn 2008, winter-spring 2009), Gettysburg ranger John Winkelman (autumn 2008-winter 2009), Drenda Gostkowski (winter-spring 2009), Billy Conn's son Tim Conn (winter-spring 2009), Valley Forge's Supervisory Ranger William J. Troppman (winter 2008-spring 2009), professional nature photographer Glenn E. Mucy (spring 2009), Johnny Appleseed Educational Center and Museum Director Joe Besecker (spring 2009), and former Pittsburgh mayor, Sophie Masloff (spring 2009), I also drew from and recommend further reading and exploration in the following ...

Books

Alcott, Louisa May. *Little Women.* New York, NY: Little, Brown, 1868.

Alleman, Mrs. Matilda (Pierce). *At Gettysburg: What a Girl Saw and Heard of the Battle, a True Narrative.* New York: W. Lake Borland, 1888.

Bachelder, Louise. *Abraham Lincoln, Wisdom and Wit.* Mount Vernon, NY: The Peter Pauper Press, 1965.

Brooks, Paul. *The House of Life: Rachel Carson at Work.* Boston, MA: Houghton Mifflin Company, 1972.

Carson, Rachel. *Silent Spring.* Boston, MA: Houghton Mifflin Company, 1962, 1990, 2002.

Eldridge, Dan. *Pittsburgh.* Moon Handbooks/Travel Guides, 2008.

Fleming, Thomas. *Washington's Secret War, the Hidden History of Valley Forge.* New York, NY: Harper Collins Publishers, 2005.

Grey, Zane. *Tales of Lonely Trails.* New York, NY: Blue Ribbon Books, 1922.

Grey, Zane. *Riders of the Purple Sage.* New York, NY: The Modern Library, 1912.

Griffing, Robert. *The Art of Robert Griffing, His Journey into the Eastern Frontier*, with text by George Irvin, Editing and Additional Text by Ann Trondle-Price, Introduction by Donald Miller, and Conclusion by Ted Brasser. Ashville, NY: East/West Visions, Paramount Press, Inc., 2000.

Griffing, Robert. *The Narrative Art of Robert Griffing Volume II, the Journey Continues.* Text and Introduction by Tim J. Todish. Foreword by Fred Anderson. Gibsonia, PA: Paramount Press, Inc., 2007.

Harbison, Massy. *Narrative of the Sufferings of Massy Harbison*. Pittsburgh, PA: S. Engels, 1825. Copyright 2005 by Doris Herceg and Drenda Gostkowski.

Harbison, Francis. *Flood Tides Along the Allegheny*. Apollo, PA: Closson Press, 2000.

Jackson, John W. *Valley Forge, Pinnacle of Courage*. Gettysburg, PA: Thomas Publications, 1992.

Jehrio, Peter and Sprague, Terry. *Baltimore & Ohio Steam Locomotives*. Lynchburg, VA: TLC Publishing, 2003.

Johns, Robert H. Edited by Cole, Robert E. *The Incident that Could Have Killed Pittsburgh*. Apollo, PA: Closson Press, 2008.

Kennedy, Billy. *Women of the Frontier*. Greenville, SC: Ambassador Emerald International, 2004.

Kennedy, Paul F. *Billy Conn, the Pittsburgh Kid*. Bloomington, IN: Author House, 2007.

Kidney, Walter C. *Pittsburgh Then and Now*. San Diego, CA: Thunder Bay Press, 2004.

Krensky, Stephen. *Hanukkah at Valley Forge*. New York, NY: Dutton/Penguin Group, 2006.

Kudlinski, Kathleen, V. *Rachel Carson, Pioneer of Ecology*. New York, NY: Puffin Books, 1988.

Lear, Linda. *Rachel Carson, Witness for Nature*. New York, NY: Henry Holt and Company, 1997.

Loudon, Archibald. *Loudon's Indian Narratives*. Lewisburg, PA: Wennawoods Publishing, 1996.

McCullough, David. *Truman*. New York, NY: Simon and Schuster, 1992.

McKinney, Gary S. *Oil on the Brain*. Chicora, PA: Mechling Books/Bookbindery, 2003.

Miller, Randall M. and Pencak, William. *Pennsylvania, a History of the Commonwealth*. University Park: The Pennsylvania State University Press *and* Harrisburg, PA: The Pennsylvania Historical and Museum Commission, 2002.

National Park Service and Aperture Foundation, Inc. *Ellis Island, Echoes From a Nation's Past*. New York, NY, 1988.

Nesbitt, Mark. *Ghosts of Gettysburg, Volumes I-VI*. Gettysburg, PA: Thomas Publications, 1991-2004.

O'Hanlon-Lincoln, Ceane. *County Chronicles* (Volume I). Chicora, PA: Mechling Books/Mechling Bookbindery, 2004.

O'Hanlon-Lincoln, Ceane. *County Chronicles Volume II*. Chicora, PA: Mechling Books/Mechling Bookbindery, 2006.

O'Hanlon-Lincoln, Ceane. *County Chronicles Volume III*. Chicora, PA: Mechling Books/Mechling Bookbindery, 2007.

O'Hanlon-Lincoln, Ceane. *County Chronicles Volume IV*. Chicora, PA: Mechling Books/Mechling Bookbindery, 2008.

O'Toole, Andrew. *Sweet William, the Life of Billy Conn*. Chicago, IL: University of Illinois Press, 2008.

Pauly, Thomas H. *Zane Grey, His Life, His Adventures, His Women*. Chicago, IL: University of Illinois Press, 2005.

Sabin, Francene. *Rachel Carson, Friend of the Earth*. Troll Communications, 1993.

Scaife, Richard M. Publisher, Inc./Trib Total Media. *Forging Ahead: Pittsburgh at 250*. Pittsburgh, PA: Reed and Witting Co., 2008.

Sharfman, Rabbi I. Harold. *Jews on the Frontier*. Washington, DC: Henry Regnery Publishing, 1977.

Truman, Harry S. *Truman Speaks*. New York, NY: Columbia University Press, 1960.

Wilson, Patty A. *The Pennsylvania Ghost Guide Series*, Roaring Spring, PA: Piney Creek Press.

Zitzler, Paula. *Unscheduled Stop: The Town of Tyrone and the Wreck of the Walter L. Main Circus Train.* Tyrone, PA: America's Stories, Inc., 2008.

Booklets, Magazines and Newspapers, etc.

Behe, Rege. "Stephen Foster: Pittsburgh's Forgotten Phenom." Entertainment section of the *Tribune-Review*, Sunday, June 28, 2009.

Cooke, Louis E. "Walter L. Main." *Bandwagon*, Vol. 11, No. 3, May-June, 1967, pp. 3-13.

Forbes, Marilyn. "Dunbar Buzzes as Beehive Forms." Fay-West section of the *Tribune-Review*, Sunday, August 23, 2009.

Schofield, Paul. "Legendary Chat, Heisman Winner Returns Home." Sports segment of the *Daily Courier*, Saturday, July 18, 2009.

Series Editor Weaver, Kyle R. *Drake Well Museum and Park Guide, a Pennsylvania Trail of History Guide.* Mechanicsburg, PA: Stackpole Books, 2002.

Browning, Mark. "Feeling Right at Home." "Focus" section of the *Tribune-Review*, Sunday, November 2, 2008.

Thomas, Mary Ann. "Making Tracks." "Focus" section of the *Tribune-Review*, Sunday, August 3, 2008.

Videos and Films

The Winter of Red Snow, Valley Forge, Pennsylvania, 1777. Scholastic Dear America Series, 1999.

Web Sites

Altoonapa.gov
The American Experience
The American Revolution
Armstrong Cable Television: Hometown Favorites: *Faces of Fayette*, "Author Ceane O'Hanlon-Lincoln and her *County Chronicles*, a Pennsylvania history series"
Carnegie Museum of Art, Pittsburgh, PA
Circushistory.org
ConnellsvilleCulturalTrust.org
Doodahdays.com
Drake Well Museum and Park
Dunbar Historical Society (www.dunbarhistoricalsociety.com)
Encyclopedia Smithsonian: The Smithsonian from A–Z
Ghosts of Gettysburg
Great and Historical Trees
Greater Connellsville Chamber of Commerce
Historic Cashtown Inn
Johnny Appleseed Education Center and Museum
Mechling Books/Mechling Bookbindery
National Baseball Hall of Fame
The National Civil War Museum, Harrisburg, PA
National First Ladies' Library
National Museum of the American Indian
Nativetreesociety.org/historic
Paramountpress.com
Pennsylvania Cable Network (PCN): *PA BOOKS*, "Author Ceane O'Hanlon-Lincoln and her *County Chronicles*, a Pennsylvania history series."
Railroadcity.com
Senator John Heinz Pittsburgh Regional History Center/Heinz History Center
Shawnee Traditions, Language, Culture, and Ethnohistory
The Smithsonian Institute
The Smithsonian Magazine
Tomandjoes.com
The United States Military Academy at West Point
The United States Naval Academy at Annapolis
Tillie Pierce House
United States Olympic Committee
Valley Forge National Historical Park
Visit Pittsburgh
Wikipedia
Wildlife Works, Inc.
Witness Trees
Women's Military History
YouTube: John Woodruff

To read all about *County Chronicles*, its dynamic author Ceane O'Hanlon-Lincoln, the awards the series has thus far garnered, and additional reader feedback visit: www.mechlingbooks.com.

County Chronicles may be ordered online or by telephoning Mechling Books/Bookbindery toll free (where the caller will speak to a live person), weekdays 8 a.m. to 4:30 p.m., at 1-800-941-3735.

School and public libraries, historical societies, clubs, church and school organizations, etc., be certain to ask about Mechling's special fundraising offers.

In Memory of
Dr. William F. Colvin
1921-2009

William F. Colvin, M.D., 88, was a beloved figure in my hometown of Connellsville, Pennsylvania. While I was preparing this volume for publication, in fact, proofing the segment about Dr. Colvin's son and grandsons in "Historic Connellsville ... Hometown Memories," Dr. Colvin passed away.

He was born and reared in Pittsburgh, graduated from Peabody High School there, and the University of Pittsburgh as well as the Pitt Medical School. His medical practice was in the tri-town (Liberty/Vanderbilt/Dawson) area of greater Connellsville from 1948 until 1985 when he retired. Dr. Colvin served in the Army Medical Corps in World War II and afterward, with the rank of captain, in Korea.

Duty and serving were his life's credo. Dr. Colvin was an active member of the East Liberty Presbyterian Church, where he served as an elder for many years. He was also a member of the Connellsville VFW and the Vanderbilt American Legion Post 586. From 1953 to 1976, he was manager of the Tri-Town Little League Team, leading the team to sixteen Connellsville league championships, and three league All-Star teams to state championships in 1963, 1964, and again in 1976. In 1960, he received the Manager of the Year award for District Nine Little League.

During his exemplary life, Dr. Colvin garnered a myriad of accolades, including, during the 1970s, Connellsville Little League Outstanding Man of the Year, the St. Rita Award for outstanding service to the area's youth, the Kiwanis Citizen of the Year Award, and the Outstanding Citizen award for the tri-town community.

He was recognized by the Senate of Pennsylvania for leadership and his numerous contributions to his community. In 1976, he was presented with Connellsville's Key to the City. In 1990, this well-known local hero was inducted into the Pennsylvania State Sports Hall of Fame.

Dr. Colvin was preceded in death by his wife, the former Betty Lou Dolquest, with whom he shared nearly thirty-one years of

Captain William F. Colvin, M.D.

a loving, successful married life. A notable family man, Dr. Colvin is survived by his son William D. Colvin and wife Judith, daughter Pandy Colvin Shumar and husband James, daughter Cherie Colvin Angelini and husband David, eight grandchildren, and four great-grandchildren.

A golf and model train enthusiast, Dr. Colvin was also known for his ready smile and his benevolent practical jokes. He was a success at everything he did, and he did everything with such gusto! But, as someone once said, if success is justly measured by the number of friends one has made in a lifetime, Dr. William F. Colvin has entered Heaven a successful man, indeed!

He will be sorely missed.

Pennsylvania County Map

COURTESY FAYETTE COUNTY MAPPING DEPARTMENT
DAVID M. DOMEN, MAPPING SUPERVISOR